GL9100

£21-65

C W Potter

GL9100

Exeter Archaeological Reports: Volume I

THE LEGIONARY BATH-HOUSE AND BASILICA AND FORUM AT EXETER

with a summary account of the legionary fortress

by

PAUL T. BIDWELL

Preface by Aileen Fox and contributions by
D. Bailey, D. Charlesworth, G. B. Dannell, B. Dickinson, K. T. Greene,
K. Hartley, M. W. C. Hassall, D. Mackreth, H. Miles, D. P. S. Peacock,
R. Reece, V. Rigby, R. G. Scrivener, N. Shiel, D. J. Smith, V. G. Swan,
J. M. C. Toynbee and the late C. M. Wells

EXETER CITY COUNCIL
AND
THE UNIVERSITY OF EXETER
1979

ISBN 0 85989 094 5

Set in Monotype Bembo 12/13 pt.

Printed by The Devonshire Press, Torquay

To
Aileen Fox

FOREWORD: THE ORIGIN OF THE EXCAVATIONS IN THE CATHEDRAL CLOSE

Aileen Fox

It was a very long time ago when the perceptive W. G. Hoskins put the idea into my mind that there might be something worth excavating beneath the solid Heavitree stone edifice of St Mary Major, the early Victorian church in the western part of the Cathedral Close. It arose out of a discussion of the Saxon occupation of Exeter, when my husband, the late Sir Cyril Fox, was investigating the early monastic well pool (Fox, 1965), south of the present Lady Chapel, in the Bishop's Palace gardens. W.G. was firmly of the opinion that the earliest Saxon church in Exeter would be found on the site of St Mary Major but it seemed improbable that any archaeologist would be given an opportunity to look for it. It was also obvious from the various excavations which had taken place in Exeter from 1945 onwards (Fox, 1952), that the centre of the Roman city, like that of its medieval successor, lay on the plateau, above the steep rise from the river Exe and the Longbrook. The site of St Mary's adjoined the known site of the Public Baths in the Deanery garden (Montgomerie-Neilson and Montague, 1933–6), and although it is easy to be wise after the event, it was clear even then that the church site was of potential importance in determining the Roman town plan.

Accordingly in 1968 when the church was closed and had been declared redundant and the possibility of its demolition was mooted, I informed the Chief Inspector of Ancient Monuments at the Ministry of Public Buildings and Works that something would have to be done if the scheme eventuated. When one of the inspectors, Mr Peter White, was on a routine visit to the West Country in April 1968, there was an opportunity for us to go together to see the Dean, The Very Rev. Marcus Knight and to make a case for a future excavation. He was interested in and sympathetic to our proposals, and agreed in principle; and this decision was subsequently confirmed by the Chapter.

The project then remained dormant until 1970 when, at long last, the City Council overcame all obstacles and decided to go ahead with the redevelopment of the Guildhall site, on the lines laid down by their consultant, the late Lord Holford. The Ancient Monuments Branch had been alerted to the scheme and their Inspector, Miss Sarnia Butcher, came to Exeter to discuss a plan of campaign. With the agreement of Professor Frank Barlow, it was agreed that John Collis who had just been appointed lecturer in the archaeology section of the History Department would undertake the excavations which would be sponsored jointly by the Department of the Environment and the University. At the same time, at the instigation of the energetic Director of the Royal Albert Memorial Museum, Patrick Boylan, the City Council had approached the Department with a proposal for the founding of an Archaeological Field Unit to carry out excavations in Exeter, financed jointly by the City and the Department. This was something of a novelty at the time and Exeter became one of the first Local Authorities to make such a provision for archaeology, which has since become a commonplace. Michael Griffiths of Durham University was appointed as the first Field Officer in 1971, and an Excavation Committee was subsequently set up, with the representatives of the City, the University, the Department of the Environment (Ancient Monuments) and of the relevant local and national Archaeological Societies. It held its first meeting in April 1971.

By this time, the Dean and Chapter had decided to demolish St Mary's to improve the appearance of the Close and had made provision in the contract for time for excavation. Thus the new Excavation Committee was faced with the prospect of staffing and funding two major excavations, both of the utmost urgency. Opinion was divided and it was only after some vigorous argument, in which I strongly supported the claims of St Mary Major, that it was decided that both projects should go ahead. It was agreed that Griffiths should investigate St Mary's and that Collis should tackle the Guildhall. Additional finance was generously provided by the University at the request of the Vice Chancellor, Dr F. J. Llewellyn, by the Dean and Chapter, as well as by the Department and other contributors to the Appeal.

The return exceeded all expectations. I shall long remember seeing in one of the first cuttings the monumental flight of steps which subsequently proved to belong to Isca's basilica, superimposed on the hypocaust of what could only be a military Bath Building.

Auckland, New Zealand.
February, 1978.

INTRODUCTION

The excavations reported on in this monograph took place at various times between June 1971 and August 1977; most of the work was occasioned by an extensive replanning of the west end of the Cathedral Close, which has already been referred to in the Preface (see p. v). Excavations were begun on the site of the church of St Mary Major, where the construction of an underground car-park had been proposed. The uncovering of the substantial remains of a Neronian legionary bath-house and of a later civil *basilica* and *forum* led to the abandonment of the project.

As the excavations proceeded, it became apparent that the Roman structures warranted preservation and public display, if possible. The interested parties were consulted, and it was agreed that if the remains were to be preserved, some form of covering was essential. Apart from the difficulties of protecting the walls and hypocausts from the effects of the weather, an open site was thought likely to spoil the appearance of the Close. Ove Arup Associates were commissioned to draw up a feasibility study for the construction of an underground museum to display the remains. This was to have had a concrete roof at ground level covered by lawns; an entrance was to have been sited unobtrusively next to the buildings on the western side of the site. The roof was to have had an uninterrupted span across the bath-house, which would have involved considerable feats of engineering. Accordingly, the cost of the project was estimated to be about £320,000. At first this sum was thought to be prohibitive, but a significant proportion of the total was taken up by landscaping work which had to be carried out irrespective of whether the underground structure was built. For a time it seemed quite likely that the money would be raised. Then, in 1974, severe curbs were imposed on local authority spending and Exeter City Council decided that they could not provide any financial support for the scheme. Hopes of raising the necessary funds faded rapidly and in the summer of 1974 the site was filled in. Over a thousand tons of sand were spread over the site to make the task of re-excavation easier. A more prosperous future may yet see a revival of interest in the site and the ultimate fulfilment of the plans for its preservation and public display.

Work was begun on the final stage of landscaping in 1976. A 'processional way' was to be constructed from Broadgate to the West Front of the Cathedral, where an area of paving about 30 m square was to be laid down. This involved the destruction of extensive late Roman and medieval deposits; these were removed by archaeological excavation. Unfortunately funds were not made available for the investigation of the early Roman deposits; these were only examined when revealed by the removal of the filling of robber-trenches.

Archaeological work was carried out on a smaller scale in 1975 when a sewer heading was dug on the north side of the Cathedral, and in 1977 when alterations were made to the National Westminster Bank.

The reader is referred to pp. 22–4 for further details of the excavation programme.

Funds for the excavations were provided by the Department of the Environment, Exeter City Council, the University of Exeter, the Dean and Chapter, the Northcott Trust, the Marc Fitch Fund, the Society for the Promotion of Roman Studies and the British Academy (Albert Reckitt Archaeological Fund). Several individuals who wish to remain anonymous also donated considerable sums. The excavations attracted considerable interest from the general public, whose donations and purchases of booklets and postcards also helped to defray the cost of excavation.

The excavation of the sewer heading in 1975 was paid for by the South Western Water Authority. Half the costs of the excavations in 1977 were paid for by the National Westminster Bank and half by the Department of the Environment.

Most of the costs of preparing this monograph for publication were borne by Exeter City Council, with a substantial contribution from the Department of the Environment. Three-quarters of the costs of publication were paid by the Department of the Environment and the remainder by Exeter City Council, the University of Exeter and Devon County Council.

Permission to carry out the excavations of 1971–6 were granted by the Dean and Chapter; a particular debt of gratitude for their cooperation is owed to Mr P. Gundry, the Cathedral Surveyor and to Mr J. Eden, Clerk to the Dean and Chapter. There can scarcely be a more pleasant setting for an excavation than the Close of an English cathedral city. Unfortunately, at times, work on the site intruded on the tranquillity of the surroundings and caused some inconvenience to the staff of the Cathedral. The latter must be thanked for their forbearance and assistance. In particular, Mr P. Dare, head of the masons' department, gave much practical help and advice on various matters; in 1976 he willingly varied his programme of work to take account of delays in the progress of the excavations.

I wish to thank Messrs Collins, Dodgson and Evans of the National Westminster Bank and Miss Holt, the architect of the project, for their assistance in arranging the excavations in 1977.

In 1971 the excavations were directed by M. Griffiths and supervised by A. E. Johnson, the writer and Miss M. Dale; the site was planned by Miss Anne Gentry and the finds were processed by Mrs C. Griffiths. In 1972 the writer took charge of the day-to-day running of the site under the general direction of M. Griffiths. J. R. L. Thorp and R. Potts acted as supervisors, the site was planned by Miss Penny English and the processing of the finds was organised by Miss Edith Walker and Miss Susan Haynes. In 1975 and 1977 the excavations were supervised by S. Brown and in 1976 by J. Pamment. All the photographs were taken by N. Cheffers-Heard and R. Turner.

It is not possible to name all those who took part in the excavations, but mention must be made of Messrs Rex Bridgwater and Bernard Joy who gave up many hours of their leisure to work on the site. Despite the pleasant setting of the excavations there were times when working conditions left much to be desired. The work in 1976 was carried out during an exceptional drought when water was rationed. In the strong-rooms of the National Westminster Bank, where work took place in 1977, concrete floors two feet in depth had to be drilled out in order to reach the Roman deposits. Nevertheless, the enthusiasm of those working on the various sites ensured that the excavations were brought to a successful conclusion.

This monograph was written at various times between 1973 and 1978 while the writer held the post of Assistant Field Archaeologist at Exeter City Museums. Most of the plans and finds drawings are the work of Miss Penny English; the small finds and the mosaic were drawn by Mrs Susan Hill and Miss Susan Wilson, and the ironwork by Miss Avril Hoogenburg; Miss Barbara Jupp and Miss Francine Epifanoff also helped with the drawings. I am grateful to my successive Directors for much encouragement in the writing of this report.

I wish to express my thanks to those who supplied reports on various types of artifacts. Pottery reports have been supplied by Mr D. M. Bailey (lamps), Mr G. B. Dannell (decorated samian and also the dating of the plain samian), Miss B. M. Dickinson (samian stamps), Dr K. T. Greene (pre-Flavian fine wares), Mrs K. Hartley (mortaria), Dr D. P. S. Peacock (amphora), Miss V. Rigby (terra nigra) and Mrs V. G. Swan (Flavian and later fine wares). Miss V. Rigby and Mrs V. G. Swan have also discussed more general aspects of the Exeter pottery with me. The coins were identified by Dr R. Reece and Mr N. Shiel. I am particularly indebted to Mr N. Shiel for making available, at short notice, some of the results of his researches on coins from Exeter, and for a full discussion of their significance. Mr D. F. Mackreth reported on the brooches, Dr R. G. Scrivener on the sources of various types of building-stone, Dr M. Hassall on the *graffiti*, Mrs H. Miles on flints and the late Dr C. Wells on five skeletons. Dr D. J. Smith contributed a note on the mosaic fragments from the legionary bath-house and Professor J. M. C. Toynbee reported on the Purbeck-marble carving of an eagle from the Guildhall site.

Lady Fox, Mr Michael Griffiths and Dr Valerie Maxfield read a draft of this report and made many useful comments and suggestions. Mr G. C. Boon and Professor S. S. Frere read and commented on a more complete draft; I am grateful to them for pointing out ways in which the presentation of the report could be improved, for supplying additional information about some of the topics discussed in the report, and for correcting errors of fact. The complete draft was also read by Mr C. G. Henderson and Dr C. J. Young, who made further comments and suggestions. Cross-references were checked by Messrs. S. Brown and C. G. Henderson. I am grateful to Miss S. M. Pearce for comments on the cemetery; in the course of constructing the model of the bath-house Mr E. W. Haddon discussed several important aspects of the reconstruction. Final responsibility for the report rests with the author.

The excavations in the Cathedral Close have formed only part of the work carried out in Exeter by the City Museums Archaeological Field Unit under its successive Directors, Messrs M. Griffiths and C. G. Henderson. Work on other sites has thrown much light on the history of Roman Exeter. The discovery of the legionary fortress has been the most important result of this work. A summary account of the fortress has been included in this report and forms a necessary preface to the description and discussion of the legionary baths. I am grateful to Mr C. G. Henderson for allowing me to publish details of his excavation of the barrack-blocks, *fabrica* and granaries. I have also drawn on Mr G. B. Dannell's comments on the samian and Mr N. Shiel's identification of coins from as yet unpublished sites.

I am also grateful to Professor Frank Barlow and Mr R. A. Erskine for assistance in preparing the manuscript for publication.

It is a pleasure to be able to dedicate this report to Aileen Fox, who was largely responsible for bringing about the excavations. Aileen Fox visited the excavations which took place in 1971 and 1972 at frequent intervals and greatly encouraged the progress of the work. Were it not for the excavations she carried out at Exeter in the twenty years following the Second World War, when so much of the surviving medieval city and the underlying Roman deposits were obliterated, the recovery of the outline plan of the *basilica* and *forum* would not have been possible, and much of the evidence on which various conclusions in this report are based would have vanished into oblivion. The work which Aileen Fox carried out in Exeter drew on slender financial resources and sometimes took place, especially just after the War, in a local climate of opinion which was less tolerant of the needs of archaeology than it is now. All those who are concerned with Exeter's Roman past are deeply indebted to Aileen Fox.

PAUL T. BIDWELL

May, 1978

Royal Albert Memorial Museum,
Exeter.

CONTENTS

LIST OF PLATES

ACKNOWLEDGMENTS TO PLATES

R. Turner, Plates I–VII, VIIIB–XA, XI; N. Cheffers-Heard, Plates VIIIA, XB, XIIA–XXI.

LIST OF FIGURES

SECTIONS AND ELEVATIONS:

TABLES

BIBLIOGRAPHY

Antal, 1962.   Antal, F., *Hogarth and his place in European Art*, London, 1962.

Anderson, Spiers and Ashby, 1927.   Anderson, W. J., Spiers, R. P. and Ashby, T., *The Architecture of Ancient Rome*, London, 1927.

Ashby, 1906.   Ashby, T., 'Excavations at Caerwent, Monmouthshire, on the Site of the Romano-British City of Venta Silurum, in the year 1905', *Archaeologia*, **60** (1906) 111–130.

Ashby, 1935.   Ashby, T., *The Aqueducts of Ancient Rome*, Oxford, 1935.

Ashby, Hudd and King, 1909.   Ashby, T., Hudd, A. E. and King, F., 'Excavations at Caerwent, Monmouthshire, on the Site of the Romano-British City of Venta Silurum, in the years 1907 and 1909', *Archaeologia*, **61** (1909) 565–82.

Atkinson, 1914.   Atkinson, D. 'A Hoard of Samian Ware from Pompeii', *J. Roman Stud.*, **4** (1914) 27–64.

Atkinson, 1942.   Atkinson, D., *Report on the Excavations at Wroxeter, 1923–1927*, Oxford, 1942.

Baatz, 1962.   Baatz, D., *Mogontiacum, Neue Untersuchungen am römischen Legionslager in Mainz* (*Limesforschungen, Band* 4), Berlin, 1962.

Bailey, forthcoming.   Bailey, D., *British Museum Catalogue of Lamps, ii*.

Baker, 1970.   Baker, R. S., 'A Circular Kimmeridge Shale Tray from Wareham', *Proc. Dorset Natur. Hist. Archaeol. Soc.*, **92** (1970) 148–50.

Bandinelli, Caffarelli and Caputo, 1966.   Bandinelli, R. R., Caffarelli, E. V. and Caputo, G., *The Buried City: Excavations at Leptis Magna*, London, 1966.

Beavis, 1970.   Beavis, J., 'Some Aspects of the Use of Purbeck Marble in Roman Britain', *Proc. Dorset Natur. Hist. Archaeol. Soc.*, **92** (1970), 181–204.

Berger and Moussat, 1927.   Berger, M. and Moussat, E., *Anthologie des Textes Sportifs de l'Antiquité*, Paris, 1927.

Bidwell, 1977.   Bidwell, P. T., 'Early Black-Burnished Ware at Exeter' in (Ed.) Dore, J. and Greene, K. T., *Roman Pottery Studies in Britain and Beyond*, (pp. 189–198), Oxford, 1977.

Bidwell and Boon, 1976.   Bidwell, P. T. and Boon, G. C., 'An Antefix Type of the Second Augustan Legion from Exeter', *Britannia*, **7** (1976) 278–80.

Bishop and Prideaux, 1922.   Bishop, H. E. and Prideaux, E. K., *The Building of the Cathedral Church of St Peter in Exeter*, Exeter, 1922.

Blagg, 1976.   Blagg, T. F. C., 'Tools and Techniques of the Roman Stonemason in Britain', *Britannia*, **7** (1976) 152–72.

Blake, 1947.   Blake, M. E., *Ancient Roman Construction in Italy from the Prehistoric Period to Augustus*, Washington, 1947.

Blake, 1959.   Blake, M. E., *Roman Construction in Italy from Tiberius through the Flavians*, Washington, 1959.

Blake, 1973.   Blake, M. E., *Roman Construction in Italy from Nerva through the Antonines*, Philadelphia, 1973.

Böhme, 1972.   Böhme, A., 'Die Fibeln der Kastelle Saalburg und Zugmantel', *Saalburg Jahrbuch*, **29** (1972).

Boon, 1958.   Boon, G. C., 'A Note on the Byzantine Æ Coins said to have been found at Caerwent', *Bulletin of the Board of Celtic Studies*, **17** (1958) 316–9.

Boon, 1966.   Boon, G. C., 'Roman Window Glass from Wales', *J. Glass Stud.*, **8** (1966) 41f.

Boon, 1972.   Boon, G. C., *Isca, the Roman Legionary Fortress at Caerleon, Mon.*, Cardiff, 1972.

Boon, 1973. Boon, G. C., 'Roman Glassware from Caerwent, 1855–1925', *Monmouthshire Antiquary*, **3** (1972–3) 118f.

Boon, 1973a. Boon, G. C., 'Sarapis and Tutela: A Silchester Coincidence', *Britannia*, **4** (1973) 107–114.

Boon, 1974. Boon, G. C., *Silchester, The Roman Town of Calleva*, Newton Abbot, 1974.

Boon, 1974a. Boon, G. C., 'Counterfeit Coins in Roman Britain', in (Ed.) Casey, J. and Reece, R., *Coins and the Archaeologist* (pp. 95–172), Oxford, 1974.

Boon, 1975. Boon, G. C., 'Three Caerleon Sculptures', *Bulletin of the Board of Celtic Studies*, **26** (1975) 227–30.

Boon, 1977. Boon, G. C., 'A Greco-Roman Anchor-Stock from North Wales', *Antiq. J.*, **57** (1977) 10–30.

Boon, 1978. Boon, G. C., 'A Counterstamped and Defaced *As* of Nero from Exeter', *Numis. Chron. ser.* 7, **18** (1978) 178–80.

Borquin, 1954. Borquin, J., 'Fouilles de Pro Aventico; les Thermes de "Perruet" ', *Bulletin de l'Association Pro Aventico*, **16** (1954) 93–114.

Brailsford, 1962. Brailsford, J. W., *Hod Hill, volume one: Antiquities from Hod Hill in the Durden Collection*, London, 1962.

Branigan, 1974. Branigan, K., 'Vespasian and the South-West', *Proc. Dorset Natur. Hist. Archaeol. Soc.*, **96** (1974) 50–7.

Breeze and Dobson, 1976. Breeze, D. J. and Dobson, B., *Hadrian's Wall*, London, 1976.

Brock and Mackworth Young, 1949. Brock, J. K. and Mackworth Young, G., 'Excavations at Siphnos', *Annual of the British School at Athens*, **44** (1949) 1–92.

Brödner, 1951. Brödner, E., *Untersuchungen an den Caracallathermen*, Berlin, 1951.

Burckhardt-Biedermann, 1909. Burckhardt-Biedermann, Th., 'Römische Zimmer mit Hypokausten in Baselaugst', *Anzeiger für Schweizerische Altertumskunde*, **11** (1909) 206–14.

Bushe-Fox, 1916. Bushe-Fox, J. P., *Excavations on the Site of the Roman Town at Wroxeter, Shropshire, 1914*, London, 1916.

Bushe-Fox, 1932. Bushe-Fox, J. P., *Third Report on the Excavations of the Roman Fort at Richborough, Kent*, Oxford, 1932.

Bushe-Fox, 1949. Bushe-Fox, J. P., *Fourth Report on the Excavations of the Roman Fort at Richborough, Kent*, Oxford, 1949.

Cagnat, 1913. Cagnat, R., *L'Armée Romaine d'Afrique*, Paris, 1913.

Calkin, 1935. Calkin, J. B., 'An Early Romano-British Kiln at Corfe Mullen, Dorset', *Antiq. J.*, **15** (1935) 42–55.

Carcopino, 1941. Carcopino, J., *Daily Life in Ancient Rome*, London, 1941.

Charlesworth, 1959. Charlesworth, D., 'Roman Glass in Northern Britain', *Archaeol. Aeliana ser.* 4., **37** (1959) 33–58.

Charlesworth, 1966. Charlesworth, D., 'Roman Square Bottles', *J. Glass Stud.*, **8** (1966) 26–40.

Charlesworth, 1971. Charlesworth, D., 'A Group of Vessels from the Commandant's House, Housesteads, *J. Glass Stud.*, **13** (1971) 34–40.

Charlesworth, 1977. Charlesworth, D., forthcoming, *J. Glass Stud.*, **19** (1977).

Chenet, 1941. Chenet, G., *La Céramique gallo-romaine d'Argonne du IVe Siècle et la Terre sigilleé décorée à la Molette*, Mâcon, 1941.

CIL. *Corpus Inscriptionum Latinarum*, Berlin, 1863–.

CK. Carson, R. A. G., Hill, P. V. and Kent, J. P. C., *Late Roman Bronze Coinage, part* 1, London, 1960.

Clarke, 1971. Clarke, P. J., 'The Neolithic, Bronze Age and Iron Age, and Romano-British Finds from Mount Batten, Plymouth, 1832–1939', *Proc. Devon Archaeol. Soc.*, **29** (1971) 137–161.

Courtois, 1941. Courtois, C., *Timgad, Antique Thamugadi*, Algiers, 1951.

Cramp, 1975. Cramp, R., 'Window Glass from the Monastic Site at Jarrow', *J. Glass Stud.*, **17** (1975) 88–96.

Crummy, 1977. Crummy, P., 'Colchester, Fortress and Colonia', *Britannia*, **8** (1977) 65–106.

Cunliffe, 1969. Cunliffe, B. W., *Roman Bath*, London, 1969.

Cunliffe, 1971. Cunliffe, B. W., *Excavations at Fishbourne*, 1961–9 (2 vols.) London, 1971.

Cunliffe, 1975. Cunliffe, B. W., *Excavations at Portchester Castle, Vol. I: Roman*, London, 1975.

Dameski, 1974. Dameski, V., 'A Survey of Types of Glass on the Territory of Croatia during the Roman Empire', *Arheolovski Vestnik*, **25** (1974), 69 (English summary).

Daniels, 1959. Daniels, C. M., 'The Roman Bath House at Red House, Beaufront, near Corbridge', *Archaeol. Aeliana ser.* 4, **37** (1959) 85–176.

Darling, 1977. Darling, M., 'Pottery from Early Military Sites in Western Britain' in (Ed.) Dore, J. and Greene, K. T., *Roman Pottery Studies in Britain and Beyond* (pp. 57–100) Oxford, 1977.

Davey, 1961. Davey, N., *A History of Building Materials*, London, 1961.

Davey, 1972. Davey, N., 'The Conservation of Romano-British Painted Plaster', *Britannia*, **3** (1972) 251–68.

Déchelette, 1904. Déchelette, J., *Les Vases Céramique Ornés de la Gaule Romaine, Vol. 2*, Paris, 1904.

Dore and Greene, 1977. (Ed.) Dore, J. and Greene, K. T., *Roman Pottery Studies in Britain and Beyond*, Oxford, 1977.

Douch and Beard, 1970. Douch, H. L. and Beard, S. W., 'Excavations at Carvossa, Probus, 1968–70: Interim Report', *Cornish Archaeology*, **9** (1970) 93–7.

Down and Rule, 1971. Down, A. and Rule, M., *Chichester Excavations, I*, Chichester, 1971.

Down, forthcoming. Down, A., *Chichester Excavations, III*.

Drack, 1950. Drack, W., *Die Römische Wandmalerei der Schweiz*, Geneva, 1950.

Dudley, 1967. Dudley, D., 'Excavations on Nor'nour in the Isles of Scilly, 1962–6', *Archaeol. J.*, **124** (1967) 1–64.

Duncan-Jones, 1964. Duncan-Jones, R., 'An Epigraphic Survey of Costs in Roman Italy', *Pap. Brit. Sch. Rome*, **33** (1965) 175–88.

Duncan-Jones, 1974. Duncan-Jones, R., *The Economy of the Roman Empire*, Cambridge, 1974.

Dunning, 1949. Dunning, G. C., 'The Purbeck Marble Industry in the Roman Period', *Archaeol. Newsletter* (March, 1949), 15.

Duval, 1961. Duval, P-M., *Paris Antique*, Paris, 1961.

Eschebach, 1973. Eschebach, H., 'Untersuchungen in den Stabianer Thermen zu Pompeji', *Mitteilungen des Deutschen Archaeologischen Instituts, Römische Abteilung*, **80** (1973) 235–42.

Espérandieu, 1931. Espérandieu, E., *Recueil Général des Bas-Reliefs, Statues et Bustes de la Germanie Romaine*, Paris and Brussels, 1931.

Exner, 1939. Exner, K., 'Die provincialrömischen Emailfibeln der Rheinlande'. *Bericht der Römisch-germanischen Kommission*, **29** (1939) 31ff.

Farrar, 1973. Farrar, R. A. H., 'The Techniques and Sources of Romano-British black-burnished Ware', in (Ed.) Detsicas, A., *Current Research in Romano-British Coarse Pottery*, (pp. 67–103) London, 1973.

Fellmann, 1958. Fellmann, R., *Die Principia des Legionslagers Vindonissa und das Zentralgebäude der römischer Lager und Kastelle*, Brugg, 1958.

Fels, 1927. Fels, C., 'Grabungen der Gesellschaft Pro Vindonissa: Grabung auf des Sudfront des Prätoriums im Herbst 1925', *Anzeiger für Schweizerische Altertumskunde*, **29** (1927) 91–6.

Fowler, 1962. Fowler, P. J., 'A Native Homestead of the Roman Period at Porth Godrevy, Gwithian', *Cornish Archaeology*, **1** (1962) 17–60.

Fox, 1952. Fox, A., *Roman Exeter (Isca Dumnoniorum): Excavations in the War-damaged Areas, 1945–7*, Manchester, 1952.

Fox, 1952. Fox, A., 'Roman Discoveries in Exeter, 1951–2', *Proc. Devon Archaeol. Soc.*, **10** (1952) 106–114.

Fox, 1953.   Fox, A., 'Excavations in Bear St., Exeter,' *Proc. Devon Archaeol. Soc.*, **11** (1953) 30–41.

Fox, 1966.   Fox, A., 'Roman Exeter (*Isca Dumnoniorum*), Origins and Early Development', in (Ed.) Wacher, J. S., *The Civitas Capitals of Roman Britain* (pp. 46–51), Leicester, 1966.

Fox, 1968.   Fox, A., 'Excavations at the South Gate, Exeter, 1964–5', *Proc. Devon Archaeol. Soc.*, **26** (1968) 1–20.

Fox, 1974.   Fox, A., 'New Light on the Military Occupation of South-West England', in (Ed.) Birley, E., Dobson, B. and Jarrett, M., *Roman Frontier Studies 1969*, Cardiff, 1974.

Fox, 1965.   Fox, C., 'The Siting of the Monastery of St Mary and St Peter in Exeter', in (Ed.) Harden, D. B., *Dark Age Britain*, London, 1965.

Fox and Dunning, 1957.   Fox, A. and Dunning, G. C., 'A Medieval Pottery Kiln in Exeter', *Antiq. J.*, **37** (1957) 43–53.

Fox and Ravenhill, 1959.   Fox, A. and Ravenhill, W., 'The Stoke Hill Roman Signal Station, Excavations 1956–7', *Trans. Devon Ass.*, **91** (1959) 71–82.

Fox and Ravenhill, 1972.   Fox, A. and Ravenhill, W., 'The Roman Fort at Nanstallon, Cornwall', *Britannia*, **3** (1972) 56–111.

Fremersdorf, 1967.   Fremersdorf, F., *Die Römischen Gläser mit Schliff, Bemalung und Goldauflagen aus Köln*, Cologne, 1967.

Frere, 1967.   Frere, S. S., *Britannia*, London, 1967.

Frere, 1971.   Frere, S. S., 'The Forum and Baths at Caistor by Norwich', *Britannia*, **2** (1971) 1–26.

Frere, 1972.   Frere, S. S., *Verulamium Excavations: I*, London, 1972.

Frere, 1975.   Frere, S. S., 'The Silchester Church: The Excavations by Sir Ian Richmond in 1961', *Archaeologia*, **105** (1975) 277–303.

Frere and St Joseph, 1974.   Frere, S. S. and St Joseph, J. K., 'The Roman Fortress at Longthorpe', *Britannia*, **5** (1974) 1–129.

Fulford, 1977.   Fulford, M., 'Pottery and Britain's Foreign Trade in the Later Roman Period', in (Ed.) Peacock, D. P. S., *Pottery and Early Commerce* (pp. 35–84), London, 1977.

Furtwängler, 1969.   Furtwängler, A. E., 'Bruchstücke von Grossbronzen in Avenches', *Bulletin de l'Association pro Aventico*, **20** (1969) 42–52.

Germania Romana, II.   *Germania Romana, II* (*Die Bürglericher Siedlung*), Bamberg, 1924.

van Giffen, 1948.   van Giffen, A. E., 'Thermen en Castella te Heerlen (L.): Een Rapport en een Werkhypothese', *L'Antiquité Classique*, **17** (1948) 199–236.

Gillam, 1970.   Gillam, J. P., *Types of Roman Coarse Pottery in Northern Britain*, (3rd edn.), Newcastle-upon-Tyne, 1970.

Gillam, 1976.   Gillam, J. P., 'Coarse Fumed Ware in North Britain and Beyond', *Glasgow Archaeol. J.*, **4** (1976) 57–80.

Goodchild, 1946.   Goodchild, R. G., 'The Origins of the Romano-British Forum', *Antiquity*, **10** (1946) 70–7.

Goodchild and Milne, 1937.   Goodchild, R. G. and Milne, J. G., 'The Greek Coins from Exeter Reconsidered', *Numis, Chron. ser. 5.*, **17** (1937) 124–41.

von Gonzenbach, 1961.   von Gonzenbach, V., *Die Römische Mosaik der Schweiz*, 1961.

Green, 1977.   Green, C. J. S., 'The Significance of Plaster Burials for the recognition of Christian Cemeteries', in (Ed.) Reece, R., *Burial in the Roman World* (pp. 46–53), London, 1977.

Green, 1959.   Green, H. J. M., 'An Architectural Survey of the Roman Baths at Godmanchester', *Archaeol. News Letter*, **6** (1959) 223–330.

Greenaway and Henig, 1975.   Greenaway, J. and Henig, M., 'A Moulded Glass Cameo from Silchester', *Britannia*, **6** (1975) 209–10.

Greene, 1972.   Greene, K. T., *Guide to Pre-Flavian Fine Wares*, Cardiff, 1972.

Greene and Greene, 1970.   Greene, J. P. and Greene, K. T., 'A Trial Excavation on a Romano-British Site at Clanacombe, Thurlestone, 1969', *Proc. Devon Archaeol. Soc.*, **28** (1970) 130–6.

Greenfield, 1964.   Greenfield, E., 'Excavation of a Bombed Site in Chapel St., Exeter', *Trans. Devon Ass.*, **96** (1964) 339–79.

Grenier, 1958.   Grenier, A., *Manuel d'Archéologie Gallo-Romaine, Troisième Partie: L'Architecture*, Paris, 1958.

Haberey, 1942.   Haberey, W., 'Spätantike Gläser aus Gräben von Mayen', *Bonner Jahrbücher*, **142** (1942) 249–84.

Harden, 1966.   Harden, D. B., 'New Light on Roman and Early Medieval Window Glass', *Glastechnische Berichte*, **8** (1966) 8–16.

Harden, 1969.   Harden, D. B., 'Ancient Glass II: Roman', *Archaeol. J.*, **126** (1969) 44–77.

Harris, 1972.   Harris, H. A., *Sport in Greece and Rome*, London, 1972.

Hartley, 1972.   Hartley, B. R., 'The Roman Occupation of Scotland: the evidence of samian ware', *Britannia*, **3** (1972) 1–55.

Hauser, 1901.   Hauser, O., 'Die Arbeiten der Antiquarischen Geschellschaft von Brugg im Jahre 1900', *Anzeiger für Schweizerische Altertumskunde*, **3** (1901) 31–5.

Haverfield and MacDonald, 1907.   Haverfield, F. and MacDonald, S., 'Greek Coins at Exeter', *Numis. Chron. ser. 4*, **7** (1907) 145–55.

Hebditch and Mellor, 1973.   Hebditch, M. and Mellor, J., 'The Forum and Basilica of Roman Leicester', *Britannia*, **4** (1973) 1–83.

Hellenkemper, 1975.   Hellenkemper, H., 'Architektur als Beitrag zur Geschichte der Colonia Claudia Ara Agrippinensium', in (Ed.) Temporini, H., *Aufstieg und Niedergang der Römischen Welt: II (Prinzipat)*, 4, Berlin, 1974.

Hermet, 1934.   Hermet, F., *La Graufesenque*, Paris, 1934.

Hinz, 1961.   Hinz, H., 'I. Bericht über die Ausgrabungen in der *Colonia Ulpia Traiana* nordlich der Xanten', *Bonner Jahrbücher*, **161** (1961) 343–95.

Hinz, 1975.   Hinz, H., 'Colonia Ulpia Traiana', in (Ed.) Temporini, H., *Aufstieg und Niedergang der Römischen Welt: II (Prinzipat)*, 4, Berlin, 1974.

HK.   Carson, R. A. G., Hill, P. V. and Kent, J. P. C., *Late Roman Bronze Coinage, part 2*, London, 1960.

Hooker.   John Vowell *alias* Hoker, *The Description of the Citie of Excester*, (Ed.) Harte, W. J., Schopp, J. W. and Tapley-Soper, H. (3 vols.), Exeter, 1947.

Hoskins, 1960.   Hoskins, W. G., *Two Thousand Years in Exeter*, Exeter, 1960.

Hull, 1963.   Hull, M. R., *The Roman Potters' Kilns of Colchester*, Oxford, 1963.

Hurst, 1972.   Hurst, H., 'Excavations in Gloucester, 1968–71', *Antiq. J.*, **52** (1972) 24–69.

Isings, 1957.   Isings, C., *Roman Glass from Dated Finds*, Gröningen, 1957.

Jahn, 1909.   Jahn, V., 'Das römischen Dachziegel von Windisch', *Anzeiger für Schweizerische Altertumskunde*, **11** (1909) 111–129.

Jarrett, 1969.   (Ed.) Jarrett, M. G., *The Roman Frontier in Wales*, Cardiff, 1969.

Jarvis and Maxfield, 1975.   Jarvis, K. and Maxfield, V. A., 'The Excavation of a First-Century Roman Farmstead and a Late Neolithic Settlement, Topsham, Devon', *Proc. Devon Arch. Soc.*, **33** (1975) 209–66.

Kähler, 1950.   Kähler, H., *Hadrian und seine Villa bei Tivoli*, Berlin, 1950.

Keller, 1913.   Keller, O., *Die Antike Tierwelt*, 1913.

Kenyon, 1935.   Kenyon, K. M., 'The Roman Theatre at Verulamium, St Albans', *Archaeologia*, **84** (1935) 213–81.

Kenyon, 1948.   Kenyon, K. M., *Excavations at the Jewry Wall Site, Leicester*, Oxford, 1948.

Kleiss, 1962.   Kleiss, W., 'Die Öffentlichen Bauten von Cambodunum', *Materialhefte zur Bayerischen Vorgeschichte*, **18** (1962).

Knorr, 1919.   Knorr, R., *Töpfer und Fabriken verzierter Terra-Sigillata des ersten Jahrhunderts*, Stuttgart, 1919.

Knorr, 1952.   Knorr, R., *Terra Sigillata-Gefässe des ersten Jahrhunderts mit Töpfernamen*, Stuttgart, 1952.

Koenen, 1904.   Koenen, C., 'Novaesium, Das im Auftrag des rheinischen Provincialverbandes vom Bonner Provinzialmuseum 1887–1900 gegrabene Legionslager', *Bonner Jahrbücher*, **111/112** (1904).

Krencker, 1929.   Krencker, D., *Die Trierer Kaiserthermen*, Augsburg, 1929.

Kretzschmer, 1961.   Kretzschmer, F., 'Die Entwicklungsgeschichte des Antiken Bades und das Bad auf dem Magdalensberg', *Carinthia I*, **151** (1961) 213–75.

Landels, 1978.   Landels, J. G., *Engineering in the Ancient World*, London, 1978.

Laur-Belart, 1928.   Laur-Belart, R., 'Grabungen der Gesellschaft Pro Vindonissa in den Jahren 1926–7', *Anzeiger für Schweizerische Altertumskunde*, **30** (1928) 18–36.

Laur-Belart, 1930.   Laur-Belart, R., 'Grabungen der Gesellschaft Pro Vindonissa im Jahre 1929', *ibid.*, **32** (1930) 65–102.

Laur-Belart, 1931.   Laur-Belart, R., 'Grabungen der Gesellschaft Pro Vindonissa im Jahre 1930', *ibid.*, **33** (1931) 203–36.

Laur-Belart, 1935.   Laur-Belart, R., *Vindonissa, Lager und Vicus*, (Römisch-germanische Forschungen, **10** (1935)).

Laur-Belart, 1966.   Laur-Belart, R., *Führer durch Augusta Raurica*, Basle, 1966.

Lawrence, 1957.   Lawrence, A. W., *Greek Architecture*, London, 1957.

Lega-Weekes, 1912.   Lega-Weekes, E., 'An Account of the Hospitium de le Egle, etc.', *Trans. Devon Ass.*, **44** (1912) 480–551.

Lethbridge, 1952.   Lethbridge, T. C., 'Excavations at Kilpheder, South Uist, and the Problem of Broch and Wheel-houses', *Proc. Prehist. Soc.*, **18** (1952) 179–94.

Levison, 1905.   (Ed.) Levison, W., *Vitae Sancti Bonifatii*, Hanover, 1905.

Ling, 1971.   Ling, R., 'Cylinders in Campanian Art', *Antiq. J.*, **51** (1971) 267–80.

Loeschke, 1919.   Loeschke, S., *Lampen aus Vindonissa*, Zurich, 1919.

Lugli, 1946.   Lugli, G., *Roma Antica: Il Centro Monumentale*, Rome, 1946.

Lugli, 1957.   Lugli, G., *La Tecnica Edilizia Romana*, Rome, 1957.

MacDonald and Curle, 1929.   MacDonald, G. and Curle, A. O., 'The Roman Fort at Mumrills, near Falkirk', *Proc. Soc. Antiq. Scot.*, **63** (1928–9) 396–575.

MacMullen, 1959.   MacMullen, R., 'Roman Imperial Building in the Provinces', *Harvard Studies in Classical Philology*, **64** (1959) 207–235.

Maiuri, 1942.   Maiuri, A., *L'Ultima Fase Edilizia di Pompeii*, Naples, 1942.

Maiuri, 1950a.   Maiuri, A., 'Significato e Natura del Solium nelle Terme Romane', *La Parola del Passato*, **15** (1950) 223–7.

Maiuri, 1950b.   Maiuri, A., 'Scoperta di un edificio termale nella Regio VIII, Insula 5, nr. 36', *Notizie degli scavi di antichità*, **66** (1950) 116–36.

Maiuri, 1957.   Maiuri, A., *Le pitture di Pompeii, Ercolano e Stabia nel Museo Nazionale di Napoli*, Naples, 1957.

Maiuri, 1958.   Maiuri, A., *Ercolano, I Nuovi Scavi*, (2 vols), Rome, 1958.

Manning, 1975.   Manning, W. H., 'Roman Military Granaries in Britain', *Saalburg Jahrbuch*, **32** (1975) 105–29.

Manning, 1976.   Manning, W. H., 'The Conquest of the West Country', in (Ed.) Branigan, K. and Fowler, P. J., *The Roman West Country* (pp. 15–41), Newton Abbot, 1976.

Margary, 1967.   Margary, I. D., *Roman Roads in Britain*, London, 1967.

Martin, 1957.   Martin, R., *Lehrbuch der Anthropologie*, Stuttgart, 1957.

Masson Phillips, 1966.   Masson Phillips, E. N., 'Excavation of a Romano-British site at Lower Well Farm, Stoke Gabriel, Devon', *Proc. Devon Archaeol. Soc.*, **23** (1966) 3–34.

Mau-Kelsey, 1899.   Mau, A. (trans. Kelsey, F. W.), *Pompeii, Its Life and Art*, London, 1899.

May, 1916.   May, T., *The Pottery found at Silchester*, London, 1916.

Meaney and Hawkes, 1970.   Meaney, A. L. and Hawkes, S. C., *Two Anglo-Saxon Cemeteries at Winnall*, (*Soc. for Medieval Archaeol Monograph Ser.* 4), London, 1970.

Merrifield, 1965.   Merrifield, R., *The Roman City of London*, London, 1965.

Miles, 1977.   Miles, H., 'The Honeyditches Villa, Seaton', *Britannia*, **8** (1977) 107–48.

Miles and Miles, 1973.   Miles, H. and Miles, T., 'Excavations at Trethurgy, St Austell: Interim Report', *Cornish Archaeology*, **12** (19i73) 25–30.

Milles, 1782.   Milles, J., 'Account of some Roman Antiquities discovered at Exeter', *Archaeologia*, **6** (1782) 1–5.

Mócsy, 1974.   Mócsy, A., *Pannonia and Upper Moesia*, London, 1974.

Montague and Morris, 1933.   Montague, L. A. D. and Morris, P., 'Report of the Exeter Excavation Committee: Roman Remains in the Cathedral Close, Exeter', *Proc. Devon Archaeol. Explor. Soc.*, **2** (1933–6) 224–37.

Montgomerie-Neilson and Montague, 1933.   Montgomerie-Neilson, E. and Montague, L. A. D., 'Report on the Excavations in the Deanery Garden, Exeter, 1932–3', *Proc. Devon Archaeol. Explor. Soc.*, **2** (1933–6), 72–8.

Morant, 1922.   Morant, G. M., 'A First Study of the Tibetan Skull', *Biometrika*, **14** (1922) 193–260.

Morris, 1941.   Morris, P. in 'Roman Britain in 1940', *J. Roman Stud.*, **31** (1941) 138.

Münten and Heimberg, 1976.   Münten, F. and Heimburg, U., 'Bonn' in 'Jahresberichte des Staatlichen Vertrauensmannes für Kulturgeschichtliche Bodenaltertümer', *Bonner Jahrbücher*, **176** (1976) 397–401.

Murray-Thriepland, 1956.   Murray-Thriepland, L., 'An Excavation in St Mawgan-in-Pyder, North Cornwall', *Archaeol. J.*, **113** (1956) 33–83.

Murray-Thriepland, 1965.   Murray-Thriepland, L., 'The Museum Street Site, 1965', *Archaeol. Cambrensis*, **114** (1965) 130–45.

Nash-Williams, 1930.   Nash-Williams, V. E., 'Further Excavations at Caerwent, Mon., 1923–5', *Archaeologia*, **80** (1930) 229–88.

Nash-Williams, 1932.   Nash-Williams, V. E., 'The Roman Legionary Fortress at Caerleon in Monmouthshire: Report on the Excavations in Prysg Field, 1927–9, Part II', *Archaeol. Cambrensis*, **87** (1932) 48–104.

Nash-Williams, 1953.   Nash-Williams, V. E., 'The Forum-and-Basilica and Public Baths of the Roman Town of Venta Silurum at Caerwent in Monmouthshire', *Bull. Board Celtic Stud.*, **15** (1953) 159–67.

Nash-Williams, 1953a.   Nash-Williams, V. E., 'The Roman Villa at Llantwit Major, Glamorgan', *Archaeol. Cambrensis*, **102** (1953) 89–163.

Neal, 1974.   Neal, D. S., *The Excavation of the Roman Villa in Gadebridge Park, Hemel Hempstead, 1963–8*, London, 1974.

Neal, 1974–6.   Neal, D. S., 'Three Roman Buildings in the Bulbourne Valley', *Hertfordshire Archaeol.*, **4** (1974–6) 1–95.

Neumann, 1967.   Neumann, A., 'Forschungen in Vindobona, 1948–67: I, Lager und Lager-territorium', *Der Römische Limes in Österreich*, **23** (1967).

Newstead, 1928.   Newstead, R., 'Report on the Excavations on the Site of the Roman Fortress at the Deanery Field, Chester, (No. 2)', *Annals Archaeol. Anthropology*, **15** (1928) 3–32.

Noel-Hume, 1950.   Noel-Hume, I., *Discoveries in the Walbrook*, London, 1950.

O'Sullivan, 1969.   O'Sullivan, J. C., 'Wooden Pumps', *Folk Life*, **7** (1969) 101–116.

Panella, 1972.   Panella, C., 'Annotazioni in Margine alle Stratigrafie delle Terme Ostiensi del Nuotatore', in *Recherches sur les Amphores Romaines* (*Collection de l'École Française de Rome*, 10) Rome, 1972.

Peacock, 1975.   Peacock, D. P. S., 'Amphorae and the Baetican Fish Industry', *Antiq. J.*, **55**(1975) 232–243.

Peacock, 1977. Peacock, D. P. S., 'Pompeian Red Ware', in (Ed.) Peacock, D. P. S., *Pottery and Early Commerce* (pp. 147–62), London, 1977.

Peacock, forthcoming. Peacock, D. P. S., 'Roman Amphorae, Typology, Fabric and Origin', *Collection de l'École Française de Rome*, forthcoming.

Peate, 1970. Peate, I. C., *The Denbigh Cockpit and Cockfighting in Wales*, National Museum of Wales (Welsh Folk Museum), 1970.

von Petrikovits, 1975. von Petrikovits, H., *Die Innenbauten römischer Legionslager während der Prinzipatszeit*, Opladen, 1975.

Philp, 1977. Philp, B. J., 'The Forum of Roman London, 1968–9', *Britannia*, **8** (1977) 1–64.

Pirling, 1966. Pirling, R., *Das Römisch-Frankische Gräberfeld von Krefeld-Gellep*, (Germanische Denkmäler der Völkerwanderungzeit, Serie B.2), 1966.

Platner and Ashby, 1929. Platner, S. B. and Ashby, T., *A Topographical Dictionary of Ancient Rome*, Oxford, 1929.

Plommer, 1956. Plommer, H., *Ancient and Classical Architecture* (Simpson's History of Architectural Development, I), London, 1966.

Plommer, 1973. Plommer, H., *Vitruvius and Later Building Manuals*, Cambridge, 1973.

Pollard, 1974. Pollard, S., 'A Late Iron Age Settlement and a Romano-British Villa at Holcombe, near Uplyme, Devon'. *Proc. Devon Archaeol. Soc.*, **32** (1974) 59–161.

Price, 1973. Price, J., 'Some Roman Glass from Spain', in *Annales du 6ᵉ Congrès de l'Association Internationale pour l'Histoire du Verre*, Cologne, 1973.

Rahtz, 1977. Rahtz, P., 'Late Roman cemeteries and beyond', in (Ed.) Reece, R., *Burial in the Roman World* (pp. 53–64), London, 1977.

Raimbault, 1973. Raimbault, M., 'La Céramique Gallo-Romaine dite "à l'éponge" dans l'Ouest de la Gaulle', *Gallia*, **31** (1973) 185–206.

Ralegh Radford, 1937–47. Ralegh Radford, C. A., 'The Roman Site at Topsham', *Proc. Devon Archaeol. Explor. Soc.*, **3** (1937–47) 6–23.

Ralegh Radford and Morris, 1933–6. Ralegh Radford, C. A. and Morris, P., 'Report of the Exeter Excavation Committee', *ibid.* **2** (1933–6) 225–240.

R.C.H.M., 1962. Royal Commission on Historical Monuments, *An Inventory of the Historical Monuments in the City of York, I: Eburacum, Roman York*, London, 1962.

R.C.H.M., 1970. Royal Commission on Historical Monuments, *Dorset*, vol. 2 (south-east), pt. 3, London, 1970.

RIB(i). Collingwood, R. G. and Wright, R. P., *The Roman Inscriptions of Britain: I, Inscriptions on Stone*, Oxford, 1965.

RIC. Mattingly, H. and others, *The Roman Imperial Coinage*, London, 1923–67.

Richardson, 1940. Richardson, K. M., 'Excavations at Poundbury, Dorchester, Dorset, 1939', *Antiq. J.*, **20** (1940) 429–448.

Richmond, 1968. Richmond, I. A., *Hod Hill, volume 2: Excavations carried out between 1951 and 1958*, London, 1968.

Rivet, 1969. (Ed.) Rivet, A. L. F., *The Roman Villa in Britain*, London, 1969.

Rolland, 1946. Rolland, H., *Fouilles de Glanum (Saint-Rémy-de-Provence)* (Supplément de Gallia) Paris, 1946.

Russell, 1968. Russell, J., 'The Origin and Development of Republican Forums', *Phoenix*, **22** (1968), 304–36.

S. Sydenham, E. A., *The Coinage of the Roman Republic*, London, 1952.

Schleiermacher, 1972. Schleiermacher, W., *Cambodunum-Kempten: Eine Römerstadt in Allgau*, Bonn, 1972.

Schultze, 1928. Schultze, R., *Basilika: Untersuchungen zur Antiken und Frühmittelalterlichen Baukunst* (*Römisch-Germanische Forschungen*, 2), Berlin, 1928.

Schwarz, 1969. Schwarz, G. Th., 'Die Flavischen Thermen "En Perruet" in Aventicum', *Bulletin de l'Association Pro Aventico*, **20** (1969) 59–68.

Shiel, 1975. Shiel, N., 'Finds of Æ Coins', *Numis. Circ.*, **83** (1975) 475.

Shipley, 1933. Shipley, F. W., *Agrippa's Building Activities in Rome*, St Louis, 1933.

Shortt, 1840. Shortt, W. T. P., *Sylva Antiqua Iscana*, London, 1840.

Shortt, 1841. Shortt, W. T. P., *Collectanea Curiosa Antiqua Dumnonia*, London, 1841.

Simonett, 1936. Simonett, C., 'Grabungen der Gesellschaft Pro Vindonissa in den Jahren 1934 und 1935 auf der Breite', *Anzeiger für Schweizerische Altertumskunde*, **38** (1936) 161–73.

Simpson, 1976. Simpson, G., 'Decorated Terra Sigillata at Montans', *Britannia*, **7** (1976) 244–73.

Smith, 1852. Smith, H. E., *Reliquiae Isurianae*, London, 1852.

Stead, 1967. Stead, I. M., 'A La Tène III Burial from Welwyn Garden City', *Archaeologia*, **101** (1967) 1–62.

Stevens, 1942. Stevens, C. E., 'Notes on Roman Chester', *J. Chester Archaeol. Soc.*, **35** (1942) 49–52.

St John Hope and Fox, 1905. St John Hope, W. H. and Fox, G. E., 'Excavations on the Site of the Roman City of Silchester, Hants, in 1903 and 1904', *Archaeologia*, **59** (1905) 333–70.

St. Joseph, 1977. St. Joseph, J. K., 'Aerial Reconnaisance in Britain', *J. Roman Stud.*, **67** (1977) 125–161.

Strong, 1968. Strong, D., 'The Monument' in (Ed.) Cunliffe, B., *Fifth Report on the Excavations of the Roman Fort at Richborough, Kent* (pp. 40–73), London, 1968.

Taylor, 1959. (Ed.) Taylor, M. V., 'Roman Britain in 1958', *J. Roman Stud.*, **49** (1959) 102–35.

Thatcher, 1956. Thatcher, E. D., 'The Open Rooms of the Terme del Foro at Ostia', *Memoirs of the American Academy at Rome*, **24** (1956) 169–220.

Thomas 1971. Thomas, C., *The Early Christian Archaeology of Northern Britain*, Glasgow, 1971.

Todd, 1977. Todd, M., '*Famosa Pestis* and Britain in the Fifth Century', *Britannia*, **8** (1977) 319–326.

Toynbee, 1973. Toynbee, J. M. C., *Animals in Roman Life and Art*, London, 1973.

VCH. *Victoria County Histories*.

Vegas, 1966. Vegas, M., *Die römische Lampen von Neuss (Novaesium ii)*, Berlin, 1966.

Vetters, 1953. Vetters, H., 'Das Legionsbad von Lauriacum', *Forschungen in Lauriacum*, **1** (1953) 49–53.

Wacher, 1962. Wacher, J. S., 'Cirencester 1961: Second Interim Report', *Antiq. J.*, **42** (1962) 1–14.

Wacher, 1971. Wacher, J. S., 'Roman Iron Beams', *Britannia*, **2** (1971) 200–3.

Wacher, 1974. Wacher, J. S., *The Towns of Roman Britain*, London, 1974.

Ward-Perkins, 1970. Boethius, A. and Ward-Perkins, J. B., *Etruscan and Roman Architecture*, London, 1970.

Ward-Perkins, 1970a. Ward-Perkins, J. B., 'From Republic to Empire: Reflections on the Early Provincial Architecture of the Roman West', *J. Roman Stud.*, **60** (1970) 1–19.

Ward-Perkins and Goodchild, 1953. Ward-Perkins, J. B. and Goodchild, R. G., 'The Christian Antiquities of Tripolitania', *Archaeologia*, **95** (1953) 1–82.

Warmington, 1976. Warmington, B. H., 'Nero, Boudicca and the Frontier in the West', in (Ed.) Branigan, K. and Fowler, P. J., *The Roman West Country* (pp. 42–51), Newton Abbot, 1976.

Webster, 1959. Webster, G., 'Roman Windows and Grilles', *Antiquity*, **33** (1959) 10–14.

Webster, 1975. Webster, G., *The Cornovii*, London, 1975.

Webster, 1977. (Ed.) Webster, G., *Romano-British Coarse Pottery: a Student's Guide* (3rd edn.), London, 1977.

Webster and Woodfield, 1966. Webster, G. and Woodfield, P., ' "The Old Work" at the Roman Public Baths at Wroxeter', *Antiq. J.*, **46** (1966) 229–39.

Wedlake, 1958. Wedlake, W. J., *Excavations at Camerton, Somerset, 1926–50*, Camerton, 1958.

Weinberg, 1965. Weinberg, G. D., 'The Antikythera Shipwreck Reconsidered', *Transactions of the American Philosophical Society*, **55** (1965) 1–33.

Wheeler, 1929.   Wheeler, R. E. M., 'The Roman Lighthouses at Dover', *Archaeol. J.*, **36** (1929) 29–46.

Wheeler, 1930.   Wheeler, R. E. M., *London in Roman Times*, London, 1930.

Wheeler, 1932.   Wheeler, R. E. M., 'Notes on Building Construction in Roman Britain', *J. Roman Stud.*, **22** (1932) 117–34.

Wheeler, 1943.   Wheeler, R. E. M., *Maiden Castle, Dorset*, Oxford, 1943.

Whitwell, 1974.   Whitwell, J. B., in Addyman, P., 'Excavations in York, 1972–3', *Antiq. J.*, **54** (1974) 200–32.

Wilkes, 1969.   Wilkes, J. J., *Dalmatia*, London, 1969.

Wilson, 1970.   (Ed.) Wilson, D. R., 'Roman Britain in 1969. I: Sites Explored', *Britannia*, **1** (1970) 269–305.

Wilson, 1971.   (Ed.) Wilson, D. R., 'Roman Britain in 1970, I: Sites Explored', *Britannia*, **2** (1971) 243–288.

SUMMARY

The Legionary Fortress (c. 55/60–75):

In a brief account of the newly-discovered fortress of the Second Augustan Legion at Exeter, the defences, plan and internal buildings, including barrack-blocks, a *fabrica* and granaries, are discussed. There is a resumé of the relevant dating evidence, which suggests a foundation-date in the fifties of the first century A.D., probably during the latter half of the decade; occupation by the Second Augustan Legion can be shown to have continued into the early Flavian period and appears to have terminated c. 75. Other military sites in the Exeter area are described, most notably an establishment sited south-east of the fortress. The evidence for *canabae*, cemeteries, an aqueduct and industries is also considered.

The Legionary Bath-House (c. 60/65–80):

Period 1A (*c.* 60/65–75): the baths were erected on a reserved site, probably some 4000 sq.m in extent, in the angle between the *viae principalis* and *praetoria*. Their construction-date lies in the sixties, probably c. 65. Excavation revealed the *caldarium*, part of the *tepidarium*, a small area of the *palaestra*, which contained a feature interpreted as a cock-fighting pit, a furnace-house and service-buildings. It is suggested that the plan of the bath-house has very strong affinities with broadly contemporary examples at Vindonissa and Avenches, and that the axially-symmetrical plans of these buildings point to a connection with the development of the 'Imperial' type of bath-house.

Period 1B (*c.* 75–80): a reduction in the size of the bath-house is thought to have occurred when the fortress was dismantled c. 75. Demolition-deposits associated with the construction-work of Period 2A produced much decorative material, including fragments of one or more figured pavements, two types of antefix, and Purbeck-marble mouldings and veneers. Three-dimensional reconstructions of the internal and external appearances of the bath-house are attempted.

The Forum and Basilica (c. 80–the late fourth century):

Period 2A (construction) (*c.* 80): parts of the legionary bath-house were incorporated into a civil *basilica*, which originally consisted of a nave without aisles but with a range of rooms on its north-east side. The *basilica* had an open front but this was soon closed off by the construction of an aisle or passage. Parts of the *forum*-courtyard and south-east *forum* portico and range were also explored. The results of the excavations carried out in 1945–6 are reconsidered and the walls and metalled surfaces which were traced at that time can now be seen to have lain on the south-west side of the *forum*. It has been possible to reconstruct an outline plan of the *basilica* and *forum*, which measured 106.5 m by 67 m overall. Outside the south-west range there was an open market-place (67 m by 32 m). The planning of the central area of the Roman town and the evidence for the site of the public baths is also considered.

Periods 2B–3A (alterations to the *basilica* and *forum*, late Antonine to late fourth century): at the beginning of Period 2B a room was built on the site of the south-east *forum* portico and a range of rooms was constructed along the south-east side of the *basilica*. Period 2C (last quarter of the third century) saw the reconstruction of the aisle or passage at the front of the *basilica* and alterations were made to the range south-east of the *basilica*. In Period 3A (after *c.* 340) the *basilica* was extended south-eastwards to accommodate a tribunal.

Other Sites in the Cathedral Close:

South-east of the *basilica* and *forum* a considerable length of Roman street was explored. Buildings on its south-east side were also investigated; one contained a badly damaged mosaic pavement. Evidence was recovered for the position of a street running down the north-west side of the *basilica* and *forum*, which had originally functioned as the *via praetoria* of the fortress.

Post-Roman Activities on the Site of the Basilica and Forum:

The *basilica* was demolished before the middle of the fifth century. For a time its site appears to have been given over to casual occupation; a few pits are known from this period. Six graves on the Roman alignment are thought to represent the remains of a Christian cemetery of unknown extent. Two of the graves were dated by Carbon 14 to about the middle of the fifth century.

Later remains which have been excavated in the Cathedral Close will form the subject of another monograph.

I. THE LEGIONARY FORTRESS AND ITS SETTING

1. THE LEGIONARY FORTRESS (Figs 1–3)

Ptolemy placed the Second Augustan Legion at the Dumnonian *Isca* (Exeter) rather than the Silurian *Isca* (Caerleon) where it was stationed from *c.* A.D. 75 (Bidwell and Boon, 1976, 279). In the nineteenth century this ascription was accepted and an enthusiastic local antiquary, W. T. P. Shortt, published a plan of the *Castrametatio Romana Iscana* which plotted various finds of Roman material made at Exeter within the lay-out of a legionary 'camp' (Shortt, 1840, section entitled 'Roman Camp of Isca', (not paginated)). However when the first scientific excavations were carried out in Exeter during the early 1930's, no evidence of early military occupation was recovered (details summarised in Fox, 1952, 98–104). These investigations were carried out on a very small scale but, when larger areas were explored following the Second World War, the absence of any signs of a military occupation appeared to be confirmed.

In 1964, however, a short length of military ditch was found below the town rampart; its excavator suggested that it belonged to a six-acre fort in the Holloway Street area (Fox, 1968, 3–6). In 1971–2 timber barrack-blocks of legionary size and part of a *fabrica* were excavated on the Guildhall site, and a Neronian bath-house of substantial size was uncovered in the Cathedral Close. Since then excavations have been carried out elsewhere within the fortress and the outline of its plan has been recovered.

It is the purpose of this section to provide a brief account of the legionary fortress and its setting. The internal buildings are not described in detail; greater attention has been paid to establishing the overall plan and to setting out the dating evidence, since these particular aspects have a direct bearing on the site which forms the subject of the following report.

Siting:

The fortress occupied a position on a spur which overlooked the lowest fordable point on the River Exe (Fig. 1). It was ideally placed to control the Exe valley which, as recent aerial photography has shown, was probably intensively settled in the late pre-Roman Iron Age. Land communications to the east were by means of an extension of the Fosse Way which appears to have originally terminated near Axminster. Roads also led off into north and central Devon and towards the South Hams, a rich agricultural area (Margary, 1967, 113–21). The Exe was probably navigable as far as Exeter and so the fortress would have been accessible by water.

Defences:

In 1975 the discovery of two ditches established the position of the southern corner of the fortress defences. The larger outer ditch was 2.5 m deep and 4 m wide with a marked 'Punic' profile (i.e. with the outer side nearly vertical); its course was traced over a distance of 50 m. The smaller ditch occupied a position less than 2 m from the inner lip of the larger ditch; it had a V-shaped profile and was 2.5 m in width and 1.5 m in depth. These two ditches were sectioned again in December 1977–January 1978 and this time it was possible to demonstrate that the larger ditch cut the smaller. The fill of the latter consisted of layers of clay which contained a small group of

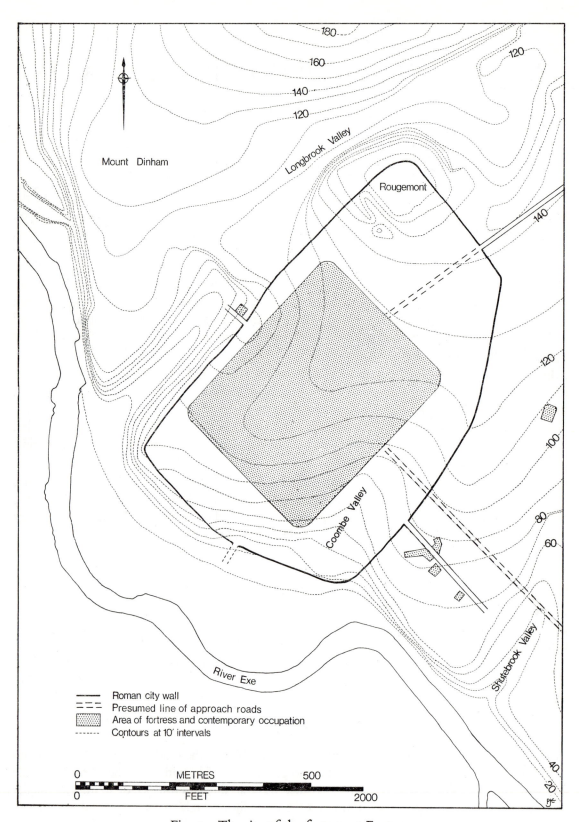

Fig. 1. The site of the fortress at Exeter.

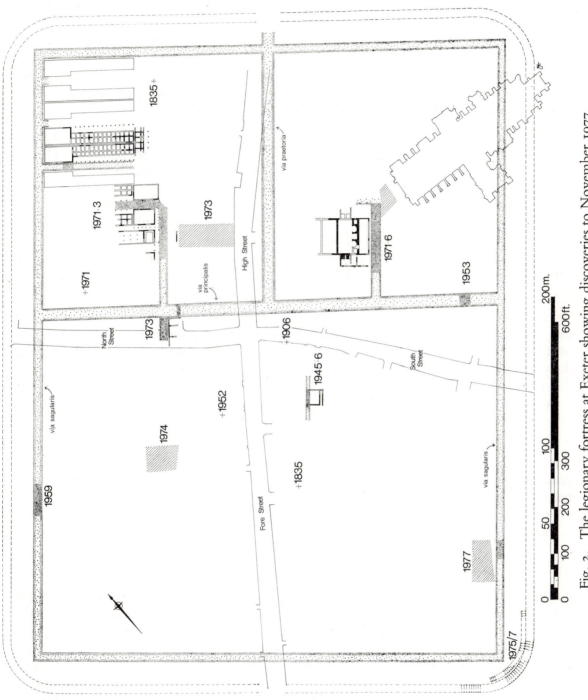

Fig. 2. The legionary fortress at Exeter showing discoveries to November 1977.

pre-Flavian material. The rapid silting of the larger ditch contained a sherd of late first-century date. At one point the silt was sealed by a rubbish deposit which contained a group of 38 samian vessels, the latest example providing a *terminus post quem* of *c.* 80 (see further, pp. 187–8). Elsewhere the ditch was left open until the early second century when it was partly filled. However, its course must have been visible on the ground until well into the third century. Eventually it was filled in completely and buildings were erected on its site.

A short length of the south-western ditch was revealed nearby in the course of building work. It allows a closer calculation of the curve which the ditch described at the corner and from this the line of the defences on the south-east side can be fixed with some certainty. The line of the *via sagularis* on this side was located in 1977; it ran about 15 m north-west of the projected line of the inner ditch.

Some indication of the position of the defences on the north-east side of the fortress was given by the partial excavation of two pairs of barrack-blocks on the Guildhall site in 1971–2. Here it seems justifiable to restore a third pair to the north-east of those already investigated in order to provide accommodation for a full cohort (see below). If this cohort-block stood at the northern corner of the fortress, the distance between the lips of the inner ditches, from south-west to north-east, would have been approximately 430 m, after allowing a further 20 m for the *via sagularis*, intervallum and rampart on the north-east side. The possibility of another *scamnum* to the north-east can be dismissed because no traces of early timber buildings were observed in a G.P.O. trench dug along the length of Queen Street.

In 1959 at Bartholomew Street East a 25 m length of road at least 4 m in width was excavated (brief account in Fox, 1966, 49). It was originally thought to have been civil, but now appears to date to the period of the legionary fortress. If its line is extended northwards, it can be seen to have bounded the centurions' quarters of the cohort-block at the northern corner of the fortress, showing that the barracks had an overall length of *c.* 62 m. Thus it must have represented part of the *via sagularis*. To the north-west two periods of activity were distinguished in what must have been the *intervallum*, an area at least 9 m in width. At first the site was used for metal-working[1]; subsequently in *c.* 65–70 a series of timber buildings was erected. These structures stood until *c.* 80–5 when they were apparently destroyed by fire[2].

If it is assumed that the Bartholomew Street road represents part of the *via sagularis*, the overall breadth of the fortress would be *c.* 350 m, again allowing for the *intervallum* and rampart on the north-west side. These tentative estimates of the length and breadth of the fortress produce a ground area of *c.* 15.4 ha or 38 acres (*c.* 440 m by 350 m, measured from the conjectured position of the inner lip of the inner ditch)[3]. The fortress was thus remarkably small (see further, p. 13).

The internal buildings:

Barracks: parts of five barrack-blocks have been explored at the northern corner of the fortress. The plans of two which lay back-to-back can be partly reconstructed. They were approximately 62 m in length, their north-western limits being indicated by the line of the *via sagularis* excavated in Bartholomew Street (see above). The centurions' quarters measured roughly 20 m by 10 m and the men's accommodation consisted of 14 *contubernia*. The two barrack-blocks belonged to two separate pairs; the presence of a third pair of barrack-blocks to the north-east can be postulated in order to provide a full cohort-block. Immediately to the south-east five more *contubernia* were excavated; they must have formed part of another barrack-block with its centurion's quarters next to the north-eastern *via sagularis*.

These barrack-blocks are notable for their small size. Most legionary barrack-blocks vary in length from between 70 m (as at Noviomagus) to almost 100 m (as at Vindonissa and Lambaesis (von Petrikovits, 1975, 36); it is argued below that the Exeter barrack-blocks were scaled down in accordance with the small size of the fortress).

All these barrack-blocks showed three phases of construction. The first two cannot be closely dated, but the third phase was associated with early Flavian material.

Another pair of barrack-blocks was found on the north-east side of the *fabrica*. At the south-eastern end of their *contubernia* were two rectangular buildings, one measuring 14.5 m by 10.5 m, the other 17 m by 10.5 m. These barracks may have had a special function because they do not appear to belong to a full cohort-block. If they extended as far north-west as the *via sagularis*, they would have been considerably larger than their neighbours to the north-east. The two rectangular buildings adjoining the *contubernia* resemble centurions' quarters, but these were usually placed next to the defences. H. v. Petrikovits has suggested that these two barracks provided accommodation for *immunes* (1975, 42).

Fabrica: the *fabrica* and the possible *immunes* barrack-blocks immediately to the north-east were apparently built at the same time. Their sites had previously been occupied by small timber buildings and some pits associated with metal-working. In the *fabrica* the principal structure was an aisled hall 9 m wide which consisted of at least four bays. Its floor was covered with charcoal and slag and was cut through by a series of rectangular plank-lined troughs; these contained slag, charcoal and bronze off-cuts, as well as scraps of military fittings and personal objects such as tweezers; one trough contained bronze filings. Clearly this part of the hall was used for bronze-working. At the south-east end of the hall a room measuring 9 m by 7.5 m was found; a narrow slot running around three sides of the room may have represented the base of a work-bench or of shelving. Next to the aisled hall there was an entrance from the street. On the other side of the entrance part of a room was excavated; its function cannot be determined.

The *via principalis* (see p. 9) probably marked the south-west limit of the *fabrica*. There is no firm evidence as to the position of its north-west side, but a small pit excavated on the north-east side of North Street in 1971 may have been associated with the *fabrica;* it contained a bronze ladle 30 cm in length and what appeared to have been an iron helmet.

It is possible that the ground-plan of the *fabrica* resembled those at Inchtuthil and Lambaesis where continuous aisled halls were ranged around three sides of a central courtyard. But aisled halls are a prominent feature of other *fabrica* types, and the Exeter building may have resembled the more common 'Basartyp', rectangular buildings containing a multiplicity of rooms and courtyards (von Petrikovits, 1975, 82–98).

Granaries: south-east of the *fabrica* evidence was recovered for the existence of one or more granaries covering an area of at least 40 m by 15 m. The granaries were supported on a grid of posts pile-driven into the ground, their construction-technique resembling that of examples at Usk (Wilson, 1970, 273 and Wilson, 1971, 247, Fig. 4; see also Manning, 1975, 105, 'Group II' granaries). They showed at least two periods of construction.

Building on the south-west side of the via principalis: part of a building in the angle between the *via principalis* and the continuation of the street which flanked the south-east side of the *fabrica* was excavated in 1973. Too little is known of its plan to determine its function.

At various times traces of buildings and substantial finds of pre- or early Flavian material have been made within the area of the fortress. The two 'houses' explored by A. Fox near South Street in 1945–6 must certainly be military buildings of some type (Fox, 1952, 31–7). 'House 2' was about 9 m wide and consisted of at least two rooms; one appeared to have measured about 9 m by 7.5 m and had a clay floor with a rectangular tile-built hearth. On the south-east side of this building there was a veranda, but on the north-west side the wall of the building bounded a narrow road about 3 m in width with a central drain. The fragmentary plan of this building does not readily suggest its function.

In 1974 in Mary Arches Street observations of builder's trenches revealed traces of substantial early timber buildings, presumably associated with the fortress. Unfortunately no intelligible plan could be recovered.

An area which included part of the south-eastern *via sagularis* was investigated in 1977. Later activity had removed much of the evidence for the military period, but traces of one building, possibly a barrack-block running *per strigas*, were recovered immediately to the north-west of the *via sagularis*. North-east of this building there was an area which contained a number of pits, some with a fill of cess.

When the Western (or Lower) Market was constructed from 1835 onwards, in a position near the centre of the fortress, there came to light a 'prodigious quantity of Roman pottery of various kinds', a 'Praefericulum, or sacred vase' of bronze (not illustrated by Shortt), an *aureus* and five bronze coins of Nero, nine coins of Claudius and five of Vespasian as well as two complete *disci* from lamps of pre-Flavian type[4]. The site of the New (or Higher) Market which straddles the north-eastern defences produced two coins of Claudius, two of Nero and four of Vespasian, together with a considerable quantity of samian (Shortt, 1840, 35–42). It is likely that two pits recorded by A. Fox in 1952 near the centre of the fortress were filled towards the end of the fortress period[5].

Sites within the fortress defences are currently being explored and will doubtless reveal more building-plans. Most deposits of legionary date probably remain intact under the centre of the modern city because they are sufficiently far below the present ground-level to have escaped destruction by the digging-out of basements and cellars. Practical considerations, of course, will prevent the excavation of most of these deposits within the foreseeable future.

The internal plan:

Apart from the *via sagularis* four streets crossing the fortress from north-east to south-west have been investigated. The street immediately to the south-east of the *fabrica* did not run down the whole length of the fortress; north-east of the *fabrica* it must have turned to run up between the two possible *immunes* barrack-blocks, and to the south-west it appeared to terminate before reaching the area explored in Mary Arches Street in 1974. The street which bounded the south-east side of the bath-house is described in this volume (see p. 26). A third street on this alignment, running between two buildings of unknown function, was excavated in 1945–6 (see above); since its width was only *c*. 3 m, it must have been of little importance. A fourth street was represented by the line of the *via praetoria*, which would have bisected the *praetentura*. Unfortunately an excavation which straddled this line failed to produce any trace of such a street because the Roman deposits had been largely destroyed. However it is very likely that an early civil street which crossed this site, bounding the north-western side of the *forum* and *basilica*, in fact followed the course of the earlier fortress *via praetoria* (see pp. 120–1).

Two roads which appear to cross the width of the fortress from north-west to south-east have been investigated. One was clearly of minor importance; to the north-west it passed between the possible *immunes* barrack-blocks and to the south-east its line may have been represented by a narrow road which passed along the rear of the later civil *basilica* and *forum* (see p. 35).

A more important road has also been investigated. It skirted the south-west side of the *fabrica* and must have marked the south-west limit of the bath-house site. Its course further to the south-east was marked by a stretch of metalling excavated in 1953 (Fox, 1953, 2–3). Here the street appeared to date to the late first century: 'the only finds from the metalling were a rim and small fragment of a South Gaulish form 37, worn scraps of form 18 and a bit of a buff jug, all of late first century date'. It is possible that two or more road surfaces were mistaken for one; the depth of make-up for the 'lower road' (c. 75 cm) is much greater than that of other fortress or early civil streets[6].

If it can be accepted that the street cut right across the fortress, its width shows that it was the *via principalis*[7]. It would follow that the road which must have passed under Broadgate was the *via praetoria* and that the fortress faced north-east[8]. The baths would thus occupy the corner between the *viae principalis* and *praetoria* as at Caerleon, Vindobona and also Lauriacum where the baths were only separated from the *via principalis* by a narrow range of buildings (von Petrikovits, 1975, Taf. 3 and 10; for Vindobona, see Neumann, 1967, 58 and Abb. 18). The site of the *principia* can also be fixed. The position of the buildings excavated in 1945–6 suggests that it could not have measured more than about 45 m from north-east to south-west and thus it was likely to have been rather smaller than most legionary *principia*[9]. The distance of the *via principalis* from the north-east stretch of the *via sagularis* was c. 160 m and from the south-west stretch, c. 215 m. This gives a proportion of 1 : 1.35[10].

2. CONTEMPORARY SITES IN THE NEIGHBOURHOOD OF THE FORTRESS

Buildings south of the fortress:

In 1964, as remarked above, the discovery of a substantial Roman ditch had provided the first evidence of a military presence at Exeter (Fox, 1968, 3–6). The ditch was found below the rampart of the Roman town next to the South Gate, running on a line at right angles to these later defences. The recovery of a short length of a post-trench and associated post-holes, and the general topography of the area were taken to indicate that a rampart was situated on the north-east side of the ditch and that together they formed part of the south-west defences of a possible six-acre fort.

Recent excavations on both sides of the projected line of the ditch have revealed a more complex state of affairs (Fig. 3): (1) A site south-west of the line of the ditch (i.e. outside the conjectured fort) revealed several phases of early occupation. The north-eastern part of the site was deeply truncated but still preserved evidence for a gate in a wooden fence running parallel to the line of the ditch. The south-west part of the site was reduced by later disturbance to a narrow strip of stratigraphy which ran across the site of one or more timber buildings; these showed at least three major building phases. The floor-levels were covered with charcoal and slag, and metal-working had obviously taken place in the area. (2) About 25 m north-east of this site on the other side of the projected line of the ditch a better preserved group of buildings was excavated. It consisted of three rectangular buildings each about 10 m in length which were grouped around three sides of a courtyard measuring 13.5 m by 9 m; the fourth side was partly closed off by a fence. These buildings showed only one major constructional phase. (3) Two smaller sites to the south-east have also produced slight traces of early timber buildings together with a series of pits back-filled at the end of the military period. The buildings north-east of the projected line of the ditch were erected after c. 65 because they covered two cremations of this date, while those to the south-west could well have been earlier. Both sets of buildings were demolished in the early Flavian period; the dating evidence includes a scattered hoard of ten coins.

Any discussion of the function of these buildings needs to take their setting into account. Those to the north-east must have been built on the site of a cemetery; the two cremations so far recovered were presumably outliers of a larger group near the road leading to the *porta principalis dextra*, some 50 m to the north-east. The buildings to the south-east were built on the edge of an easily defensible spur overlooking the River Exe.

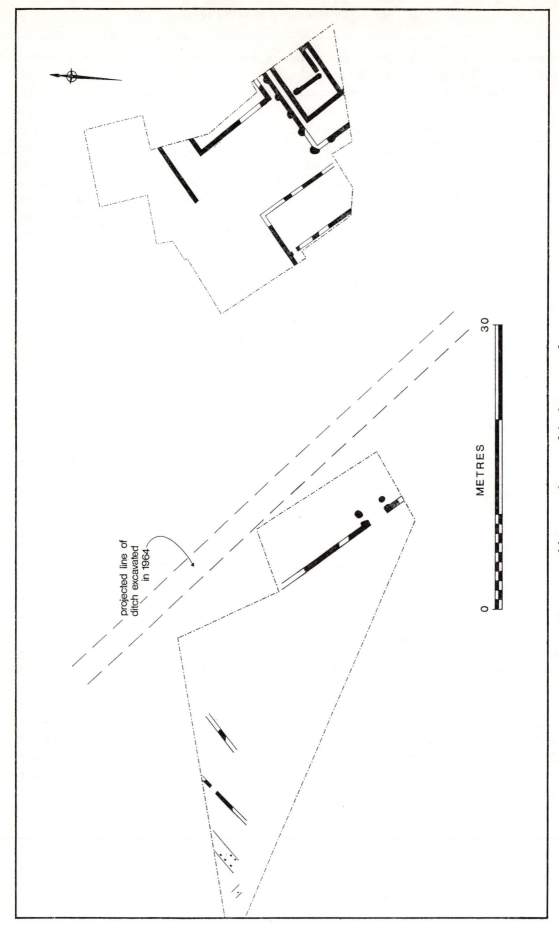

METRES

0   30

projected line of
ditch excavated
in 1964

Fig. 3. Buildings south-east of the legionary fortress.

The main problem is whether the occupation here was military or civil in character. The presence of a ditch certainly suggests military activity in the area at some stage, but the ditch itself cannot be firmly associated with any of the excavated buildings, and may have preceded them. However several points weigh against an interpretation of the buildings as part of a civil settlement:

(1)   As far as can be seen the buildings consisted of rectangular structures grouped around courtyards and enclosed within fenced compounds. Although few legionary *canabae* have been explored in detail, it seems reasonable to expect more evidence of purely domestic occupation such as strip-houses, rubbish pits, wells etc.

(2)   The buildings north-east of the ditch were erected on the site of a cremation-cemetery probably dedicated to military use (see below). It seems very unlikely that civil occupation would be allowed to encroach on such a cemetery.

(3)   There is some evidence for the location of the *canabae* 0.5 km further to the north (see below).

If it is accepted that the buildings were military in character, the following account of the activities south of the fortress can be proposed. The buildings south-west of the projected line of the ditch were earlier than those to the north-east; they showed three periods of construction rather than just one, and only pre-Flavian material was recovered from their earliest levels. They were enclosed by the ditch located in 1964. A cremation cemetery developed in the zone between this establishment and the road leading to the *porta principalis dextra*[11]. In the late Neronian or early Flavian period the establishment was enlarged, the ditch on the north-east side being filled in and built over[12]. Demolition took place in the early Flavian period, certainly no earlier than 72–3, the terminal date of the scattered hoard referred to above.

Little can be said at present about the specific military functions of these buildings. The topography of the area makes it unlikely that the establishment was a physical annexe of the fortress, as at Colchester (Crummy, 1977, Fig. 3, 70–1), York (R.C.H.M., 1962, p. xxxiii and p. 45a) or Caerleon (Boon, 1972, 31–3), where a ditch appeared to separate a military from a civil zone outside the fortress (Boon, 1972, 31–3 and *pers. comm.*). However, these buildings south-east of the fortress may represent a works-depot or stores-base.

The canabae:

The most likely position for the *canabae* is on the level ground beyond the north-east gate of the fortress. A site excavated about 300 m from the eastern corner of the fortress on the gravel terrace which overlooks the Shutebrook valley produced the fragmentary plans of two small timber buildings of first-century date; a few metres distant was a wattle-lined well whose fill contained pre-Flavian pottery. The post-war excavations also produced some evidence of early occupation south-east of the road which led to the north-east gate (*porta praetoria*) of the fortress (Fox, 1952, 51).

Cemeteries:

The two cremations underlying the buildings south-east of the fortress have already been referred to. They appear to be the outliers of a cemetery alongside the road leading to the *porta principalis dextra*. Although in both cases considerable parts of the cremations had been removed by later disturbance, they still yielded a rich collection of objects which included a bronze lamp and a figurine of (?) Victory; a small bronze model of a dog found in deposits associated with the buildings which superseded the cemetery may have been disturbed from another cremation nearby. Two glass vessels were also recovered (Fig. 70, 4 and 23). The wealth of the grave-goods and proximity to the *porta principalis dextra* indicate that this cemetery was dedicated to legionary rather than civilian use.

A quantity of pre-Flavian material was recovered from the parish of St David's during the first half of the nineteenth century; this probably points to the site of another early cemetery, some 0.5 km north of the fortress (Shortt, 1841, 91).

The Stoke Hill signal-station:

This was discovered in 1953 and investigated in 1956–7 (Fox and Ravenhill, 1959, 71–82). The site occupied a position on the highest point of Stoke Hill, 158 m above sea-level and some 2.5 km due north of the fortress. The signal-station commanded views extending to the mouth of the Exe estuary and a considerable distance north-eastwards to the Blackdown Hills. Its outer defences consisted of a ditch and rampart forming a subannular enclosure roughly 110 m across. At the centre there was another enclosure roughly 33.5 m square which was again defended by a ditch and rampart, with an entrance on the east side. No buildings were found in either the inner or outer enclosures, and very few finds were made. The only closely datable objects were a coin of Carausius and a Dr. 38 imitation (possibly Oxford ware, although the fabric was very decayed); neither of these finds was made in a context which could be associated with the occupation of the signal-station. At first it was thought that the earthwork was late Roman in date, but since the exploration of the out-posts at Martinhoe and Old Burrow in North Devon (Fox and Ravenhill, 1966, 3–39), the plans of which closely resemble Stoke Hill, a first-century date has come to be thought more likely, despite the absence of datable material.

Topsham:

Occasional finds of first-century material at Topsham, some 6.5 km from Exeter at the head of the Exe estuary, have been taken to indicate the presence of an early port or supply-base. The recent excavation of a 'farmstead' dating from *c.* 50–55 to *c.* 70–75 does nothing to diminish the likelihood of this since the building was some 2–300 m distant from the area where previous finds have been made (Jarvis and Maxfield, 1975, 210). Unfortunately no other building-plans have been recovered, and no finds of an undisputably military character have been made. Thus at present very little can be said about the exact nature of the first-century occupation at Topsham[13].

Industries and supplies:

To the north-east of the fortress there was an area devoted to the manufacture of tiles. In Southernhay West a scatter of tile-wasters was found in 1946–7 sealing a deposit which contained pre-Flavian pottery (Fox, 1952, 53–4 and Pl. XXV). In 1974 tile-wasters were noted in a section through a road underlying High Street. It should be noted that tiles were employed not only in the construction of the baths but also in roofing the timber buildings within the fortress. The discovery that a mould used to make antefixes at Exeter was taken to Caerleon and used there can be taken to suggest that the tile-works were under direct legionary control and were not being operated by civilian contractors (Bidwell and Boon, 1976, 279). It seems likely that pottery manufacture also took place in this area, for certain types of mortaria and coarse wares have a fabric closely resembling that of the tiles (see p. 192).

On the south-west side of the fortress part of a kiln was excavated in 1974 and later features produced wasters associated with it. The kiln was manufacturing mortaria of late Neronian/early Flavian type stamped (?) VITANI or VITANII[14], and also flagons. Unfortunately no examples of this potter's stamps are known from elsewhere in Exeter and it is uncertain how long-lived or successful his particular workshop was. For quarries, see p. 55.

Exeter must have been an important point for the distribution of supplies brought in from the Continent (cf. p. 190). It is possible that one day the study of the distribution of *terra nigra*, fine wares, amphorae, samian, glass and other supplies may shed some light on this particular function.

3. THE GARRISON

The Second Augustan Legion is known to have operated in South-West England during the early years of the conquest under the command of Vespasian, and it is presumed that this legion, together with auxiliaries, controlled the area until the end of the military occupation[15]. The identification of the Second Augustan Legion as the garrison at Exeter was confirmed by a find from the site of the legionary baths. Fragments of two antefixes, one from the construction levels of the baths, proved to come from the same mould as examples from Caerleon; the inference which can be drawn from this discovery is that the mould was part of the stock-in-trade of a legionary tiler working first at Exeter and then at Caerleon, where the Second Augustan Legion was based from c. 75 (Bidwell and Boon, 1976, 279).

The small size of the fortress at Exeter may signify that accommodation was provided for only part of the legion. This has also been suggested in the case of Lincoln (with an area of 41.5 acres, see Frere, 1967, 71), which although slightly larger than Exeter (38 acres, see p. 6) is still appreciably smaller than most legionary fortresses, the norm being about fifty acres. However at Exeter the barracks of the only cohort-block where an estimate of size is possible are only c. 62 m in length. Apart from the barracks of the first cohort, little variation can usually be detected in the size of accommodation from cohort to cohort. Thus at Exeter, it is likely that all the barracks were smaller than usual, and if so, it would probably have been possible to accommodate the whole legion within the fortress. The baths also appear to have covered much less space than is usual (4100 sq.m, cf. Caerleon, c. 8000 sq.m (Boon, 1972, 78); Chester, 6400 sq.m (Jarrett, 1967, 36); Lauriacum, 9000 sq.m (Vetters, 1953, 50)) and, as has been stated elsewhere (p. 9), the *principia* was unlikely to have measured more than about 45 m in length.

Thus the present knowledge of the fortress plan suggests that the buildings within it were smaller than usual and that its modest size does not necessarily mean that it provided accommodation for only part of the legion. The choice of site may have dictated the size of the fortress. It is remarkable that Exeter occupies a hill-top site; indeed it has been suggested that the Roman occupation succeeded a hill-fort (Hoskins, 1960, 3), although recent work has not produced the slightest evidence for any Iron Age occupation. On the north-west side the defences occupied a position on the crest of a steep slope above the Longbrook valley; the south-west and south-east sides ran along the top of fairly steep slopes. Most of the north-east side adjoined a stretch of fairly level ground, although at the northern end the ground begins to rise steeply towards Rougemont, its summit at 59.75 m O.D. Thus within the confines of the site it would have been impossible to have constructed a larger fortress without including steep slopes within its circuit.

4. SUMMARY OF DATING EVIDENCE

A. Material dating evidence[16]:

(1) *Foundation-date of the fortress*: no closely datable material has been found in association with the construction of the first phase of timber buildings within the fortress. The general character of the early coins and pottery from all contexts at Exeter provides the only clue to the foundation-date. The earliest piece of decorated samian recovered from excavations carried out between 1971 and August 1977 was thought to date to c. 45–60 or possibly c. 50–65; eleven pieces dated to c. 50–65 (see Table 1). 63 Claudian and pre-Claudian *aes* have been recorded from Exeter since the 1840s when Shortt began to publish coin-finds. However, these formed the money-supply down to A.D. 64, so need not in themselves suggest a Claudian date when set alongside the 85 coins which date from between 64 and 73. Miss V. Rigby judged that the group of about 50 *terra nigra* vessels so far recovered from Exeter 'as a whole . . . belongs to the period after A.D. 55' (see p. 190).

The coarse pottery unfortunately cannot be used as evidence in this particular discussion because it is impossible to date it within sufficiently precise limits.

There are obvious reservations about the significance of the early finds from Exeter. High standards of cleanliness prevailed within the fortress and rubbish was removed elsewhere instead of being disposed of in pits. The character of the material is likely to be distorted by the large proportion which came from demolition deposits, especially from above the buildings south of the fortress, and from the furnace-ash deposits which accumulated in the service area of the modified legionary baths when these served a civilian community in the period c. 75–80. Nevertheless there are some deposits which almost certainly date from the first decade of occupation within the fortress (e.g. the construction-levels of the baths) and it would be surprising if all the material from the first few years of occupation proved to have eluded recovery. Thus the evidence so far recovered points to a foundation-date after c. 55.

Comparison of the early material from Exeter and Usk, also a Neronian foundation, is likely to be instructive. The fortress at Usk awaits full publication, but the site has produced large numbers of Claudian copies and much samian dating from c. 55 (G. C. Boon, *pers. comm.*).

(2) *Occupation within the fortress:*

   (i) construction of the legionary baths: the building-levels on this site produced a group of pottery and coins which was Neronian in date (see pp. 55–6).

   (ii) the final construction-phase of the barrack-blocks was associated with a few pieces of early Flavian samian.

   (iii) early Flavian samian was recovered from deposits which had accumulated over the floor of the *fabrica* hall prior to its demolition.

   (iv) occupation in the 'houses' excavated near South Street in 1945–6 (Fox, 1952, 31–7); the material was pre-Flavian in character; as stated (*ibid.*, 36, n. 3) a Neronian coin of 64–66 was probably associated with the demolition rather than the construction of 'House 2'. From the silt of the ditch which ran along the centre of the road between the two 'houses' there came a Dr. 29, probably early Flavian in date.

   (v) *intervallum* and *via sagularis* in Bartholomew Street (Fox, 1966, 49); hearths and smelting-places were associated with coins of Claudius and Nero. Timber buildings were erected in c. 65–70 and these were destroyed by fire c. 80–5, according to the excavator. Thus their construction-date lies within the fortress period, but their destruction occurred rather later than the date of the fortress demolition suggested below; the dating evidence requires reassessment when it becomes available for study.

   (vi) pits next to the south-eastern stretch of the *via sagularis*: a group of pits, some containing a fill of cess, contained early Flavian samian.

Occupation within the fortress was associated with Neronian (items i, iv and v) and early Flavian (items ii, iii, v and vi) groups of samian and coins.

(3) *Occupation outside the fortress:*

   (i) cremations south of the fortress: one was furnished with ten samian vessels, the three decorated examples dating to after c. 60; the group as a whole was judged to close towards the end of the Neronian period and was associated with a coin of Nero (*RIC* 118, c. 64–66). The other cremation contained pre-Flavian material, but nothing more closely datable.

     The principal importance of this group is that it supplies a *terminus post quem* for the expansion of the establishment lying to the south-west.

   (ii) primary and secondary construction-levels of buildings south-west of the projected line

of the ditch; a few pre-Flavian samian sherds were associated with the first phase of building. The second phase produced a few early Flavian pieces and a coin of Claudius counter-marked PROB[17].

(iii) occupation in buildings north-east of the ditch: decorated samian dating from *c.* 70 was associated with floor-levels and secondary constructional features.

(iv) fill of the ditch between the two groups of buildings: this produced a small group of pre-Flavian material (Fox, 1968, 3).

(v) Southernhay Gardens: two buildings associated with a well produced a small group of material, none of which need date to later than the early Flavian period.

(vi) Roman 'farmstead' at Topsham (Jarvis and Maxfield, 1975): the samian indicates that occupation fell within the date-range *c.* 50–75; 'probably, however, all will have been made between A.D. 55 and 70'. The latest coin from the site was a *dupondius* of Vespasian (*RIC* 739, 72–3).

It would appear that the establishment south of the fortress was constructed in the pre-Flavian period; it appears to have been enlarged in the late Neronian or early Flavian period, certainly some time after *c.* 65.

The two civil sites in Southernhay and at Topsham appear to have been contemporary and roughly co-terminous with the military occupation.

(4) *Demolition deposits within the fortress:*

(i) Reduction in size of the legionary bath-house: this can almost certainly be associated with the withdrawal of the legion and is dated by samian to the early Flavian period, necessarily before *c.* 80 when work on the *basilica* and *forum* was commenced (see p. 65).

(ii) drainage ditch next to the south-eastern stretch of the *via sagularis*: the fill of this exceptionally large drainage ditch contained early Flavian samian and a slightly worn coin of 71 (*RIC* 427). The ditch presumably passed out of use when the fortress was demolished.

(iii) demolition of barrack-blocks and *fabrica*: in this area the demolition debris was removed and there were no useful associated groups of material. However the site of these buildings was given over to civil occupation associated with pits, wells, etc., which produced groups of samian dating from *c.* 80 and *c.* 85.

(iv) partial filling of ditch at the southern corner of the fortress: a group of 38 samian vessels provided a *terminus post quem* of *c.* 80 for this event. Whether this can be taken to mark the demolition date of the fortress is doubtful since the deposit contained much domestic refuse; it may merely represent the use of a short stretch of the ditch for the disposal of rubbish, substantial stretches of the defences elsewhere having been slighted already at an earlier date.

(5) *Demolition of buildings south-east of the fortress:*

(i) demolition deposits covering the north-eastern group of buildings: these deposits contained a group of early Flavian samian. Of greater importance was a scattered hoard of ten coins which had been dispersed through the demolition layers; it terminated with five unworn coins of 72–3. Although the hoard provides a *terminus post quem* for the demolition of the buildings, it was not in its primary position. It is likely that the hoard had been concealed in the wall or roof of one of the buildings and was not noticed and recovered when demolition took place; if so, the hoard signifies that the buildings were in fact still standing in 72–3.

(ii) filling of pits at Friar's Walk: three pits which were apparently back-filled at the same time contained a total of 28 samian vessels with a *terminus post quem* of *c.* 70. These pits may well lie within the establishment south-east of the fortress and may be associated with the tidying-up of the area at the end of the military period.

The dating evidence speaks for itself. Although the quantity of material from the fortress demolition levels is small, its early Flavian date is beyond doubt. The evidence for the end of the buildings south-east of the fortress is more specific; demolition took place some time after 72–3. In view of the fact that early Flavian samian was stratified in occupation- and late construction-levels in both establishments, one could hardly argue for a demolition date before c. 75. The general chronological pattern of finds confirms this view; early Flavian samian and coins from the first few years of Vespasian's reign are plentiful, but there is a dramatic falling-off in the case of later material (see Tables 1 and 3).

B. *Historical evidence:*

Although this is not an appropriate place to explore the significance of the legionary fortress at Exeter in terms of the Roman conquest of South-West England, it is necessary to try and reconcile the dating evidence set out above with the contemporary military dispositions in Southern Britain, so far as they are known.

It has been argued recently that Exeter marked the termination of the first westward thrust by Vespasian (Fox, 1974, 84); judging from the absence of early material, this is scarcely possible. Indeed there is no archaeological evidence of Roman military activity west of Waddon Hill in

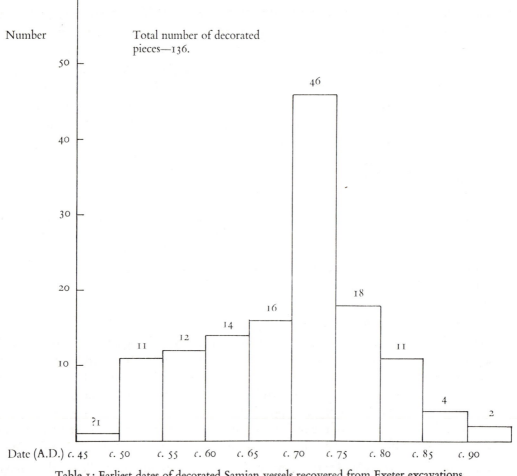

Table 1: Earliest dates of decorated Samian vessels recovered from Exeter excavations
(1971–August 1977)

Dorset that need necessarily pre-date the foundation of the fortress at Exeter in the Neronian period. The signal station at Martinhoe (Fox and Ravenhill, 1966, 24) and the two-acre fort at Nanstallon (Fox and Ravenhill, 1972, 87) are certainly Neronian; and since Old Burrow, the predecessor of Martinhoe, produced only two coins, it can scarcely be claimed as Claudian with any confidence (Fox and Ravenhill, 1966, 22).

Apart from the reference to Vespasian's activities in the first few years of the occupation (Suetonius, *Divus Vespasianus*, IV, 1) the historical sources make no mention of a campaign in the South-West. Neither does the overall strategical situation before *c.* 60 suggest a date when an advance into the territory of the Dumnonii would have been especially advantageous. The earliest date when control of the area may have been of some importance was during Boudicca's rebellion and its aftermath. B. H. Warmington has pointed to the tactical importance of South-West England if an evacuation was contemplated (Warmington, 1976, 47–8). However the attitude of the Dumnonii towards events at the time is unknown, although the increasing number of forts which are becoming known in their territory shows that they must have put up a certain amount of resistance to the occupation[18]. In short, the military situation in the late Claudian and early Neronian period does not readily suggest a date at which the annexation of the territory of the Dumnonii and the installation of a legion at Exeter would seem particularly appropriate[19].

It is clear that the military occupation of the South-West continued into the Flavian period. The fort at Nanstallon has produced coins of Vespasian (Fox and Ravenhill, 1972, 92) and at Okehampton the newly discovered fort has also produced a samian Dr. 37 dating from *c.* 70. The fortress at Exeter also continued into the Flavian period and this poses a problem. It is widely believed that the Second Augustan Legion was responsible for the construction of the Gloucester fortress *c.* 66 before moving on to Caerleon for the Welsh campaign of 74–8 (e.g. Manning, 1976, 40–1), but a change of garrison at Exeter at this date is very unlikely. It also seems scarcely possible that most of the legion moved to Gloucester *c.* 66, leaving the fortress in the hands of a 'caretaker' garrison, because coins and samian dating to the late Neronian and early Flavian period are plentiful. In addition, the excavated barracks were reconstructed after *c.* 70, the *fabrica* was still in use at this date and the bath-house was not reduced in size until the early Flavian period. The establishment south-east of the fortress was also expanded.

The demolition of the fortress occurred within the early Flavian period, but certainly some years before *c.* 80 when work on the construction of the *basilica* and *forum* was commenced. A suitable historical context for the abandonment of the fortress is the foundation date of Caerleon, *c.* 75, at the beginning of the governorship of Frontinus (Boon, 1972, 20).

Conclusions:

The fortress at Exeter was probably established after *c.* 50. On the basis of datable material a foundation date of *c.* 55–60 rather than *c.* 50–55 seems more likely. No earlier military establishments are known west of a line between the Parret and the Axe, and the placing of the Second Augustan Legion at Exeter may be contemporary with the annexation of the Dumnonian peninsula as a whole. The fortress and the establishment to the south-east remained in occupation until *c.* 75, and there is no suggestion, arising from either the building-sequences or finds, of any diminution in the intensity of occupation before that date.

NOTES

1. For metal-working in *abricae* situated in the *intervallum* area, see von Petrikovits, 1975, 90–1.

2. These dates are proposed in Fox, 1966, 49; unfortunately the material from this excavation is inaccessible at present, so a reassessment of the dating evidence in the light of the legionary occupation is not yet possible.

3. This gives the fortress a proportion of about 5 : 4, as at Gloucester, Lauriacum, Carnumtum and Lambaesis (von Petrikovits, 1975, 113). However it should be noted that the walls of the buildings in the northern quarter of the

fortress do not form right-angles, nor does the *via principalis* run at right-angles to the line of the defences. This may be taken to suggest that the plan of the fortress formed a quadrilateral rather than a true rectangle.

4. Shortt, 1840, 30–6, 47–50, 133; for the *disci*, see the Frontispiece, nos. 1 and 2. D. M. Bailey (*pers. comm.*) has commented on the lamp decorated with a ship (no. 1): 'Several lamps with this scene have been found in Britain, most recently at Usk. Others come from Gloucester, London and Colchester.'

5. Fox, 1952, 106–110; a *terminus post quem* for the filling of the pit of *c.* 70 was supplied by a mortarium stamp of Q. Valerius Veranius.

6. At Bear Street in the later Roman period the road was about 4.5 m in width, the position of its north-east edge being indicated by a line of footings. At an earlier date the road could have been up to 8.5 m in width; the deposit of 'mixed loam' at the south-west end of Trench 8 (section Z–Z) must mark its extreme possible north-west limits.

7. The *via principalis* at Caerleon was 7.5 m in width (Boon, 1972, 25).

8. cf. Pseudo-Hyginus (*Liber de munitionibus castrorum*, 56) and Vegetius (*Epitoma rei militaris*, 1, 23). Both were of the opinion that the fortress should face the enemy. In the case of Moguntiacum-Mainz, where the internal plan of the fortress is almost totally unknown, D. Baatz used these authorities to argue that the *porta praetoria* must have faced towards the Rhine (Baatz, 1962, 73). However at Exeter it is possible that trouble was anticipated not only from the Dumnonii in the west, but also from the Durotriges to the east.

9. See pp. 130–2 for a Purbeck-marble eagle possibly from the *principia*. The dimensions of the *principia* were similar to those of the Inchtuthil *principia*, which was *c.* 46 m square. However it is likely that the Inchtuthil building was a temporary structure which it was later intended to replace by a larger stone *principia* (Boon, 1972, 28); it was set back from the *via principalis* and occupied only part of a vacant plot. The Exeter *principia* could not have been rebuilt on a larger scale without the demolition of the building to the south of it.

10. Elsewhere this ratio varies from 1 : 1 at Chester to 1 : 2.3 at Lambaesis, Albano and Vindonissa; most fortresses have a proportion of between 1 : 2.1 and 1 : 1.7 (von Petrikovits, 1975, 114).

11. At Chester cremations which were perhaps associated with an earlier fort have been found below the fortress (Stevens, 1942, 50).

12. The 'gully' and associated post-holes which the excavator sought to associate with a rampart on the north-east side of the ditch may in fact represent part of a later timber building. (Fox, 1968, 4).

13. Find-spots summarised in Ralegh Radford, 1947, 6–23; apart from the discoveries referred to in this section, no further finds of early material have been made at Topsham.

14. These are the readings proposed by K. Hartley, to whom I am grateful for comments on the mortaria.

15. But see Branigan, 1974, 55 where it is suggested that part of the Twentieth Legion was involved in the campaign.

16. This survey of the dating evidence for the fortress is not, in one respect, comprehensive. An important body of evidence which it has not been possible to utilise is the largely unpublished collection of samian amassed by Shortt and now in the Rougemont House Museum, Exeter. An analysis of early decorated vessels and stamps might well provide further information about the foundation date.

17. The countermark is Claudian, see Boon, 1974a, 140, n. 37.

18. The list of relevant sites is as follows: a $6\frac{1}{2}$ acre fort (including annexe) at North Tawton; a $3\frac{1}{2}$ acre fort at Wiveliscombe; two 2 acre forts at Nanstallon and Okehampton; signal-stations or fortlets at Martinhoe, Old Burrow and probably Broadbury; also military sites in the Exeter area discussed in this section. References in Fox, 1974. Two temporary camps have recently come to light in Devon: one with an area of 3.75 acres at Alverdiscott in North Devon and another with an area of at least 17 acres near the fort at North Tawton referred to above (St Joseph, 1977, 125–6).

19. Cf. Fox and Ravenhill, 1972, 88–91, for a consideration of the historical circumstances possibly bearing on the establishment of the fort at Nanstallon in Cornwall. As stated by these authors, the fort was likely to have been planted as a result of a westward advance which would have involved a major campaign. Whether or not this campaign was launched from a newly-established legionary base at Exeter is quite beyond proof at present.

A NOTE ON EARLY COINS FROM EXETER—N. SHIEL

The coins in general may provide some pointer as to when the military occupation ceased. The Table below is a supplement to that given by Goodchild (Fox, 1952, 104), and provides a much fuller version of his statistics for the unpublished coins in the Rougemont House Museum (his column D):

DATE	A	B	C	TOTAL
Pre-Claudian	8	3	1	12
Claudius	13	27	11	51
Nero	32	16	5	53
Vespasian and Titus	31	7	11	49
Domitian	12	2	2	16
Nerva and Trajan	32	8	4	44

A—Unpublished in Rougemont House/Acc. Register.
B—Unpublished from other sites dug 1971–1976.
C—From excavations published in this volume and in Fox, 1952, 63.

Table 2: Roman *aes* coins from Exeter

There is the expected pattern of a sharp rise under Claudius; a steady total through Nero and Vespasian and then a decline under Domitian followed by a further rise under Trajan. This is very general and does little more than show that the level of occupation, as reflected in the coinage, had gone down by Domitian's reign. A more interesting pointer emerges from a chronological analysis of such Vespasianic coins as are sufficiently well preserved or documented to permit it.

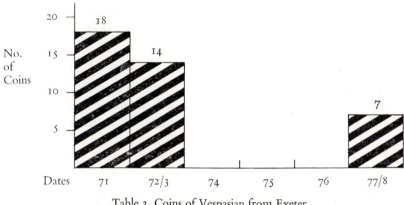

Table 3. Coins of Vespasian from Exeter

This shows a very clear break at about 73 with a subsequent resumption of the supply of coins right at the end of the reign. Such a date is very well supported by a small Vespasianic hoard which will be published in a forthcoming volume. The hoard was found in 1974 above buildings south-east of the fortress, (see p. 11), and it is terminated by five unworn coins of 72–73 which suggest a deposition date not long after that. The absence of any sign of an influx of fresh coinage during the middle years of Vespasian's reign would thus seem to suggest that there was no longer a military presence in Exeter at that time.

II. GAZETTEER OF ROMAN FINDS IN CENTRAL EXETER

(Fig. 22)

1715: a hoard of coins was found in the northern corner of the Cathedral Close (find-spot outside area of Fig. 23; see further pp. 167–79).

1778: six bronze figures were discovered in July 1778 'in digging a cellar under the house of Mr Upham situated in the High Street at Exeter at the corner of Broadgate. They were found within a very narrow space, and not more than three or four feet below the present pavement of the street.' The find consisted of two figures of Mercury and a small bronze cock, two smaller figurines representing (?) Apollo and Mars and another possibly representing Fortuna. Two bronze pedestals, one square and one circular, were also found. Finds of samian, coarse pottery and glass were also made (Milles, 1782, 1f). All these objects appear to have been lost.

There is little doubt concerning the position of the tenement under which these finds were made; it stood on the eastern side of Broadgate at the corner of High Street. For excavations on this site see pp. 60 and 120–1.

1810: about 1000 coins are said to have been dug up between Broadgate and Milk Lane in Fore Street during the construction of a main sewer at 'a depth of 20′ below the level of the present pavement'. The only coins recorded by Shortt formed an unusual collection for a Romano-British *civitas* capital: nine Ptolemaic coins, sixty Alexandrian Imperial and thirty Greek Imperial issues, eight *numismata serrata*, two 'British' coins, two Consular coins and eleven Byzantine issues (Shortt, 1840, 90f.). The authenticity of this find has been a matter for considerable debate (see p. 165).

1823: during the demolition of Broadgate 120 coins of normal late Roman type were found; in addition Shortt details two Ptolemaic coins, six coins from Syracuse and two from Sidon and two Consular coins (Shortt, 1840, 101).

1832: 'a great quantity of tessellated pavement' was found during the demolition of houses on the east side of South Street (Shortt, 1840, 21).

1833–4: further tessellated pavements were found on what is now known to have been the site of the Public Baths (Shortt, 1840, 23, 29, 139; see pp. 121–3).

1835: two Roman foundations 'as hard as stone itself and powerfully cemented' and 'an immense quadrangular Portland stone with a square cut in its centre' were found on the east side of South Street (Shortt, 1840, 41). The 'Portland' stone was probably a sandstone from east Devon since the former has never been encountered in Roman levels at Exeter; the 'square cut in its centre' may have been a lewis-hole or the seating for a post.

1838: 'massy masonry, combined with a conglomerate of powerful cement' was found on the west side of South Street; the discovery was made in the course of laying curb-stones, so presumably the foundation lay only a little way below the surface (Shortt, 1840, 67).

1866: the 1872 edition of *Murray's Handbook for Travellers in Devon and Cornwall* states that 'some fragments of a Roman tesselated pavement were found during the removal of the old church (*sc.* St Mary Major), which had a Norman tower' (p. 32; this is wrongly described by Bishop and Prideaux (1922, 20) as being found under the Norman tower). This must refer to the mosaic in the building on the south-east side of the *basilica* and *forum*, which was cut through by the chancel of the Victorian church (see pp. 117–8).

1871: a coin was found at an unspecified location within the Deanery grounds (see p. 167).

1874: coins were found in laying a gas main at Broadgate (see p. 166).

1882: coins were found on the site of the (then) National Provincial Bank (now the National Westminster Bank; see p. 60 and pp. 120–1 for recent excavations on this site).

1883: coins were found at the junction of High Street and South Street (see p. 166).

1906: coins were found in excavations at the base of the South Tower of the Cathedral (see p. 167).

c. **1906**: an *aureus* of Vespasian was found at the junction of High Street and South Street (see p. 166).

1911–12: two walls were discovered in building an extension to the National Provincial Bank (now the National Westminster Bank, see p. 120). These can now be seen to have marked the northern corner of the *basilica* and *forum*.

1932: a Roman bath was excavated in the Deanery Gardens (Montgomerie-Nielson and Montague, 1933–6, 72f; see pp. 121–3).

1940: two mortar floors were recorded during the construction of a water-tank on the site of what is now known to have been the *tepidarium* of the legionary baths (Morris, 1941, 138). The lower floor was described as 'of heavier type containing pieces of brick and pounded brick at (a depth of) 5' 3" . . . (it) rested on loose stones, but the virgin soil was not reached'. This was presumably the Period 1B floor (see pp. 62–3).

1945–6: structures were excavated on the site of the baths *insula* (discussed in detail on pp. 121–3), and on the south-west side of South Street on the south-western side of the *forum* (see p. 78).

1950: a section through Roman levels was revealed by the collapse of the west side of the Deanery Garden wall (see p. 122).

1953: a short length of what is now recognised as the fortress *via principalis* and a drain serving the Public Baths were excavated at Bear Street (Fox, 1952, 1f; see pp. 8–9 and pp. 121–3).

III. THE LEGIONARY BATH-HOUSE

1. DETAILS OF THE EXCAVATIONS AND THE RECORDING SYSTEM

Details of excavations (Fig. 4):

June 1971: excavations were begun on the site of the nave and south aisle of the Victorian church of St Mary Major. The massive foundation-walls of the church penetrated to natural and were not removed. In the nave Roman deposits were severely disturbed by burials, mostly nineteenth-century brick-lined graves; walls at the eastern end had been robbed during the demolition of the early cathedral, formerly the minster, in the twelfth century. When the Victorian south aisle was constructed, underlying deposits had been terraced away to a depth of c. 1.5 m; the surviving Roman deposits were cut by a number of early graves.

North of the church an east–west strip 5 m in width was cleared of burials to expose the top of the Roman deposits. In the course of this work the steps at the east end of the *forum* portico were revealed.

In the autumn of 1971 it was decided to extend the excavations as far north as Broadgate in the following year. A test trench (trench 8) was excavated 20 m to the south of Broadgate to obtain information about the preservation of Roman deposits in the area. Unfortunately it did not prove possible to extend the excavations this far in 1972. An outline section through trench 8 was assembled from levels taken on the Roman deposits exposed in the sides of grave-cuts.

Work on these sites continued through the winter of 1971–2.

Spring 1972: work began on the excavation of an extensive area north of the church. Considerable damage to later Roman deposits had been caused by:

(i) burials, particularly those contemporary with the minster, a few of which penetrated almost to natural.

(ii) a Second World War emergency water-tank which covered most of the northern part of the area.

(iii) the crypt of a thirteenth- or fourteenth-century charnel-chapel which cut down into natural.

On the eastern side of the site work was obstructed by a water-main which required the retention of a large baulk of unexcavated material in order to support it. Work continued until November 1972, by which time most of the site had been excavated to natural. Further work was suspended until the future of the site was decided.

1973: it proved possible to excavate features such as the Period 1A land-drains which were only sampled in 1972.

1974: the water-main was re-routed and the baulk which had supported it was excavated. Efforts to secure funds for the construction of a building to display the remains failed and the site was back-filled. The hypocausts and walls were covered with 1.5 m depth of sand to facilitate re-excavation; the remaining depth was levelled-up with top-soil.

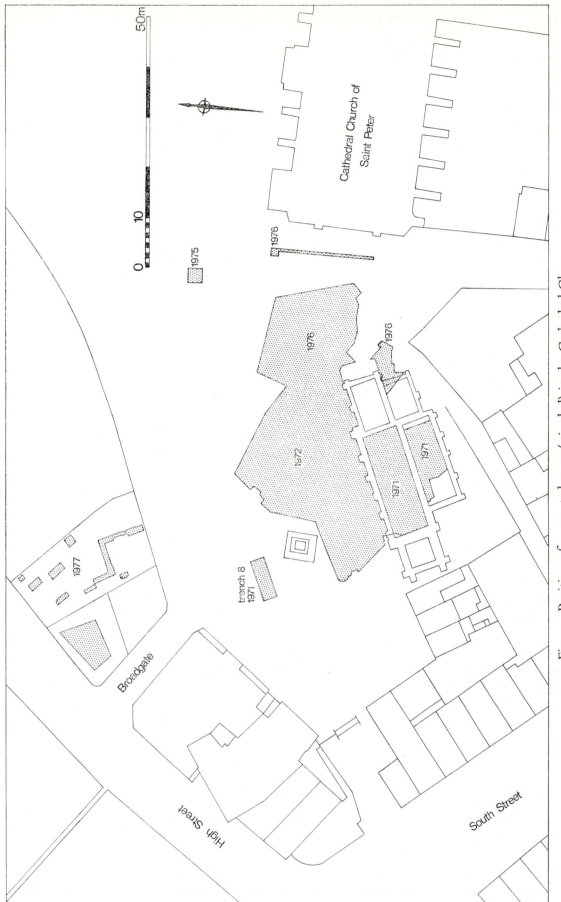

Fig. 4. Position of excavated areas (stippled) in the Cathedral Close.

1975: a heading dug to give access to a deep brick sewer was excavated to the east of the previous sites.

1976: excavations were carried out in advance of terracing and drainage works associated with the construction of a paved square next to the West Front of the Cathedral. Funds were made available for the excavation of all deposits likely to be destroyed by this work. Early Roman levels were not explored but were exposed in places where it proved necessary to clear robber-trenches in order to prevent subsidence.

1977: the cellars and strong-rooms of the National Westminster Bank and the cellars of properties adjoining Broadgate were excavated in advance of rebuilding work which involved the construction of deeper basements. Complete excavation proved impossible owing to structural considerations.

Site records and finds:

In 1971 features and layers were numbered separately with, where necessary, subdivisions indicated by lettering. This cumbersome system was simplified in 1972, when a continuous numbering system for all types of features and deposits was adopted. In this report the two different systems have been used side-by-side with no alterations in the original numbering, except in a few instances where ambiguities would seem likely to arise. Where features have numbers under both systems, the 1972 system is quoted.

Details of all features were recorded on printed forms. These, together with all drawings and notebooks, will be lodged in the Rougemont House Museum, Exeter. The animal bones from this and other Exeter excavations will form the subject of a monograph by M. Maltby (*Exeter Archaeological Reports, vol. 2* (in preparation), to be published by the University of Sheffield).

Methods of citation:

In describing stratification, references are made to the published sections in the following form: (13: 1409B–D), which is to be expanded as 'section 13: 1409B–D'. When features are referred to by single numbers only, e.g. (14), they are only to be found on the plans cited in the particular section-heading. Where a number is preceded by the abbreviation 'n.i.', this signifies that the feature to which the number refers is not illustrated in the report.

N.B. Cross-references between sections, elevations and figures are to be found on p. xviii. The arrows indicating the positions of sections on the plans represent the datum points; these are usually placed at either end of the section, although in some cases the sections continue beyond the datum points.

2. PERIOD 1A (CONSTRUCTION)

A. GENERAL DESCRIPTION (Fig. 6):

The legionary baths were erected on a site covering an area of some 4000 sq.m., which occupied the eastern angle between the *viae praetoria* and *principalis*. They were erected *c*. 60–65, perhaps as much as a decade after the foundation of the fortress; no traces of any earlier structures were found on the site. Excavation uncovered the *caldarium* (hot room), part of the *tepidarium* (warm room), one of the two furnace-houses serving the *caldarium* hypocaust, part of the *palaestra* (exercise-yard) and various service areas.

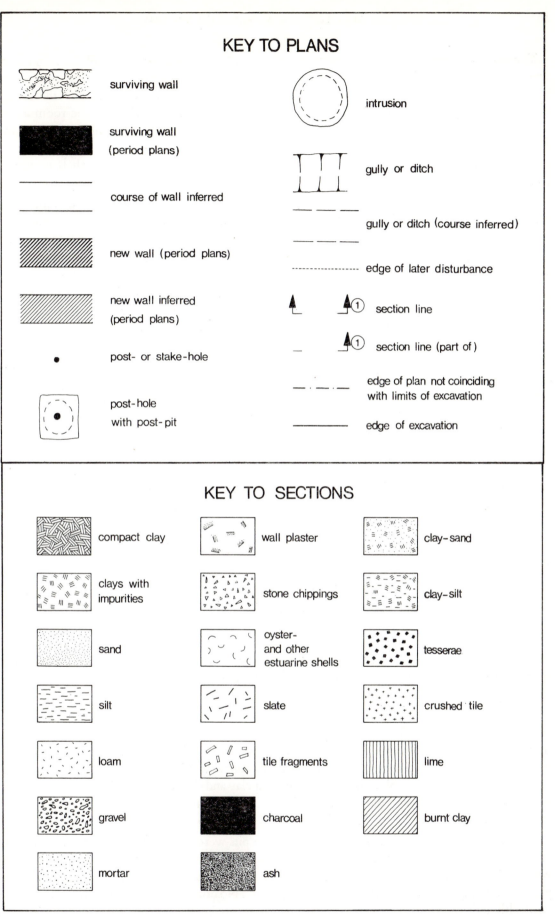

Fig. 5. Key to sections and plans.

The *caldarium* measured 22.3 m by 9.75 m internally. On the south-east side of the room there were two apses, 4.7 m in diameter and 3.75 m deep, flanking a central recess which was 3.15 m in width and 3.75 m deep; the two apses accommodated *labra* (water-basins) and the central recess may have held a statue or an altar. Baths occupied the entire width of the room at the south-west and north-east ends, adjacent to the furnace-houses. The tile-built hypocaust was divided into four parts by channels leading from the furnace-flues. The *suspensura* (floor above the hypocaust) was supported on *pilae* (tile-stacks) 80 cm in height, and also by corbels projecting from the walls.

The *tepidarium* measured 22.3 m in length; its width was not established by excavation, but certain evidence (see p. 30) indicated that it was *c.* 11.25 m in width. Its hypocaust communicated with that in the *caldarium* by means of six arches in the base of the wall between the two rooms.

The south-western furnace-house measured 7.5 m by 10.2 m internally and contained two large masonry bases on either side of the furnace-flue, which served to support the boiler and *testudo* (a device which maintained the temperature of the water in the bath). The south-eastern part of the room was probably divided off to form a fuel-store. In the angle between the furnace-house and the *caldarium* part of the *palaestra* was excavated; it had a sanded surface and contained a circular enclosure of wooden uprights 4.4 m in diameter, which has been interpreted as a cock-fighting pit. On the south-east side of the *palaestra* there appeared to have been a room about 9 m in width which had an entry from the courtyard south-east of the furnace-house. This courtyard measured 8.4 m by 7.4 m and was open to the street along its south-east side. On the south-east side of the *caldarium* there was a walled enclosure measuring 23.2 m by 6.3 m. North-east of this was another courtyard, probably opening on to the street, which was bounded by the north-east *caldarium* furnace-house on its north-west side.

On the south-east side of the street, which was laid out before the baths were constructed, there were timber buildings showing two phases of construction. These were demolished when the baths were constructed, and the street, formerly 4 m in width, was enlarged to a width in excess of 7.6 m, covering part of the site of these buildings.

B. ACTIVITIES PRE-DATING THE CONSTRUCTION OF THE BATHS (Fig. 7):

The first activity represented on the site was probably the construction of a street, 4 m in width, running from south-west to north-east, which consisted of two layers of metalling, the lower of trap rocks and chips, mixed with a little gravel and overlying an old soil-line, and the upper of river gravel and trap chips. The junction of the two layers was made especially distinct by the surface of the lower level which was compacted but uneven, with trap rocks shattered and splintered *in situ*, as if they had been pounded. The upper surface was even and compacted, with a slight slope to the south-east (8 : 49J, 49H; 9 : 49J, 49H).

South-east of the road two periods of activity were noted, both of which took place before the baths were put into use. The old soil-line was preserved here, as to the north-west; it was cut through by a small gully running parallel to the road, which, at its north-east end, turned and ran out beyond the excavated area; to the south-west its course was interrupted by a gap 50 cm wide (gully 13 A and B). A post-pit (p.h. 18), packed with clay and containing a void 15 cm square, was probably contemporary with the gully, since it was cut by a feature belonging to the later building (see below).

After the gully had been backfilled with clay, two pits were dug, both about 90 cm square and 1.0 m deep and spaced about 2.0 m apart (pits 29 and 30). Placed mid-way between the two pits was a void which represented a post 25 cm in diameter and 30 cm deep set in a rectangular post-pit with a packing of clay and trap rocks (post hole 16). No doubt the two larger pits had also held posts although careful examination did not reveal any trace of them. A substantial post-trench

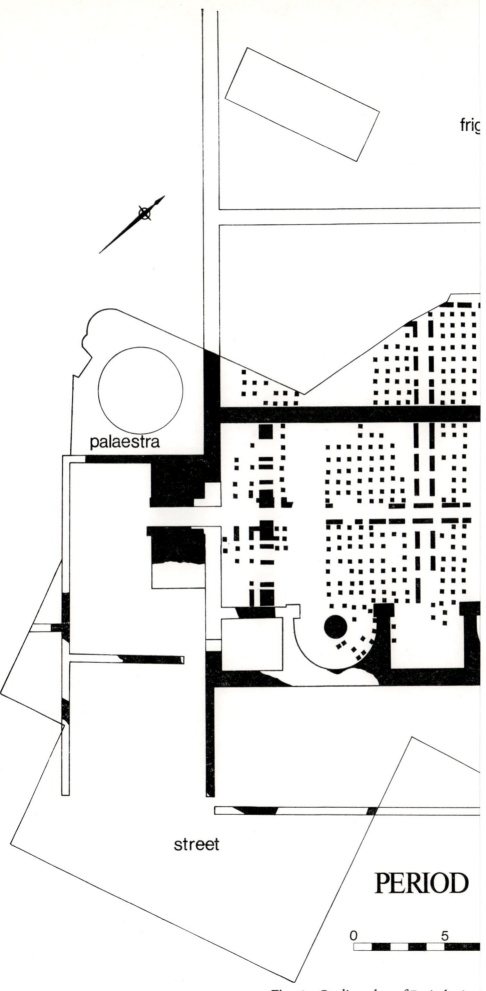

frig

palaestra

street

PERIOD

0   5

Fig. 6. Outline plan of Period 1A.

45 cm in width and 30 cm deep terminated about 75 cm south-east of the post-pits (17); there was a shallow scoop 10 cm deep on its west side (17A). All these features were back-filled with clay mixed with charcoal, food bones and a few scraps of coarse ware, and were sealed by a deposit of mixed clays flecked with charcoal, about 15 cm thick (9 : 68D). Both periods of activity must have represented the construction of timber buildings, but the area explored was so limited in size that it was not possible to determine their extent or identify their functions. A stratigraphical link with the road on the north-west side was only present at the end of the second period of activity, making it impossible to assess whether the road was present before the first timber building was erected. However common sense would suggest that this was probably the case.

C. PREPARATION OF THE SITE (Fig. 7):

The site of the baths occupied a position near the brow of a hill, but was almost completely level, save in the southern corner where the ground begins to fall away towards the Coombe Street valley (Fig. 1). The original ground surface was represented by an old turf-line, on top of which a few pockets of brown clayey silt had accumulated; unlike the old turf-line, which was sterile, the silt contained animal bones, oyster shells and a few sherds of Roman pottery, showing that it had accumulated while the site was vacant during the first few years of occupation within the fortress (see p. 56; the old turf-line was only excavated in a few places: 5: 31G; 6: 520; 7: 44E; 12: 1145; 13: 1419; 17: 78; clayey silt 4: 56C).

Preparation of the site began with the building-up of the southern corner in order to compensate for the slope; a layer of clay with a maximum thickness of 30 cm was spread over an area measuring 8 m from north-west to south-east and at least 18 m from north-east to south-west (1: 61B, 61C; 4: 56B and 46J; 5: 31F; 6: 52M; 8: 52M). By the road the level of the clay was reduced as if to form a ramp (6: 52M; 8: 52M). In places the clay was interleaved with charcoal which possibly originated from the clearance of timber buildings in the vicinity (1: 61B, 61C).

A pit, oval in plan and about 30 cm deep (f. 70), was the only feature cut in from directly above the clay deposit; on the bottom, laying face downwards, was a complete face-mask antefix (as Pl. XVIII) covered by a few trap rocks. Apotropaic powers were usually attributed to such ante-fixes; this example was probably placed in the pit to ensure the success of building operations. Beyond the area covered by the clay spread was found a small post-hole, 15 cm deep, which had been cut through by the foundation-trench of the south-west wall of the baths.

Before construction of the main building was started the site was covered by a layer of metalling consisting of trap chips and gravel (1: 61A; 4: 56A and 46H; 5: 31E; 6: 52L; 7: 44D2; 8: 52L; 12: 1161B; 17: 75; in the excavated areas represented by sections 13, 14 and 15 the metalling could not be adequately distinguished from a similar deposit immediately above). Provision of the metalled surface was obviously intended to facilitate the movement of large quantities of building materials around the site.

D. THE MAIN BUILDING (Fig. 7, Pl. I–VI):

Before the foundations of the bath-house were inserted, a trench running from north-west to south-east, 1.4 m wide and 40 cm deep, was dug in a position partly underlying the room at the eastern corner of the *caldarium* (1534). Its course was traced beyond the south-east wall of the room, where its width narrowed considerably before its termination at a point which underlay a later wall; no silting was found along its bottom, and it had been back-filled with compacted red clay. It may well be that the trench had been dug to receive a foundation, but had been set out incorrectly and was thus abandoned.

A complete section through the foundations was only exposed at the point where the wall between the *caldarium* and *tepidarium* had been robbed at a later date. The foundation-trench penetrated only 1.0 m below the level of the hypocaust floor, and was about 1.50 m in width. It was tightly packed with trap rocks with an estimated weight of up to 15 kg each; the two uppermost layers were cemented together with a very hard mortar, and, as elsewhere, the foundations were capped by a skim of mortar producing a plane surface on top of which the wall was built. The foundations of the north-east wall were 1.80 m in width; those of the south-west wall were presumably of similar dimensions, although they were only seen on the exterior of the building, where they continued beyond the wall-face for a distance of 55 cm. The foundations of the south-east wall, where the apses, central recess, and corner rooms acted as massive internal buttresses, projected for a distance of about 17.5 cm along the south-east side; in the eastern corner-room the foundations projected 60 cm beyond the wall-face, giving an overall width of about 1.65 m at this point; the foundations of the south-west apse were also exposed and were seen to project 25 cm beyond the wall-face. A test-pit was sunk on the south-east side of the north-west wall of the room at the southern corner of the main building, and showed that here the foundations were about 1.30 m in depth. Outside the main walls, where the tops of the foundations were below ground-level, the trenches so formed were filled with compacted red clay which was banked up slightly against the wall-faces (1: f.90; 13: 1420; 17: 74).

The principal load-bearing walls were all 90 cm in width, with mortared rubble cores retained by trap facing-blocks; the aggregate used in the wall-cores was, as far as could be ascertained, composed exclusively of trap rubble. At two points, one where the north-east wall had been completely robbed away, and the other where the foundations were sectioned (see above), a near vertical face across the width of the walls was available for examination; in neither instance could the superimposed layers of the wall core be distinguished, since neither air cavities nor changes in the mortar-mix were detected. The facing-blocks were laid in regular courses; below the double tile-courses and in the north-west wall of the *caldarium* below the springing of the arches, very narrow subsidiary courses were inserted to produce a perfectly level course throughout the whole length of the wall (Fig. 43). The individual blocks were, in plan, very roughly triangular, with their faces and the first few centimetres of each side trimmed flat. The blocks preserved in position never exceeded a thickness of 30 cm and a length of 40 cm, and were usually of a much smaller size. In the lower courses of the wall the blocks tended to be relatively long and thin, increasing to their greatest size at a height of about 1.0 m above the foundation level. The width of the joints varied considerably, and in many places the pointing was incised with horizontal and vertical lines to improve the appearance of the masonry.

At a height of 1.4 m above foundation level there was a double tile-course. It extended through the whole width of the south-east wall, where tiles measuring 38 cm by 25.5 cm and 20 cm square had been employed. In the arms of the apses the tiles were used only as an edging; this was demonstrated by the presence of a fragment of the mortared rubble core which was preserved to a height just above the tile-course. In the north-east wall the tiles were also used to form an edging rather than an all-through course.

The interior walls of the *caldarium* and the *tepidarium* were supplied with stone or tile corbels spaced about 60 cm apart centre-to-centre, and with their upper surfaces at a distance of 80 cm above the floor of the hypocaust basement. In the south-east and north-east walls the corbels were formed by sets of three tiles measuring 38 cm by 25.5 cm; by contrast, in the wall dividing the *tepidarium* from the *caldarium* single trap blocks were mostly used for this purpose. The function of these corbels as supports for the *suspensura* (floor above the hypocaust) is discussed on p. 30.

The wall dividing the *tepidarium* from the *caldarium* was pierced by six arches at its base, three of which survived intact. Before the arches were built the wall had been brought up to an overall level by the insertion of small subsidiary courses where necessary. Recent disturbance which had exposed the outside of the fourth arch from the south-west showed that it had been built free-standing, and that the exterior surface, the extrados, as it were, had been rendered over; no attempt was made to bond the arch with the wall subsequently built up around it. The arches were turned throughout the width of the wall with roughly-worked trap voussoir blocks.

The south-west wall of the *caldarium*, only four courses of which survived above foundation level, was pierced by an opening 3.6 m in width, probably the base of an arch intended to accommodate the furnace outlet with the *testudo* above (see p. 40). Doubtless there was an opening in the corresponding position on the opposite side of the room, but the wall at that point was not accessible for excavation.

The ends of the apse walls terminated in projecting plinths of masonry, one course in height, which supported blocks of sandstone. At the junction of the north-eastern apse with the south-east interior wall of the baths, the carefully worked stone block had been dislodged during demolition, and was restored to its original position during the course of excavation (Pl. IVB). The block between the south-western apse and the central recess was still in position. Its upper surface had been carefully worked to a plane surface in the centre of which was a lewis hole 10 cm long by 2 cm wide at the top[1]: the sides of the block had been drafted flat over a width of about a centimetre around the edges, but the centres were only roughly trimmed (Pl. VIB).

The room at the eastern corner of the building measured 3.15 m by 2.60 m internally. Apparently it could only be entered from the exterior of the building; in the north-eastern wall was preserved a door 80 cm wide, with an unpaved threshold at a height of 45 cm above foundation-level. What little could be seen of the room in a corresponding position on the south-west side of the building revealed an identical arrangement.

Half-way down the length of the wall between the *tepidarium* and the *caldarium*, the wall-top was capped by fragments of broken tile set in brick-mortar at a level of 90 cm above the hypocaust floor. This must have represented the bedding for a stone threshold; unfortunately the broken tiles were only preserved over a length of 1.0 m, giving no indication of the original width of the door (but see p. 51).

The *tepidarium* shared the same length as the *caldarium* (22.3 m). The line of the north-east wall, which was robbed to foundation-level, was indicated by the edge of a mortar floor laid down at the beginning of Period 1B. The north-west wall was situated beyond the limits of the excavation, but there was a clue to the position which it occupied: in the *caldarium*, a channel consisting of discontinuous lengths of tile-walling ran along the exact centre-line of the room, between the two

---

Level of the *caldarium* hypocaust basement floor; taken at 1 m. intervals from north-east to south-west along the heat-channel.

(1) —	(6) 37.344 m O.D.	(11) 37.316 m O.D.	(16) 37.256 m O.D.
(2) 37.384 m O.D.	(7) 37.331 m O.D.	(12) 37.285 m O.D.	(17) 37.286 m O.D.
(3) 37.357 m O.D.	(8) —	(13) 37.286 m O.D.	(18) —
(4) 37.363 m O.D.	(9) —	(14) 37.271 m O.D.	(19) 37.291 m O.D.
(5) 37.347 m O.D.	(10) 37.318 m O.D.	(15) 37.276 m O.D.	(20) 37.298 m O.D.
			(21) 37.261 m O.D.
			(22) 37.266 m O.D.
			(23) —

Levels taken from north-west to south-east along the transverse heat-channel (at 1 m intervals).

(1) 37.301 m O.D.	(6) 37.285 m O.D.	(10) 37.276 m O.D.	
(2) 37.271 m O.D.	(centre point)	(11) 37.296 m O.D.	
(3) 37.274 m O.D.	(7) 37.301 m O.D.	(12) 37.326 m O.D.	
(4) 37.278 m O.D.	(8) 37.278 m O.D.	(13) 37.336 m O.D.	
(5) 37.297 m O.D.	(9) 37.296 m O.D.		

Table 4.: levels taken on the *caldarium* hypocaust floor

furnaces; a similar feature was encountered in the *tepidarium* which, if centrally placed, would indicate that the room was 11.25 m in width (see p. 32).

North of the *tepidarium* a substantial brick-mortar floor was found at the lowest excavated level of trench 8 (21: brick-mortar, Period 1A); this presumably belonged to the *frigidarium*.

Levels taken at 1 m intervals along the course of the two heat-channels revealed a fall of 12 cm from north-east to south-west; this may well have been intended by the builders (cf. Vitruvius, V, 10, 1).

NOTES

1. A lewis-hole is used to secure a bolt for lifting a large building-block by means of a crane or hoist (Landels, 1978, 91–2).

E. THE HYPOCAUSTS IN THE MAIN BUILDING (Fig. 7; Pls. I–V, XXI):

The Hypocaust in the Caldarium: the tiled floor of the hypocaust basement was set in a matrix of brick-mortar 10 cm thick, overlying a layer of trap chips 5 cm thick. The levels beneath the basement floor were examined in only two places, near the north-eastern furnace-mouth, and where the north-west wall of the *caldarium* had been robbed out; in both cases, the old top-soil had been removed, presumably as a result of terracing. The hypocaust basement floor was lined throughout with tiles; on the north-eastern side and in the central part of the room tiles measuring 38 by 25.5 cm were used, but to the south-west roofing *tegulae* placed upside down took their place, and in the central recess *bipedales* (tiles 60 cm sq.) were employed. The main body of the *caldarium* was divided into four parts by two channels composed of tile-piers between 80 cm and 1 m in length and 20 cm wide. The gaps between the piers varied in width from 15 cm to 40 cm, and were generally aligned with the spaces between the files of *pilae*. Where the two channels crossed, the channel running from south-west to north-east blocked the course of the transverse channel. The purpose of the channels must have been to promote the circulation of hot air to all parts of the hypocaust. Thus the gaps between the piers on each side of the channel which led directly from the two furnaces were narrow in order to reduce the flow of the heat away from the middle of the room; at the mid-point of the channel there were four gaps 40 cm wide through which the hot air would have been led off into the transverse channel, where the gaps between the piers were all 40 cm in width, allowing for a freer circulation of the gases.

The south-western part of the hypocaust was built of tiles 20 cm square supported on base-tiles 25 cm square, but on the north-east side the bases were composed of four tiles 20 cm square, except in the southern and eastern corners and in the north-eastern apse. Since part of the *suspensura* must have been removed in Period 1B in order to block the transverse channel (see p. 62), it is possible that the variation in the tiles used to construct the bases signifies a replacement of the original *pilae;* on the other hand the difference may simply be attributable to fluctuations in the supply of various types of tile to the site during construction. Isolated instances of tiles 38 cm by 25.5 cm or fragments of *bipedales* used as *pila* bases were also noted.

Each of the four divisions of the hypocaust basement was equipped with 13 north-west to south-east files of *pilae* arranged in eight north-east to south-west ranks; each *pila* was placed at a distance, from centre to centre, of 60 cm from its neighbour. At the sides of the room the arrangement was rather awkward: in many places the *pilae* were situated below the stone or tile corbels, and thus could not have been built up to their full height of 80 cm. The original purpose of the corbels, which projected 20 cm where preserved, must have been to support the edge of the *suspensura*, since they are the same distance apart, centre-to-centre, as the *pilae* (that is 60 cm). However, because of the position and width of the transverse channel, it was not possible to align the files of *pilae* with the corbels. Thus, at the sides of the room, the *pilae* stood under the corbels and must have been used to give them additional support.

The *suspensura* was supported on a base composed of *bipedales* resting on the tops of the *pilae*. However, over the two channels it would not have been possible to use the *bipedales* as a covering in the normal way; the 60 cm width of the channels would have been too great to support them at all four corners and failure to do so would have caused grave structural weakness in the floor above. Material from the destruction of the hypocaust in Period 2A showed how this problem had been overcome: fragments of *bipedales* were found which showed soot-free areas about four centimetres wide running diagonally across their undersides (Pl. XXI), and in addition a number of iron bars of the same width were recovered (Fig. 76, 94–5). From this, it was clear that the *bipedales* had been supported on iron bars laid diagonally across the channels[1]. The absence of any evidence of proximity to the furnaces, such as heat-cracking or the reduction of exposed surfaces, showed that the tiles and iron bars in question were not used to support a *testudo* or a boiler, as has been found elsewhere.

The centres of the two apses were occupied by circular bases 1.3 m in diameter and constructed of broken tile set in mortar; there can be little doubt that they supported *labra*. In the south-west apse the tile base was preserved to a height of 40 cm (Pl. IVA), but in the north-east apse the base was only represented by the impression of its lowest course in mortar spread over the basement floor. In both apses the *pilae* were arranged in three concentric semicircles around the bases.

Only four *pilae* were preserved in the central recess, but their spacing appeared to be the same as in the main part of the hypocaust. For this reason the presence of a bath, which would have needed additional support, seems unlikely, but it is possible that the centre of the recess was occupied by a tile base, as in the apses, intended to support a heavy object such as a statue or an altar.

Both the north-east and south-west sides of the hypocaust were occupied throughout their entire length by lines of tile piers, which provided additional support for the weight of the baths. On the north-east side of the room, little of the original arrangement survived. The space between the furnace outlet and the south-east wall of the *caldarium* was occupied by a platform 60 cm in width, which consisted of a single layer of tiles; the platform supported four tile piers, the south-easternmost 60 cm wide and the others 40 cm wide. Traces of three other piers standing directly on top of the tiled hypocaust were found north-west of the furnace outlet.

In front of the furnace the bath was not supported by *pilae*: instead two slots were found, spaced 1.10 m apart, the south-east slot terminating against the tile platform which had been set back to accommodate it. It was clear from the iron staining and flakes of corrosion along their whole length that the slots had held iron bars about 6 cm square in section (see Fig. 7, section 16). The profiles of the slots were crisp and sharp showing that the bars must have been set into the brick-mortar before it had solidified; at several points along their course, the tiled basement floor slightly overlapped the slots. A similar pair of slots was found on the south-west side of the room in the same relative position, terminating against two tile piers; here the piers were preserved to a height of about 50 cm, and vertical grooves were observed running up their faces above the end of the slots, indicating the presence of upright bars. The horizontal bars must have formed the bases of prefabricated iron "cages" which supported the baths in front of the furnace outlets[2]. The supports for the south-western bath were constructed in a slightly different manner from those on the north-east side of the room; there were four piers along the front, each measuring 80 cm by 85 cm with two placed at either end and two flanking the opening in front of the furnace. The spaces between the main piers were filled by lengths of tile walling 25 cm wide and 80 cm in length which were separated by gaps 20 cm wide; tile walling was also used to support the bath along the sides of the north-west and south-east walls and on either side of the iron "cage". The two central piers were joined by an arch turned in tile, the springing of which was partly preserved. Behind the piers, *pilae* were found spaced 40 cm apart centre-to-centre; very few had been left in position, but the original arrangement is indicated by the alignment of the surviving *pilae* with the closely-set lengths of tile walling.

The Hypocaust in the Tepidarium: only part of the hypocaust-floor was tiled; roofing *tegulae* had been used to cover a strip 4.8 m wide on the west side of the room. A gap 60 cm wide between the *tegulae* and the south-west wall of the room was rendered over with brick-mortar which also formed the floor throughout the rest of the hypocaust basement. This inconsistency of treatment probably did not have any special significance; perhaps the supply of suitable tiles to the site had been temporarily exhausted when the hypocaust was being constructed.

The supports for the *suspensura* consisted of *pilae* arranged in the usual way and divided into four sections by tile-built channels, similar to those in the *caldarium;* their presence suggests that the hypocaust was served by at least one furnace. The north-eastern part of the hypocaust was not excavated; however, *pilae* rather than tile piers were observed at the edge of the hypocaust in the eastern corner of the room when the robbing trench of its south–east wall was emptied; this suggested that there were no baths in the *tepidarium*.

Discussion of the heating system:

The details of the hypocaust require further comment. The heat-channels and iron bars, and also the iron cages in front of the furnaces are all hitherto unparalleled features; however their functions are obvious enough. The use of tiles to line the floor of the hypocaust basement occurs commonly in baths dating to before the end of the first century A.D., for example at Pompeii (Stabian Baths, best seen in Eschebach, 1973, Abb. 3), Coriovallum-Heerlen (van Giffen, 1948, 199 ff.), and Avenches (Schwarz, 1969, Taf. 17, Abb. 2 and Taf. 18, Abb. 2). The tiles were laid down presumably to provide a level base for the *pilae* and, as the absence of a tile lining from most of the *tepidarium* at Exeter shows, this was a feature which could be safely dispensed with when tiles were in short supply or economies had to be made.

The main problem associated with the heating system concerns the use of the walls and vaults as radiant surfaces. The extension of the hypocaust system in the form of hollow walls was a comparatively recent development when the Exeter baths were built. Seneca writing in the mid first century A.D. described it as a phenomenon *quaedam nostra demum prodisse memoria scimus* (*Ep.* XC, 25; cf. *De Prov.* IV, 9 and *Ad Q.N.* III, 24). The earliest securely datable use of *tegulae mammatae*[3] to create a hollow wall space connected to a hypocaust occurred at the Baths of Regio VIII, Insula 5 at Pompeii where they were found in the men's *caldarium* on the wall behind the bath (Maiuri, 1950, 125 ff.); this building was demolished in the Augustan period. On the other hand, the Forum Baths of Herculaneum, constructed in the Julio-Claudian period, were only equipped with evacuation ducts[4], even at the time of their destruction in A.D. 79 (Maiuri, 1958, 93). Indeed in the Campanian bath-houses some of the developments in wall-heating can be seen to unfold. *Tegulae mammatae* had been installed in the *tepidarium* and *caldarium* of the Stabian Baths before A.D. 63 (Mau-Kelsey, 1899, 185; Maiuri, 1942, 70). Mau considered that this heating system was first installed in the *caldarium* where both the walls and the vaults were lined, while the *tepidarium* remained dependent on a brazier for its heating. At a later date the heating system in the *tepidarium* was modernised, but *tegulae mammatre* were used to line only the walls[5]. A further development can be seen in the Suburban Baths of Herculaneum, constructed shortly before A.D. 79, where box-tiles were employed (Maiuri, 1958, 150 ff.).

It is clear that, even in a restricted geographic area such as Campania, the innovations in heating techniques were not always instantly taken up. The same picture emerges elsewhere. The earliest use of box-tiles occurs at Vindonissa(Laur-Belart, 1935, 51) and in a bath-house at Ostia (Blake, 1959, 163) in the Claudian period; but when a bath-house was erected at Avenches in the early Flavian period, a building on much the same scale as at Vindonissa, there was no wall-heating, as was shown by the presence of evacuation ducts in both the *caldarium* and *tepidarium* (Schwarz 1969, Taf. 17, Abb. 2; Taf. 18, Abb. 2; Taf. 19, Abb. 4). Red House, Corbridge is another example of the late first century where wall-heating was apparently absent[6]. Thus the bath-house at Exeter was erected during what was still a transitional phase in the development of heating systems. However, although no box-tiles or *tegulae mammatae* were found *in situ* and no clamp-holes were noted in the wall surfaces, there is good evidence for the presence of wall-heating. Finds from the demolition levels of Period 1B and 2A included *tegulae mammatae*, box-tiles and T-shaped iron clamps. Furthermore at no point were there channels cut into the surviving walls to accommodate evacuation flues.

A further problem arises from the presence of both *tegulae mammatae* and box-tiles. At Vindonissa and Neuss[7] both types were also present although this may be due to the introduction of one type during repairs.

For the purposes of creating a radiant surface, box-tiles are more efficient than *tegulae mammatae*: the hollow space which they enclose is usually about twice as wide, and they also insulate the heating system from heat loss to the walls (Thatcher, 1956,190 n. 6). In the *caldarium* of the Suburban Baths at Herculaneum box-tiles were fixed to the walls, but the vault was lined with *tegulae mammatae* (Maiuri, 1958, 150 and 162–3). From this it can be inferred that the vault was not intended to function as a radiant surface, an inference supported by the presence of evacuation ducts running along the haunches of the vault at the top of the box-tiles. The vault was probably lined merely to prevent condensation gathering on the intrados, and the cavity so formed must have received only a small portion of the hot gases circulating in the hollow walls. The presence of the two types of tile at Vindonissa, Exeter and Neuss, all from buildings dating to the second half of the first century A.D., can be taken to indicate the possibility of a similar sort of arrangement in one or more of the heated rooms at these baths.

NOTES

1. Three large tile-fragments (8–9 cm thick) with the markings left by iron bars were recovered from the demolition-debris filling the *caldarium* hypocaust. On two of these the soot-free areas ran diagonally across the surfaces; on the third the edges of the tile had been broken away, so it was not possible to determine the alignment of the bars. Presumably the bars were laid diagonally so as to provide not only support across the width of the channels, but also across the gaps between the piers which formed the sides of the channels.

2. G. C. Boon (*in litt.*) has pointed out that, compared to the iron lintels or beams employed to support boilers (see Wacher, 1971, 200–3) or the front of baths, these iron bars were relatively feeble, and suggests that they may have formed a guard to prevent fuel from being pushed into the hypocaust.

3. *Tegulae mammatae* are flat tiles with protuberances at each corner of one face, either applied nipples or cones, or rectangular flanges. Vitruvius (VII, 4, 2) refers to *hamatae tegulae* and Pliny (*N.H.* XXXV, 159) to . . . (*figlinum opera*) . . . *ad balineas mammatis*. M. E. Blake (1947, 305) takes *hamatae* to refer to tiles with flanges at each corner and *mammatae* to those with (nipple-like) protuberances. However, there is some uncertainty about the texts, so I have followed the usual practice of referring to both types as *tegulae mammatae*.

4. This term refers to vents running up through the walls at intervals and acting as chimneys for the hypocaust. Their presence usually indicates the absence of hollow walls.

5. It is not clear what evidence there is for this sequence. Blake (1947, 307) thought the system was post-Augustan.

6. Daniels, 1959, 128–9: box-tiles and *tegulae mammatae* were recovered from the site, but evacuation ducts survived in one of the *caldarium* walls and in the *laconicum*. It was suggested that the box-tiles were used to form the evacuation ducts in places, but the function of the *tegulae mammatae* was not appreciated. Perhaps only the wall behind the bath(s) in the *caldarium* was lined with hollow tiles, as in the *caldarium* of the Baths of Regio VIII, Insula 5 (Maiuri, 1950, 124 f.).

7. At Vindonissa box-tiles are specifically mentioned, as well as *Ziegelplatten mit vier festen Nasen an den Ecken*; for Neuss see Koenen, 1904, 311 and Taf. XXII. At Red House, Corbridge (Daniels, 1959, 170) nos. 6a and b appear to be *tegulae mammatae* from their descriptions, although they are not identified as such by their excavator. There are two other finds of *tegulae mammatae* in Britain which could date to before the end of the first century A.D.; one find-spot is the site of the poorly known bath-house at Loughor (tile displayed in the Royal Institution of South Wales, Swansea) and others came from the works-depot at Holt (Grimes, 1930, 135, no. 5 "not of ordinary *tegulae* form . . . flanges are cut away in the middle of each side"); but similar tiles from the villa at Llantwit Major, Glamorgan, must date to the second half of the third century A.D. (Nash-Williams, 1953a, 132). Tiles with nipple-like protuberances instead of cut-away flanges have been found in a first-century context at Dorchester (C. J. S.

Green, *pers. comm.*) and at Usk 'a tile with conical projections . . . came from a pit some way to the west of the baths' (W. H. Manning, *in litt.*). *Tegulae mammatae* of the flanged type were recovered from the Fortress Baths, Caerleon, from contexts dating to *c.* 80 (G. C. Boon, *in litt.*). Further examples have been found in South-east England (S. S. Frere, *in litt.*) but the preceding list serves to show the different types which are to be found in Britain during the first century A.D. and later.

F. CONSTRUCTION OF THE SERVICE BUILDINGS (Figs. 7 and 16, Pl. XA):

An extensive spread of mortar overlying the trap and gravel metalling at the southern corner of the main building probably represented a mortar-mixing area (7: 44D1). To the north-east a thin layer of mixed clays, perhaps upcast from the digging of the foundation-trenches, was spread over the metalling (I: 9EC3). There was no evidence of any other activities. Subsequently the entire area surrounding the main building was remetalled with trap chips containing only a small admixture of gravel (1: 9EC2; 4: 37D; 5: 31D; 6: 52K; 7: 44D; 8: 52K; 12: 1161A; 17: 72. In the following sections the two layers of metalling could not be adequately distinguished: 13: 1418; 15: 1150).

An open gully was dug through the metalling, crossing the southern corner of the site diagonally from the north (7: gully 9); it remained open long enough for silt to accumulate along its bottom, and was finally packed with red clay. Near the southern corner of the main building, a spread of mortar was found, overlying both the metalling and the back-filled gully, and occupying much the same position as the probable mortar-mixing area described above (5: 31C; 7: 44C). When the second mortar-mixing area went out of use, mortar fragments and clay were trampled into its surface; it was eventually covered by a layer of mortar, trap chips and clay (7: 44B1 and 44B). A shallow foundation, running from south-west to north-east, 85 cm in width and about 20 cm deep, was then excavated and packed with trap rocks set in river gravel; the top of the foundation, which projected about 10 cm above the contemporary surface, was capped with white mortar (7: f. 52). At its south-west end the foundation was very much deeper, penetrating to a depth of about 60 cm, suggesting that at this point a more massive superstructure was envisaged. The methods employed in constructing the foundation were similar to those of the later service-building walls; it therefore seems probable that the foundation represented the commencement of work on the service-buildings, soon abandoned. The north-east end of the foundation was cut away by a land-drain (f. 63, 73), the presence of which provides a possible reason for the cessation of the building work: surface-water may have been accumulating on the site and it was perhaps thought necessary to make some provision for drainage. The wall which the foundation was intended to support may have been intended as the south-east side of the furnace-house: when work was recommenced, the opportunity was taken to shift its line 1.0 m to the south-east, giving covered access to the room in the southern corner of the main building.

Three land-drains were dug on the site, one running from north-west to south-east, and joining another at right angles at its south-east end, while a third connected with the former from the direction of the main building (1: f.34; 3: f.34; 4: f.63; 12: 1162; 14: 1151 and 1162; 15: 1151; 17: 73). The drains were laid in trenches varying in width between 1.0 m and 1.2 m and in depth between 85 cm and 1.25 m. Over most of its length the drain running from south-west to north-east was represented only by a clay-filled trench, which, because of the slumping of its sides, must have remained open for some time. At a distance of 4.5 m from its junction with the drain to the north-west the bottom of the trench was lined on each side with trap rocks, leaving a central channel in which fine brown silt had accumulated; the channel was capped by very large trap blocks with an estimated weight of up to 30 kg. The other two drains were constructed in a similar manner, and the upper fills of all three consisted of mixed clays. There are probably two reasons why the greater part of the drain running from north-east to south-west was not completed. First, it was dug in two parts on slightly different lines, so that where it connected there would have been a 'dog's leg'. Secondly, it may be doubted whether such drainage was really necessary, since work on the site in the moderately wet winter of 1971 was never hampered by the surface water; it is possible that exceptionally heavy rainfall had given rise to unwarranted fears about the impermeability of the sub-soil.

In some places a spread of clay continuous with the upper fill of the land-drain trenches was found (1: 9EC1; 4: 37C; 7: 44A). On the south-west side of the main building at the north-west end of the site another mortar-mixing area was encountered (17: 71; 18: 71); many lenses of different grades of mortar were observed, all cemented into a very hard mass which could only be removed with the assistance of a pneumatic drill.

After these activities had taken place, the service-building walls were constructed. Their foundations consisted of trap rubble, mortared throughout and set in shallow trenches usually 90 cm in width and penetrating no more than 10 cm below the surface of natural. The mortared rubble was built up to a height of about 15 cm above the construction level. From this point the walls themselves were constructed, all with a uniform width of 44 cm; trap facing-blocks never more than 15 cm high were employed to retain the mortared rubble core. At the extreme north-east end of the roadside wall a tile-course was found at the same level as that preserved in the walls of the main building; it was probably repeated in all the service building walls, perhaps more for the sake of appearance rather than for any structural reasons. The lowest course on the north-west face of the boundary-wall was inclined at an angle of 60°. Before the walls were built the position of the wooden water-pipe system of drainage had already been determined, and relieving arches were constructed where the pipes were intended to pass under the walls. Two examples survived, one at the north-west end of the wall abutting the southern corner of the main building, the other at the south-east end of the corresponding wall on the north-east side; both were semi-circular arches turned with tiles measuring 38 cm by 25.5 cm. On the south-west side of the main building the walls enclosed the furnace-house which measured 10.2 m by 7.5 m; the building was entered at its southern corner through a door 1.2 m wide. South-east of the furnace-house there was a courtyard which measured 8.4 m by 7.4 m. In Period 1B its size was reduced by a half; before that it was almost certainly open to the road. On the north-east side of the courtyard there was an enclosed area measuring 23.2 m by 6.3 m; it was apparently without any sub-divisions, and it is not known whether it was roofed. No doors were found in the surviving fragments of its walls; possibly there was an entry at its southern corner, opposite to that leading from the court-yard to the room by the *palaestra*. The area at the eastern corner of the main building was again probably open to the road; its north-west side was bounded by the south-east wall of the north-eastern furnace-house.

The position of the north-east boundary wall in Period 2A may have marked the earlier north-eastern limits of the service-buildings associated with the baths, but unfortunately two sections revealed in the sides of its robber trench produced no firm evidence to support this view. In the south-west section tips of clay-loam mixed with charcoal (30: 315–320) were sealed by a layer of clay which seemed to have been an extension of the post-construction levelling deposited at the beginning of Period 2A (30: 313 equivalent to 15: 1137 etc.) In the north-eastern section a deposit of loam was found, filling a feature which cut down into natural (31: 323); it is possible that the feature represented a road-side ditch, but this is far from certain.

Before the finished levels were laid down in the service area, the system of wooden water-pipes already referred to was installed. A series of trenches 80 cm wide and up to 30 cm deep were dug and baulks of timber were laid across their bottoms at intervals of about 2.0 m. The wooden water-pipes were then laid along the trenches, supported on the timber baulks which served to facilitate both the encasement of the pipes in a waterproof packing of clay, and the joining together of individual pipes with iron collars; the junctions must have been effected by placing one length of pipe in position, hammering the iron collar into one end and then hammering the adjoining pipe onto the same ring. All the pipes had been extracted at the beginning of Period 2A, leaving only their impressions, but one iron junction-collar was found discarded in the pipe-trench running south-eastwards from the north-east furnace-house.

At the south corner of the building two pipes were found, one running below the door of the furnace-house, the other running along the south-east side of the building (1: F.51 and F.68). The junction of the two pipes coincided with a small rectangular pit about 0.45 m deep, which probably served as a junction-box or inspection-chamber (4: pit 24). Leading away from the pit was a channel, square in section and not associated with a bedding-trench; this probably held a plank-lined drain (3: 74). Another pit interrupted the course of the drain, perhaps a later junction-box connected to the pipe-system installed to the north-east at the beginning of Period 1B (pit 25). The drain continued south-east after making a brief turn to the south-west and must have emptied into the roadside ditch. On the north-east side of the building a rather more complex system was found. A pipe ran south-east from the wall of the furnace-house almost to the roadside where it turned south-west, passing under a relieving arch (13: 1412, 1416; 14: 1134, 1134, 1134A). At the north-west end both bedding-trench and pipe stopped short of the furnace-house wall; at this point the pipe must have emerged above ground-level. The only evidence for a vertical pipe was a small circular pit, no doubt occasioned by its removal. Another water-pipe was found running towards this pipe at right angles; the junction of the two pipes (if indeed they joined; see below) was removed by a later wall (12: 1139A). Where the pipe leading from the furnace-house turned south-west another bedding-trench was observed, which contained no trace of a water-pipe. It is possible that the pipe leading from the furnace-house was originally intended to turn to the north-east rather than to the south-west, joining with a pipe which ran from a point by the south-east wall of the main building (see below). Instead the pipe was led away to the south-west where its course was interrupted by a plank-lined drain (14: 1148). The drain consisted of a trench 70 cm wide and 50 cm deep, the sides of which were revetted by planks held in place by opposed pairs of posts spaced at intervals of roughly 1.2 m; at one point, the planks had been embedded in the bottom of the trench leaving a slot about 3 cm wide. At the south-east end of the drain a hole had been broken through the foundations and lowest course of the roadside wall to connect with the ditch on the other side; this shows that the insertion of the drain was a modification of the original layout. The plank-lined drain terminated near the eastern corner of the main building.

The impression of a timber cross-baulk was the only evidence to show that an intrusion apparently cut by the plank-lined drain had been dug in order to remove a water-pipe running from east to west (it was probably removed at the beginning of Period 1B, although a division between the furnace-ash and similar material sealing it was not established by excavation; 14: 1147). Next to the south-east wall of the main building there was a pit with vertical sides which was probably another wood-lined junction-pit (15: 1188).

Wooden water-pipes are usually associated with the mains-supply from an aqueduct. Thus it seems likely that the water-pipe entering the site on the north-east side (12: 1139A) was a main and was connected to a branch-pipe (13: 1416) supplying the boiler in the furnace-house and the *labrum* in the north-east apse. On the other hand, the supposed water-main may have continued further to the south-west, the pipe next to the southern corner of the main building forming an extension of it (1: f.51). The pipe turned north-east and would have supplied the boiler in the south-west furnace-house. In this case the pipe by the north-eastern furnace-house (13: 1416) may have been a main leading around to the *labrum* in the north-eastern apse[1].

However, there is one problem which casts doubt on the interpretation of these pipes as water-mains: the absence of any drains to take the outfall from the baths in the *caldarium*. This raises the possibility that the pipes were, in fact, drains rather than water-mains. If so, the pipes on the south-west side (f.77 and 51) would have taken the outfall, respectively, from the south-western bath and perhaps a floor-drain in the south-west apse[2]; the pipes on the north-east side would have served a similar function (1416 and 1417). It should be noted that these pipes could well have discharged into two drains (f. 77 and 1147) which both fed into the ditch at the side of the street. This possible use of wooden pipes as drains can be paralleled by the Period 2A stylobate-drain which also fed into a wooden water-pipe system under the street to the south-east (see p. 77).

Once the pipe-system had been inserted the interior of the service-buildings was levelled up, covering the foundations of the walls and the bedding-trenches of the pipes. In the south-east part of the courtyard adjoining the south-western furnace-house, three separate lenses of well-compacted clay were deposited, the uppermost mixed with gravel to provide a roughly metalled surface (3: 46D, 46E, 46F; 4: 37A, 37A1, 37B and 46D, 46E1, 46E2, 46F; 6: 52G, 52H). Elsewhere a single layer of clay up to 40 cm thick was deposited (1: 9EC; 3: 9EC; 12: 1160; 13: 1417; 14: 1160 and 1144; 15: 1144).

In the western corner of the enclosure between the *caldarium* and the street two roughly circular clay-filled scoops were found, both approximately 40 cm in diameter; these must have been the seatings for *amphorae*-bases re-used as urinals (pits 20 and 21), which were later replaced by others, more substantial traces of which survived (see p. 64). About 2 m south of the scoops, a patch of mortar was found overlying the clay surface; it was perhaps the remains of a mortar-mixing area associated with the completion of the final details of the building.

The street: the timber building on the south-east side of the street was demolished and its site was covered by a layer of mixed clays 15 cm thick (9: 68D). The street was then resurfaced with river gravel on a bedding of mortar-debris and tile fragments; the metalling continued south-east over the site of the demolished timber buildings, indicating a minimum width of 7.6 m for the road (8: 49G1, 49G2; 9: 49G1). The only stratigraphical link between the resurfaced street and the activities to the north-west was supplied by a roadside gully (8: gully 7B; 10: gully 7B); its maximum width was 80 cm and its depth was about 35 cm. It had been cut from above the re-surfaced street and the clay levelling laid down to the north-west after the construction of the service-buildings (8: 52H, 52H1).

NOTES

1. But what little evidence there is indicates that *labra* in *caldaria* were supplied with hot water (see p. 41, n. 8).

2. *Labra* are not supplied with 'plug-holes'. The holes sometimes found at their centres are for supply-pipes (e.g. the *labrum* at Red House, Corbridge, see Daniels, 1959, 115–116). Excess water must have poured over the edge of the *labrum* onto the floor, where it would have helped to increase the steaminess of the atmosphere in the *caldarium*. There must have been drains at floor-level to take away the water.

G. THE FURNACE-HOUSES (Figs. 7 and 16, Pl. V):

The furnace-house at the north-east end of the *caldarium* was not investigated and had probably been completely destroyed in medieval times. Its existence, however, was indicated by:

(1) The supports for a bath on the east side of the *caldarium*.
(2) The presence of an iron 'cage'.
(3) An area of burnt, reduced and heat-fractured tiles in the vicinity of the 'cage'.

A short length of the south-east wall of the furnace-house was recovered at a distance of 5.22 m from the eastern corner of the main building.

The south-western furnace-house was relatively well-preserved except where the foundations of the Victorian church cut across its south-east part. It consisted of a rectangular building measuring 10.2 m by 7.5 m which had an entry at its eastern corner giving onto the courtyard by the street. From the interior access could also be had to the room in the southern corner of the main building. The most prominent features in the furnace-house were two large masonry bases, separated only by the flue of the furnace, 1.1 m in width, which had a tile-lined floor, fused into a hard grey layer by the heat. The north-west base measured 2.25 m by 2.8 m. On the north-west side it was retained by the exterior wall of the furnace-house and on the north-east partly by the south-west wall of the main building; where it passed across the front of the arch a rough wall of tile fragments was built to retain it. The south-west wall of the base was constructed of trap facing blocks built on top of a single course of tiles. The south-east wall, which formed one side of the flue, was constructed so as to take into account the high temperatures to which it would have been subjected; a course of carefully dressed trap blocks 35 cm high and 45 cm wide and of varying lengths was laid on top of a single course of tiles and capped by another; clay rather than mortar was used to cement these blocks and tiles. Although its constructional details were similar, the south-east base was much larger; its southern part was largely destroyed, but its minimum length was 4.0 m.

On both sides of the south-west end of the flue the trap blocks which lined it projected slightly beyond the bases; both the terminal blocks had symbols carefully carved on their south-western faces: on the north-west block an "X" and on the south-east block a simple diagonal line, both of which were deeply incised. It is possible that these were position-marks, the blocks having been cut to certain specifications in the masons' yard and then assembled on site.

Both bases contained a filling of trap rocks laid in coarse yellow mortar of only moderate strength; the filling also included a few chips of Purbeck marble. A spread of mortar was found running across the width of the south-east base at the same level as the tile-course above the trap blocks lining the flue; the mortar spread was capped by a spread of lime at a level about 65 cm above the floor of the flue (78 at 37.97 m O.D.). This may well represent the level at which the boiler and *testudo* were inserted.

In front of the furnace there was an apron of tiles, set in a stoking area which measured 2.4 m by 2.2 m; its floor was of clay and gravel. The stoking area was originally surrounded by a wall about 15 cm high now mostly robbed, retaining a dump of gravel capped by a mortar floor (see Section 18). A slot 10 cm deep had been cut through the south-west side of the raised floor and terminated at a distance of 20 cm from the foundations of the south-west furnace-house wall (67): its purpose is unknown.

In the angle between the masonry base and the north-west wall of the furnace-house, there was a rectangular platform 2 m in width which was constructed of trap facing blocks retaining a packing of clay (77). Its top was capped by a mortar surface at a level of 30 cm above the surrounding floor. The platform was probably the base of a flight of steps leading up to the boiler above the furnace-flue (see below).

The gravel dump capped by a mortar floor did not extend through into the south-east part of the furnace-house; here the floor was of clay (7: 44A, 32H, 32G). The different types of floor found in either part suggested the presence of a dividing wall; its position has been restored on Fig. 7. A small room in this position adjoining the service courtyard would almost certainly have been used as a fuel-store.

Discussion (Figs. 8 and 12):

The *caldarium* was served by two furnace-houses, one at each end of the room. The *tepidarium*, on the other hand, appeared to have been served only by one, situated on its north-east side (see p. 32); a second furnace-house on its south-west side would have been isolated in the *palaestra* without any access for wheeled vehicles bringing fuel. The construction of a new fuel-store on the south-east side of the north-east *caldarium* furnace-house at the beginning of Period 1B suggests that previously the fuel store had been situated between the two furnace-houses, until that serving the *tepidarium* was demolished at the beginning of Period 1B.

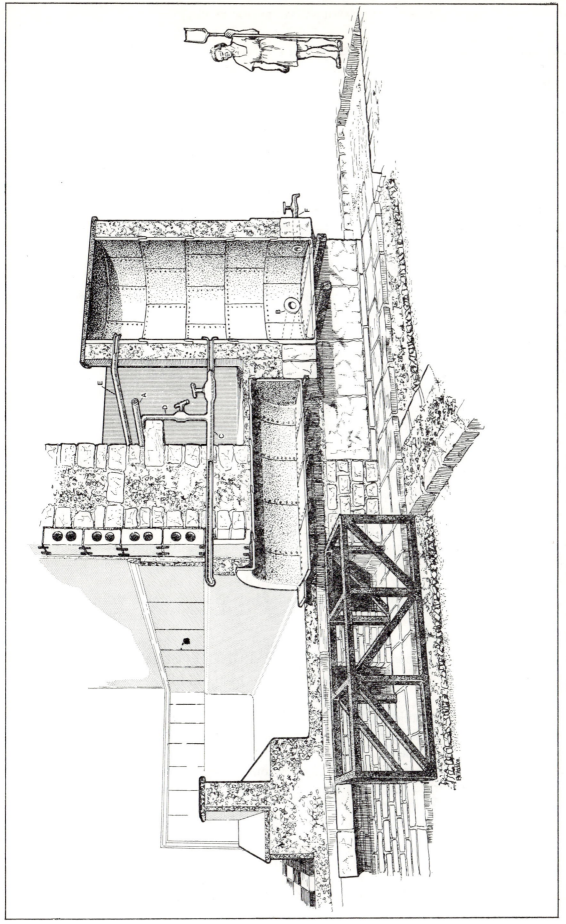

Fig. 8. Conjectural reconstruction of the south-west *caldarium* furnace-house.

Reconstruction of the south-western caldarium furnace-house (Fig. 8):

Vitruvius' account of a bath-house includes a description of the arrangements for heating water: three boilers were placed above the furnace so that the hot water taken from one was replenished with tepid water from another, which was in turn replaced with cold water from a third[1]. The description corresponds with the excavated remains in the Forum and Stabian Baths at Pompeii (Mau-Kelsey, 1899, 196–7; Stabian Baths more clearly in Kretzschmer, 1961, Bild 7) and the Forum Baths at Herculaneum (Maiuri, 1958, 109–110 and Figs. 68 and 88); in all three instances, two of the three boilers were heated directly[2].

It is clear that the heating system at Exeter was of a different type since there would not have been room to fit two boilers over the furnace-flue as well as a *testudo*. Thus we probably have at Exeter one of the earliest satisfactorily attested examples of the prevalent later system where hot water was supplied from a single boiler fed directly with cold water[3]. The earlier system probably fell out of use in the mid-first century A.D. when the size of bathrooms and level of temperature required within them increased, and it was thus no longer possible to serve a complete bath-suite satisfactorily by means of one furnace.

The greater length of the south-east masonry base is probably to be explained by the presence of a water reservoir, connected with the boiler and ultimately fed from the fortress aqueduct. Its capacity can be estimated at about 3000 gallons[4]. The boiler itself, of lead with a bronze base-plate[5], would have had an estimated diameter of 1.40 m; this would allow for a *testudo* 2.1 m in length, with a gap of 40 cm between the two. The capacity of the boiler would have been about 900 gallons[6]. A thick coating of clay or mortar would have insulated the boiler against any substantial heat loss[7]. The system of water supply has been restored according to the evidence preserved by the boilers at the Villa Rustica, Boscoreale and the Suburban Baths, Herculaneum (Maiuri, 1958, Fig. 8). Pipe A is the mains supply to the reservoir and Pipe B supplies water from the reservoir to the boiler. At Boscoreale the base of the reservoir was above the level of the boiler, and the pipe which connected them had a branch leading directly to the bath. This arrangement is not possible at Exeter and instead the pipe supplying water from the boiler to the bath is joined by another pipe (D) leading directly from the reservoir; both pipes are fitted with stop-cocks so that a supply of hot or cold water, or a mixture, could be fed into the bath by means of the same outlet (C). A pipe (E) leading from the boiler at a higher level served the *labrum* in the south-west apse[8]. Finally, again as at Boscoreale, the boiler could be drained by a bib-cock (F) immediately above the mouth of the furnace.

The lead-pipes where running for any distance along the walls were supported on grooved stone corbels. One example was found in a deposit of Period IB (Fig. 48, no. 7) and similar corbels have been found *in situ* in the *caldarium* furnace-house of the legionary baths at Lambaesis (Krencker, 1929, Abb. 286a).

In front of the furnace outlet the plunge bath was supported by an iron 'cage'. There does not yet appear to be any parallel for ironwork in this position, although iron bars were commonly used for supporting the boiler and *testudo* (as in the reconstruction) and also for supporting the front of the bath (cf. Wacher, 1970). At Exeter the front of the south-western bath was supported at its centre by a tile-turned arch spanning two tile piers. The surviving portion of the rear wall of the north-eastern bath showed that there was no 'cushion' or *pulvinus* (see. p. 155). Above the bath, the wall was protected by a splash-board of Purbeck marble (see p. 143).

The main part of the furnace-house was occupied by a sunken ash-pit, with a tile apron in front of the furnace. The apron would have provided a level base for an iron sheet closing the mouth of the furnace when it was necessary to damp down the fire: just such a sheet was found in position at the Forum Baths, Herculaneum. The base in the north corner of the furnace-house was probably part of a flight of steps leading up to the platform above the furnace, from where the water supply to the reservoir, boiler, bath and *labrum* could be regulated[9].

By means of this attempted reconstruction it has proved possible to estimate approximately the capacity of the boiler and the reservoir at respectively 900 and 3000 gallons. The estimated capacity of the bath which the boiler supplied was 4100 gallons, roughly equivalent to the total capacity of the boiler and the reservoir[10]. Thus it would have been possible to refill the bath each day; to do so, the contents of the boiler would have had to have been heated three or four times over, probably during the hours of closing, say from dusk to the sixth hour[11]. During opening hours the contents of the boiler may have been diverted to the *labrum*, which would have required a small, but continuous supply of hot water; the water in the bath would have been kept warm by the *testudo* and the underlying hypocaust. This arrangement, which, it must be admitted, is entirely hypothetical, would permit most of the water used in the *thermae*, perhaps as much as about 70,000 gallons daily, to be drawn off the aqueduct at night when demand elsewhere in the fortress was at its lowest[12].

NOTES

1. Vit. V. 10, 1: *Aenea supra hypocausim tria sunt componenda, unum caldarium, alterum tepidarium, tertium frigidarium, et ita conlocanda, uti, ex tepidario in caldarium quantum aquae caldae exierit, influat de frigidario in tepidarium ad eundem modus.*

2. At the Forum Baths, Herculaneum the installations appear to have been damaged by earlier excavators who had removed the boilers. However Maiuri's drawing shows one furnace with flues leading to the hypocausts of both the men's and women's suites, and another leading to the women's alone. Since the women's suite was much smaller than the men's, the primary purpose of the second furnace must have been to heat the boiler above it, which then must surely have been connected to its neighbour.

3. Another early example of a heating system employing only a single boiler is at the Suburban Baths, Herculaneum (Maiuri, 1958, 169).

4. The length of the base is 4 m or perhaps a little more. The reservoir occupies the entire width of the base but terminates at a distance of 80 cm from the boiler; its walls are presumed to be 44 cm thick, the standard width of the service buildings walls. Its base is at the same level as the boiler's (65 cm above the floor of the furnace) and the maximum height feasible would be 20 cm below the sills of the windows in the west wall of the *caldarium* (i.e. 3.25 m above the floor of the hypocaust basement, see p. 51). Thus the capacity of the reservoir can be estimated at 2.6 by 2.2 by 2.3 m or 2,900 gallons.

5. As at the Suburban Baths, Herculaneum: Maiuri, 1958, 169–170. Cf. Faventinus 16: *Plumbeum vas quod patenam aeream habet . . .*, in Plommer, 1973, at p. 65. The vessels in Vitruvius' description are bronze (see above, note 1).

6. Height of boiler 2.6 m, diameter 1.4 m.

7. As with the boiler at Boscoreale: Mau-Kelsey, 1899, fig. 178 and Krencker, 1929, Abb. 449, 451.

8. It is sometimes thought that a *labrum* placed in the *caldarium* would be supplied only with cold water, e.g. Daniels, 1959, 131 n. 58. However at Boscoreale the *labrum* could be provided with either hot or cold water, or a mixture (Mau-Kelsey, 1899, 357); at the Suburban Baths there appeared only to be a supply of hot water to the *labrum* in the *caldarium* (Maiuri, 1958, 170) These appear to be the only two bath-houses where the details of the water-supply to the *labra* have been preserved intact.

9. There are steps in a similar position in the furnace-room of the Suburban Baths at Herculaneum: Maiuri, 1958, 170.

10. Volume of water in the bath: 9.4 by 1.0 by 2.0 m.

11. For the opening times of *thermae* in Rome, see Carcopino, 1941, 281–2; it is doubtful whether a military bath-house would have followed the same pattern of opening hours.

12. The total daily supply required by the baths can be roughly estimated as follows:

(i) two baths in the *caldarium*	8000 gallons
(ii) a continuous supply of hot water to the *labra* in the *caldarium*	8000 gallons
(iii) cold water for plunge-baths in the *frigidarium*	6000 gallons
(iv) continuous supply of cold water for the *labra* in the *frigidarium*	8000 gallons
(v) supply to the *natatio*, refilled daily	40000 gallons

The *natatio* was a very common feature of large bath-houses (e.g. Caerleon, Boon, 1972, 81) and the presence of one at Exeter can be reasonably assumed. Baths consumed very large quantities of water; when new Imperial *thermae* were erected at Rome, an aqueduct to supply them was usually included in the building programme (Ashby, 1935, 11 and 14).

H. THE PALAESTRA (Fig. 16, Pl. VII):

The *palaestra* was bounded on its north-east side by the baths, and on its south-east side by a wall adjoining the furnace-house, of which only a very short length survived. This wall was presumably matched by another at the roadside to form a room 9 m wide, which was entered from the court-yard to the north-east. Both the *palaestra* and the interior of the room on its south side had been levelled up with a deposit of clay up to 55 cm thick (5: 31B; 17: 52; 18: 52). A trench 80 cm deep and 50 cm wide at its base crossed the *palaestra* from north-east to south-west (70), turning south-east to run towards the street at a distance of 1 m from the west wall of the service area (5: F30). The trench had probably been dug to accommodate a masonry drain robbed at the beginning of Period 1B, as the construction of a contemporary stylobate wall across its course shows.

The surface of the *palaestra* was covered by highly-compacted lenses of red and brown sand (17: 55; 18: 55). In the angle between the furnace-house and the south-west wall of the baths an enclosure 4.4 m in diameter had been constructed; it consisted of a circle of timbers, each measuring 11–12.5 cm by 42 cm in section, which had been driven into the underlying clay dump to a depth of 15–20 cm. The shallow depth of penetration suggests that the timbers could not have stood very high above ground-level. Slightly to the east of the centre point of the enclosure there was a stake-hole 20 cm deep, with a packing of small pebbles around it (54). At the beginning of Period 1B the timbers were extracted and their sockets backfilled with loam.

In the room on the south-east side of the *palaestra*, the surface of the clay dump served as a floor.

Discussion:

The identification of the courtyard south-west of the baths as a *palaestra* is made certain by its situation on the sunny side of the building and its covering of sand. *Palaestrae* were customarily sanded and Vitruvius (X, 2, 12) mentions the use of rollers to compact the sand, providing a firm footing for athletes[1]; at Caerleon there was a carefully sanded strip surrounding the *natatio* (Boon, 1972, 81). The baths of a legionary fortress would have provided the principal facilities for the relaxation of the ordinary soldier in off-duty hours; for this reason their *palaestrae* appear to have been more extensive than those of comparable civil bath-houses.

In the *palaestra* Greek athletics were less popular with the Romans, who preferred ball-games[2]; the presence of a bowling-alley at the Stabian Baths of Pompeii shows that less energetic pastimes were also pursued (Mau-Kelsey, 1899, 183). The circular enclosure in the corner of the *palaestra* at Exeter may have been associated with similar activities. It brings to mind descriptions of cock-fighting pits erected in rural England and Wales a century or more ago: 'The outdoor pit was a simple affair, generally a circular space of ground, level and covered with short grass, enclosed in a board wall about a foot high . . . Such cockpits were formerly common in Wales and were found in most localities' (Peate, 1970, 10). Hogarth's engraving, 'The Cockpit' (1759), shows a circular pit perhaps 6 m in diameter with a rim 20–30 cm in height (Antal, 1962, Plate 136a). In indoor cockpits 'the size of the fighting stage, i.e. the 'pit' itself was determined by the dimensions of the building, and ranged from a diameter of eight to ten feet to as much as twenty feet at The Royal Cockpit in London.' (Peate, 1970, 14). No plans of outdoor cock-pits appear to have survived, but they were presumably of a similar size.

Doubtless the simple plans of these outdoor cockpits would have differed little from those of antiquity, when cockfighting was as popular a sport as it was in eighteenth- and nineteenth-century England[3].

Keller (1913, ii, 136, cf. Pollard, 1977, 107ff.[4]) describes the Greek cockpit as follows: *Die Mensur bestand in einer tischähnlichen Platte,* 7ηλία, *auf der ein Kreis beschrieben oder ein erhöhter Rand angebracht war, und man wettete oft sehr namhafte Summen.* This suggests a raised stage (7ηλία *(telia)* was the name for a gaming table of any kind), similar to those found in eighteenth-century English indoor cockpits, such as the Royal Cockpit. Unfortunately no cockpits have been recovered by excavation, nor do there appear to be any pictorial representations of them surviving from antiquity. In spite of this, the identification of the circular enclosure in the *palaestra* at Exeter as a cockpit remains a strong possibility.

NOTES

1. For a roller in a scene on a Greek figured vase, see Harris, 1972, Plate 22; Ling (1971, 267–80) discusses and illustrates *palaestra*-rollers in Campanian paintings and stucco reliefs.
2. Harris, 1972, 85; see Galen, *De Parvae Pilae Exercitu* (Fr. trans. Berger and Moussat, 1927, 214) where he praises ball-games and compares the skills they require to those of a good general.
3. For cock-fighting in antiquity, see Toynbee, 1973, 257.
4. I am grateful to G. C. Boon for these two references.

I. DRAINAGE AND WATER-SUPPLY (Figs. 7, 12 and 14):

The system of wooden water-pipes in the service-area, used either as water-mains or drains for soiled water, has already been discussed (pp. 35–7). A water-main which may have supplied the baths was found on the north-west side of the *via praetoria* (see p. 160). Traces of what was probably a large masonry drain were found on the south-western side of the site, which, at the top of the excavated area of the *palaestra* turned north-east towards the main building; it presumably functioned as a drain for a large bath or *piscina* in the *frigidarium* and perhaps also for an open-air pool in the *palaestra*, similar to those found at Avenches and Caerleon (see p. 122). The flow of the drain was to the south-east, towards the street, where it probably joined and took away the contents of the road-side gully. The baths would have required a supply of water from an aqueduct; a well or rain-water collection could hardly have supplied the estimated daily consumption of some 70,000 gallons (see p. 41, n. 12). No trace of the aqueduct has yet come to light, but a probable source of supply is indicated by the medieval conduit-system, which was gravity-fed by two springs about a kilometre to the north-east of the city. The flow of the springs in the medieval period was quite considerable, because after 1411 they supplied the whole city and most of its religious houses with water (Hooker, 38–9).

J. ARCHITECTURE (Figs. 9–11):

In the works of authors of the mid and later first century A.D. there are allusions to bath-houses where high bathing temperatures were combined with great architectural ostentation[1]. Seneca and others compared these indulgences with the modest requirements of their forebears, and therein found much to sadden them. The study of the few surviving bath-houses of the Early Imperial age does not permit a close determination of the date of this transformation. However, if the introduction of more complex building plans than those seen in the earlier Pompeian bath-houses went hand in hand with improved heating arrangements, the Claudian baths within the legionary fortress at Vindonissa must have belonged to this new class of building[2]. Their plan, although still of the *Reihentyp*[3] can be regarded as more sophisticated than Pompeian examples; the principal contrast lies in the strict axial symmetry of the arrangement of the whole bathing suite. Earlier bath-houses, the baths at Glanum, the Forum and Stabian Baths at Pompeii and the Forum baths at Herculaneum[4], consisted of a looser grouping of *caldarium*, *tepidarium* and *apodyterium*, usually with an adjoining circular *frigidarium* almost entirely occupied by a bath[5]. At Vindonissa (Fig. 10) the *frigidarium* was a large room, half of whose area was occupied by a cold bath; it was flanked by two narrower rooms, each containing smaller baths at one end, but probably functioning partly as *apodyteria*. In contrast to the Pompeian baths, the *frigidarium* communicated directly with the heated rooms; the first of these heated rooms was largely destroyed by the enlargement of the *frigidarium* bath, but was apparently heated indirectly by the main *tepidarium* hypocaust. The

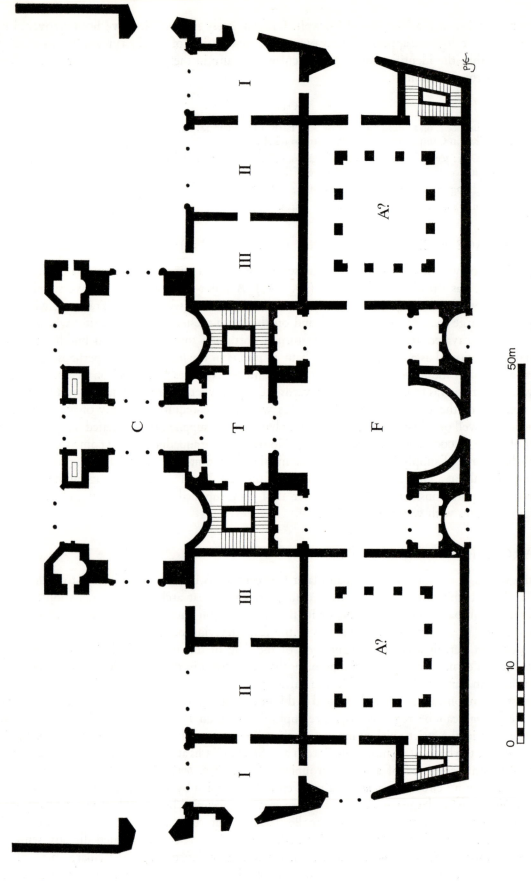

Fig. 9. Baths of Titus at Rome (after Krencker, 1929).

tepidarium was equipped with two *labra* accommodated in apses at either end of the room; the south side of the room was badly disturbed, but here Laur-Belart restored two baths flanking a central recess. Two *laconica* were situated opposite each other on either side of the main block and could probably have been entered from the passages leading through to the *caldarium*. The *caldarium* at Vindonissa was planned on a most ambitious scale; almost the entire circuit of the room was occupied by apses and recesses. The north wall was occupied by two apses which contained *labra* and flanked a central recess[6]; to either side were passages leading to the *tepidarium*. Two shallow apses at either end of the room were thought to have contained baths, although no furnaces were found communicating directly with them; the presence of baths along the south side of the room seems more certain because furnaces opened into the sides of the long recess which would have

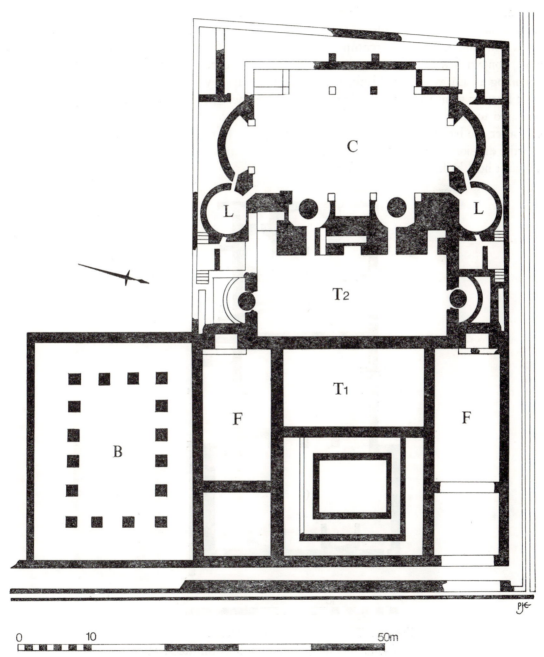

Fig. 10. The fortress bath-house at Vindonissa (after Laur-Belart, 1931).

contained them. The main body of this room must have been roofed by a vault supported over most of its length by eight massive piers, perhaps with the apses and recesses covered by subsidiary vaults at a lower level (see further p. 47 below).

The plan of the Exeter baths, so far as it is known, has more in common with the Vindonissa plan than with those of Pompeian type; the strict axial symmetry displayed in the arrangement of the *caldarium* at Exeter provides the conclusive link, and the similarity is emphasised by the presence of two apses flanking a central recess. Indeed it seems reasonable to assume the Exeter baths were planned symmetrically throughout the main suite; this assumption can almost be raised to a certainty when their plan is compared to that of the early Flavian baths 'En Perruet' at Avenches (Fig. 11). The baths at Avenches represent a simplification of the Vindonissa plan (Schwarz, 1969, synthesising accounts from 1810 onwards). The suite is somewhat smaller, but retains the symmetrical plan and the characteristic arrangement in the *caldarium* of two apses flanking a central recess, which, as at Exeter, fills up the south wall. The *frigidarium* was arranged differently from that at Vindonissa, with the accommodation for bathing (and perhaps the functions of an *apodyterium*) contained within one room[7]; the north wall was occupied by a large apse, almost certainly containing a bath, which was flanked by two smaller apses with drains and bases to support *labra*. These features seem to be a reflection of the arrangement in the *caldarium*. The room can also be compared to the partly excavated *frigidarium* in the fortress baths at Caerleon, erected about ten years after the baths at Avenches (Boon, 1972, 77 ff.). Here the north-west side again displays a tripartite division, although there was a recess rather than an apse at the centre and the apses which flanked it held baths rather than *labra*.

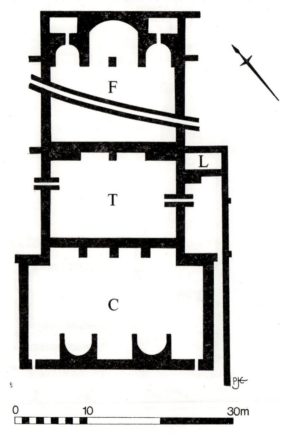

Fig. 11. The bath-house 'En Perruet' at Avenches (*palaestra* and subsidiary buildings omitted; after Schwarz, 1969).

The *tepidarium* at Avenches was probably entered from the *frigidarium* through doors placed in the two central recesses in the dividing wall. Two furnaces sited on either side of the room served the hypocaust, but there was no evidence to suggest the presence of baths or *labra*. A small rectangular room on the south side of the *tepidarium* was thought to have been a *sudatio* (*laconicum*).

The *caldarium*, which was longer than the other rooms in the suite, was, as at Vindonissa, the most ambitiously planned feature. Its layout was almost identical to that of the Exeter *caldarium* except that the north wall was set back over the width of the *tepidarium* and was occupied by four shallow recesses, separated from each other by three substantial piers. The south wall of the room was arranged in almost the same way as at Exeter with two apses accommodating *labra*, but with a recess holding a bath. Larger baths, again as at Exeter, must have been situated along the east and west walls where they were served by furnaces at the south-west and south-east corners of the room[8].

The general similarities in the planning of the baths at Vindonissa, Exeter and Avenches (perhaps also at Caerleon[9]) are evident enough, but there are other more detailed points of comparison which warrant discussion:

(1) Decorative features: from destruction levels at Vindonissa there came a Corinthian pilaster capital and part of a fluted pilaster. Many fragments of wall painting approximating to the Third Pompeian style were also recovered (illustrated fully in Drack, 1950, 121–134), as well as some decoration carried out in stucco. At both Avenches and Vindonissa fragments of statuary came to light as well as marble *labra* with channelled decoration on the underside, and at Vindonissa a tendril motif carved next to the rim. There was at least one figured mosaic at Exeter[10]. Vindonissa was furnished with black and white mosaics, and at Caerleon there were both black and white and polychrome mosaics (Boon, 1972, 79–81).

(2) Architectural features: the details of the apses which are so prominent in the plans of these baths are worth considering. In the *caldaria* at Exeter and Avenches, windows must have opened through the rear of the apses, since they occupy so much of the external wall space. In a consideration of the Central Baths at Pompeii, where windows also opened into apses in the *caldarium*, this aspect of their design was singled out by Ward-Perkins as a novel feature (Ward-Perkins, 1970a, 296). The masking of the terminations of the apses by piers occurred at both Vindonissa and Exeter; this device, which creates a greater sense of spaciousness by throwing the sides of the apses into shadow (cf. Boon, 1974, 114), was not employed in any of the Campanian baths, even those of the mid first century A.D.

The vaulting of these baths would have required cosiderable technical accomplishments on the part of their builders[11]; the spans of the *caldarium* vaults at Avenches, Exeter and Vindonissa would have been 9.0, 9.75, and 13.0 m respectively. Stone voussoir blocks found at Vindonissa were assumed to have originated from the vault. From Exeter and Avenches there was no conclusive evidence concerning the materials employed to construct the bath-house vaults.

Individual features which can be compared with those in the buildings discussed above can be found in bath-houses which date to the second half of the first century A.D. both in Italy and north of the Alps.

At the Central Baths of Pompeii (Mau-Kelsey, 1899, 203, Fig. 89) the *caldarium* was equipped with apses flanking recesses on both its longer sides; however the symmetrical axis of the room ran down its length rather than across its width. At Bath (Cunliffe, 1969, 95–100, Fig. 31) the Great Bath also had apses flanking recesses in its side walls, but again the room was laid out symmetrically about its longer axis. The arrangement of the *caldarium* of the *Frauenthermen* at Augst (Laur-Belart, 1966, 89–93 and Abb. 51) resembles that of the *caldaria* at Avenches and Exeter; baths occupied the full width of the two short sides, while the south-west wall of the room had the familiar tripartite division, with two square recesses flanking an apse, all three housing baths. The *caldarium*, however, was the only room in the bath-house suite which was symmetrical about its shorter axis.

In terms of their size and *Reihentyp* lay-out the bath-houses at Vindonissa, Exeter and Avenches find a place within a series of buildings which runs down to the middle of the second century A.D. (see Table 5). Three first-century examples make an interesting contrast to the group discussed above. The Claudian 'Great Baths' at Cambodunum have a *frigidarium* provided with a bath and a *labrum* and also a *laconicum* which stands apart from the main bathing suite (Schleiermacher, 1972, 31–6, Figs. 15–16). The later Flavian, unfinished baths at Wroxeter are similar in this respect (Atkinson, 1942, 25–54). Adjoining the *frigidarium* there was a suite of three rooms which were reminiscent of the plan at Vindonissa; at Wroxeter the central room of the three may also have been intended to contain a large *piscina*[12]. At Pompeii the Central Baths, which had not been completed at the time of the eruption in A.D. 79, also showed some advance on the plans of the earlier Campanian bath-houses (Mau-Kelsey, 1899, 208–11). There was a *frigidarium* with a plan similar to those at Wroxeter and Cambodunum and the *caldarium* took a very different form to that of the Stabian baths, for example; there was also a *laconicum* leading off the *tepidarium*. However, these three examples lack the overall axial symmetry of the bath-houses discussed above.

A similar picture results from an examination of smaller first-century bath-houses, for example those at Silchester (Boon, 1974, 121 ff.) and Inchtuthil (Macdonald and Curle, 1929, 448, Fig. 40), and the 'Cult' and 'Small' baths at Cambodunum[13].

During the course of the second century there appears to have been a tendency towards greater axial symmetry in larger bath-houses. The pattern of strict axiality is disrupted only by small inconsistencies at Xanten (*colonia*) (Hinz, 1961, 246; for a plan showing more recent discoveries, see Hinz, 1975, Abb. 6c) and at the Forum Baths of both Saint-Bertrand-des-Comminges (Sapène, 1943, 205) and Paris (Duval, 1961, 174). Again this development is matched in smaller bath-houses where J. B. Ward-Perkins has pointed to the emergence of a specifically Gallo-Roman type, distinguishable by its axiality (Ward-Perkins, 1970, 356). From the middle of the second century A.D. the simple *Reihentyp* plan appears to have been eclipsed in the case of larger bath-houses by the more complex arrangements which can be seen in the Central Baths at Augst (Laur-Belart, 1966, 93), the baths at Leicester (Kenyon, 1948, 14; but see reviews by R. G. Goodchild and M. V. Taylor in J. R. S., 39 (1949), 142 ff.) and within the fortress at Lauriacum (Vetters, 1953, 49 ff.), and also in the Northern Baths (Palais de Cluny) at Paris (Duval, 1961, 147 ff.). It is clear from this brief account that the plans of Vindonissa, Exeter and Avenches form a closely related group. They show a marked advance on the early Campanian type of bath-house plan and represent the earliest large symmetrical designs. They also precede the earliest certain example of the Imperial type, the Baths of Titus at Rome (Fig. 9).

The plan of this building conforms to what Krencker termed the Imperial type, a category sub-divided into two parts by minor differences which do not bear on the present argument. The essence of the Imperial type was the symmetrical axis of the plan and the provision of the two identical sets of supplementary heated rooms and the provision of two separate *basilicae* or *palaestrae* on either side of the *frigidarium* (Krencker, 1929, 177 f.).

In seeking the origins of the Vindonissa, Avenches and Exeter bath-house plans, it is necessary to explore certain points of resemblance to the Imperial type, which have already been noted by Laur-Belart and Schwarz in the cases of Vindonissa and Avenches respectively. The Baths of Titus have a plan which included most of the essential elements of later buildings of the Imperial type such as the Baths of Caracalla, but on a far smaller scale (Krencker, 1929, 265–266, Abb. 395, 396, 396a). The Baths, the plan of which was recorded by Palladio, consisted of a rectangular block with rooms arranged symmetrically about its shorter central axis. This axis ran through a suite of rooms containing a *frigidarium*, very small *tepidarium* and *caldarium*; on each side of the *caldarium* there were identical ranges of heated rooms, beyond which lay peristyle courtyards.

Particular details in the Baths of Titus can be paralleled amongst those in the group under discussion; the arrangement of the north wall of the *frigidarium* is reminiscent of the *frigidarium* at Avenches, where a bath contained in a large apse also occupied the same relative position; the north wall of the *caldarium*, as at Vindonissa, is divided into two apses flanking a recess, which here forms an entry from the *tepidarium*. It is the strict axiality of their plan, however, which provides this building with the most important point of resemblance to bath-houses such as Vindonissa and Exeter. The Baths of Titus can thus be viewed as an elaboration of the earlier plans; the dominant central block of rooms was retained, but the *tepidarium* was reduced in size, and the heated accommodation supplemented and varied in the rooms of the two side-ranges.

Thus it would seem possible that the axially-symmetrical *Reihentyp* plan represented a particular stage in the development of the Imperial type. The plans so far recovered may have been based on ultimate Italian prototypes. The literature of the Early Imperial period refers only to one public bath-house of any note in Rome which is earlier than the baths at Vindonissa or, for that matter, Exeter. The Baths of Agrippa were constructed on the Campus Martius in 25–19 B.C. as part of a building project which included the original Pantheon and the Stoa of Poseidon[14]. The texts make no explicit mention of any novel aspects in the design of the building, but its erection as part of a monumental complex may have provided the opportunity for an abandonment of the loose grouping of rooms typical of the Campanian tradition in favour of axial symmetry. The plan of the Baths of Nero, which is also lost to us in its original state, has been thought to represent 'a first step' towards the formation of the Imperial type (Ward-Perkins, 1970, 226). However, as we have seen, the 'first step' had already been taken at Vindonissa, and it is possible that the Baths of Nero had a fully evolved Imperial plan[15].

NOTES

1. e.g. Seneca, *Ep.* 86, 6; Martial, *Ep.* 3, 25; Columella, 1, *praef.*, 16. The evolution of Roman bath-houses is briefly described by Kretzschmer (1961) where special regard is paid to technical aspects; his conclusions about the function of *tubulatio* have been rightly challenged (Boon, 1974, 123).

2. Excavations summarised in Laur-Belart, 1935, pp. 46–56 and Taf. 16, 17; detailed excavation reports in Fels, 1900 and 1927, Laur-Belart, 1928, 1929, 1931. For a closer determination of the construction date, see Fellman, 1958, 40.

3. For this classification (which is essentially functional rather than architectural) see Krencker, 1929, 177 ff. The *Reihentyp*, the simplest bath-house plan, consists of a single row of rooms, each of a different temperature; the bather passed through the rooms and back again along the same route. In more complex types, such as the 'Imperial' type, the bather could pass through one suite of rooms to the *caldarium* and then return through a different suite.

4. Glanum: Rolland, 1946, 49–65; Stabian Baths, Pompeii: Mau-Kelsey, 1899, 180–195; Forum Baths: *ibid.*, 196–201; Forum Baths, Herculaneum: Maiuri, 1958, 91–112.

5. Except at Glanum where the building in its original state did not appear to have possessed a *frigidarium*; Rolland's *frigidarium* contains neither *labrum* nor bath, and is decorated with engaged columns, which would have diminished the space available for lockers, were the room to have served as an *apodyterium*.

6. D. Krencker's reconstruction of the *caldarium* plan omits the apses, leaving the *labra* standing behind a screen of piers (Laur-Belart, 1931, 233 ff.); however, it is clear that the substructures of the apses were found (*ibid.*, 212–3).

7. There was no *basilica* attached to the Avenches baths; at Caerleon, where the plan of the north wall of the *frigidarium* is very similar, the *basilica* would have served partly as an *apodyterium*.

8. Certainty about the position of the baths is not yet possible because the relevant areas are as yet unexcavated. Baths occupying two recesses at each end of the south wall, together with that in the central recess would not seem likely to have provided sufficient bathing facilities when compared to the provisions made at Exeter. On the other hand, if baths had occupied the entire length of the east and west walls, their southern ends would have projected into the corner recesses—a rather awkward arrangement.

9. It is worth pointing out that Exeter and Caerleon were both fortresses of the Second Augustan Legion; a similarity in the plan of their baths is thus all the more likely.

10. There was a mosaic at Vindonissa with a tendril motif, presumably a later addition to the decoration; Gonzenbach, 1961, 229 and Taf. 2.

11. See pp. 51–2 below for a discussion of the relationships of the apses to the vaults.

12. This room, which measured 13.4 m by 9 m, was called the Entrance Hall by Atkinson (1942, 51). An arch 90 cm in width passed through the base of its north wall. Atkinson thought that this was constructed to accommodate a drain leading from a *labrum* which was to have been placed near the centre of the room. However, *labra* are usually placed in niches or apses and it may have been intended to install a *piscina* in this room to supplement the cold bathing facilities in the *frigidarium*. The arch in the north wall was certainly large enough to have accommodated a drain taking the outfall from a *piscina*.

13. Schleiermacher, 1972, 26, 38. But cf. the Baths at Coriovallum-Heerlen, which show a strong tendency towards axial symmetry in plan (van Giffen, 1948, 199 ff.).

14. Platner and Ashby, 1929, 518–520; Shipley, 1933, 47–53. Ward-Perkins (1970, 3) regards the Baths of Agrippa as the Pompeian type 'writ large'.

15. Ward-Perkins, 1970, 212 and 226. They were much praised: *quid Nerone peius? quid thermis melius Neronianus?* (Mart. *Ep*. VII, 34).

Table 5: Comparison of the dimensions of legionary and larger civil bath-houses

Site	Status	Area of enclosure (sq.m)	Area of frigidarium exc. apses (sq.m)	Area of caldarium exc. apses. etc. (sq.m)
Vindonissa	Legionary Fortress	?	—	346
Exeter	Legionary Fortress	*c*. 4000	—	217
Central Baths, Pompeii	*Colonia*	3840	149	150
Frauenthermen, Augst	*Colonia*	3000	165	190
Avenches, "En Perruet"	*Colonia*	7480	180	250
Cambodunum, Larger Baths	*Civitas* capital	4300	215	250
Caerleon, Fortress Baths	Legionary Fortress	8000	—	—
Wroxeter, Early Baths	*Civitas* capital	9060	156	277
Baths of Titus, Rome	—	12600	442	382
Saint-Bertrand-des-Comminges, Forum Baths	*Colonia*	—	106	194
Chester	Legionary Fortress	6400	—	—
Xanten	*Colonia*	7400	290	304
Mainz	Legionary Fortress	—	360	420
Paris, Forum Baths	*Municipium*	?2560	117	136
Ostia, Neptune Baths	*Municipium*	5600	—	—
Lauriacum	Legionary Fortress	9000	—	—

N.B. 1: The size of the *frigidarium* at Vindonissa and of the *frigidaria* and *caldaria* at the Neptune Baths, Ostia, and at Lauriacum have been omitted since the various facilities appear to have been contained in a number of rooms.

N.B. 2: For references to these bath-houses see bibliography.

K. RECONSTRUCTION (Figs. 12 and 13, Pl. XIIB, XIII, XIV):

Interior of the *caldarium:* the evidence upon which the attempted reconstruction of the *caldarium* is based falls into four categories: the building-plan as recovered by excavation, finds of architectural materials from the site, comparisons with other baths of similar type, and knowledge of the general state of architectural development in the Neronian age.

Certain features of the interior arrangements were preserved. Indications of a threshold near the mid-point of the north-west wall were found (see p. 29); a layer of broken tile set in brick-mortar was taken to represent the bedding of stone slabs. The bedding, which survived over a length of 1.3 m, slightly overlapped the central axis of the building, and if the entry with which it was associated occupied the exact mid-point of the wall, it would have had a minimum width of 2.4 m. The arrangement of post-holes and beam-slots cut through the floor of the new *frigidarium* in the course of Period 1B, if correctly interpreted as internal porches, would point to the existence of another entry to the north-east, no doubt supplemented by another at the south-west end of the wall for the sake of symmetry. The arrangement of the north-west wall of the *caldarium* therefore appears to reflect the treatment of the south-eastern side of the room. The apparent width of the doors communicating between the *caldarium* and *tepidarium* can be contrasted with those in the Campanian bath-houses, where even in the mid-first century Suburban Baths of Herculaneum the doors were of very small size[1]. But at Avenches a threshold preserved in the north wall of the *caldarium* was 3.2 m wide (Schwarz, 1969, 60 and Taf. 17).

The north-east and south-west walls were occupied along their entire length by baths, above which were splashboards (see p. 143). Windows in these two walls would have formed the principal source of light for the room. It is possible to suggest that their sills would have been at least 3.25 m above the floor of the hypocaust basement[2]; their tops would have been situated below a cornice which was likely to have run around the room at the level from which the vault sprang. There is no indication of the width of the windows nor of their number; three have been restored in each wall in the reconstruction. The windows have also been shown with semicircular heads rather than flat lintels since this would seem to accord better with the arcuate qualities of the interior[3].

Round-headed windows have also been restored in the apses and the central recess; in Vitruvius's description of a bath-house the presence of windows illuminating the *schola labri* is mentioned (V, 10, 4).

No material from the site was recognised as coming from the vault. Certainly if voussoir blocks were used in the construction of the vault, as appears to have been the case at Vindonissa (see p. 47), the absence of any evidence would be surprising. But had concrete with a rubble or tile aggregate been used, small fragments from the demolition levels would have been indistinguishable from the debris of other features. It may be noted that the south-east side of the *caldarium* is provided with two separate lines of support, one for the vault, which would spring from the piers in front of the apses and recess and from the north-east walls of the corner rooms, and the other for the protective tiled roof with its sole-plate resting on top of the wall which ran behind the apses and recess[4].

Having ascertained what is known or may be reasonably inferred about the interior of the *caldarium*, it is possible to attempt a reconstruction. For aesthetic reasons, it can be presumed that the vault would have sprung from a height above ground level equivalent to at least one half the width of the room, i.e. in excess of 4.9 m. In all probability one of the factors determining the height of the vault would have been the elevation of the apses and recess, which it is reasonable to assume were roofed respectively by half-domes and a small barrel-vault. There appear to be two alternatives for the height of these features:

(i) as in Campanian bath-houses, the crown of the vaults would have been below the level from which the main vault sprang. If it is presumed that the height of the room was no

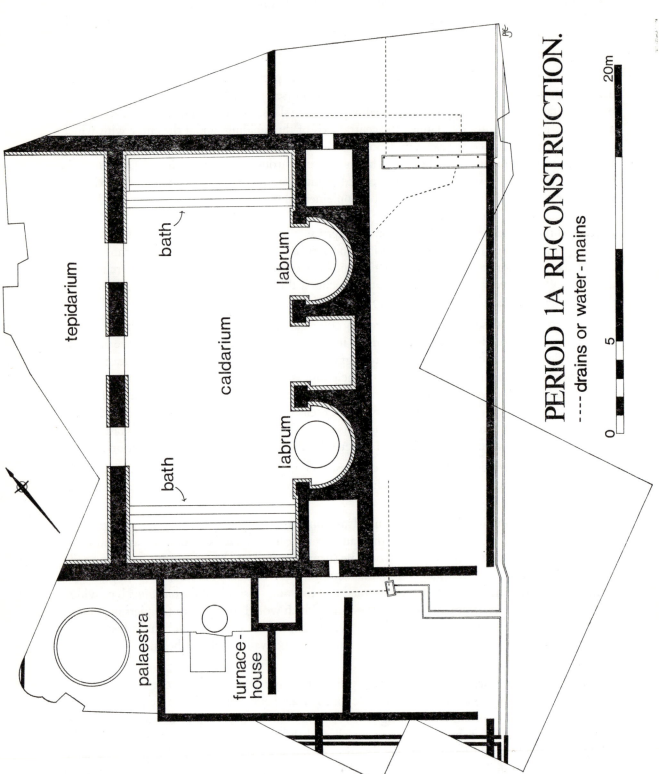

PERIOD 1A RECONSTRUCTION.
--- drains or water-mains

0   5   20m

Fig. 12. Reconstruction of baths (Period 1A, dotted lines show course of wooden water-pipes).

greater than its width, the maximum height of the apses would have been about 4.9 m, giving their elevations a rather squat proportion (width to height) of about 1 : 1.05.

(ii) additional height could have been achieved by constructing the subsidiary vaults from the same level as the main vault. The proportion of width to height would then be about 1 : 1.50. But over a cosniderable distance the main vault would have rested on the open and inward sloping ends of the subsidiary vaults, surely giving rise to a serious structural weakness. Furthermore a comparable arrangement cannot be found amongst the handful of contemporary vaults which still survive.

In the reconstruction offered here (Fig. 13), these two alternatives are dispensed with. The height of the *caldarium* is somewhat greater, with the main vault springing from a height of 7.9 m above floor level; the room has an overall proportion, width to height, of 1 : 1.31, and the apse elevations a proportion of 1 : 1.90. The treatment of the apses and recess poses another problem. In the reconstruction, undecorated piers have been shown supporting the arches in front of the half-domes and barrel-vault. At Vindonissa, part of a fluted pilaster and an associated Corinthian capital were thought to have come from piers in the *caldarium* (Laur-Belart, 1931, 226 n.2 and Abb. 5a and b). At Exeter Corinthian pilasters would have had to have been paired, if used to decorate the piers; this would be an architectural anachronism, since the device is not known to have been employed in the West before the later Roman period[5]. Similarly, the stone pier bases seem suitable to accommodate free-standing columns of the Tuscan order, framing the apses and recess, and indeed what was probably part of a *torus* moulding came from the demolition levels in the *caldarium* (see Fig. 47, 18); however, the columns would again have had to have been paired, once more an anachronism.

There is no reason to suppose that the interior decoration would have been austere; the black and white floor-quarries, mosaic and Purbeck marble would no doubt have been complemented by wall-paintings and stucco. The intrados of the vaults over the apses and recess are shown with stucco ribbing; there is evidence for this at Vindonissa (Laur-Belart, 1931, 218), where there were also wall-paintings approximating to the Third Pompeian style (Laur-Belart, 1931, Taf. XI–XIII; Drack, 1950, 121–134).

Exterior: the presence of a tiled roof over the main vault is suggested by the recovery of fragments of at least thirty-one antefixes from the site (see p. 149). Its function would have been to protect the concrete vault from the effects of rain and frost.

At intervals around the main building there would have been vents or chimneys for the hypocausts; their general form is known from the Simpelveld sarcophagus (Boon, 1974, 125 and 324 n. 8). Inside the building the vents presumably would have opened into ducts running around the top of the wall-jacketting (*ibid.*; Maiuri, 1958, 150).

It should be noted that there was no evidence for a plaster-rendering on the exterior walls of the bath-house. The only service-building wall which was rendered was that on the south side of the enclosure behind the *caldarium*, and that only on its roadside face.

NOTES

1. Maiuri, 1958, 91f.; for instance the dimensions of the entry communicating between the *caldarium* and the *sala a stucchi* are 2.2 m by 1 m. All the entries were fitted with single-leaved wooden doors.

2. On the inside we must allow 80 cm for the hypocaust, 40 cm for the *suspensura*, 1.0 m for the height of the bath, certainly a minimum height of 29 cm for the splashboard and perhaps as much as 70 cm, and 15 cm for a moulding above; this would give a maximum height of 3.25 m for the sills, allowing for an area of plain wall 20 cm high above the moulding.

3. Round-headed windows appear in the Suburban Baths of Herculaneum, but not in the Central Baths of Pompeii; Maiuri, 1958, Fig. 135; Mau-Kelsey, 1899, 202–205.

4. For the arrangement of a tiled roof over a vault, see Webster and Woodfield, 1966, 238 and Fig. 3.

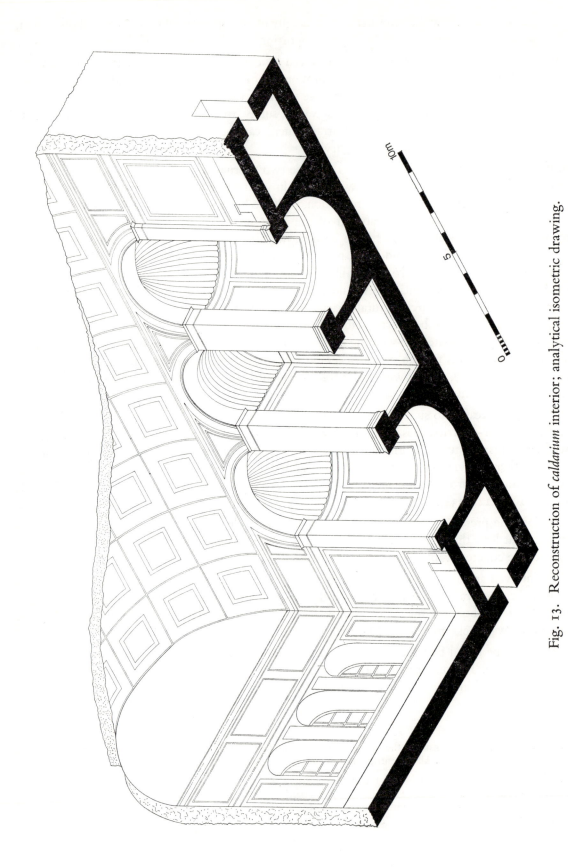

Fig. 13. Reconstruction of *caldarium* interior; analytical isometric drawing.

5. The earliest dated example of the use of paired columns is to be found in the church of Santa Constanza, Rome, which was the mausoleum of Constantine's daughter (J. B. Ward-Perkins, *in litt.*). The circumstances bearing on the introduction of this architectural device are discussed in Ward-Perkins and Goodchild, 1953, 70. Dr. Ward-Perkins, (*in litt.*) agrees that the foundations in front of the apses were most likely to have supported undecorated piers. He observes that in Rome columns are found in the Baths of Titus, although they are not a feature of bath-house architecture much before this date.

L. THE SUPPLY OF MATERIALS TO THE SITE:

The levels associated with the construction of the baths provided some information about the organisation of building-work and the supply of materials to the site. The road pre-dating the construction of the baths contained many trap rocks, making it clear that the trap quarries, probably sited on the slopes of Rougemont, had been opened during the earliest stages of occupation within the fortress in order to provide the road metalling. There was, however, no other indication that the legion was exploiting other sources of supply for building materials except wood until work on the construction of the baths commenced. When building started, in addition to trap, sandstone from East Devon was required for pier bases and architectural features. Tiles were also needed at this early stage for the bonding courses in the main walls; the area where they were produced has been identified immediately to the east of the fortress (see p. 48).

A quarry in the East Devon coastal area must have been opened to supply sandstone for the construction of the baths. On the other hand it appears that the Purbeck quarry was already functioning by *c.* 60 (Dunning, 1949, 15; Beavis, 1970, 191–4); it may have been opened by the Second Augustan Legion and may have remained under legionary control until the Flavian period or even later[1].

The recovery of Purbeck-marble chips bearing saw-marks suggests that material was being finished on the site; presumably the slabs and mouldings would have been roughly prepared at the quarry in East Dorset.

NOTES

1. For a centurion of the Third Cyrenaican supervising a quarry, see Macmullen, 1959, 216 and 231, n. 78, and for rock-cut inscriptions in quarries worked by legionary units engaged in the construction of Hadrian's Wall, see *RIB* (i), 998–1016.

M. DATING EVIDENCE:

(1) Pre-dating street:
     Samian: Dr. 18 (stamp no. 2), *c.* 50–65 (trodden into the surface of natural below the street).

(2) From post-trenches of timber buildings south-east of the street:
     A few scraps of coarse ware only.

(3a) Levelling in southern corner of site:
     Samian: Dr. 29 (stamp no. 11), *c.* 45–60 (1 : 61B); Dr. 18, first century (1 : 61B).

(3b) Trodden into the surface of the levelling:
     Samian: Dr. 29, pre-Flavian (4: 56B).
     Coin: no. 9, Claudius, copy as *RIC* 66 (41–54) (4: 56B).

(4a) Preliminary metalling of trap chips and gravel:
     Coin: no. 10, Claudius, copy as *RIC* 66 (41–54) (7: 44D2).

(4b) Trench dug across site of room in eastern corner of main building:
     Samian: Dr. 18R, Neronian (16: 1534).

(4c) Clay overlying metalling—upcast from foundations of main building (?):
     Coin: no. 5, Claudius, copy as *RIC* 66 (41–54) (1: 9EC3).

(4d) Remetalling following insertion of main building foundations:
Samian: Dr. 29, first century (5: 31D); Dr. 27, pre-Flavian (7: 44D).

(5) Land-drains:
Samian: no. 1, Dr. 29, c. 50–65 (14: 1151); Dr. 29 (stamp no. 18, unidentified), Neronian (4; F. 63); Dr. 27, pre-Flavian (12: 1162); Dr. 24/25, Neronian? (14: 1151); Dr. 24/25, Neronian (1: F.34); Dr. 15/17, pre-Flavian? (14: 1151).

(6) Levelling following insertion of service-building walls:
Samian: Dr. 27, first century (17: 52); Dr. 18, first century, and Dr. 15/17, pre-Flavian? (both 6: 52H).

(7) Levelling over site of timber buildings on south-east side of the street:
Samian: no. 2, Dr. 30, c. 60–75; Dr. 29, Claudian; Dr. 24 (stamp no. 16), pre-Flavian; Dr. 18, pre-Flavian; all 9: 68D.

Other dating factors:

The stratified finds from the construction-levels of the bath-house form only one aspect of all the factors associated with its date. Of prime importance is the association of the building with the legionary fortress. The evidence for this may be summarised as follows:

(1) no traces of timber buildings were found below the construction-levels of the baths in the area of the *palaestra* or service buildings.

(2) the dolphin-antefixes can be associated with a craftsman attached to the legion (see p. 13).

(3) the large groups of pottery and coins from the demolition levels at the beginning of Period 2A establish a *terminus post quem* of c. 80 for the reconstruction of the bath-house as a civil *basilica*. If the baths were built after the departure of the legion, their construction and one substantial modification of their plan would have had to have been compressed into a period of about five years.

In the absence of a direct stratigraphical link between the baths and other buildings within the fortress, circumstantial evidence confirms the military date which is suggested by the small collection of finds from the construction-levels.

The construction date of the building must therefore fall within the period c. 55/60–75. It has been shown that the bath-house post-dated a timber building on the south side of the road, which may itself have had a predecessor (see pp. 26–7), and it is likely that work on the construction of the baths was not started until some years after the foundation-date of the fortress. This is only to be expected; the essential buildings, especially those for residential accommodation, would have been constructed first and, although this may not have taken very long to accomplish, there would have been a shortage of manpower if the legion was also involved in a campaign in the South-West at this time, as seems likely (see p. 17). In other legionary fortresses work was not usually started on the construction of bath-houses until some years after the foundation-date. At Caerleon the construction of the baths was not begun until c. 85, about a decade after the initial occupation of the fortress (Boon, 1972, 78); work started on the stone *principia* at about the same time (Boon, 1972, 28). A similar state of affairs can be seen at Vindonissa where Fellman has shown that the erection of the baths and *principia* formed part of the same building-project (Fellman, 1958, 20–1, 40). At Caerleon the *principia* was not completed until the later second century (Boon, 1972, 28) and it seems likely that meanwhile there was a temporary wooden *principia* on the site of the intended stone *principia* courtyard; but there was no delay in the completion of the baths at Caerleon. At Inchtuthil, where the construction of the fortress was abandoned after the passage of about three years, work had not been started on a number of buildings such as the *praetorium*, some of the tribunes' houses and granaries and an internal bath-house[1]. Once again the provision of a full-size *principia* and a bath-house may have been intended as part of the same building project. The apse of an intramural bath-house has been revealed at Usk and during building-work in the nineteenth century massive stone foundations were uncovered nearby on what should be the site of the *principia* (Wilson, 1975, Fig. 2, and W. Manning, *pers. comm.*); the remainder of the buildings which have been excavated within the fortress were of timber construction. At Chester the baths appear to have been completed by A.D. 79, probably no more than six years after the foundation of the fortress (Jarrett, 1969, 32).

At Exeter, then, it seems quite likely that work on the baths might not have started until as much as a decade after the foundation of the fortress. An upper limit on the construction date is set by the absence of early Flavian material from the contemporary building-levels. The period *c.* 60–65 seems to fit the evidence quite well.

NOTES

1. An external bath-house is known at Inchtuthil but it was very small indeed. There can be little doubt that the erection of an internal bath-house was intended; by this time such buildings were an essential feature of fortress plans.

N. RELATIONSHIP OF THE BATHS TO THE FORTRESS PLAN

It would appear that the baths were taken into account when the fortress was planned, and that a site was reserved for their erection; this much can be deduced from the absence of earlier buildings under the *palaestra* and service buildings. However it is possible that some part of the baths site was occupied by temporary buildings[1], and that when construction work began, some rearrangement of the surrounding buildings was necessary in order to accommodate their replacement; certainly at this time the earlier timber building on the south side of the road was demolished, perhaps as part of such a replanning.

The baths occupied a site on the corner formed by the junction of the *viae praetoria* and *principalis*, a position which can be paralleled at Caerleon (Boon, 1972, 77), Vindobona[2] and Lauriacum (Vetters, 1953, 49). They covered an area of about 4000 sq. m.

Two factors usually influenced the siting of the baths within a fortress. Because of the importance of bathing and sweating in Roman medical treatment, the baths were often situated near the *valetudinarium* (generally cf. Boon, 1972, 75 and n. 281, and Vetters, 1953, 53, citing Galen, *De Meth. Med.*, XI, 10); such a relationship can be seen at Caerleon, Neuss and Vindonissa, and was probably intended at Inchtuthil. This does not appear to have been the case at Carnuntum where, although the site of the baths is not yet known, the *valetudinarium* was surrounded by other types of buildings.

A second set of factors which influenced the siting of the baths within a fortress is concerned with their internal functions. Special attention would have had to have been paid to both the supply and disposal of large quantities of water. In addition it was usual to place the *caldarium* at the south-western end of the building so that it was illuminated by the greatest amount of sunlight possible during the afternoon, which was the customary time for bathing (Vitruvius, V, 10, 1); however, Xanten (*colonia*) (Hinz, 1961, 346) and Saint-Bertrand-des-Comminges (Sapene, 1943) can be cited as exceptions to the rule, since their *caldaria* have a northerly aspect. The *palaestra* was also usually placed in a position of maximum sunlight, that is, on the south or west side of the main building.

NOTES

1. There appear to have been temporary buildings on the 'reserved' site of the Caerleon fortress baths (Boon, 1972, 40).
2. Neumann, 1967, 58 f.; the remains so far uncovered are very fragmentary, but the identification, which depends on the discovery of a large apse with a hypocaust and a continuous cladding of box-tiles clamped to the interior of its wall, seems fairly certain.

O. SIGNIFICANCE OF THE BATHS

Difficult as it is to measure the amount of labour involved in the construction of the baths, some notion of the effort required merely to obtain building supplies can be gained from the discussion on p. 55. Furthermore we have the 'commercial' building costs for a very roughly comparable bath-house at Ostia, which were accounted at more than two million *sestertii*[1]. Such a project would hardly be undertaken if there was any possibility of the legion being posted elsewhere in the immediate future.

It could be argued that the baths were built as much with an eye to their use by a future civilian community as for the convenience of the legion; this is certainly possible, even though the later history of the building shows that it turned out to be too large for the needs of the town. On the other hand the building would have had a considerable effect as a vehicle for Imperial propaganda, but this was one of the purposes of government-funded buildings in most circumstances.

The erection of the baths at Exeter should be viewed as part of the normal sequence of building within a legionary fortress. It should be borne in mind that the work may also have begun on the construction of a stone *principia*, as at Usk, Vindonissa and Caerleon (see pp. 56–7).

NOTES

1. *CIL* XIV, 98; Duncan-Jones, 1965, no. 439, p. 234, see also p. 292; the annual pay of a legionary at this time (i.e. at the beginning of the reign of Antoninus Pius) was 1200 *sestertii*. The building costs of the Baths of Neptune should be treated cautiously when used as a yard-stick for this type of bath-house; for instance it is not known whether the sum also included the purchase of the site, or what proportion of the cost was represented by expensive statuary and imported marbles. The Exeter baths, of course, would have been erected by legionary technicians, perhaps with the help of forced native labour.

3. ACTIVITIES IN THE COURSE OF PERIOD 1A

No alterations or overall accumulations of material occurred during the course of Period 1A. Only four activities were recorded:

(i)   Part of the land drain running from south-west to north-east collapsed, just to the south-west of its junction with the north-west/south-east drain. Subsidence in the overlying courtyard surface resulted, and was compensated for by a make-up of mortar debris and furnace ash sealed by a layer of granular clay (3: 54B, 54B1, 54C).

(ii) A series of small depressions, none more than 5 cm deep, were found in the floor of the eastern corner room. It was not clear what activities they represented.

(iii) A large sandstone block was set into the floor of the southern corner room; it was 25 cm thick, but its area could not be estimated since it was almost wholly overlaid by the foundations of the Victorian church wall. Probing established a cut for its insertion, which was filled with furnace ash and contained a coin of Nero.

(iv) A large trap rock with a weight probably in excess of 100 kg was placed immediately to the south-east of the furnace mouth in the south-western furnace-house. Its purpose is unknown.

These activities, of course, may equally belong to Period 1B.

Dating evidence:

(1)   Fill of cut for sandstone slab inserted in floor of southern corner room:
      Coin: no. 16, *as*, *RIC* 185 (64–8) (2021).

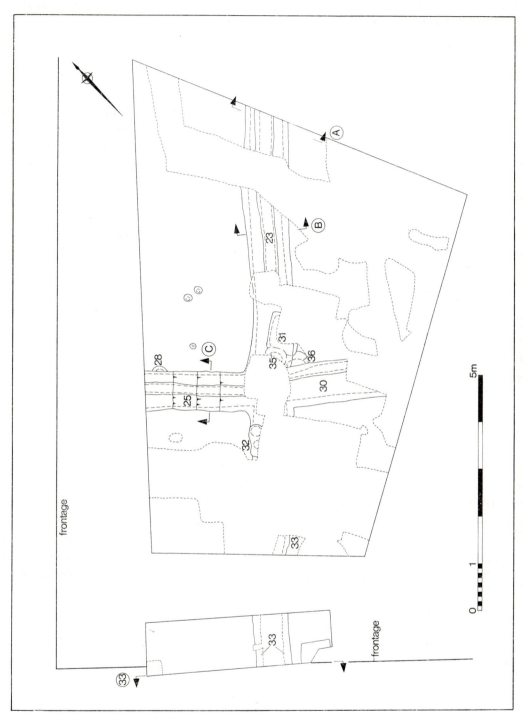

Fig. 14. National Westminster Bank site; features dating to the fortress period.

4. FEATURES NORTH-WEST AND SOUTH-EAST OF THE *VIA PRAETORIA* DATING TO PERIOD 1A (Figs. 14 and 35)

The surface of natural was only preserved in the section on the south-western side of the site, where it was at a level of about 38.45 m O.D. (33: natural). Over the rest of the site the surface of natural had been truncated to a depth of at least 20 cm by the construction of cellars.

A scatter of post-holes, some cutting each other, represented the earliest activities on the site (28, 31, 35, 36, and a scoop, 33: 53, 54). All of these features were cut by water-pipe trenches which resembled those in the service-area south-east of the *caldarium* (see p. 36). The base of the pipe-trench running from north-east to south-west showed a fall to the south-west of 12 cm over a distance of 9.6 m; the pipe itself had been robbed out (23, 33, and profiles A and B; 32: 56). This pipe-trench was joined by two others at right-angles. The north-western example showed, in a series of four distinct 'steps', a fall to the south-east of 16 cm over a distance of 2.3 m (fig. 14, 25 and profile B). The south-eastern pipe-trench was poorly preserved but the actual pipe appeared to have been laid along the north-eastern side of the trench. Unfortunately the point at which the pipes joined was cut out by a later feature. All three pipes had been robbed out (see profiles A, B and C).

A small post-pit, containing two pointed posts, which was dug into the edge of the north-east/ south-west water-pipe trench, may also have dated to the fortress period (32).

South-east of the line of the *via praetoria* the bases of two possible post-trenches were found (Figs. 35, 5, 17) but no other remains of this period survived.

Dating evidence:

Samian: Dr. 37 (?), first century, S.G. (from the clay packing of the north-west water-pipe bedding-trench: Fig. 14, 25).

There were a few scraps of first-century coarse wares from the bedding-trenches of the water-pipes.

The north-west water-pipe aligns exactly with another water-pipe which passed along the north-east side of the granaries (see p. 7), passing under the road to their north-west and then turning south-westward to run along the verandah on the south-east side of the barrack-block next to the *fabrica*. The water-pipe cut the post-pits of the verandah, which was itself a later addition to the barrack-block, and this fact, together with the recovery of the (?) Dr. 37 from the water-pipe bedding-trench, suggests that the pipe dated to late in the military period.

The north-west pipe can be traced over a distance of 72 m, so was scarcely likely to have functioned as a drain as is possible in the case of the pipes in the service-area behind the *caldarium* (see p. 36). It probably functioned as a main supplying water to the *fabrica*: the south-east branch very probably supplied the baths and the pipe crossing the site from north-east to south-west may have been the principal main from the aqueduct.

The most disappointing aspect of this excavation was the absence of any evidence for the exact position of the *via praetoria*. However traces of an early civil road bounding the north-west side of the *forum* and *basilica* were recovered (see pp. 120–1), and this must have been the successor of the *via praetoria*, the approximate line of which can be estimated by taking the mid-point between the defences on the north-west and south-east sides of the fortress (see Fig. 2).

5. PERIOD 1B (CONSTRUCTION)

A. GENERAL DESCRIPTION:

The bath-house was reduced in size *c.* 75, following the departure of the Second Augustan legion, probably in order to serve the needs of a civilian community. The hypocaust in the *tepidarium* was

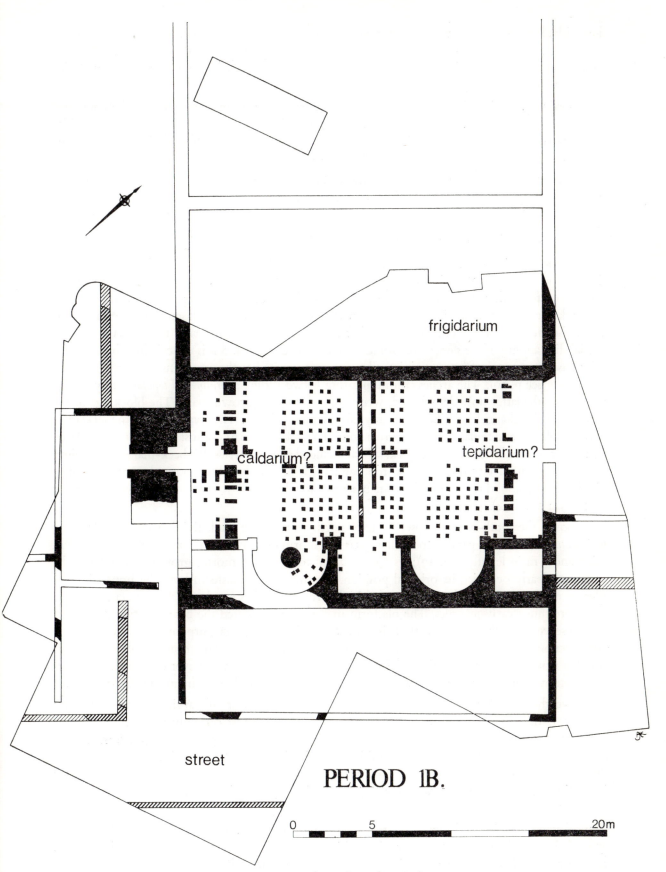

frigidarium

caldarium?

tepidarium?

street

PERIOD 1B.

0 5 20m

Fig. 15. Outline plan of Period 1B.

demolished and the room was probably adapted to serve as a *frigidarium*. The hypocaust in the *caldarium* was divided into two parts by blocking the channel which ran across the width of the room, and the north-east side of the room now probably served as a *tepidarium*, the south-west side as a *caldarium*.

A portico 4.1 m in width was built along the north-east side of the *palaestra*. The courtyard south-east of the south-west furnace-house was divided into two parts. A room 3.45 m in width was constructed on the south-east side of the north-east *caldarium* furnace-house; it probably served as a replacement for a fuel-store on the north-west side of the furnace-house.

The street south-east of the bath-house was reduced to a width of 5.2 m and was resurfaced. A timber building was constructed on its south-east side.

B. ALTERATIONS WITHIN THE MAIN BUILDING (Figs. 15–17, Pl. IIIA):

Within the *caldarium* the only activity which could be attributed with any certainty to the alterations at the beginning of Period 1B was the blocking of the channel crossing the hypocaust from north-west to south-east. Rough walling of tile fragments set in a fine white mortar had been used to block the gaps on both sides of the channel; the outer faces were rendered over with mortar while the faces towards the interior were left uneven and ragged. In order to block the channel partial dismantling of the *suspensura* would have been necessary, and it is conceivable that the *pilae* with bases composed of four adjoining tiles were constructed at the same time, as a repair to the hypocaust (see p. 30). The arches communicating between the *caldarium* and *tepidarium* hypocaust basements, the latter now demolished, were stopped up with brown loam. The blockings of the arches and the channel both bore a heavy encrustation of soot. The hypocaust in the *tepidarium* was demolished and replaced by a concrete floor. The floor of the hypocaust basement was covered by a layer of rubble about 15 cm thick, which included stone quarries, Purbeck-marble mouldings and veneers, and a few fragmentary iron bars; brick-mortar had been poured over the rubble, binding it into a solid mass and filling the basement to a height of 50 cm above the basement floor (17: 2154; 21: 2154).

Opposite the south-western apse, a metre north-west of the wall dividing the *caldarium* and *tepidarium* and running parallel to it, there was a platform of brick-mortar 20 cm in height, 48 cm wide and 3 m in length (Fig. 17); its base adhered to the brick-mortar grouting below and the platform clearly occupied its original position. The top of the platform bore the impressions of tiles set on their narrow sides and arranged in five rows; the tiles employed were 20 cm in length and were thus clearly *pila* tiles. The platform may have represented the base of a tile wall which was to serve as the lining for a bath. It is difficult to think of another purpose for it, because if the construction of a superstructure of any weight had been intended, a far stronger wall would have resulted from laying the base-tiles horizontally. The possible bath was never completed; the tiles were removed and the platform was covered by the rubble-bedding of the mortar floor above.

Above the brick-mortar there was a layer of trodden mortar of varying depth (17: 2153; 23: 2153); this was sealed by a layer of charcoal and ash, almost certainly from the hypocaust furnaces, which to the north-east gave way to a layer of clay (17: 537; 23: 2152). Immediately above, a bedding of trap rocks and demolition material, including two mosaic fragments, was laid down to support a mortar floor with an aggregate of tile fragments and river gravel (23: 2151; in Section 17 the floor was terraced away at the beginning of Period 2A).

Two holes 2 cm square were found in the mortar floor; the sides of both holes bore the impression of wood-graining and must have represented wooden posts. The mortar floor had been laid around them while they were wedged in position amongst the trap rocks of the bedding below. In one case, a skim of mortar survived above the hole, only falling away when the floor was cleaned. The posts had probably functioned as levelling pegs, their tops at a common height which would have indicated the finished level of the floor. The floor was given a *terrazzo* finish; that is, flat pebbles were impressed into its surface, and it was then ground down with stone rubbers to produce an even surface (Green, 1959, 226). The level of the floor was almost exactly 1.0 m above the bottom of the hypocaust basement, and therefore probably somewhat below the level of the floor in the *caldarium*.

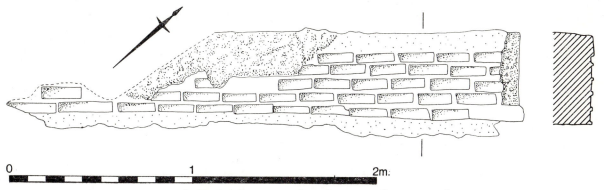

Fig. 17. Period 1B: brick-mortar foundation in former *tepidarium*.

C. ALTERATIONS MADE OUTSIDE THE MAIN BUILDING (Figs. 15 and 16):

The lack of overall levels post-dating the construction-work of Period 1A in the service buildings and *palaestra* makes the attribution of most of the features described below to Period 1B rather dubious. Nevertheless, it seems reasonable to assume that most of the replanning can be linked with the reduction in size of the baths.

In the *palaestra* the stone-lined drain which probably acted as an out-fall from the *frigidarium* was robbed out, and the trench so formed was packed with clay (5: F.30); the *frigidarium* went out of use at the beginning of Period 1B and the drain must have been robbed out at the same time. In the *palaestra* the robbing trench was cut across at right angles by a shallow foundation which terminated against the north-west wall of the furnace-house at a distance of 4.1 m from the south-west wall of the baths (17: 51). The foundation was composed of tile and trap fragments laid in mortar, and probably formed the substructure of a flimsy portico, perhaps of timber.

No alterations were recorded in the south-western furnace-house. To the south-east the court-yard was partly blocked off from the street and divided by a wall. An open gully running from the southern corner of the main building diagonally across the courtyard had previously been filled in with furnace-ash mixed with stone quarries, Purbeck-marble veneers and hypocaust tiles (4: gully 8; 6: gully 8). The wall (55 cm wide) by the street was faced with well-cut trap blocks on its south-east side, but on the other side the work was rougher with an offset 5 cm wide at the top of the foundation-level (6: profile of wall and foundation trench 52G). A spread of lime sealed the foundation-trench (6: 52F). The wall across the courtyard was 65 cm wide and was constructed of water-rolled sandstone blocks and trap blocks in about equal proportions; it stood upon a foundation no wider than the wall itself and 50 cm deep, which consisted of trap rubble and building rubbish, including part of a hypocaust stack three tiles high.

The north-west end of the wall had been destroyed by later activities, but it had terminated at least 65 cm from the wall of the furnace-house, so as to form an entry. Despite the differences in widths and construction-techniques the walls were bonded at their junction and certainly con-temporary. The roadside wall had probably been more carefully constructed in order to match the Period 1A wall to the north-east, and also that almost certainly existing to the south-west. The south-western part of the courtyard may well have been roofed over, creating a room measuring 7.45 m by 3.6 m.

In the enclosed area immediately south-east of the main building a water-pipe trench was found; it survived for a length of 3.8 m and terminated against the south-west wall (1: gully 4). The pipe had been laid in a trench 80 cm wide and 20 cm deep with two cross-baulks laid across its width. The only way in which it differed from those of Period 1A was in its shallow depth (cf. p. 35); the top of the pipe must have been covered by only a skim of clay. The arrangement at its south-west end was similar to that of the pipe leading from the wall of the north-eastern furnace-house (see p. 36); a shallow depression 60 cm in diameter and 15 cm in depth was found, which was probably dug to extract a lead pipe fed by the wooden pipe; the former was probably taken up to a certain height, and then passed through the wall, emptying into the south-eastern of the two junction-pits, which must have been dug for this purpose (4: pit 24). The wooden water-pipe to the north-west must have remained in use; otherwise there would have been no reason to lay another pipe in a different position. The supply-point of the new pipe is not known.

It was also possibly during the construction-work of Period 1B that the *amphora*-bases in the western corner of the enclosure were replaced by four others. One of the four at the south-west end of the row survived in position, and was 48 cm in diameter and 35 cm in height; fragments of the *amphora* at the north-east end of the row were also found, but there was no trace of the two middle ones. Four stake-holes were found between the *amphora*-bases; two of them were cut through the clay fillings of the depressions which the previous bases had occupied, showing that they were probably contemporary with the replacements.

At the north-east end of the enclosure, the wooden water-pipe leading to or from the south-east wall of the main building was removed by means of a wide trench backfilled with furnace-ash, leaving only the impression of a timber cross-baulk on the bottom of the trench (14: 1147, see p. 36). The junction-pit by the south-east wall of the main building had been packed with clay (15: 1188).

A wall constructed of roughly-shaped trap rocks, sometimes wedged into position with fragments of *amphora* and tile, and laid in sparse gravelly mortar, was built parallel to and 3.45 m distant from the wall of the north-east furnace-house. Its foundations were only 10 cm deep, and the roughly-constructed wall may have been intended as a base for a timber superstructure, enclosing a room for use as a fuel store. In Period 1A it is possible that the two furnace-houses on the north-east side of the main building shared a common fuel-store; when the *tepidaritm* hypocaust was demolished, its furnace-house was probably also demolished together with the fuel-store, which it would then have been necessary to replace.

The street: a large quantity of building debris had been spread over the original Period 1A surface to serve as bedding for a layer of remetalling which consisted of river gravel (8: 49F1, 49F2; 9: 49F1, 49F2). Before this took place the roadside ditch had been packed with clay mixed with a few fragments of stone quarries; when the street had been resurfaced, the ditch was recut (8: gully 7A). On the south-east side of the street, a line of timbers had been laid on the old surface before the remetalling took place (8: F.11; 9: F.11); a thin layer of clay was then spread over the area south-east of the timbers and capped with a mortar floor (9: 68B, 68A). The timbers must have acted as bedding-plates for a building, a technique often encountered in early civil contexts, but not yet attested in fortress-levels. The building had a frontage onto the street 8.2 m in length, and the absence of any internal divisions suggested that the area excavated was part of a single room at least 3.2 m wide.

D. DATING EVIDENCE:

(1a) Brick-mortar grouting of demolished *tepidarium* hypocaust:
Samian: Dr. 27, Claudian (23: 2154).

(1b) Furnace-ash deposited below bedding of mortar floor in former *tepidarium*:
Samian: two examples of Dr. 27, Nero-Vespasian; no. 2, Dr. 29, *c.* 50–65 (all 17: 537).

(1c) From bedding of mortar floor in former *tepidarium*:
      Samian: Dr. 30, base, Nero-Vespasian (23: 2152).

(2)   Fill of gully cut by wall dividing courtyard adjoining the south-west furnace-house:
      Samian: Dr. 37, Flavian; Dr. 18, Flavian, Dr. 18, Flavian (all 4: gully. 8).

(3)   Clay packing of Period 1A road-side gully;
      Samian: Dr. 27, pre-Flavian (?) and Ritt. 9, pre-Flavian (?) (both 8: gully 7B).

Finds from group 2 indicate a Flavian date for the alterations of Period 1B, prior to the construction work of Period 2A, dated to *c.* 80.

E. DISCUSSION:

The *caldarium* could not have been subdivided by anything more substantial than a timber screen; no transverse wall-foundations were found cutting through the hypocaust basement, and any form of partition, if present, must have rested on top of the *suspensura*. The south-western half of the room appeared to have been used as a *caldarium*, because here the hypocaust seemed to have deteriorated through the effects of heat more markedly than to the north-east, particularly in the area adjacent to the furnace-mouth. It seems possible that the bath on the north-east side had been partially demolished, leaving only the back wall in position. Fragments of Purbeck marble thought to have been associated with a bath came from the filling of the former *tepidarium* hypocaust basement; but these could have come from the *frigidarium*.

The reduction in size of the baths must have occurred after the departure of the Second Augustan Legion in *c.* 75. The alterations would have been undertaken partly for the purpose of economy in the running costs, but would also have resulted in freeing a large part of the former legionary baths for other purposes. It is not known whether the *frigidarium* and other rooms north-west of the excavated area were demolished at this time. However, the nature of later activities on the site suggests that they may have remained in use throughout Period 1B; during the alterations of Period 2A, a large timber hall, erected in the eastern corner of the *palaestra*, appeared to have served as a temporary building for public use while the *basilica* was being constructed. The predecessor of this temporary building may have been the former *frigidarium* or some other room in the legionary baths, used during Period 1B as an administrative *basilica*. Likewise the *palaestra*, or the greater part of it, may have been taken over to function as a market-place.

The possible presence of these makeshift public buildings at Exeter need not necessarily imply that the territory of the *Dumnonii* was constituted as a *civitas* free of military control before *c.* 80. The community which sprang up on the site of the legionary fortress would depend upon adequate trading facilities for its economic well-being, and also require buildings to house an interim administration. On analogy with the state of affairs known from some of the Danubian provinces, the latter was most likely to have been controlled by a *praefectus civitatis* (Mócsy, 1974, 69), perhaps a centurion, although civilians (Wilkes, 1969, 287–8; Mócsy, 1974, 134) are also known to have been appointed to similar positions. The former site of the fortress would have been the most convenient location for the centre of administration.

There is as yet no evidence for any continuing military occupation on the site of the fortress after the departure of the legion. Indeed, the transfer of the legion to Caerleon may have been the occasion for a general military withdrawal from South-west England[1].

NOTES

1. The fort at Nanstallon, Cornwall, was said to have been held until *c.* 80 (Fox and Ravenhill, 1972, 86–8). Although a building was erected over a level containing a Dr. 37 (*ibid.*, Fig. 21, 5, described as '. . . Flavian, but could belong to the early part of that period . . .'), there was nothing from the site to show that occupation continued beyond *c.* 75. Early in the nineteenth century three coins of Vespasian were recovered from the site (*VCH*, Cornwall, v, 5): their discovery is mentioned in the recent report (Fox and Ravenhill, 1972, 92) but they are not described and presumably they have been lost.

6. ACTIVITIES IN THE COURSE OF PERIOD 1B (Fig. 16)

In the former *tepidarium*, now serving as a *frigidarium*, a series of post-holes had been dug through the mortar floor; eight post-holes (2127B and C, 2128A, B and H, and 1811C, D and F) were all about 20 cm in depth, breaking through the mortar floor to the rubble bedding below; the rest of the post-holes were more like sockets, with a maximum depth of 10 cm. All these features were filled and sealed by the demolition-deposits of Period 2A (23: 2124). A series of eight post-holes (2128A, C, D and G, 2127B and 1811A, E and F) seemed to reflect the position of the piers fronting the apses and recess in the *caldarium*, while a slot (2127A) and two post-holes (2127C and 2128H) taken together corresponded roughly to the width of the central recess. As shown elsewhere (p. 51), it seems likely that originally there were three doors in the wall dividing the *caldarium* from the *tepidarium*, and that the doors lay directly opposite the apses and recess. The post-holes, therefore, appeared to be arranged so as to take account of the position of these doors. A plausible interpretation of their function is that they represented the remains of wooden 'internal porches', built to cut down heat-loss from the caldarium. It can be safely assumed that the original entrances were equipped with wooden doors (see p. 53, n.1), but in Period 1B it may have been found that there was too great a heat loss with the *caldarium*, *tepidarium* and *frigidarium* communicating directly; accordingly, a second set of doors may have been constructed in order to insulate the *tepidarium* and *caldarium*.

IV. THE *BASILICA* AND *FORUM*

1. GENERAL DESCRIPTION

The *basilica* and *forum* were constructed *c.* 80 and covered the site of the legionary baths and a considerable area to the south-west, *c.* 7135.5 sq.m in all (120.5 m by 67 m). On the south-west side of the *forum* there was an open market-place measuring 67 m by 31 m, which was excavated in 1945 and 1946, and originally thought to represent part of the *forum*. Within the area of the present excavations the south-east and north-east walls of the bath-house were incorporated within the fabric of the *basilica*, which consisted of an aisleless hall 10.4 m in width, reducing to 9 m in width at its south-east end. On the north-east side of the hall there was a room measuring 13 m by 7.6 m which has been identified as the *curia*. On its north-west side part of another room, 6.1 m in width and of unknown length, was explored. A flight of steps ran along the front of the central portion of the *basilica* which was probably pierced by a series of arches or openings. On the south-east side of the *forum*-courtyard there was a portico 4.9 m in width with a flight of steps leading up to the *basilica* at its north-east end. There was access to this portico from the street to the south-east by means of a passage-way 3.2 m in width; on the south-west side of the passage-way there was a room 6.08 m in width with a door which communicated with the portico. Opening off the north-east side of the passage-way there was another room measuring *c.* 3.75 m by 6.2 m. On the south-east side of the *basilica* there was an open courtyard with a passage 90 cm in width on its north-west side. At its north-east end this passage connected with a probable portico, 2.7 m in width, which ran along the north-east side of the *basilica*: beyond it was a continuation of the courtyard on the south-east side of the *basilica*. The northern corner of the courtyard behind the *basilica* was also located (p. 120).

The street on the south-east side of the *basilica* remained in use.

2. CONSTRUCTION OF THE *BASILICA* AND *FORUM*

A. CONSTRUCTION OF THE *BASILICA* (Figs. 18–21, Pls I, II, IV, VIA, IXA):

Demolition of the main building: the apses and central recess on the south-east side of the *caldarium* were filled to a depth of 70 cm with clean brown loam (n.i. 1528 and 2115), most of the *pila* tiles having been previously removed. The rubble filling the rest of the hypocaust basement lapped up against the loam, showing that demolition work had commenced on the south-east side of the room; clearly it was originally intended to remove all the tiles from the basement, but, for some reason, the attempt was abandoned. The rest of the basement was filled with rubble which had been consolidated by pouring liquid brick-mortar over its surface (11: 2017; 16: 1524; 19: 545; 22: 2139)[1]. The constituent elements of the rubble filling are of some interest because they show at what point in the sequence of demolition the hypocaust was dismantled; the rubble consisted of:

(i) debris from the *suspensura*, including tiles 60 cm square, iron bars, stone floor-quarries, mosaic fragments and *tesserae*. Except in the apses, little attempt was made to salvage the *pilae*, many of which stood five or six tiles high amidst the rubble.

(ii) the rear wall of the north-eastern bath, the central portion of which was missing, perhaps having been destroyed when the *testudo* and pipes were scrapped. Some of the Purbeck

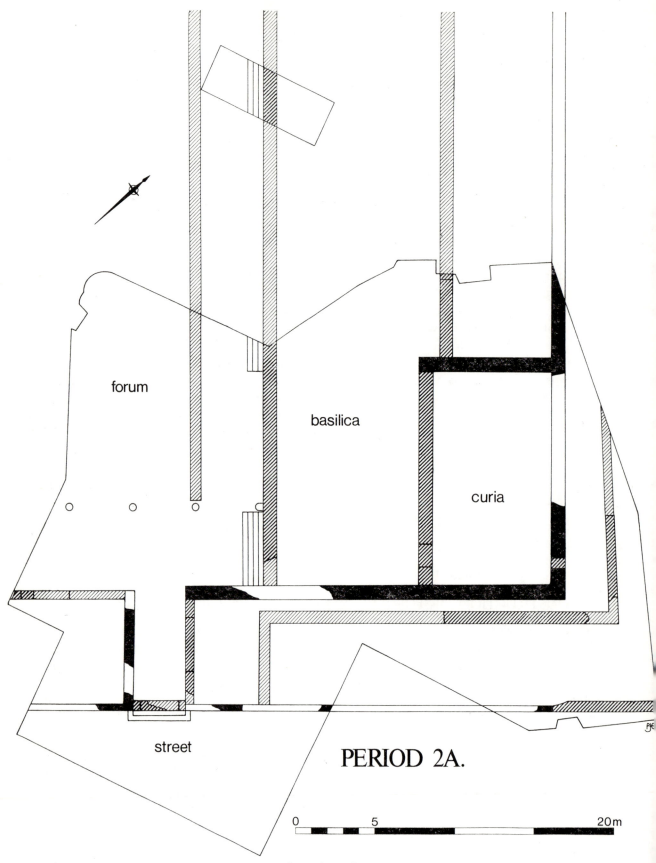

Fig. 18. Outline plan of Period 2A.

marble can definitely be shown to have been associated with the two baths in the *caldarium*: and this was a likely source of many other fragments.

(iii) a small quantity of miscellaneous material: a few *tegulae mammatae*, a very small quantity of wall-plaster, some Purbeck-marble mouldings probably from the rim of a *labrum*, nails, window-glass and some food-bones and pottery.

Most of the material originated from the *suspensura* and from the baths at either end of the room. Large amounts of wall plaster, recognisable fragments of vaulting, roof-tiles and trap facing-blocks were not represented amongst the rubble, and their absence suggests that demolition work started with the removal of the *suspensura*, and, inevitably, the baths which it supported.

Demolition of the walls and vaults took place from immediately above this level, but left little trace, the resulting debris having been cleared away. The north-west wall of the room in the eastern corner was removed leaving only four courses surviving above foundation-level (16: 1521); the apse and recess walls were partly robbed, and the mortared rubble core of the south-west wall, where exposed by the robbing, was patched over, using facing blocks bedded with wide joints which were roughly pointed and incised with horizontal and vertical lines (Elev. 1); at the same time a 14 m length of the north-west *caldarium* wall was reduced to the level of the Period 1B floor in the room to the north-west.

The filling of the hypocaust basement was covered by a thin spread of sandstone chips and sand and mortar debris, occasionally overlaid by charcoal (16: 1523; 22: 2135 and 2134; 23: 2135). A bank of sand and sandstone chips was found against the north-west wall of the *caldarium*, sloping up to seal its levelled-off top (23: 2124), and overlying the spread of sand and sandstone chips and mortar debris (23: 2135). The large quantity of sandstone chips shows that masons were already at work in the vicinity, and the presence of iron slag mixed with the charcoal deposit also points to metal-working. A dozen stake-holes were scattered over the south-eastern half of the area (not illustrated) and a small pit was filled with lenses of fine sand laminated with charcoal (16: 1534).

Construction of the basilica[2] :

Two parallel walls, spaced 8.9 m apart and running across the entire width of the *caldarium*, were built from above the levels just described. Both walls were of the same width as the main walls of the earlier building. The south-west wall was built on a foundation of mortared rubble, *c.* 1.5 m wide, including water-rolled sandstone rocks, trap rocks and broken tile; the foundation rested on the tiled floor of the hypocaust basement. At its south-east end, the wall partly overlaid the south-west arm of the south-west apse and to the north-west it was built against and lapped over the north-west wall of the *caldarium*. The foundations were capped by a layer of mortar, forming a platform on top of which the wall was constructed. The wall consisted of a mortared rubble core, faced with blocks of trap or, occasionally, sandstone, which were larger and less regular than those employed in walls of Period 1A; the joints between the blocks were up to 20 cm in width and were trowel-marked with horizontal and vertical lines. The line of the wall was extended north-westwards from where it crossed the line of the demolished south-east *tepidarium* wall by means of a shallow foundation (see p. 73).

The north-east wall was of identical dimensions and construction-technique. At its south-east end the wall incorporated part of the north-east *caldarium* apse in its fabric. To the north-west, the wall ended against the surviving portion of the *caldarium/tepidarium* wall, which was retained over a distance of 8.3 m in the new building. Its line was continued north-westwards on the other side of the cross-wall by a wall set back 1.6 m to the north-east; its foundations, which were 1.4 m wide, cut down at least 10 cm below the brick-mortar floor of the hypocaust basement. The wall continued over a length of 4.8 m; where it ended a sandstone block was found at the base of the wall, spanning its whole width. The foundations had once continued north-westwards, presumably supporting a threshold, but had been entirely robbed at a later date.

Building-activity associated with the insertion of the walls was represented by trails of dried mortar, found adhering to the foundation-platforms, and probably trimmed from the pointing of the walls; a layer of mortar debris and trap chips found covering the south-east part of the area must have represented a working surface (22: 2130). Near the north-east edge of the layer an area of mortar measuring about 1.0 by 1.5 m was found, bearing the impression of planks 25 cm wide which could have represented a wooden board for mortar-mixing.

Before the next stage of construction the small door at the eastern corner of the building was blocked with coursed masonry. On the interior face of the blocking were found the impressions of planks of wood placed horizontally against the rough mortar pointing. Boarding must have been erected against the wall-face, extending across the doorway, before it was blocked, and must have then been removed before the interior of the building was levelled-up once more; there seems to be no obvious explanation for this. Finally the exterior walls were roughly rendered over on their interior faces with plaster containing a very high proportion of lime. This may perhaps have been intended as some form of damp-proofing designed to prevent moisture from the deposits below the floor of the *basilica* from penetrating the walls.

Subsequently the interior of the building was filled to a depth of 60–70 cm with a dump of yellow clay, loam mixed with occupation-material and some demolition-debris (16: 1514 and 1516; 22: 2126; 23: 2126). The finished floor-levels were laid down directly over the levelling. In the *basilica* the floor was 25 cm thick, and was composed of a bedding of tightly-packed trap rocks, supporting a floor of mortar mixed with an abundant pebble aggregate. Only a small area of the floor survived at the south-east end of the nave (22: 2108). A similar sequence was recovered to the north in Trench 8 where a deposit of red clay 35 cm deep overlaid the brick-mortar floor of the *frigidarium*, and in turn was sealed by a layer of trap rocks and a mortar floor at a level of 38.70 m O.D., only 10 cm lower than the floor preserved at the south-east end of the nave (21: reconstructed levels).

Within the excavated area the reconstruction of the building had formed two rooms behind the nave. The north-west room was levelled up with yellow clay (n.i. 1804) which sealed a spread of mortar debris (n.i. 1807) directly overlying the Period 1B floor. The yellow clay was capped by a mortar floor 5 cm thick at 38.95–39.00 m O.D., 15–20 cm higher than the floor-level in the *basilica*; the robbed threshold (see above) must therefore also have served as a step up from the lower level to the south-west. The room to the south-east was entered through a door 1.50 m from the end of the *basilica*. Only one slab of the threshold remained in position, but the impressions of others were preserved in the mortar of the underlying wall, and showed that the door was originally 2.4 m wide. A circular hole had been cut in the surface of the surviving block, about 30 cm from its south-east edge. The hole was 6 cm in diameter and 8 cm in depth and was connected with the edge of the block by means of a channel with an 'U'-shaped profile 6 cm wide and 4 cm deep. This must represent the lower pivot-hole for a door; the circular hole would probably have held an iron bush, and the groove was provided so that the lower pivot could slide into place after the upper pivot was inserted in its socket; lead would then have been run into the groove, fixing the iron bush solidly into position[3].

The floor of the room was constructed in the same way as that in the nave of the *basilica*, but was at a higher level (39.10–39.15 m O.D.). The threshold of the door at 39.00 m O.D. therefore functioned partly as a step up from the nave. Wall-plaster from the robbed trench of the south-east wall of the room probably formed part of the original decoration (see p. 159). No evidence for the decoration of the nave or the north-west room was found except for wall-plaster found on the south-east wall of the nave, which preserved no pigment.

Insertion of the south-west aisle wall:

In Period 2C a wall was constructed parallel to and 4 m distant from the south-west wall of the *basilica*. Earlier stratification on either side of its foundation trench preserved two different sequences of activity (see Section 17); and thus the presence of an earlier wall in this position was demonstrated, although no traces of its fabric remained. This wall did not form part of the original building-plan, however, because both the stylobate gutter and *forum* portico terminated against the south-west wall of the *basilica*.

It seems probable that this early modification to the plan was carried out during the final constructional stages of Period 2A. The floor of what was now effectively the south-west aisle of the *basilica* had been covered by a discontinuous spread of mortar debris sealed in turn by a mortar floor-surface (20: 539, 546, 534; elsewhere the two mortar surfaces could not always be adequately distinguished, e.g. 17: 534); these events may have been connected with the insertion of the wall.

The purpose of the wall may have been to close off the open front of the *basilica*, creating, in effect, an aisle. The *basilica* faced south-west, the direction of the prevailing winds, which may have made it unusable in winter.

NOTES

1. At Wroxeter when the baths were demolished to make way for the *basilica* and *forum*, many of the rooms were also filled up with grouted rubble (Atkinson, 1942, 28).

2. The plan of the building is not 'basilican'; but in spite of this there can be little doubt that it would have been called a *basilica* by those who used it; this term has therefore been employed throughout the report.

3. Breeze and Dobson, 1976, 158; for pivot-holes in the threshold of an entry to the *forum* at Wroxeter, see Atkinson, 1942, 80.

B. CONSTRUCTION OF THE SOUTH-EAST *FORUM* RANGE AND STRUCTURES SOUTH-EAST AND NORTH-EAST OF THE *BASILICA* (Figs. 18 and 19):

Demolition of the service buildings: In the *palaestra* the Period 1B stylobate-foundation was dismantled and partly robbed (17: 48). To the south-east the furnace-house was filled with rubble derived from the demolished boiler-bases. The lowest tip-line, confined to the north-eastern part of the area and sealing a layer of ash which had accumulated over the stoking area (18: 65), was composed of lumps of mortar, mixed with trap chips, window glass and nails; many of the mortar lumps had been subjected to intense heat and must have come from immediately above the flue (18: 61). A second tip of larger, mostly unburnt mortar lumps (18: 60) overlaid most of the stoking-area to the south-west. Fragments of roof-tile scattered above the two tips of materials showed that the roof had been taken down only after the internal fittings had been stripped out. The interior was then levelled with a dump of clean brown clay-silt (18: 64). Finally a continuous layer of trodden mortar debris accumulated over the area formerly occupied by the *palaestra* and furnace-house (17: 49; 18: 49). In the fuel-store tips of clay and ash (7: 32C–32G) were sealed by two layers of clay, trap chips and mortar debris (7: 32A, 32B) which must have been associated with the demolition of the surrounding walls. The room south-west of the Period 1B service-entry was levelled with similar material (4: 36D, 36E; 6: 52B, C, D and E) and the demolition of the walls was again marked by an accumulation of mortar debris (4: 36C). In the service-entry ash had also been dumped, but here was capped by clean brown clay-silt (3: 46B and B1; 4: 46B, B1 and C). A layer of mortar debris was present only in the north-western half of the area (4: 46A), but had probably been terraced away to the south-east in order to provide a level floor in the completed building (c.f. 4: 12D; 3: 12D). The furnace-ash had been used to fill in the plank-lined gully (3: F.77) but the two pits or (?) junction-boxes (see p. 36) had been previously packed with clay (4: pit 24). In this area the two adjoining walls of Period 1B were retained and incorporated in the plan of the Period 2A buildings. When the water-pipes had been removed a layer of ash was spread over the whole area to the south of the main building, (1: 9EB, 9EB1; 3: 9EB, 9EB1; 12: 1139; 13: 1409B–D: 14: 1143; 15: 1143)[1].

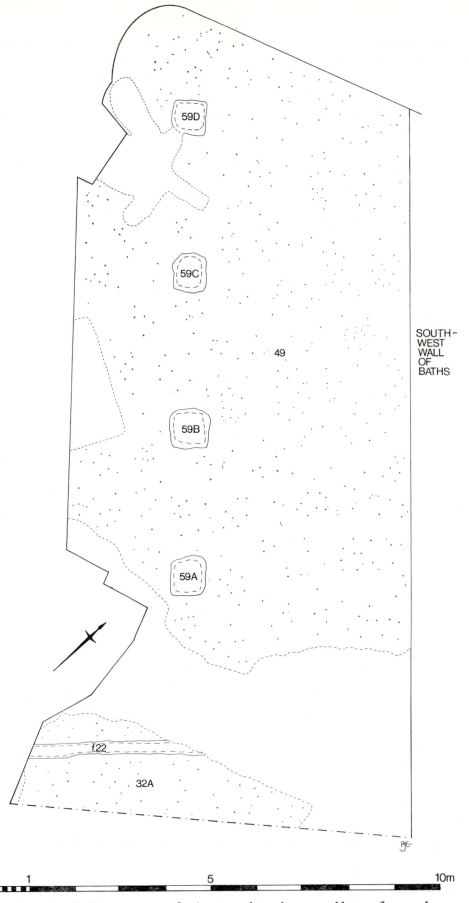

59D

59C

49

SOUTH-
WEST
WALL
OF
BATHS

59B

59A

f.22

32A

0   1   5   10m

Fig. 20. Timber building on site of *palaestra* and south-west *caldarium* furnace-house.

The bulk of the material used for levelling prior to demolition was ash from the furnaces mixed with some domestic rubbish, large piles of which must have accumulated on the site before demolition took place. The ash layers were largely devoid of demolition material; a few fragments of Purbeck-marble veneer and some stone floor-quarries were found scattered over the southern corner of the site, but they probably represented rubbish survivals from the work carried out at the beginning of Period 1B.

Temporary building (Fig. 20):

After the demolition-work was completed, a large timber building was erected in the area formerly occupied by the *palaestra* and south-west furnace-house. A sleeper beam *c.* 25 cm wide formed its south-east end-wall (7: f.22). A post-pit 75 cm square and 50 cm deep lay to the north-west, the first in a line of four spaced roughly 2.5 m apart (59A–D). There was room for a fifth post-pit to the south-east, adjacent to the beam-slot, but any possible evidence of this had been destroyed by later disturbance. The remaining post-pits were filled with river gravel and trap rocks, probably the remains of the post-packing. The timbers which occupied the post-pits could have functioned either as aisle-posts or supports for a ridge-pole. In either case, the still extant south-west wall of the baths would have formed the north-east wall of the building; its minimum dimensions were thus 15.6 by 8 m.

Forum-*courtyard*:

The site of the timber building was covered by a layer of mortar which also sealed the robber-trench of the south-west wall of the bath-house (17: 43 and 48; 18: 43; 20: 43). The mortar level, which was 35 cm thick in places, formed the surface of the *forum*-courtyard throughout Period 2A. At the north-west edge of the excavation a post-Roman robber trench was found (Int. 18), the south-east end of which coincided with a change in the construction of the south-west wall of the *basilica;* north-west of this point the foundation-raft resting on the hypocaust basement was replaced by a shallow footing of mortared rubble (17: 535). Both the robbing trench and footing were encountered 16 m to the north-west in Trench 8 (21: F.5 and F.6). The robbing trench had the same width as the steps preserved at the north-east end of the *forum* portico and was almost certainly dug in order to remove a similar feature; it would follow that the shallow footings represented the base of step-foundations.

South-east forum-*portico*:

The most prominent feature was a flight of steps, preserved intact over about half its width, which led up from the portico to the higher level within the *basilica*. The steps formed an impressive monument and were not dismantled, so it was impossible to examine their foundations closely; however they appeared merely to have rested on the grouted rubble filling of the hypocaust basement. Sandstone blocks 25 cm high, 40 cm wide and 80 cm in length were used to form the individual steps. Only three-quarters of their width was exposed as the surface of the treads; the remaining 10 cm was recessed to a depth of 1 cm to accommodate the blocks above and to provide for a tight joint. Two grades of sandstone were used, one near-white and the other a deep dull pink; the top step (from north-west to south-east) consisted of a white and two pink blocks, the step below of a white and two pink blocks, and the two lowest steps of two pink blocks flanking a white. The two shades of colour were clearly employed for decorative effect, perhaps forming a symmetrical pattern[2].

An engaged column-base, surviving to a height of 31 cm and supporting a shaft 46 cm in diameter, was found in position immediately to the north-west of the steps (Fig. 49, no. 1); it was supported on a sandstone slab which was flush with the contemporary floor-surface and re-used, to judge from its irregular shape. The lower half of the base projected at the back and was jointed

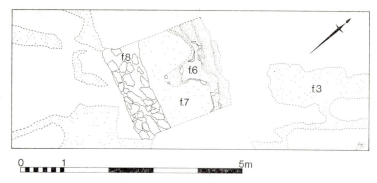

Fig. 21. Roman levels and features in Trench 8.

into the south-west wall of the *basilica*. North-west of the base was found a sandstone slab measuring 1 m by 60 cm, with a shallow depression 35 cm in width and 5 cm deep cut into its surface.

The column-base represented the termination of the portico-colonnade and the block on its north-west side the end of the stylobate-gutter. Both had been destroyed to the south-west by the foundation-trench of a wall constructed at the beginning of Period 2B. However the inter-columniation can still be estimated, because it seems likely that the later south-west aisle wall would have abutted the adjacent column to the south-west, which would then represent the termination of the portico-colonnade; this assumption is supported by the position of a small pit which could well have been associated with its removal (2022). An intercolumniation of 3.6 m can thus be established, a figure which compares well with that of the east *forum*-portico at Wroxeter where columns with a diameter of 47 cm were spaced 3.8 m (16 modules) apart from centre to centre[3]. If Vitruvius' rules for the proportions of Tuscan columns are applied (IV, 7, 2–3), where the diameter of the column at two modules gives a height of 16 modules, including base and cap, a height of 3.68 m can be calculated for the colonnade of the *forum* portico at Exeter. How closely later provincial practice reflected the traditions described by Vitruvius is uncertain.

The rear wall of the portico was formed at the north-east end by the south-east wall of the bath-house; its mortared-rubble core had been refaced where exposed by the removal of the south-west wall of the baths. At the south-western end of the excavated part of the portico a new wall had been constructed (see below).

The demolition-debris underlying the portico was sealed by a layer of brown clay, capped by a mortar level (11: 2010, 2022; 7: 13E, 13F); the latter was sealed by a compacted layer of crushed tile (11: 2008; 7: 13D) which appeared to have served as a floor throughout Period 2A.

Behind the portico there was a room lying only partly within the excavated area, and to the north-east of this room an entry-passage leading to the road. A wall of Period 1B was reused as the south-west side of the passage, but a new wall was built to form the north-east side. It utilised a demolished wall of Period 1A as a foundation, and was constructed of well-cut blocks of trap and sandstone supported on a continuous line of sandstone slabs, which also formed the paving of an entry 3.20 m in width (Elev. 4) leading into a room on the east side of the passage. A drain passed below this entry; the threshold-slab at the south-eastern end had been taken up and placed over the drain, probably at the beginning of Period 3A, when the entry was blocked off; it was restored to its original position during the course of excavation. The floor of the passage was of mortar and was continuous with that of the south-east *forum*-portico (3: 12C; 4: 12C). It overlaid a spread of clay and trap chips (3: 12D, D1; 4: 12C1, D). To the north-west the floor sealed a layer of mortar debris, which probably represented the levelling of a hollow (4: 12E). A large masonry drain ran down the centre of the passage, leading from the stylobate-gutter to a wooden drain-pipe under the street. It was constructed of trap and sandstone rubble, some reused blocks and fragments of Purbeck marble, filling a cut whose width varied between 1 and 1.2 m. The average width of the drain was about 30 cm but just to the south-east of its junction with another drain which joined it from the north-east, its width decreased to about 20 cm. At the junction there was a slight swelling on the south-west side, presumably intended to increase the acuteness of the angle at which the two bodies of water met, so as to prevent the water from "backing-up" either of the drains. Curiously, the details of construction seem to anticipate a large and rapid flow of water which the wooden water-pipe under the road (see below) would have been hard put to to cope with. Near the top of the drain ledges 4–6 cm in width had been constructed on each side along most of its length. At the junction of the two drains a jumble of *tegulae* was found spanning its width. *Tegulae* roughly trimmed to shape must have formed the original cover of the drain, sealed over by the floor of the passage; however all other traces of them were removed when the drain was partly robbed in Period 2B. The floor of the drain was of mortar, mostly worn away. At its north-west end where the stylobate-gutter fed into it, the drain floor was at a level of 37.46 m O.D. Levels taken at intervals of 50 cm along the central portion of the drain from north-west to south-east produced the following readings:

1. 37.43 m O.D.	6. 37.24 m O.D.	11. 37.27 m O.D.
2. 37.39 m O.D.	7. 37.25 m O.D.	12. 37.19 m O.D.
3. 37.39 m O.D.	8. 37.24 m O.D.	13. 37.19 m O.D.
4. 37.31 m O.D.	9. 37.24 m O.D.	14. 37.15 m O.D.
5. 37.21 m O.D.	10. 37.26 m O.D.	15. 37.12 m O.D.

Over its entire length the drain showed a fall of 31 cm.

The south-west end of the entry-passage was dignified by a monumental entry (Elev. 3). Although badly damaged, enough remained to reconstruct its original form. A 2 m length of sandstone sill was supported on a mortared-rubble foundation which penetrated almost to natural; its original width would have been 3.1 m. The upper surface of the sill was very worn and the front was chipped and scarred by later activity which had taken place in the vicinity. At the back of the blocks the surfaces were well preserved; their edges had been worked flat, but the rest of their surfaces were only roughly trimmed by means of diagonal punching. The presence of the foundations of the Victorian nave a few centimetres from the surface made it impossible to record accurately the details of the tooling. At the west end of the sill a block of stone measuring 50 cm by 80 cm by 54 cm high was left in place; no doubt it was originally matched by a block of similar size on the north-east side. The upper surface of the block was irregularly punched and scored to key mortar bedding for a superimposed stone, perhaps a column-base, which did not survive.

The entry was fronted by two steps leading up from the street. Their foundations were represented by a raft of mortared rubble overlying a street-surface which was probably in use only during the reconstruction of the building (8: 49E, F.88). Only a part of one step was preserved in position; its south-east edge was 60 cm distant from the entry-sill, suggesting that the two steps would originally have been each 30 cm wide.

South-west of the entry-passage there was a room whose south-east and north-east walls were retained from Period 1B, but whose north-west wall was newly constructed with a robbed threshold of unknown width opening onto the *forum* portico. The room was 6.08 m wide and its length was in excess of 6.6 m. The interior was levelled, after construction, with clay, loam and mortar debris (4: 36A, 36B; 6: 52A) above which in the south-east part of the room a mortar floor survived, similar in details of construction to that in the nave (6: F.56A). The floor was 40 cm higher than the level of the south-east portico; no evidence of steps leading up to the room from the portico was preserved. Another room was situated north-east of the entry-passage, communicating with it by means of the doorway already described. The north-west and south-east walls were of Period 1A construction. A large robber-trench probably marked the position of the wall on the north-east side of the room; the robber-trench must have been dug to remove a Period 3A wall, which, however, may have incorporated a Period 2A wall within its fabric (Fig. 32, f.93, see p. 106). The room measured 6.2 m by *c*. 3.75 m and entrances must have led off from it to both a narrow passage and an open area to the north-east. It was given a thick mortar floor laid directly on top of the pre-demolition levelling material (3: 9EA; 1: 9EA, see pp. 71–2), except to the extreme south-west, where it partly covered a mortar raft under the line of sandstone slabs which supported the south-west wall of the room (3: F.6). A drain crossed the room at an oblique angle, joining that under the entry passage to the south-west. Its top had been built flush with the finished mortar level, which was found adhering to its sides in many places. However the mortar floor soon cracked and became uneven because of settlement which took place in the levelling material below, and dumps of clay and loam 40 cm thick were deposited to form a new floor (1: 10EC and 10ED; 3: 10EC and 10ED). At the same time the top of the drain was rebuilt. The sandstone paving of the threshold to the south-west had also been cut through to accommodate the drain, presumably when it was heightened, although here the drain was robbed out to a depth below the rebuild. The function of this branch of the drain must have been to take water from the roof of the *basilica*; the absence of a drain running along the base of the south-west wall of the *basilica* indicated the presence of a gutter at eaves-level, probably emptying into the drain by means of a pipe[4].

Area to the south-east and north-east of the basilica:

The north-east wall of the Period 1A enclosure immediately to the south-east of the main building was demolished, but the south-east wall which ran along the roadside was retained, and a new wall extended its line north-eastwards. The junction between the old wall (44 cm wide) and the new wall (60 cm wide) was effected by a gradual widening. The new wall continued for a distance of 7.25 m and then was represented by a robbing trench which turned north-west (see Fig. 28). Examination of the sections revealed in its sides at one point suggested that the line of the new wall may have coincided with the earlier north-eastern limits of the legionary baths (see p. 35).

Another wall had been constructed along the north-east and south-east sides of the *basilica*, forming a passage or corridor which appeared to have opened into the room immediately to the north-east of the entry-passage. On the south-east side of the *basilica* the wall was 70 cm in width and survived at one point to a height of 1.3 m above foundation-level. The width of the passage on this side was only 80 cm, but on the north-eastern side of the *basilica* its width increased to 2.8 m. Here the wall had a width of 60 cm in common with other walls of Period 2A; it survived to a height of 45 cm above foundation-level, where its top was finished with a smooth skim of mortar. Along the entire length of the passage the construction-levels of Period 2A appeared to have served as a floor-level (13: 1409A; 15: 1185).

In this area the three surviving walls of Period 2A were built with foundation-trenches from one and a half to one and three-quarter times as wide as the walls themselves; the foundations penetrated to natural and were packed with rubble composed of trap and tile fragments, the top 30 cm of which was mortared to provide a solid foundation raft. The walls themselves were built with small, often square, trap and sandstone blocks facing a core of mortared rubble. Pointing was roughly executed with joints 2–4 cm in width, trowel-marked with horizontal and vertical lines in an attempt to improve the appearance of the masonry. In the main part of the area the pre-demolition levelling was covered by a layer of trap chips and mortar debris often indistinguishable from a thin skim of mortar; in the eastern corner was found a layer of trap rocks, probably discarded by masons working in the vicinity (12: 1138; 14: 1138; 15: 1138). After construction work was completed a layer of clay and loam identical to the material encountered in the room adjacent to the entry passage was deposited (12: 1135; 14: 1135 and 1136 and 1137; 15: 1137).

The layout in this area presents problems of interpretation: for instance it is far from obvious which part was roofed over and which left open. The wall of the passage south-east of the *basilica* was probably carried up to roof-level; this is suggested by the evidence for a door being cut through it at the beginning of Period 2B (see p. 94). The north-eastern return of the wall on the north-east side of the *basilica* had clearly carried a superstructure, perhaps a timber-framed wall or a dwarf colonnade. The latter alternative seems more likely, since the depth of foundation and build of the wall are the same as those elsewhere which are presumed to have been built throughout in stone. Fragments from three column-bases of the appropriate size (see p. 146) were reused in Period 3A walls at the eastern corner of the site and may have been removed from the wall, which was retained until this period. If a dwarf colonnade was present along the north-east side of the *basilica*, it would then follow that the area to the south-east and north-east was open; certainly no traces of cross-divisions were recovered in this area. The function of the passage and colonnade may have been to give covered access to rooms in the range at the rear of the *basilica;* there is evidence that the possible dwarf colonnade extended north-west for at least a distance of 16 m (see p. 95). Retention of the south-east and north-east walls of the bath-house in the plan of the *basilica* probably gave rise to this unusual arrangement; perhaps little use was made of this area until the beginning of Period 2B.

Streets: The start of building-work on the site probably occasioned the filling-in of the roadside ditch (8: gully 7A), and the demolition of the timber building south-east of the street, represented by the extraction of a sleeper-beam (8: F.11, 9: F.11). Both features were packed with clay and sealed by a roughly metalled surface consisting of river gravel and broken tile (8: 49E; 9: 49E). The foundations of the steps in front of the entry-passage rested on this surface and two trenches for wooden water-pipes were cut through it. One pipe was connected with the stone drain leading from the stylobate-gutter and joined another pipe running from north-east to south-west (8: gully 6; 9: gully 6). No iron junction-collars were found in the pipe-trench leading from the stone drain, nor was it clear how its junction with the other pipe was effected. The pipe running from north-east to south-west was later removed from its bedding-trench north-east of its junction with the pipe leading from the stone drain, but over the rest of its course it remained in use, fed solely from the stone drain and eventually rotting away *in situ.* Two iron junction-collars were thus preserved in their original position, spaced 2.2 m apart. Levels at intervals of 1.25 m taken along the bottom of the bedding trench of the east-west pipe showed a steady fall to the south-west:

1. 37.04 m O.D.	3. 36.92 m O.D.	5. 36.86 m O.D.	7. 36.79 m O.D.
2. 36.99 m O.D.	4. 36.89 m O.D.	6. 36.85 m O.D.	—

After the wooden water-pipes and the steps had been inserted, a new street-surface was laid down (8: 49C; 9: 49C). The Period 2A street was between 5.8 m and 6.5 m in width; a deep foundation-trench had destroyed its south-eastern edge and removed the relationships between later street-surface and a succession of deposits to the south-east.

The path or lane north-east of the *basilica* was probably part of the original street-plan and may even have been retained from Period 1A; some form of access to the building on this side must have been necessary. However the presence of the lane in Period 2A or at an earlier date cannot be proved by reference to the section revealed on its south-west side.

NOTES

1. Wooden water-pipes were also salvaged on the north-west side of the baths (see p. 60). The manufacture of wooden water-pipes was a laborious process, as a modern account from Kilmore, Co. Wexford makes clear (O'Sullivan, 1969, 101–116), and they were obviously worth re-using.

2. Evidence for the use of contrasting-coloured building materials for decorative effect occasionally survives in Britain. At Dover the doorways, windows and recesses of the lighthouse were turned with blocks of tufa alternating with pairs of tiles (Wheeler, 1929, 33). In the Roman villa at Boxmoor part of a (?) door-arch composed of alternating

tiles and tufa blocks had collapsed into a hypocaust (Neal, 1976, 71 and Fig. LIII). One of the most striking examples of this type of decoration survives at Cologne. The north-west corner-tower of the city wall preserves on its external face bands of diaper-pattern, a circular motif and a representation of a colonnade with pediment, all picked out in lighter-coloured stone (*Germania Romana*, II, 17, Pl. XVIII, 1; Hellenkemper, 1975, 821, Taf. IV).

3. Atkinson, 1942, 60. Columns spaced this far apart would probably have supported a wooden architrave, as was usual in Britain (S. S. Frere, *in litt*).

4. Vertical recesses for drains leading from roof-gutters can occasionally be observed in Roman buildings, for example the two *basilicae* of the Baths of Caracalla at Rome (Brodner, 1951, 28–32). Down-drains leading from the 'umbrella' vault of the so-called 'Tempio di Venere' at Baiae were embedded in its external corner-pilasters (Blake, 1973, 269).

3. DISCUSSION

A. THE PLAN OF THE *BASILICA* AND *FORUM* (Fig. 22):

The present excavations have established the south-east and north-east limits of the *basilica* and *forum*. The north-west side is marked by a street, the position of which was revealed by the providential collapse of a cellar-wall at Broadgate in 1975; accordingly the width of the *basilica* and *forum* can be estimated at about 67 m.

Work carried out in 1945 and 1946 recovered an extensive gravelled area bounded on its north-eastern side by two parallel walls, some 64 m to the south-west of the present excavations (Fox, 1952, 37f.). These features were first interpreted by their excavator as the north-eastern part of the *forum*, but more recently have been associated by J. S. Wacher with the public baths, which are known to lie immediately to the south-east (Wacher, 1974, 328). However an examination of the street-plan in the vicinity, which has been pieced together over the last twenty-five years, shows that the two parallel walls are more likely to have formed part of a narrow portico in front of the south-western range of the *forum* with an unenclosed metalled area beyond.

It appears that north-west and south-east of the *forum* there were four *insulae* similar in size to one another and partly defined by streets which continued in use following the dismantlement of the legionary fortress, and partly by streets newly laid out at the end of the first century. The dimensions of the *insulae* to the south-east are fairly well established. The street bounding their north-west sides, which dates to the fortress period, has been investigated over a length of 42 m adjoining the north-east *insula* and was traced in 1945 and 1946 next to the south-western *insula* (Fox, 1952, 43). The street running from north-west to south-east between the two *insulae* was excavated in 1953, and is now thought to have originally represented the fortress *via principalis* (see p. 9).

A gravel spread excavated at Bear Street in 1953 indicated the position of the south-eastern road (Fox, 1953, 30–41); its line was confirmed by what appears to have been a later extension traced near Chapel Street (Greenfield, 1954, 339). The fourth side of the north-eastern *insula* was bounded by a street which was partly sectioned in 1976 (see p. 118). The date of these two streets is uncertain but there is no evidence to suggest that they were laid out subsequently to the late first century A.D. The north-eastern *insula* can be shown to have sides which measured about 65 m. The dimensions of the south-western *insula* are less certain, although it can probably be safely assumed that it measured the same from north-west to south-east as its neighbour. Its width can be estimated approximately by postulating the existence of a street leading to the later south gate on the usual Roman alignment, which produces a figure close to 70 m[1].

On the north-west side of the *forum*, the south-west *insula* appeared to measure *c*. 65 m square. Its south-west side was presumably bounded by the street leading to the later south gate, and its other three sides by streets which continued in use from the fortress period. It seems reasonable to restore a fourth *insula* of a similar size immediately to the north-east.

It cannot be established beyond doubt that the remains excavated in 1945–6 and 1971–7 belong to the same building but such evidence as there is points to this conclusion. The street which ran

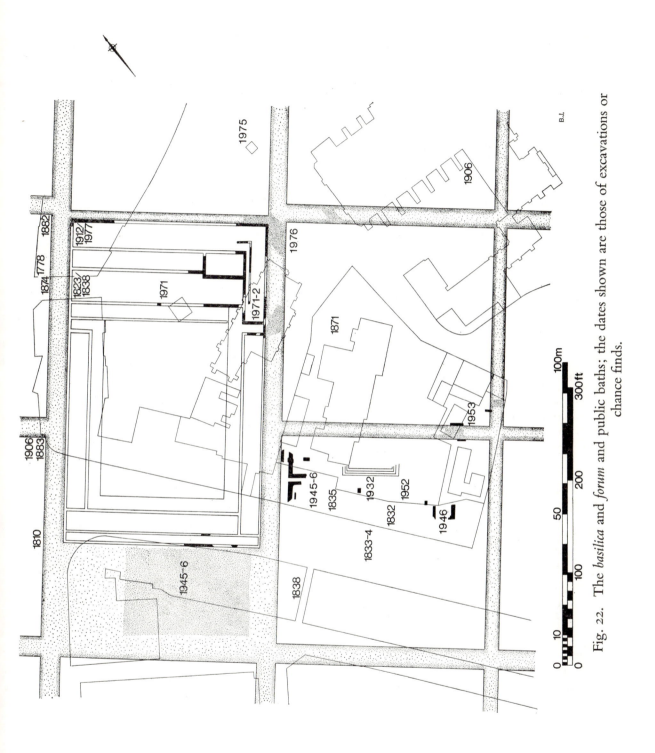

Fig. 22. The *basilica* and *forum* and public baths; the dates shown are those of excavations or chance finds.

from north-west to south-east between the two pairs of *insulae* could scarcely have formed the south-western limit of the *forum*. On the other hand it is possible that the *forum* ended against a street which ran along the north-east side of the portico found in 1945–6, the *basilica* and *forum* thus occupying the equivalent of one and a half *insulae*; if so, the portico would have belonged to another building of quite considerable extent, which unless it overlapped the *insula* adjacent to the south-west, would have occupied a rather narrow plot. This alternative hardly recommends itself.

The most convenient resolution of the problem seems, in the absence of contrary evidence, to regard the remains as part of one building. The *basilica* and *forum* would then occupy an area measuring 106.5 by 67 m with an open metalled area 67 m by 32 m in front of its south-western range. Ranges with the same width as that partly excavated to the south-east have been restored on the north-west and south-west sides of the *forum*; the area which they enclose measures 62 m by 50 m.

NOTES

1. A short length of this road was traced under the south-western tower of the South Gate (Fox, 1968).

Town	Overall dimensions (m)	Area (sq.m)	Overall width of nave and aisles (m)	Width of nave (m)	Length of nave (m)
London	169.16 × 166.1	28,097	—	—	—
Verulamium	161 × 117	18,837	36.5 ?	*c.* 18.2 ?	117
Cirencester	168 × 104	17,472	24.4	10.4	84
Leicester	132 × 90.8	11,990	18.3	6.4	52
Wroxeter	120.4 × 80.7	9,716.2	23.5	11.5	75.4
Silchester	95.5 × 84.5	8,069.7	17.5	12.0	71.25
Exeter	106.5 × 67	7,135.5	10.4	10.4	60 ?
Gloucester	97.5 × 68.6	6,688.5	—	—	—
Caerwent	79.8 × 55.5	4,428.9	18.9	7.8	38.4
Caistor	65.2 × 55.8	3,638.2	15.8	9.1	55.8

Table 6: comparison of Romano-British *fora* dimensions

B. THE MARKET-PLACE (Fig. 22):

The excavations of 1945–6 near South Street traced a metalled area which was bounded on its north-east side by two walls with foundations about 90 cm wide, spaced 2.4 m apart (Fox, 1952, 37 f.). It has been shown that these features were most probably associated with the *basilica* and *forum* (p. 78) and that the two parallel foundations could have belonged to an external portico in front of the south-western range. The metalled surface was traced by means of narrow trenches to within 3 m of the street bounding it to the south-east and 1.5 m of the presumed position of the street on its north-west side; it is clear that the portico on the north-east side did not continue around the rest of the metalled area, although the latter may have been enclosed by a wall on these other three sides. The metalled surface may have measured as much as 67 m by 32 m (2144 sq.m.) which can be compared with the estimated area of the *forum* (62 m by 50 m, i.e. 3100 sq.m). Its surface was at a level only a metre below that of the *forum* at its north-east end (about 37 m O.D.; level of *forum* just over 38 m O.D., see 17: 43).

Although the metalled area lay outside the *forum*, its function was probably still closely associated with the commercial life of the town. A number of *fora* in Britain adjoin metalled areas; these can be reasonably assumed to have provided additional market-places for traders, perhaps especially for those dealing in livestock, where it might be thought desirable to exclude the more noisesome aspects of the trade from the *forum*. At Silchester the *forum* was surrounded by a number of gravelled areas, which, except for the foundations of large timber buildings of early date, were unemcumbered by structures until a church was erected in the late Roman period. G. C. Boon has suggested that cattle markets may have been held here, and that the external *forum* porticos sheltered dealers transacting business (Boon, 1974, 111 and 175). At Leicester a gravelled area with a width of about 25 m occupied the same position relative to the *forum* as at Exeter; the street along the west side of the *forum* appeared to have been about 20 m wide and could have accommodated an additional street-market (Hebditch and Mellor, 1973, Fig. 2). On the eastern corner of Insula II at Cirencester, adjacent to the *forum*, there was a metalled area formed by an extension of the gravelled surface of the street which passed along its south-east side (Wacher, 1961, 1 f.). The area may well have functioned as a market-place from *c.* 70 until the second quarter of the second century, when a market-building was erected on the site, unless, as the excavator has suggested, the foundations of the stone building had removed all traces of a wooden structure of more or less identical plan. Behind the *basilica* at Wroxeter there was apparently an open area of considerably greater extent than the *forum* courtyard (Webster, 1975, Fig. 21). Market-places adjacent to the *forum* seem to occur quite frequently. Indeed in Britain it is only at Caerwent and Verulamium that such features can certainly be shown to have been absent.

C. THE *BASILICA*:

The *basilica* originally consisted of an aisleless hall with a range of rooms along the north-eastern side; a south-western aisle or passage was added at a later date, perhaps during the final stages of construction. The range of rooms included at its south-east end what was almost certainly the *curia*, and the centre of the range may have been occupied by a shrine for the *tutela*. It is unlikely that the south-east end of the *basilica* was occupied by a tribunal, for this would have interfered with access to the room claimed as the *curia*; the site of a tribunal is probably to be sought at the north-west end of the building. The plan of the *basilica* must have been adapted to accommodate as much of the bath-house fabric as possible; this probably explains the awkward way in which the projecting *curia* diminishes the width of the *basilica* hall at its south-east end.

The absence of aisles in the Exeter *basilica* makes it unique amongst British examples, although parallels can be found elsewhere in the Empire. Aisleless *basilicae* associated with *fora* are known at Alésia in Gaul (Grenier, 1958, 179), at Delminium and at Doclea in Dalmatia (Wilkes, 1969, 368) and at Timgad in North Africa (Courtois, 1951, 29); the Augusto-Tiberian *basilica* at Velleia was also of this type (Ward-Perkins, 1970, 7–9).

D. COMPARISON WITH OTHER ROMANO–BRITISH *BASILICAE* AND *FORA*:

The plan widely thought to be most characteristic of Romano-British *basilicae* and *fora* is the '*principia*-type'. This term was first employed by D. Atkinson (1942, 345–62) when he explored the resemblances between legionary *principia* and some *basilicae* and *fora*, although he was not the first to notice certain similarities (*ibid.*, 252–3). Legionary *principia* generally consist of a hall with two aisles, and a range of rooms, including a centrally-placed shrine, at the rear. The hall or *basilica principiorum*, which is symmetrical about its short axis, usually faces a monumental entrance across a colonnaded courtyard which is lined on three sides with ranges of rooms behind the porticos (plans conveniently collected in von Petrikovits, 1975, Bild 14). The plan of the *principia* is considered to have reached its full development by *c.* 60 at the latest, in the stone *principia* at Vetera (Atkinson, 1942, 353; von Petrikovits, 1975, 68). Allowing for certain minor modifications its similarity to the plans of *basilicae* and *fora* such as Caerwent and Silchester is obvious enough. Atkinson argued that the plan was first developed in military architecture and that the plan of the *principia* was adapted to serve as a civil administrative centre in provinces where military influence was strong. This idea was contested by R. Goodchild (1946) and now that more is known about the *fora* of Republican Italy (Russell, 1968), it seems almost certain that the plans of legionary *principia* were derived from the 'urban architecture of provincial Italy' (Ward-Perkins, 1970, 7, but see Frere, 1971, 14, n. 16). Nevertheless, in Britain, where the involvement of military technicians in the construction of public buildings is in most cases very probable, it still seems likely that some *basilicae* and *fora*, for instance Caerwent and Silchester, were modelled on legionary *principia*. Other buildings were clearly of a different type:

(i) double *fora*: no double *fora* are yet known in Britain, although there may well have been examples at Lincoln, Colchester and other *coloniae* and *municipia* (Boon, 1974, 110). The building at Verulamium may be regarded as a proto-double-*forum* because it has two entries opposite each other on the sides flanking the *basilica*: the side opposite the *basilica* is occupied by three structures, the central one probably a temple[1]. The presence of double *fora* in other Romano-British towns is not to be anticipated, for, as G. C. Boon (1973a, 108, n. 13) has pointed out, 'in the *fora* of peregrine *civitates*, there was no need to instal a *capitolium*'.

(ii) *fora* with long-axis *basilicae:* at Cirencester the main emphasis in the plan of the *basilica* was on its long axis, with a large apse at one end and possibly an entrance from the street through a portico at the other (Wacher, 1974, 296–7). The *basilicae* at Wroxeter[2] and Leicester (Hebditch and Mellor, 1973, 1–42) were probably also of this type. The *basilica* of the '*principia*-type' is essentially a short-axis building.

(iii) other types: at Caistor (Frere, 1971, 1–20) the *basilica* had an asymmetrical plan with rooms such as the *curia* tacked onto the sides in a rather haphazard manner; a continuous range of rooms at the rear was absent. It is possible that the *basilica* at Exeter had an equally untidy plan, especially since it incorporated parts of an earlier building[3].

There remain only two Romano-British *basilicae* and *fora* which conform to the '*principia*-type' as defined by Atkinson: Caerwent and Silchester.

We may conclude that the aisleless and probably asymmetrical *basilica* at Exeter represents just another example of the diverse features to be found amongst Romano-British *basilicae* and *fora*, which display as wide a range of plans as examples elsewhere in the Western Provinces.

NOTES

1. *VCH, Herts.*, iv, 32; S. S. Frere, *in litt.*

2. For the *basilica* see Atkinson, 1942, 94–9. The existence of an entrance at the north end of the *basilica* opposite the tribunal has been suggested by G. Webster (1974, Fig. 21).

3. Thus in the reconstruction of its plan (Fig. 23) considerations of symmetry have been disregarded so as to give the *basilica* the maximum possible length.

E. RECONSTRUCTION OF THE *BASILICA* (Fig. 23):

The main problem associated with the reconstruction concerns the treatment of the south-west front of the *basilica*. The two lengths of its central portion which have been investigated consisted of shallow foundations, in front of which were robbing trenches almost certainly dug to remove steps similar to those preserved at the end of the south-east *forum* portico. The existence of entries spaced at fairly frequent intervals is suggested by the absence of a continuous foundation, the weight of the walls above presumably being carried by deeply-founded piers between the entries.

The *basilicae* at Caerwent (Ashby, Hudd and King, 1909, 569–82) and Silchester (Boon, 1974, 114–5) also appear to have been 'open-fronted'. Boon, in an imaginative reconstruction (Boon, 1974, 114 and Fig. 14), introduced a colonnade which carried a wall roughly equivalent to its own height; this arrangement is scarcely possible at Exeter because the columns would have had to support a wall carrying the roof of the *basilica* rather than merely the wall of the side-aisle, as at Silchester. More powerful support would have been provided by the piers of an arcade. It is reasonable to imagine that the individual arches would have had moulded imposts, and that,

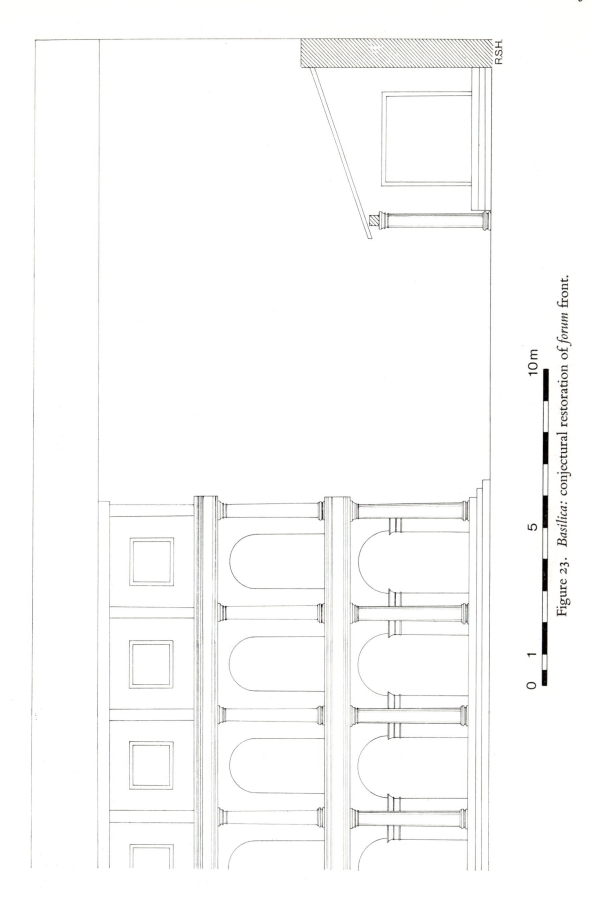

R.S.H.

0   1   5   10m

Figure 23. *Basilica:* conjectural restoration of *forum* front.

above the arcade, windows would have illuminated the interior of the *basilica*[1]. Apart from this the elevation may have been quite without interest. A reconstruction should attempt no more than the most economical interpretation of the surviving evidence in the light of contemporary architectural practice. However, it seems justifiable to wonder if the blank, drab and unpleasing facade described above would have dominated the *forum*. From other *civitas* capitals there is abundant evidence demonstrating the care taken to create impressive interiors (e.g. the provincial Corinthian order was used for the nave-colonnades at Silchester (Boon, 1974, pl. 17). Cirencester (Wacher, 1974, Fig. 57) and Caerwent (Ashby, Hudd and King, 1909, 573, Fig. 1). It follows that equal care would have been taken to create imposing exteriors. Amongst the monumental buildings of Rome, arcading was often framed by engaged Tuscan columns supporting an entablature; although these features occur most characteristically on the exteriors of theatres and amphitheatres, for example the Theatre of Marcellus (Anderson, Spiers and Ashby, 1927, Pl. XXIX) and the Colosseum (Plommer, 1956, Fig. 105), they can also be seen on the front of *basilicae* such as the *Tabularium* (Ward-Perkins, 1970, pl. 72), and on other buildings such as the porticos of the *Forum Holitorium* (Boethius and Ward-Perkins, 1970, Pl. 75). A provincial example occurs at Doclea in Dalmatia, (Wilkes, 1969, 371 and Fig. 18), where five entrances along the *forum* front of the aisleless *basilica* were placed in alternate bays separated by free-standing columns whose positions corresponded with internal buttresses. In a reconstruction of this *basilica* Iveković shows a facade with free-standing columns at ground-level and engaged pilasters in an upper tier (reproduced in Schultze, 1928, 49, Abb. 34). In Britain the *basilica* of the baths at Caerwent was embellished with a series of nine engaged columns along its front (Nash-Williams, 1953, 164).

Fig. 22 shows an attempt to reconstruct the south-western elevation of the *basilica* at Exeter along these lines[2]. A notional height of 12.5 m to roof-level has been assumed; there is evidence that many *basilicae* were rather higher than this, but the shallowness of the foundations at Exeter suggests a comparatively modest height for the walls which they supported. The facade consists of two tiers of arcading surmounted by a third tier pierced by windows. The lower arcade is framed by engaged columns, and the upper, which is blind, by pilasters; the third tier is divided vertically by flat unornamented strips between the windows, a device which can be seen on the Colosseum. The arcading was probably confined to the central portion of the facade because of the presence of a tribunal at the north-west end of the *basilica*. The rooms behind the *basilica* were probably roofed at a lower level, allowing space for a clerestory above to light the nave. This certainly seems to have been the case in Period 3A where the north-eastern foundations of the *curia* extension were much shallower than those of the nave extension.

NOTES

1. S. S. Frere (*in litt.*) has suggested that instead of arches there may have been rectangular openings with lintels constructed from blocks with joggled joints, and with relieving arches above, as in the north wall of the Hall at Bath (Cunliffe, 1969, 103, Fig. 35).
2. It must be stressed that there is no architectural material from the site to support the reconstruction proposed here.

F. THE CURIA:

The room at the eastern corner of the *basilica* measured 13 m by 7.6 m, and, because of its greater width, projected into the nave beyond the room adjoining it to the north-west. It was entered from the nave by means of a door at the south-east end of its south-west wall, and had a substantial concrete floor. At Silchester, Wroxeter and Caerwent (Frere, 1967, 258 and Boon, 1974, 111 and 175; Atkinson, 1942, 99–104; Ashby, 1906, 128–30 and Ashby, Hudd and King, 1909, 570–5), rooms of roughly equivalent size at the end of the ranges behind the *basilica* naves have been identified as *curiae*. However this identification depends upon their being the largest rooms present in the wholly excavated *basilica* and *forum*. These grounds cannot be used to establish the role of the room at Exeter, for most of the *basilica* remains unexcavated, and other positions for the *curia* are possible, for instance at one end of the nave as at Caistor (Frere, 1971, 15), or in the *forum* ranges as at Cambodunum (Kleiss, 1962, 71) or perhaps Verulamium (*VCH*, Herts, iv, 132).

However there are other features apart from size which help to identify a *curia*. In North Africa and Italy, well-preserved buildings show that the model for the *curia* was the plan best seen in the *Curia Iulia* (Lugli, 1946, 131–8). In its present state the *Curia Iulia* represents a restoration by Diocletian dedicated in 303; it consisted of three elements, the *Secretarium Senatus* housing the senatorial archives, the *Atrium Minervae*, and the *Curia* itself. The *Curia*, which is thought to reflect accurately the plan of its predecessor, consisted of a hall measuring 27 m by 18 m; it was entered by a door at the centre of one end, and the interior revealed three steps a metre wide and a few centimetres high on either side of the hall, which accommodated seats or benches for the senators. At the rear of the hall there was a *podium* for the presiding senator, an altar and a statue of Victory. The *curia* at Pompeii (Mau-Kelsey, 1899, 121–3) and those in North Africa at Lepcis Magna, Sabratha and Timgad (Bandinelli, Caffarelli and Caputo, 1966, 87; Ward-Perkins, 1970, 467; Courtois, 1951, 29) display similar arrangements. Whether or not they were actually modelled on the *Curia* of the Roman Senate is far from clear, for the building-type which they represent has a history extending back to Hellenistic times, as can be seen from the *bouleuterion* at Glanum (Grenier, 1958, 481–3) and the *ekklesiastron* at Priene (Lawrence, 1957, Fig. 161).

In the north-western Provinces, only the *curia* at Augst preserves its original fittings; the building, which lay behind the *basilica*, on its shorter central axis, comprised in plan about three-quarters of a circle 16 m in diameter, with five steps 2 m wide and 30 cm high running around its interior circuit (Laur-Belart, 1966, 40). The room was entered from the *basilica* by two doors on either side of a *podium* which measured 3 m by 1.7 m. R. Laur-Belart has shown that the room provided enough space to seat 98 people, with two presiding magistrates seated on the *podium*. Although the earlier *curia* at Cambodunum and the Caistor *curia* were square in plan, the majority of the known examples in the north-western Provinces were rectangular, the proportion of their width to length approximating more or less closely to 1 : 1.5. It seems reasonable to infer that their interiors were arranged in the same way as the African and Italian examples. This may explain

Table 7: comparison of *curia* dimensions

	Dimensions	Proportion of length to breadth	Area sq.m.
Curia Iulia	27 m × 18 m	1 : 1.5	486.0
Pompeii	15 m × 10 m	1 : 1.5	150.0
Timgad (Courtois, 1951, 29 and 33)	15 m × 8 m	1 : 1.88	120.0
Leptis Magna	15.5 m × 11.75 m	1 : 1.32	183.0
Glanum (Bouleuterion)	12.5 m × 7.5 m	1 : 1.65	94.0
Augusta Raurica	16 m dia.	—	201.0
Cambodunum I	16.8 m sq.	1 : 1	289.0
Cambodunum II	20.9 m × 13.5 m	1 : 1.5	283.5
Verulamium	18.1 m × 12.2 m	1 : 1.48	219.6
Wroxeter	14.3 m × 9.14 m	1 : 1.5	128.7
Alesia	13 m × 10 m	1 : 1.3	130.0
Caerwent	13.5 m × 10 m	1 : 1.35	135.0
Caistor	9.7 m sq.	1 : 1	96.0
Exeter	13 m × 7.6 m	1 : 1.75	92.0
Silchester[1]	19 m × 9 m	1 : 2.1	171.0
Leicester	18.29 m × 11.28 m	1 : 1.62	206.4

NOTE

1. The Silchester *curia* is by far the longest in proportion to its width; could the nineteenth-century excavators have missed a robbed cross-wall? If the length of the room had been about 13.5 m giving a proportion of breadth to length of 1 : 1.5 it would have had roughly the same floor areas as the *curiae* at Wroxeter and Caerwent.

why at Caerwent a mosaic had been set into the centre of a concrete floor; the space *c.* 2 m wide on either side of the mosaic was probably covered by wooden staging or rows of wooden benches to accommodate the decurions (Ashby, 1906, 128; cf. Wacher, 1974, 378). It also suggests that the entrance would be placed at one end of the room, for a centrally-placed entrance would interfere with the seating arrangements.

The position and size of the room at the eastern corner of the *basilica* at Exeter, together with the siting of its door near the end of the room rather than the centre, are grounds for its identification as the *curia*.

G. DATING EVIDENCE FOR PERIOD 2A (CONSTRUCTION):

1. Layer of ash (18: 65) over floor of furnace-house:

   Samian: Dr. 27, Nero-Vespasian.

   Coins: no. 21, Vespasian, *dup.*, RIC 473 (71); no. 1, *denar.*, S. 745 (79 B.C.).

   Context disturbed: coin, no. 18, Nero, *as*, RIC 329 (64–8).

2. From the furnace-ash employed as levelling material:

   Samian: no. 4, Dr. 37, *c.* 75–90 (1: 9EB1); no. 10, Dr. 37, *c.* 70–90 (13: 1409B–D); no. 7, Dr. 29, *c.* 75–90 (13: 1409B–D); Dr. 29, *c.* 70–85 (13: 1409B–D); Dr. 27g (stamp no. 5), probably Flavian (13: 1409B–D); Dr. 27 (at least two examples), Nero-Vespasian (13: 1409B–D and 1: 9EB1); Dr. 27 (Lezoux), Nero-Vespasian? (14: 1143); two examples of Dr. 18 (stamps nos. 10 and 14), *c.* 60–75 and 65–90 (13: 1409B–D and 1: 9EB1); Dr. 18 (at least six examples), Nero-Vespasian (13: 1409B–D; 3: F.77 (filling), Ritt. 12 or Curle 11, probably Nero-Vespasian (14: 1147); Dr. 29, pre-Flavian (1: 9EB1); Dr. 27, pre-Flavian (13: 1409B–D); Dr. 18, pre-Flavian (13: 1409B–D); Dr. 15/17, pre-Flavian (13: 1409B–D).

   Coins: no. 17, Nero, *sest.*, RIC 207 (64–8) (13: 1412); no. 20, Nero, *semis*, RIC 388 (64–8) (13: 1409B–D).

3. From deposits above furnace-ash levelling material:

   Samian: Dr. 27, Nero-Vespasian (13: 1409A); no. 5, Dr. 29, *c.* 60–75 (14: 1138); Dr. 29, pre-Flavian (14: 1138).

   Coins: no. 27, Vespasian, *as*, RIC 746 Lyons, *cos.* IIII (72–3) (18: 60); no. 18, Nero, *as*, RIC 329 (64–8) (14: 1138); no. 12, Claudius, copy as RIC 66 (43–54) (from foundations of passage-wall along south-east side of *basilica*); no. 3, M. Agrippa, *as*, RIC (*Tib.*) 32 (37–43) (12: 1138).

4. Levelling deposits under nave and north-east rooms in *basilica*:

   Samian: Dr. 30, possibly Flavian (22: 2126); two examples of Dr. 29, *c.* 60–75 (22: 2126); no. 6, Dr. 29 (stamp no. 9), *c.* 55–65 (22: 2126); Dr. 27, pre-Flavian (16: 1514).

   Coins: no. 26, Vespasian, *dup.* RIC 740 (72–3) (16: 1520); no. 22, Vespasian, *dup.*, RIC 475 (71) (n.i.: 1528, loam fill of north-eastern apse).

5. Clay and loam deposited throughout courtyard to south-east and north-east of *basilica*:

   Samian: Dr. 30, *c.* 70–85 (14: 1137); no. 8, Dr. 29, *c.* 70–85 (14: 1137); Dr. 27 (stamp no. 6), *c.* 65–90 (14: 1137), Dr. 27, Flavian (14: 1137); two examples of Dr. 18, Nero-Vespasian (14: 1137); no. 9, Dr. 29, probably pre-Flavian (14: 1137); two examples of Dr. 18, pre-Flavian (1: 10ED and 14: 1137); Dr. 24/25, pre-Flavian (12: 1135); Ritt. 8, pre-Flavian (12: 1135).

   Coins: no. 2, M. Antony, *denar.*, Leg. VI, S. 1223 (32–1 B.C.) (1: 10EC); no. 8, Claudius, copy as RIC 66 (41–54) (1: 10EC).

Assessment of the dating evidence:

The dating evidence for the construction-work at the beginning of Period 2A falls into five well-defined stratigraphical groups:

    (i)   finds from a layer of ash which had accumulated over the floor of the south-western *caldarium* furnace-house.

   (ii)   finds from the dump of furnace-ash which was used as levelling material. This contained much pottery and animal bones, little of which showed signs of burning; it therefore seems likely that domestic rubbish from nearby buildings was thrown on the piles of ash.

  (iii)   finds from construction-deposits above the dumps of furnace-ash.

The first two groups contain material which could have accumulated on the site over a relatively short period before the baths were taken out of service; presumably the ash-dumps would have been carted away at fairly frequent intervals and the floor of the furnace-house swept from time to time. All three deposits are likely to contain little residual material and thus can be taken to give a reliable date for the commencement of Period 2A. A well-circulated coin of Vespasian dating to 72–3, and samian produced subsequent to *c.* 75 suggest a terminal date in the late seventies or early eighties.

  (iv)   finds from levelling deposits below the *basilica* and the range behind it. Although these deposits contained lenses of construction-material, for the most part they consisted of clay, etc. brought onto the site from elsewhere.

   (v)   finds from the clay and loam deposited throughout the courtyard to the south-east and north-east of the *basilica*. This deposit also consisted of material brought onto the site from elsewhere.

These last two groups were likely to have contained more residual material than those which accumulated on the site; and this indeed appears to have been the case, although the levelling deposits below the *baslica* produced a well-circulated coin of Vespasian dating to 72–3.

The relevant dating evidence from the 1945–6 excavations at the south-west end of the *forum* is consistent with that discussed above. The latest find from the silting of the ditch which ran down the road between the two buildings was a Dr. 29, probably of early Flavian date (Fox, 1952, Fig. 9, no. 8.); from the floor of the 'principal room' of House 2 there came a characteristic pre-Flavian assemblage (Fox, 1952, 35); material of similar date came from the floor of the 'kitchen' together with a coin of Nero, 'minted in *c.* 66' (Fox, 1952, 36)[1]. From the gravel overlying these structures there came a Dr. 29, considered to date to *c.* 70–80, a coin of Vespasian of 71 and the rim of a Dr. 37, of which it was said "if the evidence of the Form 37 rim fragment be strictly interpreted (the date of the deposition of the gravel) might be brought down to *c.* A.D.100" (Fox, 1952, 40). The importance which can be attached to this sherd is diminished somewhat by the occurrence of intrusive material in the deposit: that is, a coin of Constans and two Constantinian types, as well as a sherd of "Gaulish painted ware", which is, in fact, almost certainly *à l'éponge* ware, dating to the third or fourth centuries (Raimbault, 1973, especially Fig. 1).

Setting aside the Dr. 37 from the gravel in South Street the latest material is associated with deposits of furnace-ash, and, strictly speaking, dates the latest period of use of the bath-house rather than the start of construction-work on the *forum* and *basilica*. However there is no evidence of a hiatus between the latest use of the bath-house and its demolition, so the material mixed with the furnace-ash effectively dates the commencement of demolition work to *c.* 80.

The historical context:

Frere (1967, 204) has expressed the historical significance of the construction of a *basilica* and *forum* in the following terms: 'The physical indication of a self-governing community was the possession of a *forum* with *basilica* . . . the date of the foundation of such *fora* will give us an indication of the date of the grant of local self-government'. Thus at Exeter it would seem that the grant of self-government was given *c.* 80, only a few years after the departure of the legion; it has already been suggested that a *praefectus civitatis* or some similar type of official may have controlled the area during the interregnum (see p. 65).

Elsewhere in Southern England various *civitates peregrinae* were being constituted at this time. At Cirencester the fort was evacuated in the late seventies and 'the constitution of the *civitas Dobunnorum* must have followed immediately' (Wacher, 1974, 294); presumably work on the *basilica* and *forum* was started at the same time. In the probable former territories of Cogidubnus, public buildings were being erected in the eighties. At Silchester the *basilica* and *forum* was partly built by *c.* 85 (Boon, 1974, 108), and at Winchester the equivalent building is dated to the 'end of the Flavian period or slightly later' (Wacher, 1974, 280). An inscription shows that the *basilica* and *forum* at Verulamium was dedicated in 79, perhaps in the presence of Agricola, although work on its construction probably started under Frontinus (Frere, 1967, 114, Fig. 9).

During the decade A.D. 80–90 the provincialisation of Southern Britain must have been largely completed as the construction of the *basilicae* and *fora* demonstrates; the majority of tribal territories, formerly client kingdoms or under direct military control, must have been constituted as *civitates peregrinae*. We are told that at the beginning of this period, in the winter of 79–80, Agricola 'with private encouragement and public aid pressed forward the construction of temples, *fora* and town-houses'[2]. The evidence for the start of work on the construction of the *forum* and *basilica* at Exeter would fit very well with the date of Agricola's exhortation.

NOTES

1. The actual date of the coin is *c.* 64–6 (according to N. Shiel who examined the coin in the Rougemont House Museum, Exeter).

2. Tacitus, *Agricola*, 21, 1: *hortari privatim, adiuvare publice, ut templa fora domos extruerent.* . . .

4. ACTIVITIES IN THE COURSE OF PERIOD 2A (*c.* 80–late Antonine)
(Figs. 19 and 24, Pl. IXB)

Nave of basilica, curia: no activities here could be attributed to Period 2A.

South-west aisle: a skim of mortar overlaid a layer of gravel and mortar, and represented a re-surfacing of the floor in the course of Period 2A (17: 533, 531; 19: 533, 531; 20: 533, 531). From this level a shallow foundation, represented by a robbing trench dug to remove it in Period 2C (construction), was inserted against the south-west wall of the *basilica* between the steps to the north-west and south-east (20: 527). It may have served as the base of a masonry bench.

Forum-*courtyard*: the *forum*-courtyard surface was very worn in places, and a marked depression was found running across the excavated area from west to east. It was deeper at the east end, where it had been packed with sandstone rocks (18: 47). No trace of an eaves-drip gully was found along the front of the south-west aisle; there may have been a gutter running along the eaves and emptying into the stylobate-gutter. A cross-shaped feature was cut through the mortar surface of the *forum*-courtyard in the western corner of the excavated area (Pl. 21). It was composed of four slots 1.05–1.25 m in length and 30–50 cm in width, but with a uniform depth of 15 cm and with U-shaped profiles. Its backfill of brown loam could be distinguished from the overlying level. The four arms presumably held beams to which cross-struts could have been attached, supporting an upright beam or pole. A similar, but slightly larger feature was found placed almost in the centre of the orchestra of the theatre at Verulamium, and it was said that 'the purpose of this upright, whether a maypole, gibbet or post to which baited beasts could be chained, can only be a matter of surmise' (Kenyon, 1935, 281 and Pls. 60, 2 and 68). None of these activities would be out of place in the *forum*. The only further comment that can be offered is that, at Exeter and Verulamium, the erection of the pole on bed-plates, rather than its insertion in a post-pit, may have been to allow for its removal when not in use.

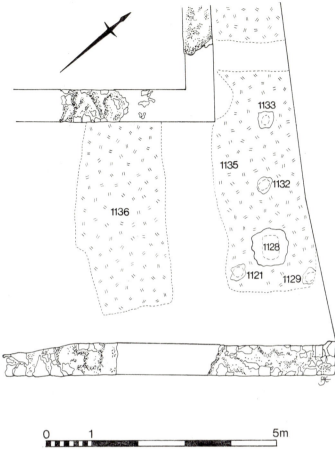

Fig. 24. Period 2A: fence across courtyard south-east of the *basilica*.

South-east forum *range:* in the portico no activities were recorded; contemporary levels were truncated in the room to the south-east. In the passage leading from the road a layer of mortar-debris and brown loam had accumulated over the original floor (3: 12B); this possibly represented material trampled in from the street to the south-east.

Courtyard, passage and portico to the south-east and north-east of the basilica: here only one set of features pre-dated Period 2B. A series of post-holes was found in a line at right-angles to the south-east boundary wall and about 1.0 m to the north-east of the junction of the portico and passage walls (1128, 1129, 1121, 1132 and 1133). Four of the post-holes were about 20 cm deep while the fifth, somewhat larger in diameter, was about 35 cm deep. They presumably formed a fence, dividing off the south-western part of the courtyard. No evidence of any activity within the passage and portico on the north-west and south-west sides of the courtyard survived.

Street: the earliest resurfacing of the street was of river gravel, well compacted and tending to even out the slight south-eastwards slope of the earlier street (8: 49B; 9: 49B). A layer of dirty brown loam mixed with food-bones, oyster-shells and pottery which had been dumped along the south-east side of this street-surface, probably represented rubbish thrown against the north-west wall of the road-side buildings (8: F.85; 9: F.85). A V-shaped trench was dug through the surface removing the north-eastern part of the wooden water-pipe. The trench stopped *c.* 1.0 m from the junction with the pipe leading from the south-east *forum* portico, which remained in use until the beginning of Period 2B. The extraction-trench was packed with trap-rocks and was sealed by a re-surfacing of the street, which was composed of river gravel mixed with some broken tile (8: 49A; 9: F.57 and 49A). A further re-surfacing which was confined to the south-west end of the street evened out the hump over the material dumped along the south-east side and was composed of river gravel, overlying a dump of gravel mixed with trap rocks (8: 29H1 and 29H2). The last resurfacing of Period 2A was underlaid by a deposit of loam, gravel, trap and tile fragments which gave the street a slight camber (8: 29G1 and 29G2; 9: 29G1 and 29G2).

The street was thus resurfaced four times during the course of Period 2A, that is, over the span of about a century; but only in one instance, when the water-pipe was removed, was this occasioned by the deterioration of the street-surface within the excavated area.

Dating evidence:

Basilica and *forum:*

Samian: none.

Coins: none.

Street:

Second re-surfacing:

Samian: no. 11, Dr. 37, *c.* 120–140 (8: 49A); Dr. 37, second century, cut as counter (8: 49A); Dr. 42, second century (8: 49A).

Third re-surfacing:

Coin: no. 34, Domitian, *as*, *RIC* 327 (86) (8: 29H2).

Fourth re-surfacing:

Samian: Dr. 27 (stamp no. 8) Trajanic or early Hadrianic, M. de V. (8: 29G2); Dr. 18R, first century (8: 29G2).

There was an almost complete absence of building activity within the *basilica* and *forum* throughout its first hundred years of life. The major alterations made at the beginning of Period 2B were connected with a re-planning of the building, and not, as far as can be determined, with the repair of a decaying fabric. The dating evidence for the second re-surfacing of the street (9: 49A) is not inconsistent with a date some thirty or forty years subsequent to the completion of the Period 2A building; the upper levels contained residual material.

V. ALTERATIONS TO THE *BASILICA* AND *FORUM* (SECOND TO FOURTH CENTURIES)

1. PERIOD 2B (CONSTRUCTION) TO PERIOD 2C: GENERAL DESCRIPTION

At the beginning of Period 2B (late Antonine) substantial alterations were made to the buildings on the south-east side of the *forum*-courtyard and the *basilica*. A room 5 m in width and at least 12.5 m in length was constructed on the site of the *forum* portico. The passage-way from the street was blocked. The courtyard on the south-east and north-east sides of the *basilica* was divided up into a series of rooms. Those on the south-east side may well have served as offices or store-rooms, while the rooms north-east of the *basilica* probably served as shops opening onto the path or lane which ran along their north-east side.

No major alterations were made during the course of Period 2B, although there was much evidence of 'domestic' occupation in the probable shops north-east of the *basilica*.

At the beginning of Period 2C (last quarter of the third century) the outer wall of the south-west aisle was rebuilt. A hypocaust was installed in the room adjoining the southern corner of the *basilica* and minor alterations were made to the ranges on the south-east and north-east sides of the *basilica*.

The remains described above were less well-preserved than earlier structures on the site and stratigraphical links between various parts of the site were often missing. It has been assumed that the various major alterations which were undertaken belonged to no more than two general programmes of reconstruction; the dating evidence, as far as it goes, confirms this.

2. PERIOD 2B (CONSTRUCTION)–LATE ANTONINE (Figs. 25, 26 and 27)

The first substantial reconstruction of the *basilica* and *forum* took place in the Antonine period. There was no stratigraphical link between the alterations carried out on the south-west and north-east sides of the site, but the dating evidence suggests that they were contemporary (see p. 96). No contemporary activities were recorded in the *basilica*. A wall (p. 93) was inserted across the south-east end of the aisle, forming a room which adjoined the *basilica* and extended across the site of the south-east *forum* portico; the north-west side of the foundation-trench was filled with a deposit of loam and gravel, which also extended up the length of the aisle, providing a new floor surface (17: 528, 19: 528; 20: 528). In places it overlaid a lens of charcoal (19: 530).

Forum-courtyard: the worn and patched surface of the *forum*-courtyard was levelled up with a dump of brown loam 20 cm thick (17: 36; 18: 36; 20: 36); the deposit contained Antonine pottery, and had rather an uneven surface, so it is likely to have represented preliminary levelling during construction work, rather than a re-surfacing of the *forum* at a slightly earlier date. A deposit of medium-grade gravel interleaved with lenses of building debris was found above (17: 35; 18: 35; 20: 35). On the south-west side of the excavated area, a square or rectangular pit 85 cm deep had been cut through one of the gravel layers (42; Fig. 27, Pl. VIIIB); it was placed slightly askew to the alignment of the surrounding buildings, and measured 2.6 m by at least 1.3 m. A slot 2–4 cm wide

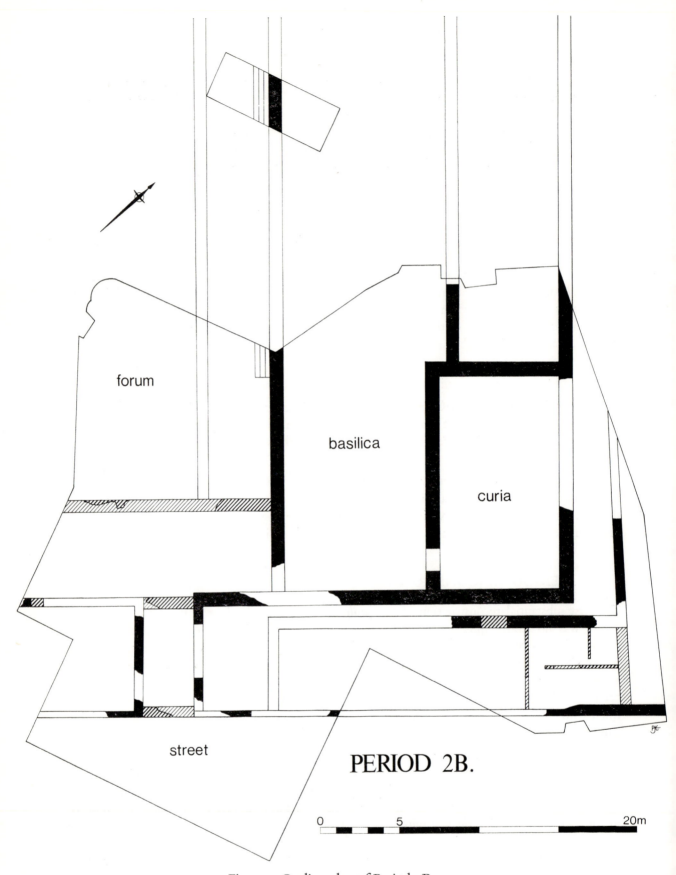

forum

basilica

curia

street

PERIOD 2B.

0   5   20m

Fig. 25. Outline plan of Period 2B.

and 5 cm deep ran around the sides of the pit to accommodate the bottom of a vertical lining of planks. Battens secured to corner posts, the triangular cross-sections of which were preserved by lime adhering to the sides of the pit, had probably held the planks in position. The bottom of the pit had also been lined with planks; lime percolating down between the joints had preserved their outline, showing that they had a uniform width of about 18 cm. The pit was used either for storing lime or perhaps for slaking it. In either case the plank lining must have been intended to prevent contamination; well-slaked, clean lime is essential for plaster-work where the paint is applied to a lime base over a mortar-rendered surface[1].

The foundation-trench for the wall which replaced the south-east *forum* portico was cut in from above the gravel layers (18: 33). It was sealed by a layer of mortar which provided the *forum* with a new surface (17: 26; 18: 26; 20: 26).

South-east forum *portico:* the floor of the portico was covered throughout its length by a layer of demolition-debris (7: 13C1; 11: 2007). The only evidence for the demolition of the colonnade was a small pit which probably was associated with the removal of the column-base against which the aisle wall is presumed to have abutted (Fig. 19, 2022). A wall 95 cm in width replaced the colonnade, and continued north-east across the south-west aisle to abut the *basilica* wall, showing that it was not a substructure for a replacement colonnade; on its south-east side it was cut in from immediately above the layer of demolition-debris (11: 2006). At the same time the north-west entrance of the passage leading to the street was blocked by a wall 75 cm in width; it was isolated from the surrounding deposits by later disturbance, but its construction-technique corresponded with that of the wall to the north-west. The threshold of the room south-west of the entry-passage was robbed and the doorway was blocked by a wall.

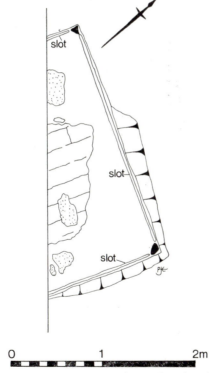

Fig. 27. Period 2B (construction): timber-lined pit in *forum*.

The construction-techniques of these three walls is in marked contrast with those of Periods 1A and 2A. The trap facing blocks were usually 10–15 cm square and were only roughly trimmed to shape; they were usually laid with joints less than 2 cm wide, employing a coarse yellow mortar with little binding power. The walls were faced for some distance below the level from which they were inserted, and, in order to facilitate this, wide, shallow foundation-trenches were excavated; below the level of the facing, the walls stood on rubble-filled trenches no wider than themselves.

These alterations formed a room 5 m wide and at least 12.5 m in length. Its floor consisted of a deposit of pure river gravel 40 cm thick, which concealed all but the uppermost surface of the top step (7: 13C, 23B; 11: 2002).

Rooms behind the south-east portico: no deposits of this period survived in the room south-west of the entry-passage. Removal of the stylobate-gutter rendered the stone drain obsolete, and after its covering and uppermost courses had been removed, the drain was filled with clay and mortar debris and a new mortar floor was laid down in the passage (3: 10D; 4: 10D). It seems likely that the blocking of the entrance from the street also took place at this time (Elev. 3); the step-foundations in front of it were cut through by a ditch, the fill of which contained second-century pottery (8: gully 5).

The area to the south-east and north-east of the basilica: in the room north-east of the entry-passage the clay floor of Period 2A was covered by a lens of silt which probably represented the breaking-down of the clay surface through the passage of feet (1: 10EB); a similar deposit overlay the courtyard-surface to the north-east, where it was mixed with lenses of charcoal, mortar debris and clay (12: 1125; 14: 1125). This deposit was sealed by dumps of clay mixed with demolition debris, which was presumably laid down immediately before construction work commenced (12: 1120 and 1113; 14: 1080, 1082 and 1120; 15: 1080). The most important change effected in this area was the construction of a range of rooms, 4.9 m wide, between the passage immediately to the south-east of the *basilica* and the boundary wall. The end wall of the range was represented by a robbing trench which extended the line of the rear portico south-eastwards; its origin as a wall of Period 2B construction was confirmed by a persisting difference in the deposits to each side above the Period 2B construction levels (14: Int. 16). The north-eastern part of the range was divided into two rooms whose limits were marked by the edge of a mortar floor which must originally have abutted a timber sill beam (14: 1055). The north-eastern room measured 4.9 m by 6 m; its mortar floor preserved a prominent ridge running down the centre, which stopped at a distance of 1.2 m from the south-west end of the room; this probably supported a timber sill-beam, the base of a partition which subdivided the room leaving an entry through to the south-west (1055B). At the rear of the north-western half of the room the mortar floor bore the impression of a timber 9 cm in width and 1.75 m in length (1079). It terminated with a small rectangular projection measuring 2.75 cm by 5 cm which was set back 3 cm from the north-eastern edge; the projection would appear to have preserved the outline of the base of a stop-frame for a door opening inwards to close the 60 cm gap between the beam and the central partition. This arrangement enclosed an area measuring 2.4 m by 1.4 m, more the dimensions of a large cupboard than of a separate room.

The adjacent room, which had a length of at least 4.45 m, was entered from the passage to the north-west by means of a door represented by a large sandstone threshold-block (15: 1085). Close to the timber wall of the north-east room the extraction-pit for a large post had been cut in from a higher level (14: 1024; see p. 101); the post may originally have been inserted at this period as a roof-support, and its position, half-way between the wall of the *basilica* and the boundary wall, shows that the passage-way and rooms to the north-east were roofed in common. Little can be said about the other room or rooms in the range; later disturbances had removed all traces of contemporary activity to the south-west. In the room north-east of the entry-passage the drain was partly robbed and back-filled with loam and occupation-material; charcoal, ash, and clay had been trodden over the floor (1: 10EA; 3: 10EA).

The passage along the south-east side of the *basilica* remained in use but its floor-level was raised by tips of demolition debris 45 cm thick (15: 1083, 1088); at one point a spread of mortar associated with the insertion of the threshold-block in the south-east wall overlay the demolition-debris (15: 1058).

The floor of the portico behind the *basilica* was raised with a deposit of brown loam containing food-bones and oyster-shells, mixed with many small fragments of roof-tile and showing a number of clear tip-lines (13: 1401, 1402, 1403, 1404, 1405). The final surface had been removed by burials but the decreasing depth of the upper tip-lines indicated that it was not much higher than the surviving level. This distinctive deposit was also seen in section at a point 16 m north-west of the east corner of the *basilica*, against its north-east wall. There was a clear contrast between the materials employed to level up the passage and the rear portico, and the finished level of the latter was at least 30 cm higher than the former. Either the passage was no longer accessible from the portico or steps had been inserted to compensate for the different levels; unfortunately the junction of the portico and passage had been destroyed at the beginning of Period 3A.

On the south-west side of the courtyard there was found a spread of mortar which was probably associated with the construction of the range of rooms to the south-east of the *basilica;* it did not extend as far as the section revealed on the north-east side (12: 1108 and 1112; 14: 1108). The courtyard was subsequently levelled with a number of easily distinguishable tip-lines of gravel, which also contained fragments of a brick-mortar floor and solidified trails of molten lead (12: 1074, 1103, 1104, 1105 and 1111, 1097, 1094; 14: 1074, 1103, 1104, 1105; 30: 309, 310).

The street: the fifth re-surfacing of the Period 2A street was the first to be bedded on a deposit of demolition-material (8: 29E1, 29E2, 29E3, 9: 29E1, 29E3); accordingly there is some reason to regard it as contemporary with the building work of Period 2B, although dating evidence is entirely lacking. If the entrance leading to the south-east portico was blocked at this time (see p. 94), then the fragment of a ditch containing Antonine pottery which cut through the step-foundations may well have been associated with the re-surfacing of the street (8: gully 5).

NOTES

1. The evidence is discussed in Davey, 1961, 113–4.

Dating evidence:

1. *Forum*-courtyard:
   Samian: no. 15, Dr. 37, *c.* 140–160, C.G. (17: 36); ?form, (stamp no. 3), *c.* 115–145 (18: 33, foundation-trench of wall replacing colonnade of portico).
   Coins: no. 24, Vespasian, *as*, RIC 486 (71); no. 23, Vespasian, *dup.*, RIC 478 (71) (both from 17: 36).

2. South-western aisle: no datable finds.

3. Portico at rear of *basilica*:
   Samian: Dr. 36, Antonine, C.G. (13: 1404); Dr. 29 (stamp no. 13) *c.* 70–85 (13: 1405); Dr. 27 (stamp no. 1) *c.* 65–80 (13: 1405); Dr. 18/31 (stamp no. 15) *c.* 105–125 (13: 1402).

4. Courtyard on the south-east side of the *basilica*:
   Samian: Curle 21, late Antonine, ?C.G. (12: 1105); Dr. 33, late Antonine, ?C.G. (12: 1105); no. 16, Dr. 37, *c.* 100–120, M. de V.; Dr. 37, *c.* 70–85; Dr. 18, Flavian (all from 14: 1082).
   Coin: no. 13, Claudius, copy as RIC 69 (41–54) (14: 1082).

5. From silt over clay floor of Period 2A in room south-east of passage:
   Samian: no. 14, Dr. 29, *c.* 75–90) (1: 10EB); Dr. 33, first century (1: 10EB); Dr. 30 base, first century (1: 10EB).

6. From road-side ditch cutting step-foundations:
   Samian: Curle 23 (rosette stamp, no. 17), early Antonine (8: gly. 5).

Discussion:

The alterations taken to mark the commencement of Period 2B occurred in two stratigraphically isolated areas, covering first the south-west aisle of the *basilica, forum, forum* portico and the range of rooms to the south-east, and secondly the range south-east of the *basilica* and the area to the north-east. Groups of samian from both areas are closed by Antonine pieces, and it seems justifiable to assume the broad contemporaneity of all the alterations. Two of the pieces in Group 4 were late Antonine and provide a *terminus post quem* for the whole reconstruction.

The sequence of activity recovered from the *forum* suggests that alterations made to the south-east portico took place after work had been started elsewhere on the site; this is suggested by the fact that the lime-pit was sealed by a layer which was cut by the foundations of the wall replacing the portico colonnade. The function of the room to which this wall belonged is obscure; presumably it communicated with the *basilica* and could be entered from the *forum* portico beyond the excavated area. Even allowing for the poor quality of their construction the substantial width of the walls and the depth of their foundations indicate that the room which they enclosed may have been quite lofty, perhaps rising above the range behind the former portico.

The range of rooms occupying the previously vacant area south-east of the *basilica* communicated with the *forum* range and the rear portico by means of the narrow passage of Period 2A construction. It is possible that the relatively well-preserved room at the north-east end of the range was used for storage purposes; some care was taken with its fitting-out, providing a mortar floor, and dividing the room into two halves; the central partition may have supported racks or shelves and extra storage was provided by the cupboard at the northern corner. Little information about the rooms to the south-west was recovered; but since access to them was to be had by only a very narrow passage, perhaps they were also intended for storage.

3. ACTIVITIES IN THE COURSE OF PERIOD 2B (LATE ANTONINE–LAST QUARTER OF THE THIRD CENTURY) (Fig. 28)

Above the construction-levels of Period 2B it was not always possible to relate the activities in various parts of the excavated area to an overall chronology. Later disturbance caused chiefly by the digging of foundations for the Victorian church had divided the site into a number of unrelated sequences of stratigraphy.

Basilica: no activities at this period.

Forum-courtyard: a small oval pit 40 cm deep was found 80 cm distant from the north-west wall of the reconstructed south-east *forum* range; it was loosely packed with sandstone rocks and pink sand, perhaps the packing for a post, although no traces of a post-tube survived (31). Subsequently a gully had been dug parallel to and 2.8 m distant from the south-western aisle, running the whole excavated length of the *forum* and cutting across and removing the south-western side of the pit (17: 25). Although there was no apparent outlet for the gully at its south-east end, it must have functioned as a drain, since silt was found along its bottom. It was back-filled with brown loam mixed with blocks of sandstone and trap.

Some time after the filling of the gully the *forum*-courtyard was levelled with a dump of clean brown loam mixed with lenses of gravel, 20 cm thick overall (17: 22; 18: 22; 20: 22). The deposit had a compacted, uneven surface, but appeared to have functioned as a surface of some duration, since it was patched in two places with similar material (17: 21; 20: 21; n.i. 17).

Rooms behind the south-east portico: a mortar floor sealing a layer of mortar debris was found in the room which had formerly served as an entry-passage (3: 10C, 10B; 4: 10C, 10B).

Range south-east of the basilica: no activities could be attributed to this period.

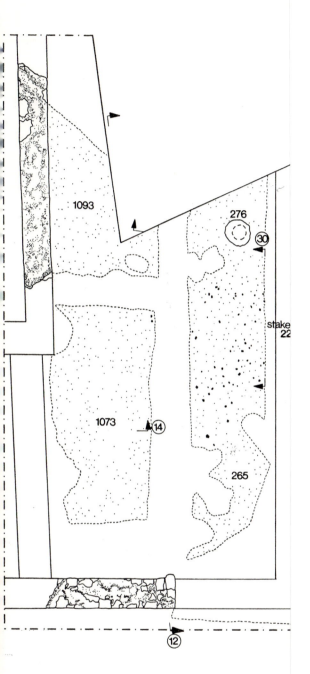

1093

276

30

1073

14

265

stake
22

12

Area to the north-east of the basilica: the original gravel surface of Period 2B date was overlaid in places by a thin lens of occupation material, on top of which a mortar floor 5–7.5 cm thick was found (12: 1093 and 1073; 14: 1073; 28: 265; 30: 265). At the north-west end of the excavated area a post-hole 23 cm deep was found cut through the floor (28: 276). Further south-east there was a group of 64 stake-holes, some square, some circular, confined to an area measuring 3.25 m by 2.5 m; they formed no readily discernible patterns and their purpose is not known. The stake-holes, which were up to 12.5 cm deep, were filled with material from the layer above—a deposit of occupation-material and loam, mixed with many burnt clay lumps and oyster-shells (28: 264; 30: 263). The next overall re-surfacing was composed of occupation material and loam, mixed with gravel in places (12: 1039 and 1092; 14: 1039; 28: 252; 30: 252). At the north-west end of the area a mortar floor was found (12: 1091; 28: 1091), its limits marked by unassociated features which were demonstrably later in date (14: Int. 21; 28: 206); these features must have removed a previous division forming a room measuring 2.3 m from north-east to south-west and at least 3.5 m from north-west to south-east. A fragmentary wall built on top of the north-west end of the stylobate must therefore represent a replacement of the portico, incidentally at its south-east end forming the south-west side of the room described above. The wall consisted of water-rolled sandstone blocks set in a coarse yellow mortar, and sat directly on top of the mortar rendering of the wall-top which may have formerly supported a colonnade (see p. 77).

The gravel and earth floor which extended over most of the area was covered at its south-east end by occupation-material mixed with trap chips (30: 251), sealed by a clay floor (Fig. 28, 225). Two successive hearth-pits filled with layers of ash and burnt clay were found by the south-east wall (242 and 243); they were sealed by a gravel surface again confined to the south-east end of the area (n.i.: 263). At the north-west end the gravel and earth floor was covered by a deposit of sandy clay mixed with demolition- and occupation-material (28: 244). The next overall surface, the last which can be attributed to Period 2B, was a compacted earth surface (28: 217; 12: 1038), above which were traces of a fire which appeared to have occasioned the alterations of Period 2C.

Street: three re-surfacings of the street can be attributed to the course of Period 2B. The lower two were made up predominantly of river gravel and were only investigated on the south-west side of the excavated area (8: 29D1, 29D2, 29C; 9: 29D1, 29C). The uppermost (Fig. 34) was exposed throughout the excavated area, and was also traced in the form of a path or narrow lane, 2.4 m wide, adjacent to the north-eastern boundary wall; the main street preserved a heavily-rutted surface and was drained by shallow gullies on each side (8: 29B; 9: 29B; 26: 212, n.w. gully 218; s.e. gully 219). A curious feature was the banking-up against the boundary wall of the silt which filled the shallow gully on the north-west side. The most likely explanation for this is that the silt was the product of mud, dung and domestic rubbish accumulating over the street-surface which had been periodically swept from the carriage-way and piled along its north-west side. The surface of the path or lane was partly excavated and found to consist of a layer of gravel 17.5 cm thick with a shallow gully on its south-western side (28: 221, (gully) 223). On its north-eastern side the street-surface overlaid a deposit of silty loam whose surface was at the same level as the street (28: 222); it may owe its origins, at least in part, to silt cleared from the previous street-surface. A further re-surfacing, which was found only along the course of the path or lane, considerably increased the camber (28: 215); it overlaid a deposit of silty loam along its north-eastern side (28: 224).

Mid or late second- to third-century ditch-deposits on the north-west side of the street:

About 5 m north-east of the steps which led up to the passage next to the south-east *forum* portico, there was found a pinnacle of strata which appeared to represent a series of successive ditch-fills. Unfortunately it was impossible to link the ditch-fills with the appropriate street-surfaces, since the latter had been removed in this area. The brown loam deposits contained pottery ranging in date from the mid to late second century to the third century (no later than *c*. 250, judging by the absence of obtuse-angled lattice on cooking-pots).

Dating evidence:

1. Re-surfacing of the *forum:* Dr. 37, Antonine, (C.G.) (17: 22).
    Coin: no. 36, Trajan, *den., RIC* 109a (103–111) (17: 22).

2. Former entry passage:
    Coin: no. 6, Claudius, copy as *RIC* 66 (41–54) (4: 10C).

3. Area north-east of the *basilica:* no closely datable material (but see below).

4. Occupation material above mortar floor in area to north-east of the *basilica:*
    Dr. 27, pre-Flavian (14: 1092); no. 17, Dr. 37, *c*. 75–95, S.G. (14: 1092).

The meagre evidence recovered does not allow for the dating of the various activities. However a sherd from a BB1 cooking pot with obtuse lattice from the highest floor level in the area behind the *basilica* (28: 217) shows that the sequence of activity runs down to *c*. 250 or later.

Discussion:

The main issue concerns the use to which the area behind the *basilica* was put. There is evidence to show that the area between the portico and the boundary-wall was roofed: remains of a large plank, burnt in the fire which preceded the alterations at the beginning of Period 2C, were found lying on the uppermost floor-surface; above were many fragments of burnt roofing tile (see p. 101). The nature of the activities recorded, with hearth-pits, stake-holes, layers of occupation-material and floors of earth and clay, is strongly 'domestic' in character; there are thus grounds for presuming the existence of 'shops' here, no doubt opening onto the path or lane on their north-east side and quite separate from the offices to the south-west. Whether or not the former portico now served as a passage leading to the rooms in the south-east range or was devoted to some other function is uncertain.

4. PERIOD 2C (CONSTRUCTION) (LAST QUARTER OF THE THIRD CENTURY)
(Figs. 29 and 30)

Extensive alterations affecting the *forum* and *basilica* can be attributed to an overall reconstruction which took place in the last quarter of the third century.

Basilica: in the room north-west of the *curia* the original Period 2A floor was covered by a layer of compacted yellow clay, 5 cm thick. The surface of the clay was capped by a layer of brick-mortar 5 cm thick, on top of which were found many loose dark grey and white *tesserae* (1805). The *tesserae* probably represented the remains of a wrecked tessellated or black and white mosaic floor. There was no associated dating evidence.

Forum-courtyard: the south-west wall of the aisle was replaced from directly above the last *forum* surface of Period 2B (17: 21, 22; 18: 22, 20; 21). The south-west side of its foundation-trench was filled by a deposit which also raised the level of the *forum* by 40 cm (17: 1; 18: 1; 20: 1); the dumped material consisted of tips of wall-plaster, mortar debris, trap and sandstone chips and the remains of a white tessellated pavement, all interleaved with lenses of loam and gravel. The surface of the dump, which was preserved in only one place (see p. 107), served as the new court-yard-level.

South-west aisle: before the south-west wall was demolished a feature, possibly a bench (see p. 88), was removed from the north-eastern side of the aisle (20: 527). The level of the aisle was then raised by up to 45 cm. A layer of broken tile which covered most of the area probably resulted

PERIOD 2C : FORUM.

0   1   5   10m

Fig. 29. Period 2C (construction): *forum*.

from the removal of the roof (17: 525); a deposit of wall-plaster and fragments of cornice-mouldings came from the stripping of the walls (17: 522; 19: 522; 20: 522), described on pp. 157–9. These demolition-deposits were capped by three distinct dumps of loam and gravel mixed with mortar debris (17: 515, 514; 19: 517, 515, 514; 20: 517, 515, 514). Reconstruction of the south-western wall took place from above this level. All traces of the earlier wall were removed by the new foundations which were laid in a trench 1.2 m in width and 1.3 m deep, packed with large trap and sandstone rocks (17: 524; 20: 524); the uppermost layer of rubble was mortared in order to support a wall 75 cm wide, which consisted of a single course of trap blocks, on top of which had been set a course of tile fragments, their finished faces carefully placed along the edges of the wall. It is possible that the tiles were inserted to provide a level base for a line of stone blocks which were intended to serve as the stylobate of a colonnade; at a later date (see p. 107), another wall of quite different construction was built on top of the tile course. The new floor-level in the aisle consisted of a layer of loam and fine gravel (20: 507).

South-east forum *range:* the north-west wall of the large room at right angles to the *basilica* nave was reconstructed: the base of the wall was retained as a foundation, but was increased to a width of 1.7 m by the addition of trenches packed with trap rocks and chips on each side (11: 2001; 18: 23; 19: 519). There was no context for the reconstruction within the sequence of stratigraphy, but it must have been earlier than the south-eastwards extension of the south-west aisle at the beginning of Period 3A (see p. 107). A layer of demolition-debris covering the original floor of the room was presumably associated with this work (7: 22D, 23A; 11: 23A); a mortar floor was found overlying it (7: 22C; 11: 22C). The small room at the eastern corner of the range was now associated functionally with its neighbour to the north-east and is described below.

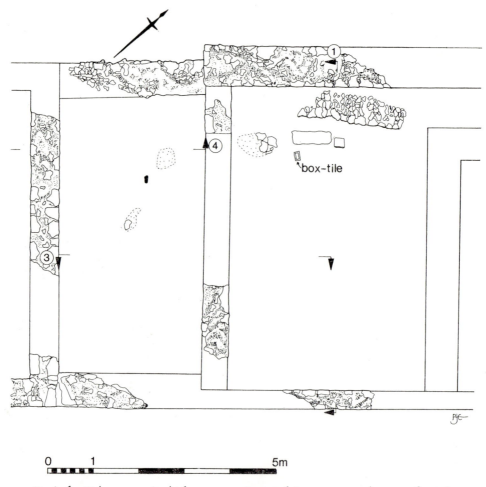

box-tile

0   1   5m

Fig. 30.   Period 2C (construction): hypocaust inserted in room south-east of south-west aisle.

Range south-east of the basilica (Fig. 30): in the room at the south-western end of the range a layer of mortar debris was found against the north-west wall; whether this represented earlier activity or demolition-debris associated with the present work is uncertain (1: 25A). It was cut through by a wall faced only on its south-east side and built of roughly-trimmed trap blocks set in red sandy mortar. Its south-east side was abutted by a thin mortar floor directly overlying the Period 2B construction-levels (1: 21A); later deposits may have been removed here. On top of the mortar floor a very large trap block was found placed 30 cm distant from, and with its long side parallel to, the wall on the north-west side; a tile-stack bonded with red sandy mortar continued its line north-eastward, and a box-tile was found standing amongst the destruction-debris on its south-west side. Further to the south-west patches of red sandy mortar and trap rocks were found. These fragmentary remains appear to represent a hypocaust consisting of a central chamber with the *suspensura* supported by tile-stacks and by whatever material came to hand, and a solid foundation around the walls, presumably pierced at intervals by channels leading to evacuation-flues and the furnace-mouth. In the room to the south-west, two patches of red sandy mortar and clay survived above the earlier levels (4: 10A); this may indicate that alterations had also been made here and that the room may have been used to serve the furnace, or even have been equipped with a hypocaust which formed an extension of that to the north-east.

The hypocaust-floor was at a lower level than the uppermost surviving course of the Period 3A foundations which cut across the south-west side of the room (1: 21A, cf. 3: F.91); the insertion of the hypocaust should therefore pre-date the construction-work of Period 3A. The red sandy mortar found in the smaller room to the south-west overlies floor-levels subsequent to the construction work of Period 2B. There are thus good grounds for placing the hypocaust within the Period 2C sequence of construction. Finds from the demolition-debris filling the hypocaust showed that the walls and possibly the ceiling of the room above were decorated with painted plaster (see p. 161) and that the roof was slate-covered.

At the north-east end of the range the wooden partitions were removed, and the floors were covered by a continuous dump of clay mixed with mortar debris (14:1032 and 1077; 15: 1032); above this level there was a mortar floor (14: 1025). The roof-post, which it has been suggested (see p. 94) was inserted at the beginning of Period 2B, was removed at a later date (14: 1024). In the passage to the north-west, there was a dump of demolition-debris, capped by a mortar floor (15: 1047,n.i. 1013, 1012). The large quantity of broken tiles found covering the adjacent street suggested that the rooms had been re-roofed; the slate roof, the presence of which was indicated by later demolition-debris in the hypocaust, presumably extended the whole length of the range.

Rooms north-east of the basilica (Fig. 28): contemporary deposits were only preserved within the 'shop'. Here the latest Period 2B floor-level was covered by a layer of charcoal along the north-east side, confined to a strip about 90 cm wide (28: 216); at one point the carbonised remains of a plank measuring 50 cm by 90 cm were found, and elsewhere the charcoal preserved the form of timbers up to about 20 cm in length. The charcoal had presumably been removed from the higher level to the south-west before a layer of burnt roof-tile fragments was spread over the area (28: 204); this deposit did not represent a collapsed roof lying *in situ*, for the tile-fragments were all of a small size, and must have been sorted through to extract re-usable material. A dump of loam mixed with charcoal and slate fragments provided a new floor (28: 202).

Streets: the last re-surfacing of Period 2B (26: 212) was covered by a layer of broken roof-tiles, wall-plaster (see p. 149) and mortar debris; charcoal was scattered through the deposit, and a few of the roof-tiles were burnt (8: 29A2; 9: 29A2; 26: 208). The tiles and wall-plaster had probably been cleared from the rooms immediately to the north-west. A thin layer of compacted trap chips and gravel provided a new surface (8: 29A1; 9: 29A1; 26: 192). The same sequence of activity occurred in the lane or path along the north-east side of the *basilica;* here the dump contained large fragments of a brick-mortar floor (28: 209; road surface, 28: 170). The north-eastern edge of the dump overlaid a deposit of silty loam (28: 211).

Dating evidence:

1. *Forum*-courtyard make-up (17: 1); sherds from BB1 cooking-pots with obtuse-angled lattice; a fragment of a stone bowl made from elvan (a quartz porphyry from Cornwall); such bowls are conventionally dated to the third or fourth centuries and later.

   Coin: no. 33, Domitian, *dup.*, as *RIC* 311 (86) (17: 1).

2. South-west aisle make-up:

   Samian: Dr. 31, Antonine, C.G. (17: 522); Dr. 33, Antonine, C.G. (19: 521); Dr. 31, second century, C.G. (17: 525); Dr. 27, first century (17: 525).

   Sherds from BB1 cooking pots with obtuse-angled lattice (17: 525, 522, 515).

   Coins: no. 38, Trajan, *dup.*, *RIC* 539 (103–111); no. 39, Trajan, *sest.*, illegible (98–117) (from north-east foundation trench of south-west aisle wall).

3. 'Shop' (28: 216):
   BB1 flanged bowl (Fig. 67, no. 200).

4. Road:
   Coin: no. 35, Nerva, *as*, illegible (96–98) (26: 208).

In these deposits the coarse ware provides the most precise dating evidence. A sherd from a BB1 cooking pot with obtuse-angled lattice came from the last Period 2B floor level in the 'shop'. In the deposits of Period 2C (Construction) these vessels were well established; since they were first introduced *c.* 250, the construction-work should date to the second half of the third century. The BB1 flanged bowl from the 'shop', (Fig. 67, no. 200) would suggest a date in the last quarter of the third century, if not later (cf. Gillam, 1976, Fig. 4, 45–9).

Discussion:

Although overall stratigraphical relationships were absent, finds from most of the areas described demonstrated the broad contemporaneity of the alterations. In addition the road make-up contained material from the stripping of the south-east range, and wall-plaster from the same deposit was similar in character to fragments found in the *forum*-courtyard make-up. It has been assumed that the alterations formed part of a single building programme. The circumstances which brought about the reconstruction are worth considering. There was clear evidence of a fire in the 'shop' but there was no reason to think that the rest of the buildings were consumed in a general conflagration. Elsewhere evidence of destruction by fire was lacking, and reconstruction must have been undertaken because of decay in the fabric of the buildings. The fire in the 'shop' may have been co-incidental, or even ignited by a demolition-bonfire or sparks from, say, a metal-working hearth associated with the building-work.

The work at the beginning of Period 2C was of reconstruction rather than replanning. The only important change was in the south-west aisle, where the exterior wall may have been replaced by a colonnade and the floor was raised to the same level as that in the *basilica* (cf. 20: 507 and 22: 2108), resulting in the concealment of the steps along the north-east side of the aisle.

5. ACTIVITIES IN THE COURSE OF PERIOD 2C (LAST QUARTER OF THE THIRD CENTURY TO *c.* 340–350) (Fig. 28)

Basilica (*nave and north-eastern range*): no contemporary activities were recorded here.

   South-west aisle: a new floor consisting of loam and fine gravel was laid down (20: 506).

Forum *and south-east* forum *range:* no activities recorded.

Range south-east of the basilica: in the room at the north-east end of the range the mortar floor was covered by a spread of clay and mortar debris, which appeared also to have served as a floor (14: 1017 and 1016). Above this level, a small area of a later floor survived above dumps composed mostly of mortar debris (14: 1015, 1014, 1011, 1010); a layer of occupation-material had accumulated over its surface (14: 1004). A slot 12 cm wide and 6 cm deep running from north-west to south-east was cut through the top of the occupation-material (n.i.: 1003).

The 'shop': the small room against the south-western wall of the 'shop' had survived the fire at the beginning of Period 2C, for, within its confines, a separate sequence of activity was encountered: a deposit of clay 22 cm thick had been laid down over the Period 2C surface (28: 245, 220). No later deposits survived here.

In the main part of the 'shop' a pit had been cut through the original floor at the south-east end (n.i.: 203); it was almost entirely destroyed by a later wall. A layer of loam mixed with tile fragments and trap chips was then spread over the earlier floor (28: 195); a layer of mortar provided the finished surface (28: 197). Another mortar floor was found above (28: 181). Only three small patches of later deposits survived: they showed that a layer of loam had been deposited to serve as a floor, and that occupation-material had accumulated over it (28: 178, loam floor).

Streets: surfaces subsequent to the construction work of Period 2C were only found at the north-eastern end of the site. A very considerable amount of silt was found to have accumulated over the original street, filling the ditch on the north-west side and spreading south-east almost to the other edge of the street (26: 191). The first re-surfacing was confined to a strip about 1.2 m wide along the south-east edge of the street (26: 187). A second re-surfacing covered a strip about 2.2 m in width (26: 162); once again a layer of silt had accumulated over the surface (26: 161). One further re-surfacing was recorded (26: 160).

At the south-western end of the street the surface contemporary with the construction-work of Period 2C was covered by a layer of mortar debris (8: 29A; 9: 29A); later deposits had been obliterated by burials. The mortar debris was not found to the north-east where the road was covered by silt, and this may suggest that the wall-foundation running across the street (Fig. 32, f. 87) was inserted during Period 2C.

In the path or lane on the south-east side of the *basilica* the original Period 2C surface (28: 170) was covered by a layer of make-up consisting of mortar lumps and tile fragments mixed with brown loam (28: 200); above was a street-surface composed of trap chips and gravel (n.i.: 184).

Dating evidence:

Only a few finds were recovered from these deposits and they do not permit a precise dating of the various activities.

Discussion:

Nothing of note occurred in the *forum* and *basilica*. The state of the street made an interesting contrast with its former condition. Until the end of Period 2B the street had been well maintained and kept clear of mud. However the last surface to be laid down before the rebuilding work was deeply rutted and mud which had accumulated over its surface had been piled against the boundary-wall (see above). Later surfaces, although not rutted, were covered with the characteristic brown silt or mud which had not even been cleared from the carriage-ways and which was overlaid in turn by later surfaces, some of which must have been no more than foot-paths along one side of the road. Thus, from the mid-third century onwards, there is clear evidence of a decline in the standards of street-maintenance at a central position in the Roman town.

VI. FOURTH-CENTURY ALTERATIONS TO THE *BASILICA* AND *FORUM* AND THE FIFTH-CENTURY USE OF THE SITE

1. PERIODS 3A AND 3B: GENERAL DESCRIPTION

At the beginning of Period 3A (*c.* 340/350 or later), within the excavated area, very extensive alterations were made to the *basilica* and *forum*. The end of the *basilica* was extended across the site of the range of rooms to the south-east to form a tribunal, replacing or supplementing the original tribunal, the existence of which at the north-east end of the *basilica* has been previously inferred (see p. 81). The *curia* and south-west aisle were also extended south-eastwards. The room built over the original south-east *forum* portico was demolished and its site now appeared to have formed part of the *forum*-courtyard. The shops on the north-east side of the *basilica* were demolished and replaced by a narrower range of rooms, which also presumably served as shops. The path or lane along their north-east side was replaced by a street 3.5 m in width. The street on the south-east side of the *basilica* and *forum* was blocked by a wall which was probably inserted at the beginning of Period 3A, if not before.

In the course of Period 3A a new floor was laid down in the *basilica* and the ditch at the side of the street on the north-east side of the *basilica* was recut. Sometime before the middle of the fifth century the buildings within the excavated area were demolished and the site was cleared. There were traces of subsequent casual occupation in the form of pits, one apparently dug as a quarry and containing debris from metal-working, and scatters of stake-holes. The site was then taken over to serve as a cemetery. Only six burials survived destruction by the graves of later cemeteries on the site, but two of these produced Carbon 14 dates which indicate that the cemetery was in use by about the middle of the fifth century. The burials shared the same north-west/south-east alignment as the buildings which had previously occupied the site. The cemetery is thought to have been Christian.

2. PERIOD 3A (CONSTRUCTION)—AFTER *c.* A.D. 340/350
(Figs. 31–2, Pls. VIA, XB, XIA)

Basilica: two walls extended the line of the nave-walls south-eastwards. The foundation-trench of the north-eastern wall was almost 3.0 m wide and probably penetrated to natural, like its pair to the south-west, although the trench was not cleared below 37.8 m O.D. At this point the foundations were 2.0 m wide and were packed with pitched trap and sandstone rubble, including many re-used facing-blocks; above, the footings took the form of a wall which was faced with re-used trap and sandstone blocks retaining a core of rubble, broken tile, slate and mortar debris. At a height of 38.45 m O.D. the wall was off-set to a width of 90 cm and overlaid at its north-west end the levelled-off wall-top of the former south-east wall of the *basilica*. Throughout its construction a very poor mortar was used, which was often difficult to distinguish from the loose mortar

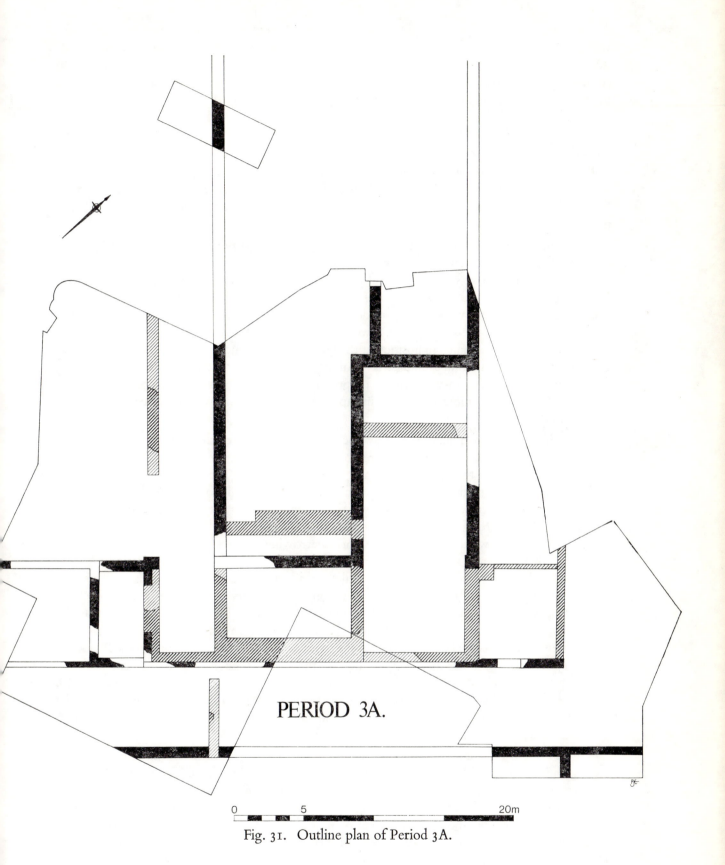

PERIOD 3A.

0   5   20m

Fig. 31. Outline plan of Period 3A.

debris within the wall-core. The sides of the foundation-trench, which were of a considerable width in order to facilitate the building of a faced wall-footing, were packed with trap and sandstone rubble, and mortar debris (14: 1027). The corresponding wall to the south-west had been completely robbed out. The base of the robber-trench was 1.50 m wide at a depth 20 cm below the surface of natural and its maximum preserved width was 2.40 m (F.93). It may have incorporated a wall constructed in Period 2A within its fabric (see p. 76). The south external corner of the wall was strengthened by a buttress measuring 40 cm × 1.6 m, penetrating 10 cm below natural; it was packed with trap and sandstone rubble (F.95).

The newly constructed end wall of the *basilica* was also thoroughly robbed. It had apparently incorporated the Period 1A boundary-wall in its fabric; to the north-west, part of the base of its foundation-trench, packed with trap rubble and 1.0 m wide, survived at the bottom of a robbing trench 3.8 m wide (F.20).

Unlike the north-east end of the former south-east wall of the *basilica* (Int. 3) the central portion between the two extended nave walls was not robbed, but survived to a height of at least 39.10 m O.D.; the wall may have owed its partial preservation to re-use as a retaining wall for a raised floor at the south-east end of the *basilica*. Two metres to the north-west another almost entirely robbed foundation 1.8 m wide and 80 cm deep ran across the nave, reducing abruptly to a width of 1.0 m near its south-west end (2104). Two large sandstone blocks and a few similar trap rocks packed around them remained in position at the bottom of the trench. North-west of this foundation a mortar floor was found capping a layer of loam (22: 2107, 2106); a similar floor was present at the same level in the south-west aisle and is presumed to have been a continuation of that in the *basilica* (see p. 107). The mortar floor, again capping a layer of loam, was also traced in Trench 8 (see Section 21).

Curia: the foundation-trench in the nave occupied a position which would have blocked the entrance to the *curia* and thus the entry-threshold had been robbed, presumably during the reconstruction, leaving only the south-easternmost block in position. The robbing trench had been packed with trap and sandstone rubble, which served as the foundations for the blocking of the door. The north-eastern wall of the *curia* was also extended south-eastwards. The foundations of the extension wall were of a less substantial nature than those of the walls to the south-west, with a maximum preserved width of 2.2 m at the north narrowing to a width of 1.9 m to the extreme south-east; they were also shallower, penetrating only to the levelled-off top of a Period 1A wall. The faced wall-footing, which was 90 cm wide, sat directly on the rubble foundations without any off-sets; fragments of two column-bases, amongst much other material, were re-used in its fabric (see p. 146). At the north-west end of the wall on the north-east side there was a rectangular foundation packed with large trap rocks—the base of a buttress reinforcing the junction of the old and new work (1406). The foundations of the south-east wall which incorporated the Period 1A boundary wall were also less massive than those of the nave extension. A trench 30 cm wide had been dug along the north-west face of the boundary-wall down to a depth of about 37.8 m O.D. and had been packed with trap and sandstone blocks. The foundation supported a somewhat wider wall-footing faced only on its north-west side and surviving only for a height of three courses. The greatest surviving width of the whole foundation was 1.6 m.

A wall divided off the north-west end of the *curia* to form a room measuring 7.6 m by 4 m. Its foundation trench, which was 1.2 m wide, had been dug down to the tile floor of the hypocaust basement and was packed with trap and sandstone rubble (16: 1504, 1505). The wall itself was 1.1 m wide and was constructed of courses of roughly shaped blocks laid on their sides in herring-bone fashion; each course was bedded on a layer of mortar up to 5 cm thick. On its south-east side, sealing the foundation-trench, there was found a layer of occupation-material and loam, capped by a mortar floor at 39.20 m O.D. (n.i. 1503 and 1502, 1501); this was perhaps the remains of a dump deposited in order to raise the floor. On either side of the former passage-wall south-east of the *basilica* two pinnacles of strata preserved small fragments of apparently identical deposits of mortar debris (14: 1001 to the south-east; 1006 to the north-west). It would seem that these deposits marked the removal of the passage-wall during the construction-work of Period 3A, since they overlaid two separate and easily distinguishable sequences of activity (see pp. 101, 103). The heights of the deposits in the north-west and south-east pinnacles were respectively 39.21 m and 39.28 m O.D., which showed that the floor of the reconstructed *curia* at its south-east end must have been at least 10 cm higher than the level of the deposits which had survived to the north-west.

South-west aisle: the south-west aisle, like the *curia* and the *basilica*, was extended south-eastwards. In the room covered by the extension the hypocaust was filled with demolition-debris (1: 8, 8A). Its south-east and south-west walls, however, were retained. A foundation-trench 40 cm wide had been dug alongside the south-east wall (1: f.89). The entry through the south-western wall was filled with a blocking, represented by a pitched-rubble foundation, after one of the original threshold-slabs had been placed over the Period 2A masonry drain to prevent subsidence (3: F.92); in addition a foundation-trench 80 cm wide had been dug along the north-east side of the wall (3: F.91). This method of re-using and strengthening existing walls was the same as that employed in the extension of the *curia* (see above). Further north-west the reconstruction of the south-west aisle wall can also be attributed to Period 3A; here the remains of one course of water-rolled sandstone blocks, crudely lopped to shape and laid in a very rough mortar, overlaid the tile-course of the earlier wall. The later wall can certainly be shown to post-date the re-surfacing of the *forum*-courtyard in Period 2C but other relationships were lacking.

The room in the range south-east of the *forum*, which formerly abutted the nave of the *basilica* at right angles, appeared to have been demolished at this time (see below); its removal left a gap which was not built over and which must have served as an entry from the *forum*-courtyard.

Just north-west of the presumed entry there was a rectangular pit measuring 2.2 m by 1.2 m and 80 cm deep (19: 516); in each of its corners there were post-holes with a depth of up to 40 cm, which presumably had held timbers intended to secure a wooden lining in place. Its function may have been similar to that of the lime-pit found in the *forum*-courtyard (see p. 91). Since it was cut through levels of Period 2C and was probably associated with building-work, it is likely to be contemporary with the reconstruction of the aisle.

Part of a mortar floor overlying a deposit of loam was found in the centre of the aisle (20: 505, 504); it was of the same character as that in the *basilica* and at an equivalent level.

Forum-courtyard: in one corner a dump of loam mixed with occupation-material was found above the Period 2C surface (n.i. 12); it represented a further re-surfacing of the *forum*-courtyard, presumably to be associated with Period 3A.

Range south-east of the forum-*courtyard:* the north-west wall of the room immediately adjacent to the *forum*-courtyard was robbed over its entire length (11: 2000; 18: 2000; 19: 2000); the robber-trench was filled for the most part with sand and sandstone chips—the debris from dressing stone—and some large sandstone blocks. The character of the fill is the only evidence for the date of the robbing; since there was no evidence of alterations to the building subsequent to Period 3A, it would be difficult to explain the origin of the stone-working debris were the robbing any later. A layer of demolition-debris above the Period 2C floor may have been associated with the removal of the wall (7: 22B and 22A; 11: 22B).

Little can be said about the two rooms adjacent to the street. It is assumed that they remained in use and now formed the south-east side of the *forum*-courtyard.

Rooms north-east of the basilica: no contemporary deposits survived here. However 5.75 m from the rear of the *basilica* a wall running from north-west to south-east had been constructed (28: 206; 32: 206 section through foundations); only its foundations survived but amongst them was found a fragment from a column-base similar to those found re-used in the extension of the north-eastern wall of the *basilica* (see p. 146). A trench was found running between the north-east wall of the *basilica* and the newly-constructed wall (12: Int. 21); presumably it had accommodated timber uprights (although no post-holes were found), forming the north-west wall of a room measuring 5.75 m by 5.6 m. A small robbing trench (Int. 15A), which removed a 2 m length of the south-east wall, may indicate the position of a door communicating with the street on the south-east side.

The rest of the earlier walls to the north-east of the *basilica* appear to have been demolished.

Streets: in the street on the south-east side of the *basilica* a small area of trap chips and gravel metalling survived above a make-up level of demolition-debris (26: 158, 159). This was the first level above that contemporary with the alterations of Period 2C to contain material from building work, so there are grounds for attributing it to the beginning of Period 3A. To the south-west a foundation packed with trap rocks, 1.1 m in depth and at least 55 cm wide, was found at a distance of 25 m from the eastern corner of the *forum-insula* (f.87); there is some slight evidence which might be taken to suggest that it dates to Period 2C (see p. 103), but the possibility that it belongs to the present work cannot be excluded.

The surfaces of the path or lane north-east of the *basilica* were cut by a ditch 70 cm in depth and 80 cm wide (28: 168), which at its south-east end turned to the north-east along the side of the street running from south-west to north-east. The space (3.5 m wide) between the ditch and the newly-constructed north-east wall of the range behind the *basilica* was probably occupied by a street which replaced the old path or lane slightly to the north-east. A fragment of gravel metalling over a make-up of mortar mixed with trap and sandstone chips which was found near the south-west lip of the ditch may represent the remains of a street-surface (n.i. 157).

Dating evidence:

1. *Curia:*

   Coin: no. 77, Helena, *HK* 104 (337–41) (1502 and 1503: the coin was found on the surface of the layer at the bottom of a grave-cut; its provenance is thus slightly suspect).

2. South-west aisle:

   1: 8A (demolition-debris in the hypocaust), fragment of an Oxford ware rosette-stamped necked bowl. Present evidence suggests that this class of vessel did not come into production until *c.* 340/350 (Fig. 67, 207). 19: 516 (plank-lined pit), sherd from a red-slipped New Forest vessel (fourth century, see p. 216).

   Coin: no. 7, Claudius, copy as *RIC* 66 (41–54) (3: F.91).

A *terminus post quem* of *c.* 340/350 is provided by the Oxford-ware bowl; the coin of Helena was unlikely to have been lost before *c.* 340. The reconstruction was therefore likely to have been undertaken around the middle of the fourth century or later.

Discussion:

At the beginning of Period 3A the south-east wall of the *basilica* was demolished and the building was extended south-eastwards over the site of the range of rooms next to the street. A cross-foundation was inserted in the *basilica* at a distance of 8 m from the new south-east wall and it has been suggested that the demolished former south-east wall could have been left standing to a certain level in order to retain a raised floor. This would have resulted in an arrangement similar to that of the tribunal identified at the south end of the *basilica* at Wroxeter (Atkinson, 1942, 97). Here the front of the tribunal was marked off by a 'sleeper wall, no doubt to support one or two steps down to the level of the nave pavement beyond'. A cross-wall dividing the tribunal into roughly equal parts ran across a well into which it had subsided; because of this D. Atkinson decided that the wall could not have supported anything heavier than a balustrade. The Wroxeter tribunal measured 11.28 m by 10.78 m. At Exeter the north-west cross-foundation would seem to have been too substantial for merely a small flight of steps. The foundations would have probably have been strong enough to support a screen of columns; in the *basilica* at Pompeii the tribunal was fronted by columns arranged in two storeys (Mau-Kelsey, 1899, 76–7) and cross-walls in front of the apsidal tribunal of the London *basilica* may also have supported a colonnade (Merrifield, 1965, 138, Fig. 24).

The room which probably functioned as the *curia* was extended south-eastwards at the same time. This may have been necessary for structural reasons; its new south-east wall would have buttressed the eastern corner of the *basilica* extension. The possibly contemporary insertion of a cross-wall dividing off the north-west end of the room would more or less have restored the original dimensions of the probable *curia* (formerly 13 m by 7.6 m; after reconstruction 14.46 m by 7.6 m). The tribunal blocked the original entry to the room, and a new one must have been inserted at the north-west end. The room north-west of the cross-wall may have been used as an 'office' but it is possible to suggest a more specific function. At Wroxeter there was a room measuring 8.85 m by 5.83 m, which adjoined the *curia* and which produced evidence that it had been used for the storage of records (Atkinson, 1942, 102); a layer of burnt debris over the floor, which was associated with the first of two fires in the Wroxeter *basilica*, contained a number of fittings which can plausibly be claimed to have come from chests or cupboards, and, in addition, a fragment of a bronze diploma. The room may thus have been used as an archive or *tabularium* for the storage of records, perhaps those directly relating to the proceedings of the *curia*. In the range behind the *basilica* at Caerwent, there was a room measuring 6.55 m by 5.18 m with access from the *curia* (Nash-Williams, 1953, 162); this room and the room at the north-west end of the probable *curia* at Exeter may also have been used to house archives.

Significance of the alterations: it would appear that in Exeter *c.* 340/350 there was wealth and civic pride sufficient not only for the upkeep of a public building, but also for its substantial reconstruction; that is, unless the work of rebuilding was a duty imposed on the *civitas* by the provincial authorities. The construction of a tribunal and the apparent retention of the *curia* attest the continuing executive and juridical functions of the building.

3. ACTIVITIES IN THE COURSE OF PERIOD 3A (*c.* 340/350 TO BEFORE THE MID FIFTH CENTURY)

Basilica: a new floor consisting of a mortar surface above a deposit of loam was laid down in the south-west aisle (20: 502, 501). Loam covering the earlier floor in the *basilica* was probably bedding for the same surface (22: 2105); further to the north-west in Trench 8 both the loam bedding and mortar surface were found (Section 21).

Streets: the ditch bounding the street on the north-east side of the *basilica* was re-cut (28: 168–1, 168–2). Its final fill, consisting of loam mixed with slate and tile-fragments, was sealed by a street-surface of gravel and trap chips above a dump of loam (n.i. 179, 172).

No contemporary activities were observed elsewhere on the site.

Dating evidence:

1. *Basilica:*

   Loam bedding for mortar floor (Section 21: uppermost two deposits, R.H.S.):

   Coin: no. 90, Valens, AE3; o) DN VALEN(S P F AUG) ,r) (GLORIA RO)MANORUM $\left(\frac{|}{P\ ///}\right)$ (?Lyons) (365–78). This coin was found when cleaning the grave-cut of a charcoal-burial.

2. *Streets* (28: 168–1, 168–2):

Both the original and re-cut fills of the ditch contained sherds of North African *amphorae*.

The terminal date of Period 3A, marked by the demolition of the *basilica* and *forum*, is discussed below (p. 112).

4. PERIOD 3B (Fig. 32)

Sometime in the late fourth or fifth century the site was cleared. Pits and stake-holes constituted the only evidence for subsequent activity, until the site was used as a cemetery.

Evidence for the clearance of the site: whether or not the buildings suffered from neglect or decay before their removal cannot be determined. Nonetheless there is clear evidence that at some point the *basilica*, whatever its state of repair, was dismantled and that the resulting demolition-debris was removed from the site. The fills of all early post-Roman features, excluding robber-trenches, were for the most part free of building debris; for instance the fill of the early graves consisted of clean brown loam and the quarry-pit contained only a small quantity of building material; the robber-trenches themselves contained scarcely any material from the superstructures of walls, such as wall-plaster. The charnel soil covering the site must have consisted largely of comminuted late and post-Roman deposits, yet it contained little building material; it may also be noted that amongst all the architectural material from the site, only two fragments were recovered from graveyard levels. When demolition took place, most of the walls seem merely to have been reduced to the contemporary ground surface. Despite sporadic robbing in later periods some walls retained or constructed in Period 3A survived to a height above that of the latest Roman deposits, i.e. the walls of the south-east *forum* range, the south-east end of the south-west wall of the nave, the retaining wall of the tribunal (formerly the south-east wall of the *basilica*), part of the north-east wall of the *curia* and the south-west wall of the room to the north-west of the *curia*. Only two robber-trenches could have dated to the period in question, since the remainder contained human bones in their fill; these were the robbing trench of the tribunal stylobate and of the north-east wall of the shop at the rear of the *basilica*, where only the uppermost courses of the foundation were removed (32: 206).

A *terminus ante quem* of *c.* 450 for the dismantling of the *basilica* is provided by OBs (ordinary burials) 485, 486 and 278 which were laid out in a line which crosses the south-west nave-wall. Indeed an earlier date may be suggested by the quarry-pit cut through the floor of the *curia*, which was unlikely to have been dug inside a standing building.

Pits: a number of pits scattered over the site were cut through later Roman levels, but did not include human bones in their fill. They are attributed to a period of occupation falling between the clearance of the site and its use as a graveyard.

Int. 22: a large pit, *c.* 3 m in diameter, had been dug through the floor of the *curia* to a depth probably in excess of 2 m from the contemporary surface. It penetrated to the grouted rubble filling of the hypocaust basement of the *caldarium* and appeared to have been immediately back-filled with lumps of burnt clay, charcoal, slag and bronze fragments, mixed with clay and mortar debris. This material came up to the top of the grouted rubble, above which the pit cut through a layer of clay which had been deposited during the construction work of Period 2A. To the south-west, the side of the pit had been cut back into the clay through a width of 40 cm over a distance of 70 cm. The north-west and north-east sides of the pit had also been cut back 40 cm through half its total circumference; a baulk of undisturbed material had been left in place at the mid-point, perhaps to support material above. The sides must have been cut away in order to obtain the clay and this suggests that the pit was dug as a quarry. The pit was opened and clay was reached but the layer was soon dug through and gave way to rubble, so as much clay as possible was obtained from delving into the sides. The presence of bronze-working debris in the fill showed that the clay was most likely to have been required for crucibles and furnace-linings. A possible secondary use of the pit was represented by charcoal and trap rubble scattered over the surface of the first infilling. Near the north-west side of the pit a few broken tiles covered with a skim of burnt clay were found, possibly the remains of a hearth; however at no point were the sides of the pit discoloured or baked by heat. Subsequently the pit was back-filled with clay lumps, mortar debris and rubbish from bronze-working, including a piece of furnace-lining (?), large lumps of slag and some snippets of sheet bronze.

Int. 32 and 33: these two pits were dug against the south-west wall of the *curia* and were about 30 cm deep.

Int. 34: this pit was about 40 cm deep.

Int. 30: in the western corner of the site, a pit with a surviving depth of 25 cm was found; it was filled with black loam containing a lens of green staining, which probably represented cess.

2–8, 508–10 and 512: these were two lines of stake-holes, the more westerly of which was sealed by OB 480.

The cemetery: six graves on the Roman alignment were found. One, the burial of a woman, was cut through the *forum* levels and was in a rather fragmentary state. Four more burials were arranged in a line which cut across the south-west wall of the *basilica* nave. The south-westernmost grave was almost entirely destroyed and no traces of the burial remained. The others, males, were relatively well-preserved and all three were sealed by burials belonging to the seventh- to tenth-century cemetery. No traces of grave goods or coffins survived. The neat ranking of the four burials suggested that they may have belonged to a planned cemetery, with rows laid out by markers. A sixth burial was found cut through the street-levels. The extent of the cemetery may have been considerable; the three burials in the nave of the *basilica* only escaped destruction by later graves because they were cut through a concrete floor (22: OB 278, 485, 486). The robber trench of the south-west wall of the nave, which was sealed by five burials of eighth- to tenth-century date (see p. 113), contained a number of human bones, presumably disturbed from other early graves in the vicinity.

Dating evidence:

Demolition of the *basilica:*

Coin: no. 67, Diocletian, *follis*, RIC 188a, Trier (296–7) (2104, robbing trench of tribunal screen). See also C14 dates of burials (below).

5. PERIOD 3B: RADIOCARBON DATING OF THREE BURIALS

The three burials cut through the floor of the *basilica* in Period 3B were submitted to the Harwell Carbon 14/Tritium Measurements Laboratory. The following results were obtained:

Burial	Harwell Ref.	Delc. (%/10)	Age b.p. (Yrs.)	b.p. 1950
O.B. 278	HAR–1614	−21.4	1530±70	A.D. 420
O.B. 485	HAR–1611	−20.7	880±70	A.D. 1070
O.B. 486	HAR–1613	−21.4	1460±80	A.D. 490

The determination for O.B. 485 is clearly anomalous and should be disregarded.

6. PERIODS 3A AND 3B: DISCUSSION

Chronology: at the beginning of Period 3A the *basilica* was remodelled and the range of shops on its north-east side was rebuilt; these events took place after *c.* 340/350. A floor laid down in the south-west aisle, and probably also the *basilica*, was the only evidence of later activity which can be confidently associated with the standing buildings. Later floors would have been removed by grave-cuts but the possibility of any further rebuilding of a substantial nature can safely be excluded, since traces of foundation-trenches might be expected to have survived. The demolition of the *basilica*, which is taken to mark the commencement of Period 3B, is not closely datable, although it can be shown to have taken place before the site was taken over to serve as a cemetery in the mid fifth century, and probably before the quarry-pit was dug.

The Cemetery: the burials were oriented with their heads to the north-west and their feet to the south-east. The bodies had been interred without coffins, to judge from the absence of nails, and were not accompanied by any grave-goods. Since they were found on a site which accommodated a monastic cemetery from the seventh century onwards, they fall within Type D of a classification of certain inhumation cemeteries found in 'Roman and later' Britain, which has been proposed by P. Rahtz (1977, 56). This type includes cemeteries at such places as Monkwearmouth and Jarrow, where burials precede the earliest known monastic structures or other remains of an indisputably Christian character. Rahtz accepts that, because of the later history of such sites, there are grounds for thinking that the earlier burials may themselves be Christian, and that, indeed, 'there may be a direct association between them and the location of the monastery' (*ibid.*, 56). It is thus possible that the burials at Exeter were Christian. The alignment of the burials from north-west to south-east certainly does not indicate that they were pagan, although many Christian cemeteries at this time were carefully oriented east–west (Thomas, 1971, 48–9). The alignment of the Exeter burials was clearly dictated by some surviving element in the lay-out of the Roman streets or roads in the vicinity. They can be compared with certain fourth-century Christian cemeteries outside Roman cities, where strict east–west alignment was not practised, for example at Bonn where some Christian cemeteries were aligned on nearby roads, although there was a 'tendency to place the head at the more westerly end of the grave' (Green, 1977, 49–50). At Exeter there is no evidence to show what particular topographical feature decided the alignment of the burials, but there are two possibilities:

(i) the cemetery was bounded on one or more sides by the surviving walls of Roman buildings or by streets still in use. It is interesting to note that the north-eastern limits of the two later cemeteries (see p. 113) coincided roughly with the line of the north-eastern wall of the range of rooms which included the *curia;* the earliest cemetery may also have extended as far north-east as this.

(ii) the burials were liturgically aligned on a church or shrine, possibly housed in a surviving Roman building (for example, part of the town-house investigated on the south-east side of the *forum,* or a structure situated in the *forum*-courtyard).

These two possibilities are not mutually exclusive.

The fact that the cemetery occupied a central position in the Roman town at a date in the fifth century may shed some light on its precise character. The law of the Twelve Tables was rigidly adhered to throughout the Roman period, probably because it did no more than formalise a natural aversion to the presence of the dead in the midst of a community. It might be thought that more than the passage of a few decades would be required to erase a social custom once backed by the force of law. It is interesting to note that in Wessex there was a similar aversion to the presence of cemeteries in settlements, which was not overcome until about a hundred years after the Conversion (Hawkes and Meaney, 1970, 51).

There are other possible instances of early post-Roman burials in Romano-British towns. At

Wroxeter, on the east side of the *forum*, there was one burial, its head removed and placed at the feet, which was perhaps pagan[1]; human bones were found in disturbed levels over the site of the *forum* and there were two burials in stone-lined graves close-by above House VI, which were aligned east–west (Bushe-Fox, 1916, 19). At Caerwent there were two burials near the building on the site of the baths which has been falsely claimed as a church (Nash-Williams, 1930, 230). Corpses have also been found at Cirencester, some in positions which have been taken to suggest that they represented the victims of epidemics who fell by the wayside and whose bodies were gradually engulfed by natural silting (Wacher, 1974, 389). It is very difficult to imagine how this could have happened; the corpses would surely have been dismembered by scavenging animals within the course of a few days (cf. Todd, 1977).

Although some of these burials may well be of fifth-century date, none can be shown to have belonged to planned cemeteries, as, apparently, the Exeter burials did. However, churches associated with cemeteries were established in some North African towns during the first half of the fifth century (Ward-Perkins and Goodchild, 1953). At Sabratha the civil *basilica* was converted into a church and in the adjacent *forum* a 'very large cemetery' developed (Ward-Perkins and Goodchild, 1953, 12). The *basilica* at Lepcis Magna was also converted into a church, although not until the time of Justinian: an earlier church established in the *Forum Vetus* in the same city contained contemporary burials.

These two instances of cemeteries developing within towns can be cited as parallels to the situation now revealed at Exeter and two aspects are particularly pertinent. First, a more Romanised community than Exeter can be shown to have abandoned the practice of exclusively extra-mural burial at an early date, perhaps because of a desire for burial close to where the sacraments of the Christian religion were celebrated. Secondly, at both these towns public buildings no longer needed for their original purposes were made over to the Church, presumably by the municipal authorities in whom ownership was vested. At Exeter it was perhaps a vacant plot rather than a set of buildings which may have fallen into the hands of the Church. In this connection mention might be made of the church at Silchester, which was built on a site probably serving, at an earlier date, as a cattle market attached to the *forum* (Boon, 1974, 111; for the church, see *ibid.*, 173–84 and Frere, 1975, 277–303).

The cemetery as possible evidence of continuity of occupation through the fifth to seventh centuries: the earliest reference to Exeter in the post-Roman period appears in Willibald's 'Life of St Boniface', where it is stated that the saint received his education at a monastery in Exeter: *ad monasterium, quod priscorum nuncupatur vocabulo Ad-Escancastre* (*Vitae Sancti Bonifiatii*, I, (Levison, 1905, 6)). The abbot of this monastery had an English name, Wulfhard, which has been taken to imply that by *c*. 680 Exeter had been annexed by the West Saxons. It seems highly probable that a second phase of the cemetery, from which 59 burials were recovered, related to this monastery[2]. Two centuries elapsed between the period when the burials were made on the site of the *basilica* and the first mention of the monastery. But this *lacuna* in our knowledge may be more apparent than real: the early cemetery may have remained in use for a considerable time and the second phase of the cemetery may extend back a great deal earlier than *c*. 680. Unfortunately finds of this period from Exeter cannot be used as evidence for continuity of occupation. The authenticity of finds of sixth- and seventh-century Byzantine copper coins has been rightly questioned (Shortt, 1840, 79–109; Boon, 1958, 317) and imported pottery of late fifth- to seventh-century date has not yet been recognised, although *amphorae* from North Africa, and perhaps also Palestine, reached Exeter in the late fourth and fifth centuries[3].

NOTES

1. Atkinson, 1942, 112–3; G. Webster points out that this was a common late Roman rite (1975, 121).
2. Traditionally the site of the monastery has been thought to lie under, or near, the Lady Chapel of the Cathedral;

this received apparent confirmation from Sir Cyril Fox's excavation of a well-pool, claimed to have a Saxon phase, on the exterior of the south side of the Choir (his 1965, 217).

3. The absence of late fifth- to seventh-century imported pottery can scarcely be used as grounds to argue against the possibility of contemporary occupation at Exeter. The area covered by such occupation would probably have been relatively small and many areas in the vicinity of the excavated site have escaped disturbance by modern building-activity. The site of the Choir School, immediately to the west of the excavations, was not examined when the present building was erected about twenty years ago.

VII. OTHER ROMAN SITES IN THE CATHEDRAL CLOSE AND A NOTE ON THE PUBLIC BATHS

1. THE *INSULA* SOUTH-EAST OF THE *BASILICA* AND *FORUM*
(Figs. 26 and 32)

This insula was laid out *c.* 80, when the central area was replanned (see pp. 78–9); to the south-west of it lay the public baths and to the north-west the *basilica* and *forum*. Its north-west side was investigated at three points over a length of 40 m extending from its northern corner south-westwards. The most south-westerly point, examined in 1971, displayed a sequence of occupation which differed markedly from that investigated at the other two points and is thus described separately.

The southern insula (1971):

The activities of Period 1A and 1B are described on pp. 26–7 and 64.

Two successive clay floors, the upper one covered by a spread of occupation-material, may have been associated with a building replacing the structure with sill-beams which was demolished at the beginning of Period 2A (9: 39E, 39D1, 39D, see p. 77). A mortar floor sealed the occupation-material (9: 39C); two layers of similar material which had accumulated over the mortar floor were cut through by a scoop, possibly a hearth-pit (9: 39B, 39A, 38G8). A further layer of occupation-material mixed with oyster-shells was found above (9: 39G7); it was overlaid by a thin gravel surface (9: 38G6) capped by a layer of loam which contained material dating to the later second century (9: 38G5). The deposit of loam seemed to have served as a floor; a scoop back-filled with loam, oyster-shells and tile-fragments had been cut through its surface (9: 38G4) and was sealed by a lens of mortar debris and charcoal (9:38G3). A dump of loam 10–15 cm thick underlaid a mortar floor which had seen considerable wear (9: 38G1; mortar floor, Fig. 4, 38G). A wooden plank measuring 1 m by 15 cm had been set into the floor and nearby three stake-holes were found (Fig. 4, F.54). The plank had been burnt in position, the stake-holes were full of charcoal and the layer above contained much burnt daub, wall-plaster and charcoal (9: 38F4); this material clearly resulted from the destruction by fire of a timber building. The destruction-level had been cobbled over with large-grade river gravel (9: 38F3); the surface of this deposit was cut through by the base of an oven, originally about 1.0 m in diameter, which had a floor lined with tile-fragments and sides revetted with small trap blocks (9: pit 12). Occupation-material had accumulated over the cobbled floor sealing the oven-base which had previously been back-filled with loam and charcoal (9: 38F1). Above there was a gravel surface capped by a thin spread of clay (9: 38E2, 38E1). A deposit of loam 15–20 cm thick underlaid two superimposed mortar floors (9: 38D, 38C, 38B) which were capped by another deposit of loam (9: 38A).

The relationship of the sequence just described to the street-surfaces on the north-west side had been destroyed by a large wall-foundation cut in from some point above the penultimate mortar floor (9: F.50). The foundations were placed in a trench 1.2 m wide, and consisted of trap and sandstone rocks (none re-used), bedded on layers of loam. It is possible that this wall was a continuation of that found further to the north-east in 1976.

Dating evidence:

9: 39A. no. 12, Dr. 37, early second century. Montans.

9: 38G7. Dr. 18, first century.

9: 38G5. no. 13, Dr. 37, *c.* 130–150.

9: 38G3. Dr. 37, Antonine.

9: 38F1 and F2. Samian sherd, late second century or early third century; jar, late second century, E.G.; Dr. 37, Antonine, C.G.

In general the sequence was poorly dated. However, there was sufficient material to date the destruction of the timber building by fire to the late second or early third century, showing that there could be no possible connection with the fire which occurred to the north-west at the beginning of Period 2C (see p. 101).

The southern insula (1976) (*Fig.* 33; *Pls* XB, XIIA):

In 1976 scarcely any information was obtained concerning the history of this *insula* during the early civil period. A section revealed on the east side of the robber-trench (F.147) was the only complete record of the occupation sequence from natural upwards. Two dumps of dirty clay 50 cm thick overlaid natural (27: 31, 30); the surface of the upper dump appeared to have served as a floor, since two lenses of charcoal were found over it (27: 28, 29). Above were dumps of loam containing wall-plaster and mortar debris (27: 27, 26, 25, 24); the surface of the uppermost dump had a hearth cut into it, and must have served as a floor (27: 23). The hearth was sealed by a series of tip-lines representing a dump 25 cm thick (27: 22, 21, 19, 18, 17) with an earth floor above: the top of the dump was about the same level as that from which the wall represented by F.147 was inserted to the west (see below). Elsewhere our knowledge of the activities on the site commences with the construction of an extensive building with walls about 55 cm in width. Their relatively slight character when compared with the later third-century town-house walls suggested that they were dwarf-walls carrying sill-beams; but it is worth remembering that the service-building walls of the legionary baths, some of which carried tiled roofs of considerable span, were only 44 cm in width (see p. 35).

Levels contemporary with this building were not excavated and its plan could only be reconstructed from a few surviving fragments of wall and their robber-trenches, which could be distinguished from those of the later town-house by their narrower width. The building probably consisted of an L-shaped range, containing at least five rooms, which, as a cursory examination of the sides of robber trenches showed, had floors of clay or earth. The north-east wing was traced over a length of 10.2 m. The position of its north-eastern wall could only be fixed approximately, by reference to the south-western limits of the adjacent street; the cross-divisions within the range terminated against a later wall running from north-west to south-east which was obviously a rebuild of the original north-west wall. At the north-west end of the wing there was a room measuring 4.6 m by about 5 m; its south-east wall was not retained in the later building but was only partly robbed. To the south-east there was a room only 2.2 m in width; again its south-east wall was not retained in the second building, although a fragment survived under an upstand of later material. The south-west wing was of uncertain width; its north-west wall had been replaced at a later date and its south-east wall was not located. At the north-east end a wall divided off a room 3 m wide. The cross-division was located at a distance of 8.5 m to the south-west. Here the wall survived to a height of 40 cm above foundation-level; its foundation-trench was represented by a scoop 40 cm wide and 10 cm deep, which was packed with clay and covered with mortar, probably trimmed from the pointing of the wall (29: 243–1, 243–2). The wall (width 55 cm) was constructed of trap blocks about 15 cm square, which had only been roughly lopped to shape. A dump of loam served as a floor, over which a layer of occupation-material had accumulated

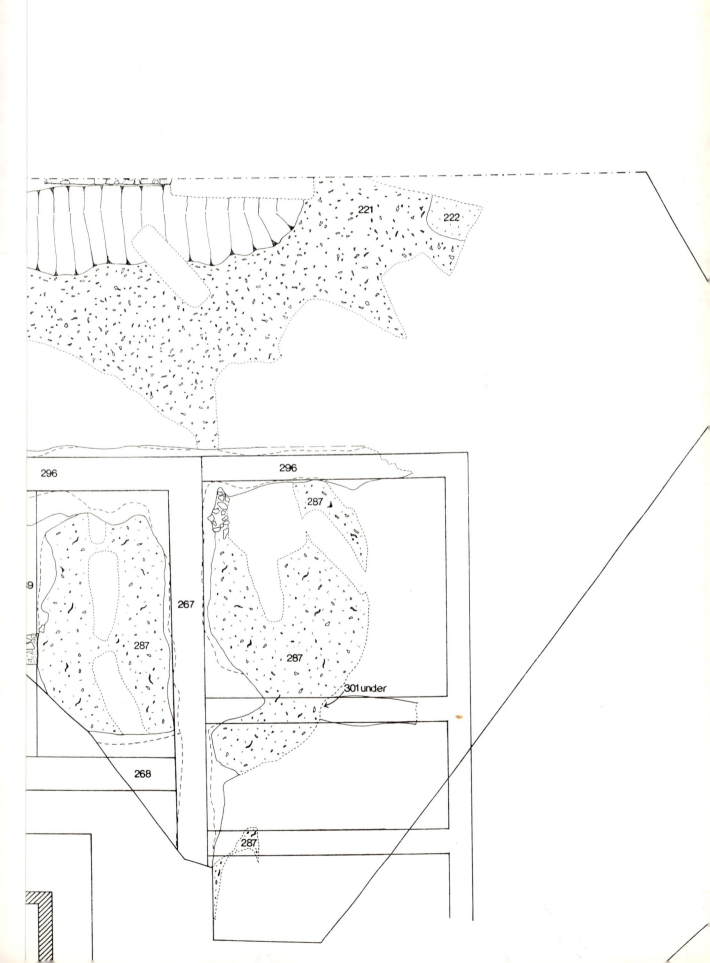

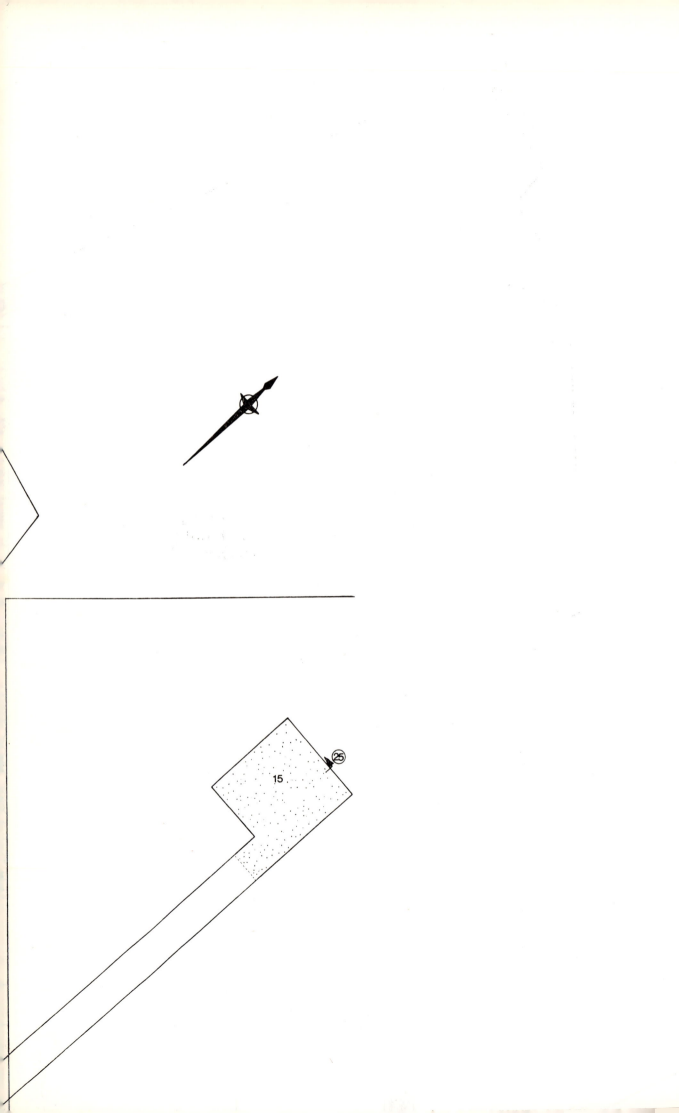

15

㉕

(29:233, 231); above were found two further floors, of clay and of mortar (29: 232, 230). A dump, consisting of clay, burnt daub and occupation-material mixed with trap fragments and mortar, covered the upper floor (29: 229, 228, 227). The demolition of the wall, which took place from immediately above the dump-level, may have been broadly contemporary with their deposition; only a layer of trampled loam (29: 226) underlay the mosaic bedding. A similar depth of dumped deposits was revealed in the section to the north-east at about the same level (27: 22, 21, 19, 18, 17) and may indicate an overall raising of levels as the first stage of reconstruction. Two rooms in the new building fell within the excavated area; it seems quite likely that the north-eastern wing of the older building was retained, its cross-walls having been removed to form a third room. To the south-west there was a room measuring 8 m by 5 m; all four of its walls were newly built. It adjoined a room equipped with a mosaic floor (described below) which measured 5 m square. The south-west wall of the room survived to a height of 10 cm above floor-level and was built of trap and sandstone rocks laid in a very coarse yellow mortar and faced with roughly worked trap blocks which had been rendered with a layer of plaster before the mosaic was laid.

Later activities were recorded in only two places. The mosaic was covered by a deposit of loam containing *tesserae* and slate fragments, which was preserved only above the plain border next to the south-west wall (118). In the room to the north-east a hearth overlaid the earth floor at one point (27: 16, 15). Above the hearth there was a deposit of dark brown loam mixed with many slates and trap rocks (27: 14): a similar deposit excavated to the south-west above the mosaic was found to contain many human bones.

Dating evidence:

From levels excavated below the mosaic:

29: F.234 and L.233, second-century coarse wares.

29: 229, 228, 227, Dr. 38, late second century; second- and early third-century coarse wares.

The sequence suggests that the first-period building dated from some time in the second century. The absence of obtuse-angled lattice on black-burnished cooking pots from dump-levels below the mosaic indicates a date in the first half of the third century or earlier for the reconstruction of the building.

Description of mosaic (Pl. XV, cf. p. 32):

The mosaic was laid on a bedding of mortar which was no more than 8 cm thick at any point (29: 139). It was surrounded by a plain red border about 75 cm in width on the south-west and north-east sides; the *tesserae* employed here were cubes with sides measuring up to 5 cm, and came from tiles (probably *tegulae*) in both the normal red and paler buff shell-gritted fabrics (see p. 153).

Only the outer edges of the mosaic survived. The principal feature was a guilloche which employed three types of *tesserae:*

(i) white, made from limestone probably quarried in East Devon.
(ii) grey-blue, siderite, available locally.

These specimens were identified by R. G. Scrivener, and represent the same types of stone employed in the mosaic(s) of the legionary baths (see p. 132).

(iii) tile; these were carefully selected from over-fired tiles so that they were of the same rather dark tone.

The guilloche enclosed two bands of blue-grey *tesserae;* in the north-east angle part of a square or rectangle survived. The rest of the design had been obliterated.

This is only the fourth mosaic to have been recovered from the town. One was found in Pancras Lane during the construction of the Police Station in 1887,[1] and fragments of two more were revealed during the excavation of a building at Catherine Street in 1945 and 1947 (Fox, 1952, 47–9).

NOTE

1. Fox, 1952, 99. There is an unpublished coloured drawing of this mosaic in the Devon and Exeter Institution.

2. TRENCH PARALLEL TO THE WEST FRONT OF THE CATHEDRAL (Fig. 33)

This trench was excavated in 1976 to remove an obsolete Victorian drain and exposed a section through Roman and later deposits. At its south end a number of surfaces belonging to a road running from north-west to south-east were revealed (25: 43–44, 46–50); they were covered by two layers of mortar debris (25: 40, 41). To the north a clay floor-surface was separated from a gravel spread by a beam-slot (24: 31, F.29); a larger feature, possibly a wall-foundation, was also cut through this deposit (25: F.11). The latter was sealed by a layer of mixed clays (24: 39).

At the extreme north end natural was covered by a deposit of mixed clays (25: 27), which had been cut through by two intrusions, possibly post-trenches. Two dumps of loam were found at the north end of the trench (25: 20, 19); they had been partly terraced away to accommodate a mortar floor bedded on a layer of pitched trap and sandstone rubble (25: 21, 22). A deposit of clay overlaid the mortar floor (25: 18). A second mortar floor supported on a bedding of pitched rubble was found above (25: 18, 15); its surface was covered by two spreads of mortar debris (25: 16, 17). These deposits were explored over an area measuring 2.2 m, by 1.4 m without establishing their limits.

The possibility that these two mortar floors are post-Roman in date should be noted; a few metres to the west there was a reduced area surrounding the apsidal east end of the eleventh-century cathedral, which also had a mortar floor on a pitched rubble bedding. The uppermost layer which was preserved over a distance of 9 m, was a deposit of dark humic soil, similar in character to the 'post-Roman dark soil' found covering later Roman levels elsewhere at Exeter; however, the deposit in this section contained a considerable quantity of human bones.

Dating evidence:
None recovered.

3. TRENCHES EXCAVATED IN 1975 AND 1976 (Fig. 34)

The trench was situated 20 m from the street which ran along the north-east side of the *basilica* and *forum* and 4.5 m from the continuation of the street which bounded its south-eastern side.

Early Roman: evidence was found for the existence of three successive timber buildings, the first two of which were represented by substantial post-trenches, a characteristic military constructional feature. Remains of the earliest building consisted of a post-trench 40 cm deep (24: 30), 1.45 m south-east of a scarp which may represent the edge of another post-trench, almost entirely cut out by a later feature (23–1). The southern post-trench apparently formed one side of an area which had been reduced to a level 30 cm below the surface of natural; the reduced area had a floor of gravel associated with a post-hole (24: 28, 31), which was superseded by a mortar floor overlying a clay dump (24: 27). In the second phase the possible post-trench to the north-west was replaced by another occupying almost the same position (24: F.23). The south-east post-trench was cut out by a shallow trench 80 cm wide and 20–30 cm deep; its profile and dimensions were similar to those of water-pipe trenches excavated in the service-area of the baths but no traces of a pipe were found along its course. The third phase of activity was represented by a structure of somewhat slighter construction: two post-trenches separated by a post set in a pit 60 cm sq. (24: 21). An extraction-pit for the post pointed to the methodical demolition of this structure; its site was covered by a thin spread of clay and loam (24: 20).

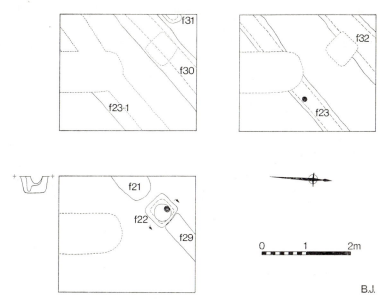

Fig. 34. Early Roman features in trench to the north-east
of the *basilica*.

Dating evidence:

Samian: body sherd, pre-Flavian? (24: 25); Dr. 18, Flavian? (24: 22); Dr. 27, pre-Flavian, and jar, pre-Flavian (both 24: 20).

Coarse wares consistent with a pre-Flavian/early Flavian date.

The dating evidence, such as it is, confirms the view that these buildings are associated with the fortress.

Late Roman: the early features and the spread of clay and loam which sealed them were overlaid by a mixed deposit containing early material together with sherds dating to the second half of the third century or later (24: 19). The remainder of the Roman sequence consisted of dump levels deposited to a depth of 65 cm; although the contents of the tip-lines were varied, adjoining sherds from the lower and uppermost levels suggested that they were contemporary (24: 14–18). The lower tip-lines consisted of loam or clay mixed with a little occupation material (24: 17A and B,18); they were capped by a tip of loose soil mixed with much occupation material (24: 16). The two uppermost tip-lines contained much building debris, trap rocks, tiles, slates and lumps of mortar and *opus signinum*, mixed with loam (24: 14, 15); the highest level also contained a large quantity of pottery.

The chronological gap between the deposit sealing the military features and the mixed deposit of mid third-century date or later must signify the removal of an intervening stratigraphical sequence; it seems scarcely credible that at such a central position within the town, no deposits should have accumulated over a period of two centuries. The layer below the tips could perhaps be interpreted as a mixed and trampled level resulting from the digging out of earlier deposits (24: 19); the tip-lines, which all save the uppermost decreased in thickness towards the south-east, probably represent a later levelling-up of the reduced area.

Dating evidence (24: 14):

Coins: no. 81, Constantinian, *Gloria Exercitus* type (337–41); no. 58, barbarous radiate (270–85); no. 42, Postumus, *ant.* RIC 303 (259–69); from graveyard levels but probably derived from this deposit: no. 59, barbarous radiate (270–85); no. 43, R, *quin.*, RIC 363 (261–9).

The *Gloria Exercitus* issue provides a *terminus post quem* of A.D. 337 for the group, but the presence of North African amphorae may suggest that its true date is somewhat later. The deposit contained a certain amount of residual material, notably many fragments of a Dressel 30 amphora (Fig. 67, no. 208).

In October 1976, an irregularly-shaped pit was dug in order to grub out the roots of a dead elm-tree which had occupied a position 6 m north of the trench described above. At the bottom of the pit a layer of loam 40 cm thick was observed, lying roughly at the same level as the dumped deposits to the south-west (24:15). The loam contained much building material, including fragments of brick-mortar, tiles and volcanic blocks; of particular interest were fragments of box-tiles identical to those from Period 2A (construction) deposits (Fig. 41, 12 and 13) and a fragment of a chamfered tile (as Fig. 47, 10). The deposit in which they were found was too high to represent a dump associated with the construction of the *basilica;* it was more likely to have been associated with the in-filling of the reduced level to the west.

4. EXCAVATIONS AT THE NORTHERN CORNER OF THE *BASILICA* AND *FORUM* (ON THE SITE OF THE NATIONAL WESTMINSTER BANK)
(Fig. 35)

The remains of Period 1A have already been described (see p. 60).

In 1911–12, during alterations to the (then) National Provincial Bank, two walls, each forming an angle, were found at the lowest levels; the stone used in them was described as limestone (Lega-Weekes, 1912). Recent work in the very same cellars recovered two short lengths of a foundation composed of trap-rocks, which filled a trench 75 cm in width; slight traces of another foundation at right angles were found to the north-west. Taken together the two walls which these foundations represented more or less reflect the position of the outer angle recorded in 1911–12; their alignment differs slightly and presumably the 1911–12 discovery was inaccurately plotted. The wall running from north-west to south-east is on exactly the same line as the north-eastern boundary-wall behind the *basilica* and must represent a north-westwards continuation of it. Thus the outer angle in fact represents the northern corner of the whole *basilica* and *forum* site; the foundations were undated but presumably were associated with the construction-work at the beginning of Period 2A. The inner angle recorded in 1911–12 appears to have been correctly plotted since its north-eastern side coincided exactly with the one surviving side of a foundation-trench packed with trap rocks (Fig. 35, 42); this wall may well be later than the original construction-work of Period 2A.

On the south-western side a ditch showing a fall of about 15 cm towards the south-west was traced over a distance of 12 m; it was cut through a layer of metalling, preserved only in the south-western section, which probably represented the north-west side of an early civil street (32: 50= Fig. 35, 24). The width of this street could have been no greater than 6.8 m, the distance between the ditch and the north-west boundary-wall of the *basilica* and *forum.*

At some time the width of the street had been reduced by at least 1.8 m. A large pit with a surviving depth of 30 cm had been dug through its north-west edge (Fig. 35, 27). After this was filled a structure represented by four pits dug for posts of a substantial size was erected (Fig. 54, 11, 13, 22, 34); one of the posts appeared to have been renewed (Fig. 35, 26).

The evidence preserved in the south-western section suggests that the street was reduced in width at a fairly early date in the civil period. However before this took place the street was apparently widened by about 3 m on its north-west side. The ditch-fill was sealed by a layer of heavy river-gravel with a compacted surface which extended across the entire width of the section (32: 46, 47); at the north-west end it was cut by a square or rectangular feature, possibly a post-pit (32: 43). Another layer of metalling with a compacted surface was found immediately above (32: 42); to the north-west it was cut through by a shallow scoop containing silty loam, which resembled the shallow road-side ditches found in the higher levels of the street on the south-east side of the *basilica* and *forum* (32: 40; cf. 26: 191, 218). Above this level street-surfaces were no longer present in the section, and buildings covered the former north-west edge of the street. A possible post-trench was associated with clay floors and occupation-levels (32: 38); the post-built structure referred to above was presumably associated with this period of activity.

The upper part of the section was separated from the lower by a depth (50 cm) of deposits which it was not possible to record. The most prominent feature was a trap-built wall some 70 cm in width (32: 8); it was cut through what appeared to be mostly levelling-up material (32: 7, 9–12, 2–22). On the north-west side of the wall a clay-sand deposit seemed to have served as a contemporary floor-surface (32: 20); to the south-east a mixed deposit seemed to have had the same function, although its surface was about 10 cm higher. Above these levels were what appeared to be demolition-deposits containing yellow-painted wall-plaster (32: 6, 14–19). Evidence of activity post-dating demolition was provided by a number of layers, predominantly of loam, which sealed the wall-top (32: 1–3, 5, 13, 23).

Dating evidence:

No closely datable material was recovered from the features described above. It should be noted that the western part of this site produced an important group of bronze figurines in the eighteenth century (see p. 20).

5. THE PUBLIC BATHS (Fig. 23)

The presence of an important public building underlying South Street and the Deanery Gardens had been suspected for many years before the discovery of a large *natatio* or swimming-pool led to its identification as the public baths. The first discovery of structural remains was made in August 1833 when a tessellated pavement was uncovered near the Deanery Kitchen; its exact position was not recorded (*Woolmer's Exeter and Plymouth Gazette* for August 17th and 24th, 1833). Other remains of later date led Shortt to conclude that he was dealing with a Roman bath refurbished by the College of Vicars for their own use. In April of the following year a report in the *Western Times* describes the discovery of a strong wall under South Street when water-pipes were being laid and its removal by blasting (*The Western Times* for April 26th, 1834). Further finds made in the nineteenth century can now be seen to have fallen within the Baths insula: in Guinea Street a 'mass of masonry combined with a conglomerate of powerful cement' was encountered; a tessellated pavement was found on the west side of South Street; and on the east side 'an immense quadrangular Portland Stone, with a square cut in its centre' (Shortt, 1840, 41, presumably a block of Beer stone with a lewis hole: the use of Portland stone is not otherwise attested in Roman Exeter).

No further discoveries were made until excavations took place in the Deanery Gardens in 1932 (Montgomerie-Nielson and Montague, 1933/6, 73f.). Part of a *natatio* was found, just over 1.0 m deep, 16.75 m in length and of unknown width; it was surrounded by a pavement of sandstone, 2.5 m wide, with a shallow gutter cut down its centre. A column-base 50 cm in diameter was found on the floor of the bath but was unfortunately not illustrated in the report. Traces of 'the position occupied by similar columns' were found on the inner edge of the pavement; what exactly constituted these traces was not explained nor does the published photograph of the pavement show any evidence for the position of the bases (*ibid.*, 75, Fig. 2). A coin of Claudius II described in the finds catalogue as 'Deanery, found in filling' (*ibid.*, 42–44) presumably came from the "filling" of the bath, and is thus the latest object recorded from it. Some distance to the south-east a wall with what may have been the springing of an arch was found, and also much 'sooty carbon'. This was interpreted as part of an arch from a hypocaust-furnace.

In 1945–6 a room dated to later than *c.* 80 was excavated to the north-west of the *natatio* (Fox, 1952, 42–4); it was represented by a wall running from with a return to the south-west. The interior of the room was occupied by a masonry base. Subsequently the wall was rebuilt and a pier was cut into it; a wall was constructed to the north-west alongside the street, probably forming the base of a portico. Another room was constructed to the south-west at the same time. The mortar used in constructing these later walls was similar to that in two walls discovered on the south-east side of the *insula*, and dated to *c.* 200 or later (Fox, 1952, 45). In 1950 two more walls were found when a section through Roman levels was revealed by the collapse of the western wall of the Deanery Garden (Fox, 1952, 1f.). In 1953 a road was found which marked the north-eastern limit of the baths *insula* (Fox, 1953, 1f.). It is argued elsewhere that the street originally functioned as the fortress *via principalis* (see p. 9). It was later resurfaced with gravel after its level had been raised by a dump of clay and gravel; associated pottery was dated to the late first and early second centuries. On the south-west side of the street a stone-lined drain 37.5 cm wide was found, whose construction A. Fox sought to associate with the resurfacing. Unfortunately its partial robbing had destroyed the relationships necessary to prove this, although the lower silting of the drain contained pottery of second-century date. The upper silting contained pottery of third- or fourth-century date, including the rim of a purple-gloss New Forest beaker datable to after *c.* 270. The drain was almost certainly one of the principal outfalls from the baths.

These various and fragmentary records of the public baths at Exeter tell us a little about the general layout of the building and its date of construction. The baths may well have been built at the same time as the *forum;* there is nothing amongst the stratified material from past excavations to show otherwise. Rebuilding and extensions took place around or after 200. The coin of Claudius II from the filling of the *natatio* and the pottery from the upper silting of the drain show that the baths may have fallen into disuse as early as the late third century.

The *natatio* is of such a large size that it must have been an external feature; it would otherwise be necessary to postulate the existence of baths quite at variance in scale and character with the status of the community which they were intended to serve. External *natationes* are known from the later public baths at Wroxeter (Webster, 1975, Fig. 23, measuring 7 m by 12.5 m) and from the baths in the fortress at Caerleon (Boon, 1972, 81, measuring 41 m (later 33 m) by 6.7 m); elsewhere in the north-western Provinces there are first-century examples at Augst (Frauenthermen, Laur-Belart, 1966, Abb. 51) and at the Flavian Baths "En Perruet" at Avenches (Schwarz, 1969, Taf. 22).

The excavation report refers to the 'traces of the position' occupied by a row of columns on the inner edge of the pavement on the west side of the *natatio*. At first sight the colonnade would seem to suggest the existence of a portico on the south-west side of the *natatio*. However the portico would have been situated just 12.5 m south-west of the street which runs down the north-eastern side of the *insula*, and thus the *natatio* would have been situated in a rather narrow courtyard or *palaestra*. On the other hand, it is possible that the colonnade was a free-standing, purely decorative feature, enclosing all four sides of the *natatio*. In a reconstruction drawing of the *natatio* at Wroxeter, the late A. Sorrell restored a similar feature with two *exedrae* at the centre of the narrow ends (Webster, 1975, at 64, Fig. 24). At Hadrian's Villa, both *Canopus* and the *Teatro Marittimo* have free-standing colonnades bordering the edges of pools (Kähler, 1950, 44f. and 137f.). Other finds contribute little to an understanding of the lay-out of the baths within the *insula*.

Monumental remains have been discovered on both the north-east and south-east sides of the *insula* as well as in the northern corner. This may be taken to suggest that the whole *insula*, which measured *c.* 75 m square (*c.* 5625 sq.m.) was given over to the baths; their extent would compare well with baths at other *civitas* capitals, e.g. Cambodunum (see Table 5).

The only hint as to the position of the main building within the *insula* comes from South Street where massive foundations were found in the nineteenth century. If the axis of the main building had been from north-west to south-east in order to give the *caldarium* the usual southerly aspect, terracing into the slope would have been necessary, explaining the presence of powerful substructures.

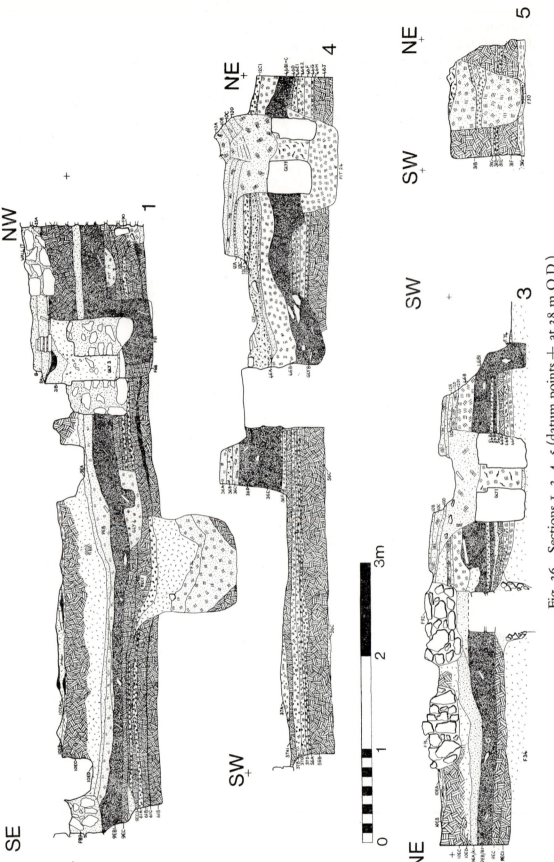

Fig. 36. Sections 1, 3, 4, 5 (datum points + at 38 m O.D.).

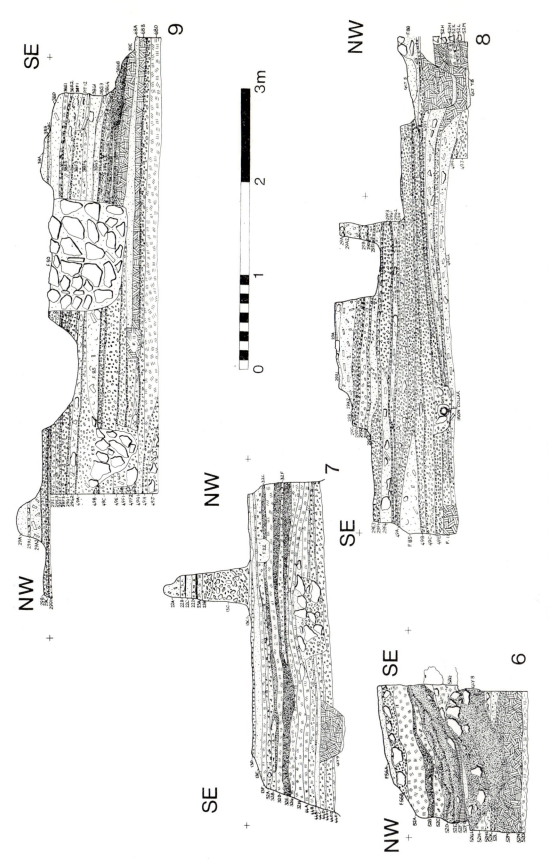

Fig. 37. Sections 6, 7, 8, 9 (datum points + at 38 m O.D.).

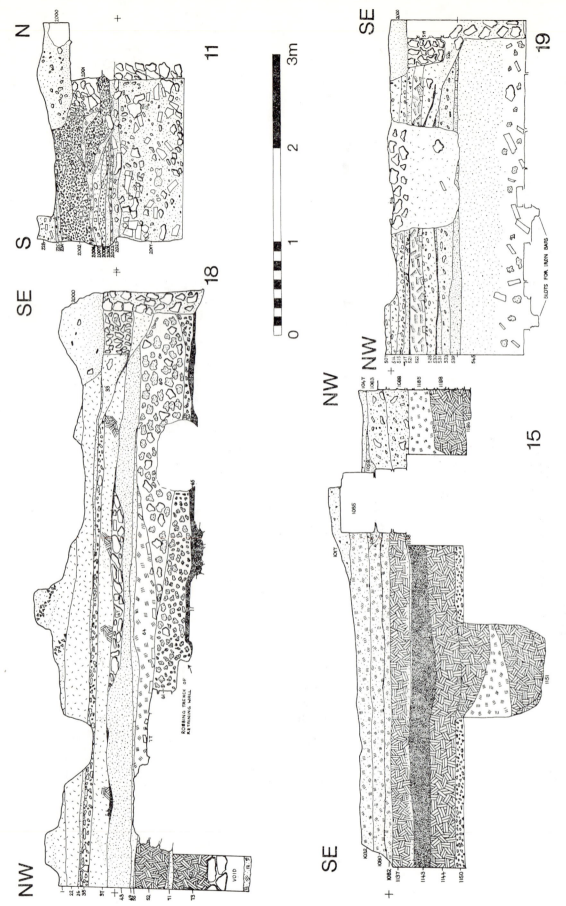

Fig. 38. Sections 11, 15, 18, 19 (datum points + at 38 m O.D.).

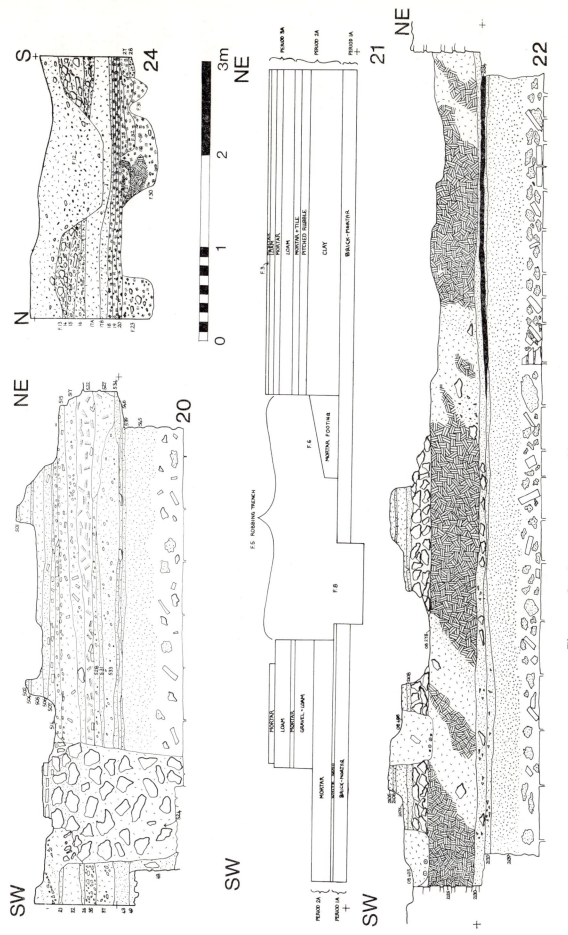

Fig. 39. Sections 20, 21, 22, 24 (datum points + at 38 m O.D.).

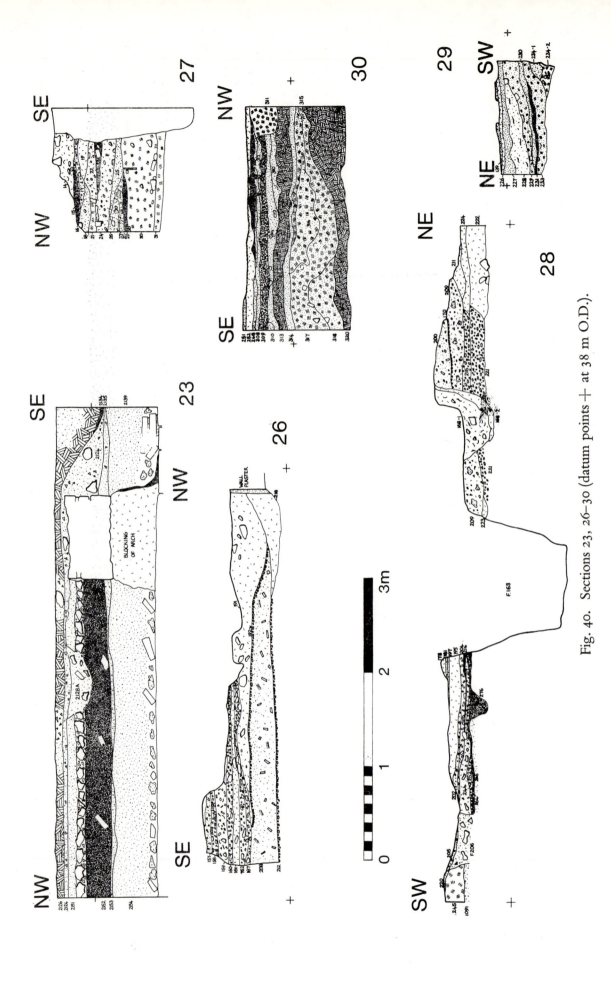

Fig. 40. Sections 23, 26–30 (datum points + at 38 m O.D.).

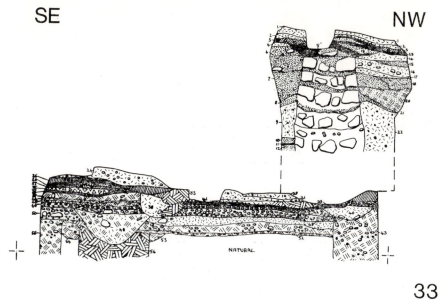

SE   NW

33

A   B   C

SW   NE

32

0   1   2   3m

SE   NW

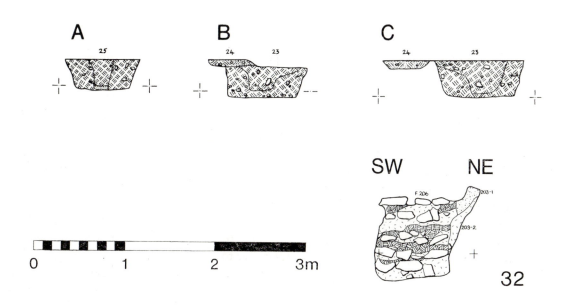

Elev 5

Fig. 41. Sections 32–33; Profiles A–C; Elevation 5 (datum points + at 38 m O.D.).

VIII. BUILDING MATERIALS AND CARVED STONE

Chronological summary

Foundation of fortress	..	..	*c.* 55–60
Period 1A (construction)	..	..	*c.* 60–65
Period 1B (construction)	..	..	*c.* 75
Period 2A (construction)	..	..	*c.* 80
Period 2B (construction)	..	..	late Antonine
Period 2C (construction)	..	..	last quarter of the third century
Period 3A (construction)	..	..	*c.* 340–350.
Period 3B (cemetery)	..	..	mid-fifth to (?) seventh centuries.

1. A NOTE ON THE SCUPTURED TORSO OF A BIRD (Pl. XX)
by J. M. C. TOYNBEE

In 1972 there came to light in Trichay Street, Exeter, the roughly life-size torso of a large bird carved in Purbeck marble. It was found in a rubbish pit, associated with late-first-century pottery, near the centre of the Roman city, on a site that had been in military occupation from *c.* A.D. 55–60 until the mid seventies of the first century. The sculpture represents the front portion of the bird's body and the upper section of each of its legs. The back of the piece, which is completely flat, is 20 cm long and 15.5 cm wide at its greatest extent; and the fragment measures *c.* 9 cm from the flat surface behind to the greatest projection of the body in front. In the centre of the flat surface, nearer to the top than to the bottom, is a small round hole, *c.* 1.5 cm deep, into which could have been fitted a peg uniting the piece that we have to a separate, missing piece of marble on which the bird's wings and back would have been carved. At the top of the fragment there is a clean horizontal cut well below the base of the lost neck, suggestive of the bird's deliberate decapitation. The lower portions of both legs and the claws are gone. Behind the upper portions of the legs the sculpture tapers towards the missing tail. The remainder of the legs, the chest, and the sides of the body are carved with a series of curved relief-lines running in different directions, which represent feathers very naturalistically and sensitively rendered. A very slightly projecting ridge along the left-hand (spectator's) side of the piece, at the top of the edge of the flat surface behind, may be the beginning of the right wing.

Of the species of bird portrayed there is no quite conclusive evidence. But the notably massive proportions of the breast and the military character of the find-spot make an eagle the most likely candidate for its identity. It might, if an eagle, have stood, facing the spectator, on the ground beside the right leg of a life-size statue of Jupiter or of an emperor in Jupiter's guise; and such a group would have found a natural place in the headquarters building of a legionary fortress. Of such a statue of a god or emperor not a trace has survived. But chronologically the personage depicted could well have been Nero, most of whose portraits, at the time of his *damnatio memoriae*, were either completely destroyed or provided with a new head, that of one of his immediate successors. As for the imperial eagle, it might have been thought sufficient to mutilate it, smashing

S

NE

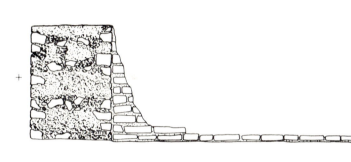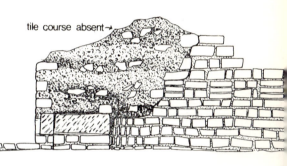

tile course absent→

SW

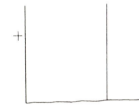

NW

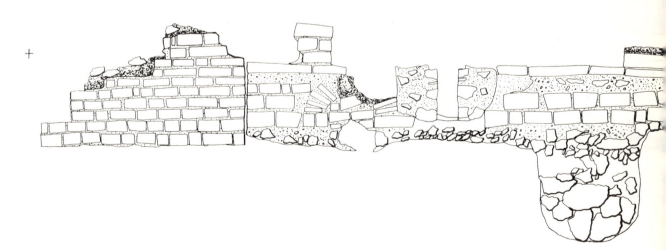

SE

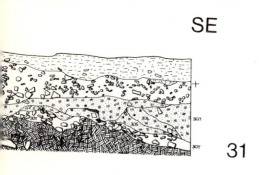

31

SW

Elev

NE

Elev.

NE

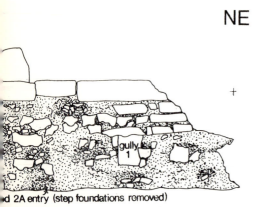

d 2A entry (step foundations removed)

Elev. 3

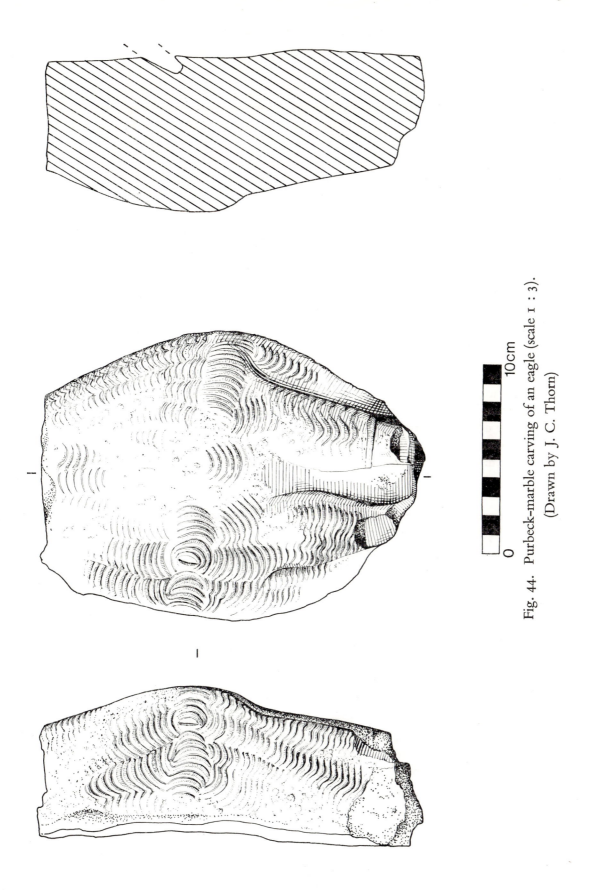

Fig. 44. Purbeck-marble carving of an eagle (scale 1 : 3).
(Drawn by J. C. Thorn)

to bits its head, wings, back and claws and consigning what was left to a rubbish pit. Such a reconstruction of the story of the piece is, of course, purely speculative; but at least it offers a possible explanation of it.[1]

Imperial portraits there must have been in Britain from the earliest days of the Roman province. But whether they were of bronze or foreign marble and imported ready-made, or were carved in this island in local materials by immigrant artists associated with the army is a question that cannot be answered. Of the Exeter (?) eagle it can, however, be said with certainty that it was worked in Britain by an artist from abroad. Its delicate sculpting betrays the hand of a very competent craftsman trained in the naturalistic tradition of classical art. In this respect it is in sharp contrast to the limestone statuette of an eagle found in 1948 about half a mile from the Roman villa at Spoonley Wood in Gloucestershire, where it might have formed part of a shrine of Jupiter. In this case the feathers of the breast and folded wings (the head, the legs, and the tip of the tail are gone) are roughly indicated by purely conventional, incised, criss-cross lines; and the bird was obviously the work of a native carver (Taylor, 1959, 127, Pl. 18). On the other hand, another limestone eagle, about life-size, found in the summer of 1972 near the *forum* of Corinium (Cirencester), of which the head and legs are lost, has most naturalistically sculptured feathers on breast, back, tail and wing (not yet published). This bird was probably carved in the second century by a skilful and highly trained artist, perhaps from Gaul, and it ranks among the best sculptures in the local oolite that grace the Corinium Museum.

One of the most interesting features of the Exeter bird is its material. So far as the present writer is aware, it is the first figure-sculpture in Purbeck marble known from Roman Britain. In G. C. Dunning's survey of the Purbeck-marble industry in the Roman period (1949, 15) the use of this stone during the first hundred years after the conquest for inscription-slabs, tombstones, pilasters, columns, cornices and wall-veneering is fully-documented. But of sculpture nothing is said; and no discoveries of such sculptures subsequent to 1949 spring to mind.

NOTE

1. We cannot completely rule out the possibility that this sculpture was part of a large high-relief and was pegged, by means of the hole in its flat rear surface, onto a stone slab, the accompanying figure of a god or emperor, assuming that it existed, being in high-relief likewise. The bird's wings, whether spread or folded, would then have been merely incised on the background. But so monumental a relief is, perhaps, unlikely to have been carved for a fortress at this early date, when the locations of the various legions were still in a state of flux. A statue in the round could have been more easily acclimatised in a new military context when a legion moved on to fresh quarters.

2. FRAGMENTS OF MOSAIC FROM THE LEGIONARY BATHS (Pls. XVIA and B)

by D. J. SMITH

The following notes are based upon personal study of all the available fragments in September, 1975, but I am indebted to Mr Paul Bidwell for discussing them with me, as well as for providing photographs and data, and also to Mr David S. Neal for communicating to me his own observations, likewise resulting from personal examination.

The fragments, twelve in number, and many loose tesserae, are believed to have come from a mosaic or mosaics contemporary with the construction of the baths, i.e. *c*. A.D.60. Three (nos. 1, 2, 10; see below) were found in the demolition deposit of *c*. 75, the rest in that of *c*. 80 (pp. 62, 67).

Only three colours are represented, namely red, white, and grey-blue. The red 'tesserae' preserved only in fragments 1, 2 and 3, are chips of samian[1]; but Dr M. Stone, Department of

Geology, University of Exeter, has reported that the white are of a fine-grained limestone, possibly from the Beer quarries near Lyme Regis, and the grey-blue are of calcium iron carbonate or siderite of uncertain origin. It is important to note that the latter have acquired a brown scale and, except where this has flaked off, consequently appear as brown tesserae.

Three of the fragments consist of no more than grey-blue tesserae, mostly *c.* 2.0 by 1.5 cm, far from closely set (Pl. XVIA, nos. 10, 11 and 12). These must have come from a plain surround, if not from an entirely plain pavement; one came from the demolition deposit of *c.* 75 (no. 10), the other two from that of *c.* 80.

The remaining nine fragments all preserve smaller tesserae of two or three colours and must be described individually.

Fragment 1. Pl. XVIA:

This formed part of the rubble make-up of a concrete floor which was laid *c.* 75 over the hypocaust of the *tepidarium*, when this chamber was converted into a *frigidarium* (p. 62).

The fragment measures 14.0 by 15.5 cm. The tesserae and their bedding of very fine mortar mixed with crushed tile have together a thickness of 1.5 cm. All three colours are represented.

Centrally at the 'top' of the fragment is a disc of small, irregular grey-blue tesserae across which runs a broken, slightly curving line of samian chips. The diameter of the disc varies from *c.* 4.5 to *c.* 5.0 cm. To the right (as one looks at the fragment) are the forelegs and part of the head, neck and body of an animal, facing the disc. This is executed in small grey-blue tesserae and set against a background of larger, white tesserae. The feet are unmistakably like hooves. On the opposite side of the disc, and also facing it, there was evidently a corresponding creature; in particular, a leg with a hoof can be clearly seen.

Below, separated from the disc by white oblong tesserae only *c.* 0.3 cm wide, a grey-blue band three tesserae wide extends across the fragment. Immediately below this are the remains of an arrangement of grey-blue lines on a white ground. To the writer these suggest a pattern of stylised leaves (acanthus?) curving upward in opposite directions from a slightly arched line near the bottom of the fragment; beyond this is a line of white tesserae and then, on the edge of the fragment, a repetition of the slightly arched line in very much smaller grey-blue tesserae which are oblong rather than square. To Mr Neal this arrangement seems possibly the top of the head of an aquatic deity with excrescent conventionalised lobster's legs and claws.

The disc flanked by hoofed creatures was first thought to be part of a scene depicting a chariot race, the disc being seen as a chariot wheel (*Current Archaeology* IV (No. 39, July, 1973), 109). This interpretation, however, does not stand scrutiny. Any resemblance between the disc and a wheel disappears with the recognition that what appeared to be brown tesserae forming spokes are actually grey-blue tesserae, as in the rest of the disc, on which there survives the brown scale already mentioned. Even the curving line of samian chips does not extend entirely across the disc. Moreover, both the flanking creatures are clearly facing *towards* the disc.

In fact, a disc flanked by confronted hoofed creatures is the only safe description of the remains; but it may perhaps be added that the creatures were possibly sea-horses or—recalling the emblem of the legion whose baths these were—capricorns. For the disc, which presumably occupied an axial position in the design, no satisfactory interpretation comes to mind.

Fragment 2. Pl. XVIB:

This was found with fragment 1 and is of the same materials and construction but regrettably does not join it. It measures 9.0 by 6.5 cm. The mosaic can hardly be described otherwise than as a jumble of smallish tesserae of different shapes and sizes, including a few chips of samian set together in a line, with the exception of a small group forming what appears to represent a human eye; if so, an adjacent line of grey-blue tesserae (including two oblong), and the line of samian chips beside it, must together represent the eyebrow. The eye, then, would be a right eye. There is, however, no indication of a left eye where, allowing for the scale of the fragment, one would expect it. The 'eye' may therefore be illusory.

Fragment 3, Pl. XVIB:

This came from the demolition deposits dated to *c.* 80 in the *caldarium*. It measures 10.50 by 7.5 cm. The backing of *opus signinum* survives to a thickness of *c.* 2.5 cm. The thickness of the tesserae and their bedding mortar together is 1.5 cm.

In terms of technique this is the best of the fragments. The tesserae are generally larger and squarish, one if not both dimensions being *c.* 1.0 cm. The fragment is roughly the shape of an isosceles triangle. Most of it is white and evidently a background. The 'apex', however, preserves grey-blue tesserae in what appears to be part of a straight band, possibly a linear border, and one of the other 'angles' preserves part of a feature executed in grey-blue tesserae and samian chips, some of which are much smaller and less regular than those in the rest of the fragment. Mr Neal has suggested to the writer that, if the fragment is viewed with the 'apex' at the bottom, one can see the remains of this feature part of a typical handle and part of the body of a cantharus; and this seems indeed the case.

Fragments 4–12, Pl. XVIB:

These came from the same deposits as fragment 3. Fragments 4–9 are smaller but similar in technique. None, however, preserves any samian chips. The most interesting of these is fragment 5, with grey-blue lines on a white ground; but it would be risky to suggest possible interpretations of this. Fragments 10–12, which incorporate larger and more oblong tesserae, appear to be remains of a plain grey-blue surround. In fragment 12 the backing of *opus signinum* rises on the jagged side some 0.5 cm above the level of the tesserae, suggesting a quarter-round moulding such as is sometimes found in the angle, between a pavement and the surrounding walls.

Commentary

These fragments are much more important than their small size and generally unimpressive technique might suggest. They constitute the earliest evidence for mosaic so far discovered in Britain, antedating by some fifteen years the pavements of *c.* 75/80 at Fishbourne (Sussex) (Cunliffe, 1971, vol. I, 145–50, Pl. LXXIV–LXXXII); and, while the latter are almost entirely and con- servatively black and white and non-representational,[2] the fragments from Exeter include one with figures, though admittedly rudimentary, one very probably representing part of a cantharus, and one apparently depicting an eye. To these indications of a craftsman less orthodox than the Flavian mosaicists at Fishbourne may be added the employment of samian chips as 'tesserae'. In short, these fragments conceivably represent the work not of a professional mosaicist but of a legionary craftsman uninhibited by conventional training. If so, it is possible for the first time to postulate a military mosaicist.[3]

NOTES

1. To the best of my knowledge this is the earliest recorded instance of the employment of samian sherds as 'tesserae'; for later instances see Rivet, 1969, 76, 78.

2. In fact, among the fifteen pavements of which substantial remains survive there is only one significant exception to this generalisation, i.e. the mosaic of Room N 20: Cunliffe, 1971, vol. I, 149, Pls. XXVI, XXVII, LXXXI, XCI.

3. For a wall-painting probably by a legionary painter see Davey, 1972, 260, Pl. XIX, A.

3. GEOLOGICAL REPORT ON BUILDING MATERIALS

by R. G. Scrivener

Six specimens of building stone were presented to the Institute of Geological Sciences for examination. Comparisons were made with rocks of known provenance and age in order to establish the sources of the archaeological specimens. The results of this examination are summarised below. Colour descriptions are based on the rock colour chart published by the Geological Society of America.

Specimen A—building stone (employed in both the legionary baths and *basilica* and *forum* for architectural details such as column-bases).

Rock type: Greyish-pink, calcareous sandstone.

Probable stratigraphical horizon: Upper (Keuper) Sandstone, Trias.

Locality: Uncertain, extensive outcrop in East Devon, particularly along the coast between Budleigh Salterton and Sidmouth.

Specimen B—floor-quarry (from the legionary baths).

Rock type: Porcellanous, white limestone.

Stratigraphical horizon: White Lias (Rhaetic).

Locality: White Lias limestones of this type have a fairly wide distribution, the principal localities being the Langport (Somerset) district and an area near Axminster. A closely comparable specimen comes from Tolcis Quarry (ST 280010).

Specimen C—building stone (trap, the principal building material in all building periods on the site).

Rock type: Altered, red basalt.

Stratigraphical horizon: Permian.

Locality: Local to site, probably Rougemont area.

Specimen D—roof-tile.

Rock type: Flaggy, grey limestone.

Stratigraphical horizon: Lowest part of Lower Lias (Jurassic) or White Lias (Rhaetic).

Locality: As for Specimen B. A similar specimen noted from the Axminster district.

Specimen E—roof-slate.

Rock type: Greenish-grey slate.

Stratigraphical horizon: Devonian, probably Upper Devonian.

Locality: Extensive outcrop in S. Devon. Roofing slates were formerly worked from the Gurrington Slate near Ashburton.

Specimen F—floor-quarry (from the legionary baths).

Rock type: Olive-grey, calcareous and sideritic mudstone.

Stratigraphical horizon: Crackington Formation (Upper Carboniferous).

Locality: Local to site, outcrops over much of Exeter district.

Other identifications of the origins of building-materials and other stone objects are included elsewhere in the finds-section, and at the appropriate places in the description of the excavated remains.

4. STONEWORK FROM THE LEGIONARY BATHS

(i) *Labrum fragments:*

Twelve pieces of a circular Purbeck-marble moulding were recovered from the rubble immediately above the demolished hypocaust-basement and from the brown loam filling the north-eastern apse. The profile of the fragments suggests that they formed part of the rim of a free-standing circular basin. Their outer circumferences were vertical and smoothly finished with a bevel at an angle of about 45° at their bases; their upper surfaces were horizontal over a distance of about 5.5 cm and then sloped towards the interior, again at an angle of about 45°. Iron clamps set in lead were inserted from the top of the fragments, apparently at frequent intervals: eight of the twelve fragments preserved dowel-holes, in one case spaced only 17 cm apart (Fig. 45, 3) but in another, at a distance of at least 36 cm. Although the undersides of all the rims were broken away, the length of the clamp preserved in one fragment (Fig. 45, 2) indicates that their original height was not much more than that now surviving. The fragments formed the rim of a *labrum* or shallow basin with a profile similar to examples from the late first-century bath-houses at Red House, Corbridge (Daniels, 1959, 116, Fig. 9) and from a Tiberian context within the legionary fortress at Vindonissa (Simonett, 1936, 172, Abb. 12). These two *labra*, respectively 1.54 m and 2 m in diameter, were carved from single blocks of stone, as was also the Purbeck-marble *labrum* from Caerleon with a diameter of 1.7 m, the rim profile of which was not complete (Boon, 1974–6, 228–30). Purbeck-marble *labra* have also been found at Silchester (St. John Hope and Fox, 1905, 345–6, Figs. 4 and 5) and Fishbourne (Cunliffe, 1971, vol. 2, 39, 2).

The Exeter *labrum* must have been clamped to a base, either of Purbeck marble (cf. miscellaneous stone objects, p. 141) or of mortar and tile rendered over with plaster. A diameter of 3–3.5 m was estimated from the circumferences of fragments 1 and 4; if such short lengths can be taken to give a reliable estimate, it would seem that the *labrum* was too large to have been installed in either of the *caldarium* apses and must have been placed in the *frigidarium*.

Fig. 45:

(1) Two adjoining fragments; length 36 cm; dowel-hole passing through fragment with traces of corrosion adhering to its sides; underside broken away (22: 2139).

(2) Fragment; length 20 cm; dowel-hole with iron clamp set in lead still in position; the top of the dowel-hole is filled with lead and capped by a skim of plaster 2–3 mm thick. The clamp protrudes 5 cm below the broken-away underside of the fragment and finishes with a rounded end (16: 1524).

(3) Fragment; length 19.5 cm. Two dowel-holes 19.5 cm apart at either end of the fragment; underside broken away (16: 1524).

Fragment (not illustrated); length 36 cm. Dowel-hole at one end, diameter 1.2 cm (16: 1524).

Eight other recognisable *labrum* fragments were recovered from the following contexts: 16: 1524 (6), 22: 2139 (2); four of the fragments had dowel-holes.

(ii) *Purbeck marble mouldings:*

Three types of mouldings which varied only in size and in the presence or absence of beading below the mouldings were recovered from the construction-levels of Period 1A and the demolition-levels which marked the commencement of Periods 1B and 2A. A fourth type with a more complex profile than the others was recovered from a late Roman feature (18: 516) and probably came from the *basilica* (see Fig. 49, 6). The use to which the three types of moulding may have been put is a matter for conjecture. In themselves they contain no hint as to their position within the building; for instance, dowel-holes are cut into both the zone below the moulding on the front

Fig. 45. Purbeck-marble mouldings from the bath-house (scale 1 : 4).

Fig. 46. Purbeck-marble mouldings from the bath-house (scale 1 : 4).

of the blocks, and also the rear of the blocks. Borders around doors or windows, above the splash-boards of baths or the dados around the walls, or cornices below the springing of the vaults would all have been possible contexts for the mouldings. As far as can be seen, the mouldings were worked up from rough, unsawn blanks and were trimmed to shape with a point. It has been suggested by Blagg (1976, 162) that a claw chisel was used on the surface of some blocks (e.g. Fig. 45, 4) but elsewhere it seems likely that an ordinary chisel was employed. The surfaces of the mouldings had been polished, presumably with stone rubbers, which left many faint striations; these surfaces were often marred by pitting which was caused by the point biting too deeply before polishing took place. The upper rear part of the mouldings and faces adjoining other blocks were also polished, presumably to facilitate a tight fit. Normally the joints between blocks were vertical, sometimes with slight off-sets or overlaps (e.g. Fig. 46, 11); however where diagonal corner-joints were made, *anathyrosis* (a technique whereby the ends of adjoining blocks were hollowed out to provide a tight fit) was employed in two instances (Figs. 45, 6 and 46, 12). Elsewhere in Britain use of this technique has been noted at Richborough on the marble casing of the monument (Strong, 1968, 62) and in the construction of a statue base in the *forum* at Gloucester (Hurst, 1972, 57), both dating to the late first century. In Roman building-work generally it was commonly used in the applica-tion of marble wall-veneers (Lugli, 1957, 207).

Type A: neither of these mouldings has been polished. Because of their relatively large size and rough finish it seems likely that they would have occupied a position at some height above floor level where their details would not have been seen clearly.

Fig. 45:

(4) (Pl. XIXa, 2). Length 52 cm. The surface of the moulding has been worked over with a point and then a claw-chisel; the back of the block has only been roughly trimmed and the bottom has been broken away. One end has broken off diagonally (? along a vein of quartz) but the other end is vertical and shows a rough finish (22: 2136).

(5) Length 18 cm. The fragment is rather battered, but appears to have had a profile similar to no. 4 (23: 2153).

Type B: this is a similar version of Type A, represented by only one example.

Fig. 45:

(6) Length 33 cm. A triangular depression 1.4 cm deep has been chiselled out of the zone below the moulding: the surface of the moulding has been polished but still bears many pits left by the point; one end has broken off, but the other shows a diagonal joint with *anathyrosis;* the centre of this joint has been chiselled out to a depth of about 1.5 cm and the sides have been worked flat (23: 2153).

Type C: the profile of this moulding is similar to Type B except that there is beading at the base of the *cyma recta.*

Figs. 46–7:

(7) Length 29.5 cm. There is a line of chisel-marks immediately below the beading; both ends are broken away (23: 2152).

(8) Length 35 cm. On the rear face of the block there is a dowel-hole 2.5 cm deep positioned 4 cm below the top of the block (23: 2153).

(9) Length 24.5 cm. One end has been broken away but the other preserves a vertical smoothed face. There is a dowel-hole 1.4 cm deep, 6 cm below the top of the block and 9.25 cm from the worked end (22: 2130).

(10) Length 21 cm. A corner piece. The lower part of the front face below the moulding has been worked to a level surface with a point but has not been polished; two dowel-holes have been cut and drilled into this surface, one 2.5 cm deep and connected to the edge of the block by a

Fig. 47. Purbeck-marble mouldings, carved stone and brick-mortar objects from the bathhouse (scale 1 : 4).

groove 0.9 cm deep, and the other 5 cm in depth. The surface of the horizontal moulding is polished but the vertical moulding has only been roughly worked to shape with a point and at the bottom part of it has been cut away to accommodate an adjacent overlapping block. The back of the block is polished over a width of 4 cm from the top and the remainder has been roughly drafted flat. The underside next to the vertical moulding has been worked flat over a distance of 10 cm in order to accommodate an adjacent block (23: 2153).

(11) (Pl. XIXA, 1). Length 44 cm. A corner piece. The entire front surface is polished; there are two rectangular sockets cut into the surface below the moulding, both showing traces of iron corrosion, and a groove running parallel to the vertical moulding where one might otherwise have expected to find beading; at the other end the beading stops 4 cm from the worked vertical face. The back is polished over a width of 4 cm from the top and the remainder has been roughly worked flat. Two dowel-holes have been drilled into the back. The underside is only roughly drafted even on the corner, where on a similar fragment (Fig. 46, 10) the surface was cut back smoothly to receive an adjacent block. The end of the block has a vertical face, except at the top where the moulding projects to form an overlapping joint (22: 2139).

(12) Length 35 cm. The lower part of the front has broken away revealing a dowel-hole 1.7 cm in length drilled from one end of the block. There is another dowel-hole 1 cm in diameter and 2.2 cm deep in the rear of the block. One end is broken away and the other, a diagonal joint, shows *anathyrosis*, with the centre cut out to a depth of 1.2 cm (22: 2139).

(13) Length 19.5 cm. A corner piece. There are slight traces of beading parallel to both the horizontal and vertical parts of the moulding. The underside was not worked flat at the edge to accommodate an adjacent block (22: 2139).

(14) Length 12.5 cm. The front of the moulding has been broken away; near one edge are the remains of a dowel-hole sunk in a rectangular socket. Both ends are broken away (22: 2139).

(15) Length 5.75 cm. A corner piece. There is a dowel-hole in one side with iron corrosion adhering to it (22: 2139).

There were six other mouldings with profiles of this type from the following contexts: 14: 1082; 23: 2153; 22: 2139 (2); 12: 1162; 17: 521. These have no special features and are not illustrated.

(iii) *Miscellaneous stone objects:*
Fig. 47.

(16) Height 11.5 cm, dia. 6.5 cm. Part of a roughly worked cylinder, probably the lower half of a phallus. The surface has been roughly dressed with a point. The top is broken away and the bottom is only roughly worked (22: 2130).

(17) Length 11.25 cm. The lower part of the front has been broken away, but still preserves part of a horizontal depression with a curving profile; the top is stepped back. The surviving edge terminates with two curves, apparently related to the profile at the front of the block; the rear is worked flat and the underside has been broken away; probably a variant of a Type C moulding (16: 1512).

(Not illustrated). A roughly worked fragment 32 cm long, 9.5 cm high and 6 cm wide. The upper part of the sides taper towards the top which is 3.5 cm wide and drafted flat; the sides are roughly worked and the lower parts are broken, as are also the underside of the block and both ends. Purpose unknown but possibly an unfinished piece (23: 2152).

(Not illustrated). Two fragments each composed of two joining pieces; they preserve only one finished surface, and appear to have come from an approximately hemi-spherical object whose diameter can be estimated (very tentatively) at about 1.5 m. The fragments could possibly represent part of the curved underside of one of the *caldarium labra* (16: 1512).

Fig. 48. Purbeck-marble veneers, etc., from the bath-house (scale 1 : 4).

(iv) *Slabs and wall-veneers:*

One hundred and sixty-three substantial fragments of Purbeck marble slabs were recovered from the site, predominantly from levels associated with the demolition of the baths at the beginning of Period 2A (substantial fragments are regarded as those measuring 10 cm square or more). Four particular types of slab could be distinguished from amongst this number and the use to which two of them had been put was clear. Type A had been used to form splash-boards above the baths, while Type B slabs had been used to form the treads of steps, probably positioned in front of the baths. Little can be said about the positions originally occupied by the rest of the slabs; the majority were presumably employed as wall-veneers or for paving. Most of the exterior faces of the slabs were sawn. There was no evidence for the use of multiple saw-blades, which were employed at Fishbourne for cutting veneers (Cunliffe, 1971, vol. 1, 59). The edges of slabs were often worked to a vertical face, or cut away towards the underside; overlapping joints also occurred (Fig. 48, 3 and 4) and joints were sometimes reinforced with iron clamps. None of the slabs have dowel-holes at the back.

Type A:

(Fig. 48, 1). Pl. XIXB. Adjoining fragments of a slab with a height of 43 cm and a thickness of 4 cm. The surface of the lower part of the sawn face is preserved under a coating of brick-mortar which has been stained brown, probably by the action of water; the remaining 29 cm height is pitted and the surface has flaked away—once more, presumably, through the action of water. The upper edge is chamfered towards the rear at an angle of about 45 degrees; the rear of the slab is roughly worked flat (15: 1185 and 12: 1103). Another fragment may have come from the same splash-board; its lower edge is chamfered outwards and forms a perfect joint when placed above the fragment just described; a groove describing a shallow arc has been cut across its face, which is pitted (12: 1185).

Fig. 48, 2. Length 22.5 cm; similar to the large fragment (Fig. 48, 1) but at the bottom of the slab at one corner are the remains of a semicircular 'notch' with a restorable diameter of about 5 cm, probably cut in order to accommodate a pipe (23: 2153).

There were similar fragments from the following contexts: 23: 2152; 22: 2136; 16: 1521; 1: 9EB.

On the larger fragment (Fig. 48, 1) the strip at the base which is covered with brick-mortar has exactly the same depth (14 cm) as the ledge behind the top of the rear bath-wall (see p. 155). Together with the erosion of the exposed surface by water, and the 'notch' probably cut for a water-pipe this feature makes it reasonably certain that the slabs came from splash-boards on the walls at the rear of the baths in the *caldarium* (see Fig. 8). Such fittings can be seen still in position in the *caldarium* of the Suburban Baths, Herculaneum.

Type B:

(1) (Fig. 48, 3). Four adjoining fragments of a sheet 35 cm wide by at least 22.5 cm in length and 2.75 cm thick; the upper surface has a depression 6 cm wide and 0.3 cm deep running along one side and the opposite edge is vertical but is deeply pitted, presumably through the action of water; on the bottom of the slab, 0.75 cm from this edge, there is a dowel-hole 1.1 cm in diameter and 0.6 cm in depth. 20: 545.

(2) A slab 35 cm wide with similar details. 1: 9EB.

(3) A fragment with a surviving length of 17.5 cm; a depression 4 cm wide and 0.5 cm deep runs along the preserved edge of the slab, which is not pitted; near this edge a dowel-hole passes through the entire thickness of the slab. 16: 1524.

(4) A corner-fragment measuring 11.5 cm by 10 cm; one edge is deeply pitted and there is a dowel-hole adjoining it. 16: 1524.

There were three other fragments with a similar thickness and with pitted edges from the following contexts: 23: 2153; 1: 9EB; 16: 1521.

The most plausible interpretation of these slabs is that they formed step-treads. The depressions running along the rear of their upper surfaces were probably the seatings for upright slabs, secured in position by iron clamps; at the front the treads were again fixed to the tops of upright slabs by clamps. Pitting on the front edge of the slabs must have been caused by the action of water and therefore the most likely position for these steps would have been in front of the baths in the *caldarium* (see Fig. 8). No upright slabs were recognised amongst the material from the site.

Type C:

(1) Two adjoining fragments with a length of 40 cm, a surviving width of 21.5 cm and a thickness of 4 cm. The upper surface has been sawn and polished. The underside has been roughly worked and the edges slope in towards the underside. 23: 2153.

(2) Corner of a slab measuring at least 30.5 cm by 34 cm, and 4 cm thick; details as above. 1: 9EB.

(3) Corner of a slab with a surviving length of 21.5 cm and width of 20 cm. Its thickness tapers away from 6 cm at the front edge, which is curved with a bevel at its base, to 3.5 cm at the rear where the slab is broken away. 22: 2139.

There were many other smaller fragments of slabs, the majority of which must have come from wall-veneers. It is possible that some of the thicker slabs were used as floor-quarries, along with the black and white stone quarries described below.

Type D:

Fragments of at least eight rectangular slabs were recovered; the largest and only complete example measured 44.5 cm by 10.5 cm, and was 3.75 cm thick. Five other examples had widths varying between 6.5 cm and 7.8 cm and may have been used to form borders around the chequer-board arrangement of the stone floor-tiles (see below).

(v) *Miscellaneous slabs:*

(1) Fragment of a slab with its full height of 36 cm preserved and with a thickness of 3 cm. The lower 5 cm of the external sawn surface is preserved below a coating of brick-mortar but the rest of the surface is deeply pitted; the lower edge has been roughly trimmed flat and a dowel-hole 1.5 cm in diameter and 2.5 cm deep has been drilled through it; the upper edge has been worked flat with fine punching, and the rear of the slab has been drafted roughly flat—possibly a variant of the Type D slabs. 23: 2152.

(2) A slab with a surviving length of 42 cm, a width of 18.5 cm and a thickness of 4 cm; the front has a sawn surface with the cut stopping 3.75 cm from the lower edge: the broken edge below has not been trimmed away so that the 5 mm width of the saw-cut is preserved; the upper and lower edges are both only roughly trimmed and both ends are broken away; this appears to have been an unfinished block which was discarded. 22: 2130.

(3) Two adjoining fragments of a slab with a sawn face, 3.5 cm thick and at least 43 cm by 18 cm in area; there are two parallel lines of chisel marks running down the length of the fragment, spaced 12 cm apart. 23: 2153.

(4) Three other fragments with parallel lines of chisel marks spaced from 6 to 13 cm apart were recovered from the following contexts: two from 13: 1409B–D and one from 20: 545. The

latter represented the corner of a slab with a dowel-hole (Fig. 48, 4): all these fragments are probably off-cuts discarded from the reworking of veneers from the baths.

(7) A fragment with two partly sawn sides; on both surfaces the saw blade appears to have twisted outwards near the bottom of the cut, and on one side the cut is 0.75 cm deeper than on the other; this fragment constitutes evidence for the cutting of very thin veneers; however none were recovered from the site. 1: 9EC.

(vi) *Sandstone column-base:*

Fig. 47, 18. Probably a fragment from a Tuscan column-base with a *torus* surmounted by a quarter-round moulding. Surviving circumference of 10 cm insufficient to estimate diameter. 16: 1512.

(vii) *Stone floor-quarries:*

Two sizes and colours were represented amongst the stone quarries from the baths. It seems reasonably certain that the quarries would have been laid in a chequer-board pattern with the rectangular quarries used to form borders. Similar quarries have been found in the *basilica* of the fortress baths, Caerleon (Boon, 1972, 79). The quarries did not appear to have been sawn; two partly worked blanks from a context dated to the beginning of Period 1B had been only roughly trimmed to shape (1: 9EB). Generally the upper parts of the edges, which sloped back towards the underside, were finely chiselled, while the remainder and the undersides were only roughly worked.

(a) Dark grey quarries (calcareous and sideritic mudstone):

(1) A complete rectangular quarry measuring 31 cm by 15 cm and with a thickness of 6 cm (23: 2153).

(2) A complete quarry 14.5 cm square and 4 cm thick with traces of brick-mortar on its underside (22: 2139).

(3) A complete quarry 15 cm square and 5.75 cm thick (22: 2136).

(4) Two half-worked blanks, one 16 cm square and 5 cm thick and the other 16 cm by 16.5 cm and 5 cm thick (1: 9EB).

There were also fragments from the following contexts: 20: 545; 16: 1524; 22: 2139; 16:1521 (all from Period 2A (construction) deposits).

(b) White quarries (white lias):

Three complete quarries were recovered from the following contexts: 1: 9EB1; 22: 2130; 22: 2139; measuring respectively 15 cm square by 5 cm, 14.75 cm by 15.25 cm by 6.5 cm and 14.25 cm square by 5.5 cm. In addition there was one fragment from a Period 1A (construction) context (1: 9EC1), five came from Period 1B (construction) deposits, eighteen from Period 2A (construction) deposits and four from later contexts.

(viii) *" Masons' " marks:*

Two marks were carved on the facing blocks of the main building's walls; one, a phallus, was certainly apotropaic, and the other may have had a similar function.

South-east wall of room at eastern corner of *caldarium:* facing block measuring 16 cm by 10 cm, deeply incised with two lines of zig-zag divided by a horizontal line and within a rectangular frame. Pl. XVIIc.

North-east side of *caldarium* central recess: phallus, length 7.5 cm, carved in relief on a block measuring 28.5 cm by 8.25 cm. The block was in a position below the level of the *suspensura*. Pl. XVIID.

(ix) *Corbel:*

Fig. 48, 7. Length 44 cm. A corbel worked in trap. Corbels of a similar type were used in the fortress baths at Lambaesis as brackets to support lead pipes (see further, p. 40).

5. STONEWORK FROM THE *BASILICA* AND *FORUM*

(i) *Column-bases* (Fig. 49):

(1) (and Pl. IXA). Engaged column-base of the Tuscan order, found *in situ* immediately to the north-west of the steps at the north-east end of the *forum* portico; the base consists of two *torus* mouldings divided by a *scotia* and surmounted by a fillet of flattened profile, above which there is a short length of shaft with a diameter of 46 cm. Even allowing for the fact that the base was exposed to the weather for only a short time—this end of the portico being enclosed at the beginning or during the course of Period 2A—the workmanship displayed is of a far higher order than that of the three bases described below; sandstone.

(2) Fragment of a column-base with an estimated maximum diameter of 50 cm; two *torus* mouldings with a fillet above. The top and underside are roughly worked flat; sandstone, weathered; re-used in Period 3A foundations of north-east wall of the 'shop'.

(3) Fragment of a column-base similar to the above; the profile of the *torus* is rather more square; sandstone; from the foundations of the Period 3A north-east wall of the *curia*.

(4) Upper part of a column-base similar to the above; in the base of the *scotia* there are a number of small pits about 0.5 cm in diameter, which, as T. F. C. Blagg (1976, 165) has noted, were caused by a drill "used as a preliminary to the definition of the *torus* mouldings". Sandstone, weathered; context as above.

(5) Fragment of a capital with a maximum diameter of 65 cm; above the moulding there is a square cap, the upper surface of which preserves a number of concentric striations; the outer circumference has been cut away sharply to a depth of 0.8 cm. This capital was clearly turned on a lathe. Red sandstone with traces of lime wash, unweathered; found in 1976, re-used in a fourteenth century stone-lined grave. There is another red sandstone capital with a similar profile in the Archive Room of the Cathedral; it is unprovenanced but was presumably found somewhere in the Close.

(ii) *Mouldings:*

(6) The moulding and the zone below are polished, but the top has been chiselled flat; the rear and underside of the moulding appear to have sawn surfaces; the junction between these two surfaces is bevelled; both ends are broken away; Purbeck marble (19: 516).

(Not illustrated). Fragment from the top part of a moulding identical to the above; Purbeck marble; unstratified.

(7) Large moulding with quarter round recess, the surface of which bears many pits caused by trimming. Both the upper part and rear of the moulding have been broken away; Purbeck marble, heavily weathered; from the northern foundations of the Norman tower of St Mary Major, and therefore presumably Roman since this material is not known to have been in use during the Saxon period.

(8) The corner of a small moulding; the upper surface is rounded and carefully smoothed; sandstone, unweathered; 17: 22.

(iii) *Carved object:*

(9) Phallus; lower end broken away; probably an external feature, perhaps built into the corner

Fig. 49. Architectural material from the *basilica* and *forum* (scale 1 : 4).

of a building to project at eaves-level, where it would have performed an apotropaic function; trap, weathered; 15: 1083.

The presence of only a small quantity of architectural material from the *basilica* could be explained by the systematic clearance of buildings on the site in the fifth century (see p. 110). For two architectural fragments incorporated in the fabric of the Saxon church of St George, see Fox, 1952, 25, n. 5.

(iv) *Inscribed and carved stones:*

North-east side of the south-west nave wall: trap block, its external surface measuring 50 cm by 16 cm, with an axe carved in relief on its face; next to the handle of the axe are two identical objects with concave sides, each 6.5 cm in length (Pl. XVIIA). The axe does not resemble the type used for dressing stone, which was usually double-headed (Blagg, 1976, 156, Fig. 1E), or the *ascia* (*ibid.*, Fig. 1D) which is often found carved on tombstones abroad. Axes are often figured, together with knives, as sacrificial implements on the sides of altars; our example resembles this type very closely (e.g. Espérandieu, 1931, no. 348). The two objects next to the handle of the axe look rather like crude representations of *astragali* (knucklebones). These were used as gaming-pieces and were thrown in a variety of ways; the throw in which each of the four landed a different way up, as seen on a Greco-Roman lead anchor-stock found off the North Wales coast (Boon, 1977, 201), represents the 'Venus' throw, invoking the protection of that deity. The bones are normally grouped in fours, but are sometimes shown in pairs, and they clearly had an apotropaic significance.

It seems possible that the carving was cut down from a larger object, perhaps an altar; the axe is not centrally placed and its blade lies along one edge of the block. If an apotropaic function was intended, it would have been augmented by this act because the block itself would have had religious associations, as well as the objects carved on its face. However there are three objections to this interpretation. First, the eccentric position of the axe may be fortuitous. Secondly, it has not been possible to locate an altar where axe and *astragali* are figured together. Thirdly, the re-use of an altar in this particular fashion cannot be paralleled, although we may suspect that when obsolete altars are incorporated into the walls or floors of later buildings, some sort of apotropaic function may occasionally be intended.

The carving would have been buried by the make-up for the *basilica* floor and thus, like the phallus carved on the east wall of the recess in the *caldarium* (see p. 110 and Pl. XVIID), it would only have been visible during construction work.

North-east side of south-west *curia* wall: block measuring 24 cm by 19.5 cm with 'M' 3.5 cm high incised on its face. The block would have been concealed by the make-up for the *curia* floor.

6. TILES

Periods 1A–2A:

A spread of tile-making debris immediately to the north-east of the fortress must mark the position of the tile-kilns producing material for the construction of the baths.[1] The occurence of antefixes in early levels at Caerleon which were produced from the same moulds as examples from the Exeter baths suggests very strongly that the kilns were being operated by legionary craftsmen (Bidwell and Boon, 1976, 278–80).

(i) *Building tiles:*

(1) *Pilae* tiles (as Vitruvius V, 10, 2) 18–20 cm sq. and 5 cm thick; used in the hypocaust and the bonding courses of walls.

(2) Tiles 24–25 cm sq. and 5 cm thick; used as base-tiles for *pilae* in the hypocaust. Fig. 50.1; tally mark ?.

(3) Tiles 38 cm by 25.5 cm by 5 cm; used as base-tiles for *pilae* (rarely), for walls of tile-built heat-ducts and piers supporting the baths, and as backing for the bath walls; also employed in bonding courses and for turning the relieving arches in the service-building walls.

Fig. 50, 2. Letter 'P' inscribed with finger before firing.

(4) Tiles about 60 cm sq. and 8 cm thick (*bipedales*); used for lining floor of hypocaust basement and as a base for the *suspensura*, also broken fragments used as *pila* bases.

Fig. 50, 3; impression of brooch pin.

Fig. 50, 4; impression of hob-nails.

Fig. 50, 5; tally mark?

Fig. 50, 6; tally mark?

(ii) *Roofing tiles:*

(1) *Tegulae* 55 cm by 40 cm by 2.5–3 cm; height including flanges 6.5–7 cm, width of flanges 2.75–3 cm. As usual notches to accommodate overlapping tiles were cut into the ends. Apart from roofing, they were also inverted and used for lining part of the *caldarium* and *tepidarium* hypocaust basements.

Fig. 50, 7; profile of flange (no complete example available for illustration).

(2) *Imbrices:* a number of fragments including an example with luting to secure an antefix to one end.

Fig. 50, 8; the only complete example. 47 cm long and 21.5 cm wide and 10.5 cm high at one end tapering to a width of 14.5 cm and a height of 7.5 cm at the other. At the larger end there was a coating of mortar 7.5 cm wide adhering to the underside.

(iii) *Antefixes:*

(1) 20 cm high by 17.5 cm wide by 3 cm thick. The antefix portrays a human face (?female) framed by hair; the top of the head is surmounted by a small projection which may be a residual representation of some form of head-dress or crown. The facial features are moulded in quite sharp relief. Without exception, the backs of the antefixes show scars where they were detached from their *imbrices*. They are closely paralleled by a common type at Vindonissa (Jahn, 1909, 112, Taf. VI 4) showing a female face with straight hair parted at the centre and an open mouth. See Pl. XVIII, 1 and 2.

Contexts: Period 1A (construction)—4; Period 2A (construction)—16; nine examples from later deposits or graveyard levels.

(2) Two fragments of antefixes. Complete antefixes from the same mould at Caerleon show two dolphins, heads downwards, flanking a rosette (Bidwell and Boon, 1976, 278–80). The two Exeter fragments show the tails of the dolphins on the upper part of the antefix. 12: 1162 and 15: 1083. Pl. XVIII, 3 and 4.[2]

(iv) *Tegulae mammatae:*

Eight fragments were recovered from the demolition-levels at the beginning of Period 2A, and one from those at the beginning of Period 1B. One fragment preserved its full original width of 37.5 cm; the maximum preserved height of any fragment was 31 cm, to which can be added 13 cm for the second flange (which was not preserved) to give a minimum length of 46 cm.[3] The thickness of the tiles varied between 2 and 3.5 cm, and the height of the flanges was about 7 cm. The tiles were probably made on a form and were knife-trimmed in places.

Fig. 51, 9; tally mark ?.

Fig. 51, 10; tally mark ?.

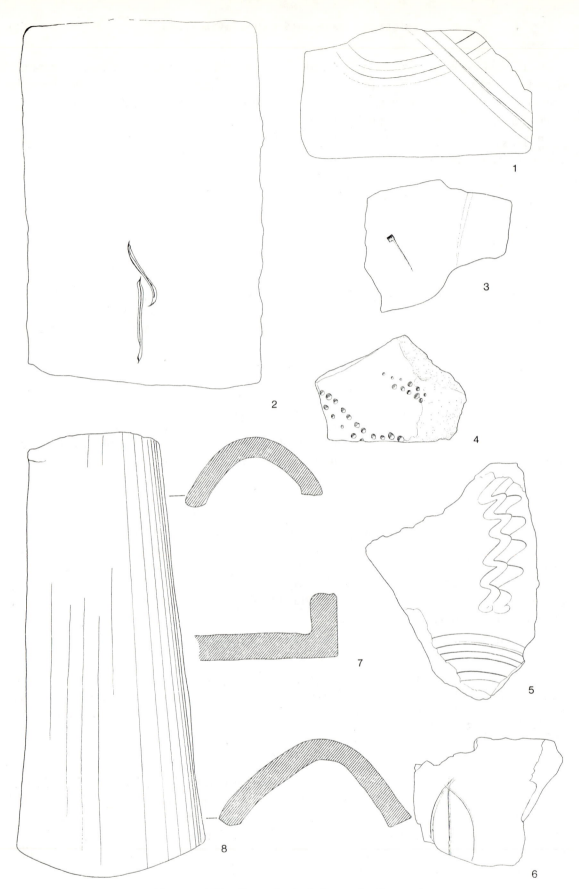

Fig. 50. Tiles from the bath-house (scale 1 : 4).

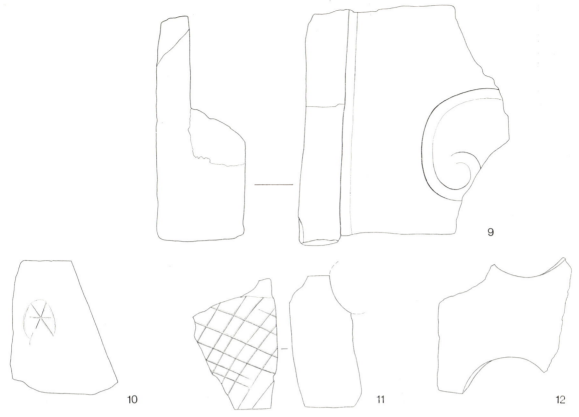

Fig. 51. Tiles from the bath-house (scale 1 : 4).

(v) *Box-tiles:*

Two fragments were recovered from demolition levels at the beginning of Period 2A. The face of one fragment was scored across diagonally to key mortar. The adjacent face was pierced by two holes 9.5 cm in diameter; a width of about 17.5 cm can be estimated for the tiles. They can be compared to smaller box-tiles from the Roman villa in Gadebridge Park, Herts., decorated with roller stamps but pierced at the sides by circular holes and probably attributable to Period 1, dated to *c.* A.D. 75 (Neal, 1974, 195–7 and Fig. 86).

Fig. 51, 11 and 12.

For the use to which the box-tiles and *tegulae mammatae* were put, see pp. 32–3.

Period 2A onwards:

The production of tiles in the vicinity of Exeter continued down to the second half of the third century and perhaps later. Deposits subsequent to the construction-levels of Period 2A produced types of tile not found in earlier deposits, but all in the characteristic fabric of those of Period 1A and 1B. In the later Roman age at Exeter tiles appear to become less common, and other materials were used in their place. Present evidence suggests that slates from the various beds in the vicinity of Newton Abbot and Ashburton, as well as stone tiles from the Salcombe area were widely used for roofing from some time in the third century; channelled rather than tile-built hypocausts became common at this time. Whether or not the production of tiles at Exeter actually ceased at any time within the Roman period is far from certain; re-use of old materials in new buildings and the occurrence of tiles residually in later deposits will probably make it impossible to determine this beyond doubt. The most commonly occurring types of tile, *tegulae* and *imbrices*, certainly show

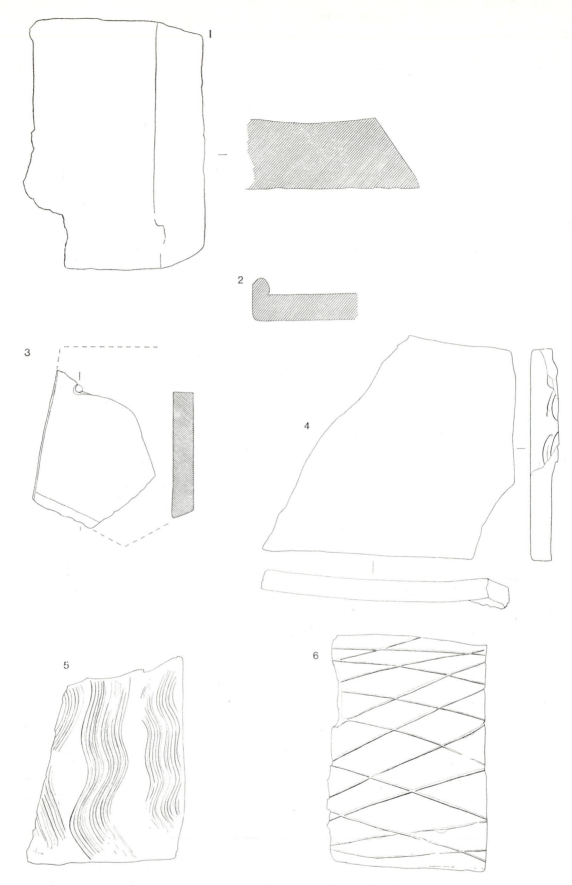

Fig. 52. Tiles from the *basilica* and *forum* (scale 1 : 4).

some evolution of form; the flanges of *tegulae* become smaller, while *imbrices* become much thinner. In the second half of the third century roofing tiles fired to a light buff colour and in a fabric which contains visible inclusions of shell first appear; their place of manufacture is not yet known.

(i) *Building tiles:*

(1) *Pila* tiles (*besales*): four tiles were found in position in the channelled hypocaust inserted in the room south of the basilica in the course of Period 2B. They were less than half as thick as those of Period 1 (thickness 2.5 cm) and were 20 cm square.

(2) Tiles with a chamfered edge, 7.5 cm thick, 26 cm wide and at least 25 cm long; there were four from a deposit of Period 2B. Their purpose is unknown. Fig. 52, 1.

(ii) *Roofing tiles:*

Fragments occurred in many deposits, but no complete examples were recovered. A large group was retrieved from dump layers in the *forum*-courtyard associated with the replacement of the south-west aisle in the last quarter of the third century (see p. 98); roofing tiles with small flanges 2.5 cm high and 1.5 cm wide in the usual red fabric predominated. Fragments of *imbrices* were also

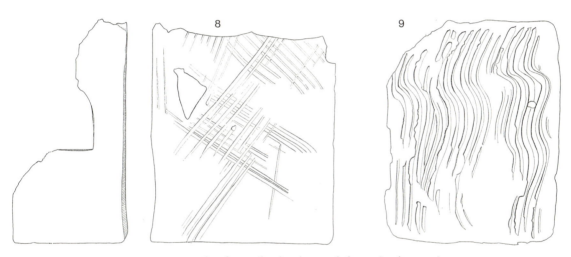

Fig. 53. Tiles from the *basilica* and *forum* (scale 1 : 4).

found with a thickness of 1.25 cm (cf. Fig. 51, 9). One indeterminate fragment in the buff fabric was also represented; this is the earliest context for it so far known. There was a large quantity of *tegulae* and *imbrices* in this buff fabric in the mid fourth-century deposit to the north-east of the *basilica;* the *tegulae* flanges were 1.5–2.25 cm wide and 1.5–2.5 cm high with their tops rounded (Fig. 52, 2), rather than of the squarish profile found with tiles in the red fabric. From this deposit there were also two fragments of possibly pentagonal tiles, with their lower edges slightly chamfered and a nail hole near the upper edge; their shape is reminiscent of the contemporary roofing slates (Fig. 52, 3).

(iii) *Floor tiles:*

The deposit north-east of the *basilica* produced four tiles in the red fabric, 6–7 cm square and 1.5cm thick with sides sloping in slightly towards the underside. Their upper surfaces were worn and there can be little doubt that they had been used as floor tiles. A similar example occurred residually in a mediaeval deposit on the Guildhall site.

(iv) *Voussoir-tiles:*

One voussoir-tile in the red fabric, with its underside combed, was recovered from a context dating to the beginning of Period 2B (1: 10EB). (Fig. 52, 4).

(v) *Box-tiles:*

The earliest deposit containing box-tiles (except those used in the baths) was a make-up under a re-surfacing of the street on the south-east side of the *basilica*, probably to be dated to the second half of the second century (9: 29H1); fragments of five were recovered, four with surfaces combed with implements set with six, eight or nine teeth, and one scored across diagonally. Fragments of similar tiles were recovered from many later contexts; they possessed no features sufficiently distinctive to suggest the possibility of chronological study.

(1) Box-tile with combed surface; from a context dating to the beginning of Period 2B (14: 1082). Fig. 52, 5.

(2) Box-tile with scored surface; context as 1. Fig. 52, 6.

(3) Box-tile with scored surface; re-used in channelled hypocaust south-east of the *basilica*, which was constructed in the course of Period 2B. Fig. 53, 7.

(4) Box-tile with combed surface; from a context dating to the beginning of Period 2B (13: 1402). Fig. 53, 8.

NOTES

1. Ralegh Radford and Morris, 1935, 185; Fox, 1952, 53–54 and Pl. XXV; a G.P.O. service trench in the High Street (1974) revealed large quantities of tile-debris incorporated in the earliest make-up levels of a road leading to the later East Gate.

2. The large quantity of fragments recovered from the site of the baths suggests that the antefixes were used to mask the ends of *imbrices* at eaves-level. On other buildings such as barrack-blocks they were probably used only as gable-ornaments, as apparently at Caerleon (Boon, 1972, 27, n. 75); this would account for the fact that only one fragment (from a face-mask antefix found in the filling of the fortress ditch at Rack St in 1975) has come to light from elsewhere within the fortress.

3. A *tegula mammata* from an early Flavian pit at Mermaid Yard (excavated in 1977) measured 38 cm in width and must have had a length of at least 54 cm.

7. OBJECTS MOULDED FROM BRICK-MORTAR

Fig. 54:

Rear wall of the bath on the north-east side of the *caldarium*. The wall was detached from the main north-east wall during demolition and was found lying where it had fallen in the destruction-debris filling the hypocaust basement (16: 1524). Two fragments were found in opposite corners on the north-east side of the *caldarium;* the central portion had been destroyed in the course of the demolition, perhaps in order to extract the *testudo*, and another substantial fragment had been removed by later disturbance. The fragment in the north corner of the room was very small and represented part of the top of the wall (not illustrated). The larger fragment measured 117 cm by 290 cm and had been built up with brick-mortar in five stages which were clearly indicated by mortar changes: (1) A layer of large fragments of broken tile had been spread over either the *suspensura* or the *bipedales* which supported it; (2) Brick-mortar had been poured over the fragments in order to bind them together and was banked up against the wall over a width of 5 cm. (3) A layer of brick-mortar 15 cm thick with a very high lime content was then laid down to provide a water-proof floor for the bath. (4) The wall of the bath was of brick-mortar 17 cm thick, which presumably had been poured against shuttering. (5) The interior of the bath was water-proofed with a rendering of brick-mortar containing much crushed tile; this was applied to the wall as a layer 1.5–2 cm thick, but at the top was used to form a moulding 14 cm high and 12 cm wide. The gap

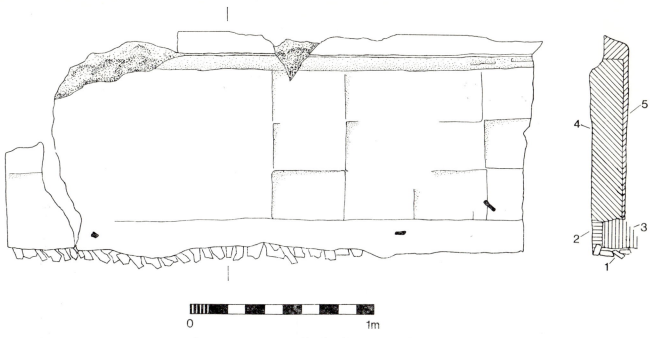

Fig. 54. Brick-mortar; rear wall of *caldarium* north-east bath (scale 1 : 20).

between the back of the moulding and the wall, which was 8 cm wide, must have been left in order to accommodate the lower parts of Purbeck-marble mouldings forming a splash-board above the bath (cf. the height of the zone of brick-mortar adhering to the bottom of the Type A facing slabs, see p. 143, and the height of the back of the moulding—both 14 cm). The rear of the bath wall preserved the impression of tiles measuring 38 cm by 25.5 cm (see p. 149) which, as the heads of three examples preserved in the brick-mortar showed, had been fixed in place with iron T-clamps. Their function was probably to protect the lining of box-tiles behind from the pressure of the bath wall.

It is clear that the bath was not lined with slabs, and that a quarter-round moulding was not present at the junction of the floor and the wall. The absence of a *pulvinus* is also worth noting.[1]

Fig. 47, 19:

Part of a moulding, perhaps from the junction of the floor and wall in the *tepidarium;* coarse brick-mortar with a very thin (2 mm) external coating of mortar containing pulverised tile. The partly-preserved underside, if originally resting horizontally on the floor, would suggest that the top of the moulding was also horizontal, and that its side sloped back at an angle of about 20° to the vertical. 23 : 2154.

NOTE

1. The *pulvinus* was the sloping rear wall of a bath, against which bathers reclined when immersing themselves (Vit. V, 10, 4; Maiuri, 1950a, 227). A well-preserved example was found at Pompeii in the Baths of *Regio VIII, Insula 5* (Maiuri, 1950b, Fig. 5).

8. WALL-PLASTER

Wall-plaster from the Legionary Baths:

A surprisingly small quantity of wall-plaster was recovered from the excavation of Period 1B and 2A construction-levels. Most of the fragments were painted white, but a few were also painted with black stripes 8 cm or more in width. Some of the larger fragments preserved irregular concave

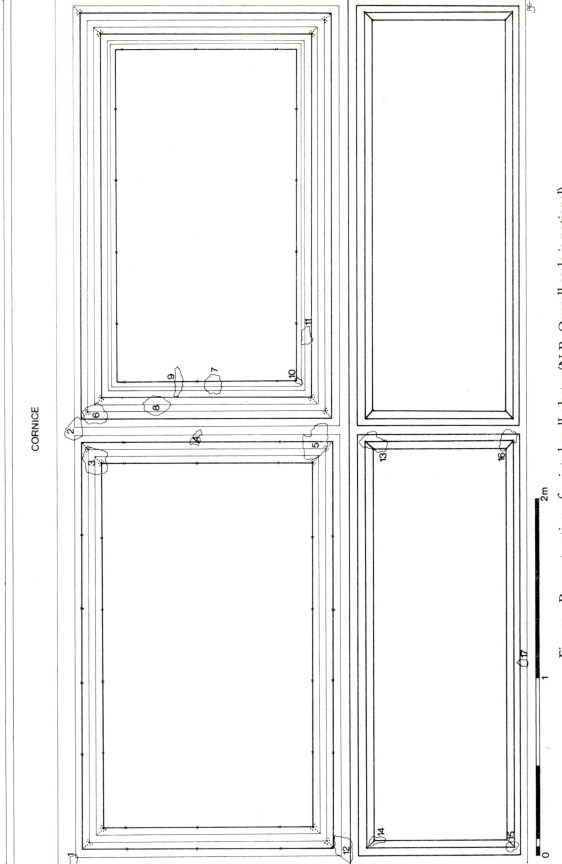

CORNICE

Fig. 55. Reconstruction of painted wall-plaster (N.B. Overall scale is notional).

0   1   2m

surfaces, and could conceivably have come from the vault. A hint that the decoration of the walls may have been less austere in character was provided by half a dozen very small fragments with blue paint from building-rubbish dumped below the Period 1B street-surface. 8: 49F1.

Fig. 47, 20:
Fragment with a chamfered edge; the surfaces are painted white and there was a black band with a width of at least 3 cm painted at right angles to the edge of the chamfer, but not continuing across the top of the fragment. 22: 2139.

Wall-plaster from the basilica *and forum:*
About three-quarters of a ton of painted wall-plaster was recovered from levels contemporary with the *basilica* and *forum*; most of it came from a single deposit in the western aisle. The plaster is described below according to its various find-spots.

Period 2C (construction), south-western aisle (Figs. 55 and 56):
One of the levelling deposits associated with the reconstruction of the south-west wall of the aisle was composed entirely of painted wall-plaster fragments (17: 522; 19: 522; 20: 522, see p. 99). The plaster presumably originated from the walls of the aisle.

The plaster was about 5 cm thick overall and was composed of three layers of mortar. The first to be applied was a layer about 1 cm thick, pinkish in colour with a fine gravel aggregate; on larger fragments the impressions of facing blocks could be made out quite clearly. The other two layers were each about 2 cm thick; the aggregate of both layers was coarser than of that adjacent to the wall. The red paint of the dado was applied directly to the uppermost mortar surface, as was also the white ground of the main zone, which was composed of a lime-wash about 0.1 cm thick.

Two thousand and thirty fragments with painted surfaces more than 2 cm square were counted; of these 37.5% were painted purple/red and 62.5% white, suggesting that the dado occupied three-eighths of the wall height. The white ground was applied with vertical brush-strokes which on most fragments could still be made out; this was evident from the 'T' junctions of the green bands (Figs. 56, 1 and 2), where the paint striations were at right angles to the cross-bar, and from fragments where the green band ran along the top of the dado (Fig. 56, 12).

There were 177 fragments with coloured bands and red and black lines on a white ground; of these 39% had bands or lines parallel to, and 61% at right angles to the paint striations. For the rectangles on the white ground, a proportion of height to width of about 1 : 1.5 was thus suggested; the position of the rectangles on the red-painted ground presumably matched those on the white ground above (Fig. 55).

At the base of the dado there appeared to have been a moulding; one red painted fragment had a projecting 'toe' of plaster which may have marked its position (Fig. 56, 17). The design on the dado was painted white, but the surface of many fragments was so worn that little trace of it survived. The border dividing the panels appeared to have been painted entirely in white; flakes of white paint often survived in this position (Fig. 56, 13, 16 and 17).

A green band masked the junction between the white and red painted grounds. Vertical green bands served to frame panels of two different types, one edged with bands and lines in black, and another by both black and red bands and lines. Some of the coloured bands had black lines at the edges; it is difficult to say whether their presence or absence played a significant part in the design. The corners of the black lines and bands were connected with lines of dots and the junctions of lines were masked with small blobs of paint. Spaced at intervals along the black lines there were pairs of short cross-strokes, perhaps painted to imitate the heads of metal clamps (Figs. 56, 4). The

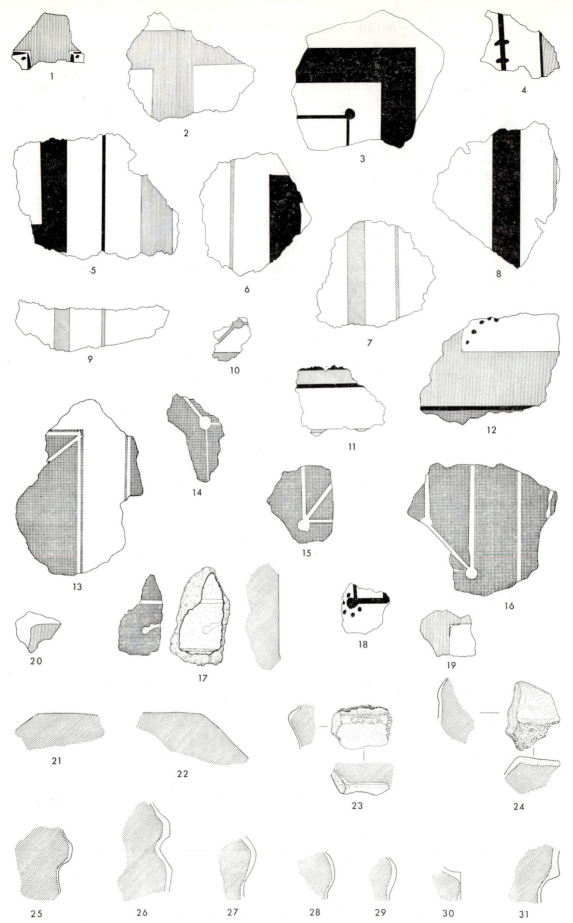

Fig. 56. Wall-plaster from the *basilica* and *forum* (for colour-code, see Fig. 78).

position of the rectangles was set out by means of small marks incised in the plaster at their corners (Fig. 56, 19). One fragment showed a possible example of lines painted in the wrong position; two overlapping corners appear to have resulted (Fig. 56, 18).

The upper border of the painted zone was formed by another green band. On several fragments at a height of 6 cm above the border, the plaster had a broken projecting edge which probably indicated the position of the stucco cornice. The shape of the cornice was roughly moulded in the backing plaster and completed by the application of another layer of plaster, consisting of pure lime. The surviving fragments represented four parts of the moulding and showed that its height was at least 25 cm (Fig. 56, 25–26; 27–29; 30–31); its full profile could not be restored.

Fragments of red painted plaster with chamfered edges probably came from the reveals of doors or windows (Fig. 56, 21–22); two fragments of the stucco cornice with corners must have occupied the same relative positions (Fig. 56, 23–24). The original surfaces of two fragments, one from the dado and one from the green band above, had been plastered over. The replastering was 0.6 cm thick, but no trace of a repainted surface survived.

N.B. The scale of the reconstruction (Fig. 55) is purely notional.

Period 2B (construction): forum (17: 36):

Fig. 57, 1–4: four fragments from a moulding painted white.

Period 2C (construction): forum (17: 1):

Fragments from at least seven highly-coloured panels came from this deposit.

Fig. 57, 5–14: fragments from two adjacent panels divided by a green band; one panel has a yellow ground with meandering red lines, imitating the veining of marble, and the other shows random splodges of yellow and red on a darker purple/red ground. One fragment of the yellow panel is recessed to a depth of 2.3 cm, perhaps to accommodate a stone moulding (Fig. 57, 11).

Fig. 57, 15–20: from a panel showing a plant with green and light red stalks and leaves, with spindly white flowers.

Fig. 57, 22–23: from a panel with a green ground and apparently random splodges of light green, red and black. The border, framed by white and black lines, is yellow.

Fig. 57, 24–25: from a panel with purple/red ground and a black border edged with a white line, its corner masked by a blob of white paint.

Fig. 57, 26: perhaps from the same panel as above; a purple/red ground with a lighter red band and black bordering line running across it.

Fig. 57, 27–31: from a panel with a white ground and red lines; at the side of the panel there is a grey band with a yellow border. On one fragment the grey band is adjacent to a red painted zone, another fragment preserves a markedly curved surface.

Fig. 57, 32–38: miscellaneous fragments.

Road make-up (26: 208):

Not illustrated: a number of fragments from a scheme of decoration identical to one represented on fragments from the contemporary *forum* make-up (Fig. 57, 24–26).

Period 3A (construction):

Robber trench of former south wall of *curia* (15: Int. 3):

Fig. 57, 39: purple/red border and a white ground painted with two black lines, possibly forming one corner of an octagon.

Fig. 57, 40: yellow ground with green veining.

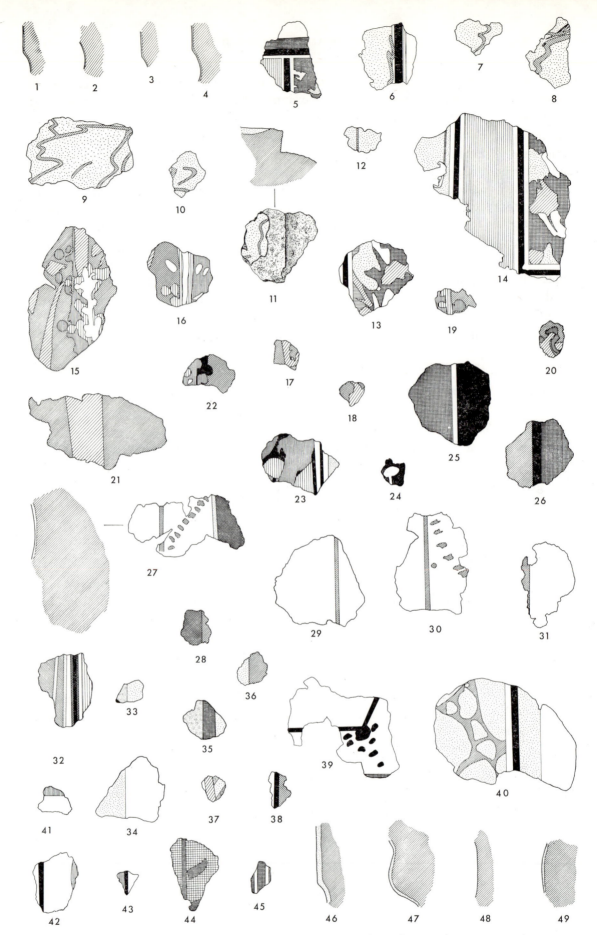

Fig. 57. Wall-plaster from the *basilica* and *forum* (for colour-code, see Fig. 78).

Fig. 57, 41–43: miscellaneous fragments.

These fragments may well have come from the interior decoration of the *curia*.

Demolition debris filling the hypocaust (1: 8A):

Unillustrated: a number of fragments painted white, and in one case painted with a red ground and a white stripe. The plaster was reddish in colour and the surface to which the paint was applied was rather rough. Most of the fragments bore the impression on their backs of twigs, straws, or reeds about 0.5 cm in diameter; these may have been secured to rafters to form a reinforcing mesh for ceiling plaster.

Residual in later features:

Fig. 57, 44: plant leaf and stem painted purple/red on a light red ground.

Fig. 57, 45: two white stripes on a red ground.

Fig. 57, 46–49: mouldings.

Discussion: much of the plaster may date to the original construction of the buildings at the beginning of Period 2A. Only the fragments from the hypocausted room show any marked difference in treatment, and they can be attributed to Period 2C (construction), when extensive alterations were carried out in this area.

The style of decoration in the south-west aisle was austere and economical, and can be compared to the designs in some of the corridors of the Fishbourne palace. The more florid decoration of the remainder was perhaps more suitable for offices and semi-private rooms such as the *curia*.

IX. THE COINS

1. COINS FROM THE EXCAVATIONS CARRIED OUT BETWEEN
1971 AND 1977

by N. Shiel and R. Reece

The precise significance of individual coins from this series of excavations has been discussed in the main body of the excavation report. The only coin which requires further comment here is the *As* of Nero (No. 19) because of the defacements it has suffered; I am indebted to Mr George Boon for his valuable comments on this. A radiate crown has been very weakly scratched on the head, presumably to enable the defacer to pass the coin off as a *dupondius*. On the reverse there is a modern-looking incusely stamped letter 'R'. Roman counterstamps are usually of letters in relief within a frame (i.e. they were engraved on the punch); the present type, however, is paralleled by discoveries in France. It appears to have been applied, as were similar stamps (or hand-engraved letters, etc.), on gold and silver coins to test for plating; plated coins with iron cores are well-known in the early *aes* series (Boon, 1978, 178–80).

As a whole, the coins suggest no major break in the occupation from its inception under Claudius or the early years of Nero's reign down to the later part of the fourth century.

THE COINS

A=Virtually fresh.
B=Little wear.
C=Well circulated.
D=Very worn.

1=Diameter in mm.
2=Die axis
3=Weight in gm.
4=Date (approximate).

		Republic	1	2	3	4
1	D	*Denarius. S.* 745; *Cr.* 372.1.	18	↗	2.54	79 BC
2	D	*Denarius. S.* 1223; *Cr.* 544.19.	16	↓	2.11	32–1 BC
		Empire				A.D.
3	D	*M. Agrippa. As RIC (Tib.)* 32.	28	↓	6.88	c. 23–39
4	D	*Claudius. As* Copy as *RIC* 66 Burnt ?	21	?	4.63	43–54
5	D	*Claudius. As* Crude copy as *RIC* 66	24	↓	5.35	43–54
6	D	*Claudius. As* Crude copy as *RIC* 66	25	↓	4.43	43–54
7	D	*Claudius. As* Literate copy as *RIC* 66	26	↓	8.24	43–54
8	D	*Claudius. As* Copy as *RIC* 66 Burnt ?	26	↓	5.67	43–54
9	D	*Claudius. As* Literate Copy as *RIC* 66	26	↙	7.35	43–54
10	D	*Claudius. As* Literate copy as *RIC* 66	25	↖	6.15	43–54
11	D	*Claudius. As* Literate copy as *RIC* 66	25	→	4.74	43–54
12	D	*Claudius. As* Literate copy as *RIC* 66	24	↓	5.29	43–54
13	C	*Claudius. As* Excellent copy as *RIC* 69	27	↓	8.65	43–54
14	D	*Antonia. Dup. RIC (Claudius)* 82.	28	↑	12.46	41–45
15	D	*Nero. Den. RIC* 52	16	↓	3.04	63–68

			1	2	3	4
16	A	*Nero. As RIC* 185	28	↓	9.05	64–68
17	A	*Nero. Sest. RIC* 207	35	↓	23–90	64–68
18	A	*Nero. As RIC* 329	31	↓	11.24	64–68
19	B	*Nero. As RIC* 329	29	↓	9.23	64–68
20	C	*Nero. Semis RIC* 388	22	↓	5.38	64–68
21	A	*Vespasian. Dup. RIC* 473	28	↓	12.18	71
22	B	*Vespasian. Dup. RIC* 475	28	↓	4.21	71
23	A	*Vespasian. Dup. RIC* 478	30	↓	12.06	71
24	C	*Vespasian. As RIC* 486	28	↓	11.59	71
25	C	*Vespasian. As RIC* 500 var. (legend 3).	27	↓	9.38	71
26	B	*Vespasian. Dup. RIC* 740	28	↓	12.76	72–73
27	C	*Vespasian. As RIC* 746	28	↓	10.06	72–73
28	C	*Vespasian. As RIC* 747	27	↓	10.20	72–73
29	D	*Vespasian. As* Illegible, chipped	26	?	7.48	69–79
30	D	*Vespasian. Dup.* Illegible, chipped	25	↓	6.88	69–79
31	C	*Titus. As RIC (Vespasian)* 785	27	↙	11.55	77–78
32	A	*Domitian. Den. RIC* 171	18	↓	3.20	92–93
33	D	*Domitian. Dup. RIC* 311	29	↓	13.17	86
34	D	*Domitian. As RIC* 327	26	↓	8.14	86
35	D	*Nerva. As* Illegible.	28	↓	9.07	96–98
36	C	*Trajan. Den. RIC* 190a	18	↙	3.20	103–111
37	D	*Trajan. Sest. RIC* 503	34	↓	24.05	103–111
38	D	*Trajan. Dup. RIC* 539	26	↓	9.70	103–111
39	D	*Trajan. Dup.* Illegible.	27	↓	9.21	98–117
40	D	*M. Aurelius. (as Caes.) Sest.* Illegible	28	↓	18.36	139–161
41	D	*Faustina II. Sest. RIC (Aurelius)* 1663	29	↑	14.45	161–175
42	B	*Postumus. Ant. RIC* 303	22	↓	2.81	259–69
43	B	*Postumus. AR Quin. RIC* 363	14	↓	0.75	261–69
44	C	*Claudius II Ant. RIC* 65	19	↓	2.41	268–70
45	C	*Claudius II Ant. RIC* 109	19	↑	2.13	268–70
46	D	*Claudius II. Ant. RIC* 265	16	↑	2.61	270
47	C	*Claudius II. Copy as RIC* 266	14	↓	1.55	270
48	C	*Victorinus. Ant. RIC* 55	18	↑	2.26	268–70
49	C	*Tetricus I. Ant. RIC* 115 o)[ ]VS PI AVG	18	↑	2.48	270–73
50	D	*Tetricus I. Ant. RIC* 129 var.	17	↑	2.55	270–73
51	D	*Tetricus I. Ant.* o) PIVESV R) Illegible	17	↓	1.80	270–73
52	D	*Tetricus II. Ant. RIC* 245	16	↘	1.05	270–73
53	C	*Tetricus II. Ant. RIC* 258	19	↓	1.83	270–73
54	C	Barbarous radiate as *Tetricus I, RIC* 81 Good copy	14	↘	1.35	270–85
55	D	Barbarous radiate as *Tetricus I, RIC* 130	18	↘	1.96	270–85
56	C	Barbarous radiate as *Tetricus I, RIC* 130	15	↑	1.90	270–85
57	B	Barbarous radiate as *Tetricus. Pax* type Pierced.	13	↙	0.80	270–85
58	C	Barbarous radiate as R) figure L.	15× 13	↓	1.37	270–85
59	D	Barbarous radiate as R) illegible	12	↘	0.57	270–85

			1	2	3	4
60	D	Barbarous radiate R) figure L.	12×10	↑	0.64	270–85
61	D	Barbarous radiate R) figure L.	15×13	?	1.85	270–85
62	D	Barbarous radiate R) figure L.	11×9	↙	0.45	270–85
63	C	Barbarous radiate R) figure L.	10	↓	0.51	270–85
64	C	Barbarous radiate R) figure L.	17×14	↙	1.33	270–85
65	D	Indeterminate radiate.	21	?	2.11	260–90
66	D	Large fragment of indeterminate radiate? *Gallienus?*	..	..	....	260–90
67	B	*Diocletian. Follis. Tr. RIC* 188a	26	↓	7.88	296–97
68	C	*Diocletian. Follis. Tr. RIC* 523	29	↓	6.95	302–03
69	D	*Constantine I. Follis* Lon. *RIC* 145	22	↓	2.25	310–12
70	B	*Constantine I. Follis.* Lug. *RIC* 153	19	↑	2.70	322–23
71	C	*Constantine I. Follis.* Tr. *RIC* 305	18	↓	2.40	302–03
72	B	*Constantine I. Follis.* Tr. *RIC* 435	18	↑	2.10	323
73	C	Hybrid o)Constantinus MAX AVG bust r. diad. dr. & cuir. R) Wolf & twins. Two stars. $\left(\frac{|}{\text{PLG}}\right)$	15	↓	0.97	330–35
74	A	*Constantinopolos* $\left(\frac{|}{\text{PLG}}\right)$ *HK* 185	17	↑	2.32	330–35
75	D	Fragments of *Urbs Roma*	..	..	....	330–35
76	B	*Constantine II* $\left(\frac{|}{\cdot\text{PLG}}\right)$ *HK* 198	17	↓	1.99	330–35
77	C	*Helena* $\left(\frac{|}{\text{TRP}}\right)$ *HK* 104	16	↑	1.25	337–41
78	D	*Theodora.* Fragments as *HK* 113	17	↓	....	337–41
79	B	*Constantius II.* TRP. *HK* 116	14	↑	1.80	337–41
80	B	*Constantius II.* TRP. as *HK* 116	13	↓	1.53	337–41
81	D	Constantinian R)*Gloria Exercitus* type One standard	14	↓	0.90	337–41
82	C	*Constans.* $\left(\frac{\text{X}}{\text{PCON}}\right)$ *HK* 431	15	↓	1.16	337–41
83	C	*Constans.* $\left(\frac{\text{D}}{\text{TRP}}\right)$ *HK* 149	15	↑	1.43	341–46
84	D	*Constans.* $\left(\frac{\text{M}}{\text{PARL}}\right)$ *HK* 456/7	14	↓	1.35	341–46
85	D	Copy as .... *HK* 48	14	↓	0.90	330–45
86	D	Copy as .... *CK* 25 (chipped)	12	↓	0.53	350–60
87	A	*Magnentius.* $\left(\frac{|\text{a}}{\text{TRP}}\right)$ *CK* 50	22	↑	3.96	350–53
88	D	*Valentinian I* as *CK* 92	16	↑	0.96	364–78
89	C	*Valentinian I* R) *Gloria Romanorum* type (O|FII)	16	↓	1.46	364–78
90	C	*Valens.* Large fragment of *Gloria* type	17	↑	....	365–78

2. UNPUBLISHED COINS FOUND IN THE AREA COVERED BY THE GAZETTEER PRIOR TO 1971 (Fig. 23, pp. 20–1)

by N. Shiel

The opportunity has been taken to supplement the Gazetteer by publishing in addition, for the first time, various other coins which have been previously discovered in the relevant areas. Of these, the majority were examined in the Rougemont House Museum but in some cases the information has come directly from the Accessions Register as it is no longer possible to isolate with certainty all coins referred to there. The first group, from Broadgate, is part of the extensive Norton Collection which was put together in the nineteenth century, primarily from local finds, and donated to the Museum. This collection contains many of the problematical, worn Greek bronzes which were allegedly found in great numbers at Broadgate in 1810 and later (Haverfield and Macdonald, 1907, 145f; Goodchild and Milne, 1937, 124f.; Boon, 1958, 316–9). These have provoked rather acrimonious discussion in the past. I am indebted to Mr George Boon for his valuable comments on this, and a fuller treatment is forthcoming.

The *aureus* of Vespasian from the junction of High Street and South Street is worthy of note. This was found in about 1906 and bought by the Museum in 1909. It is one of the three early *aurei* from Exeter (for the other two see Shortt, 1840, 30–1, 79, Pl. 11, no. 15, also Shiel, 1975, 475). The specimen of Nero from the Western Market was unfortunately sold out of Exeter in 1975. These three coins form a high proportion of the few early *aurei* that have been found in the South-West as a whole, and would only be expected under a military occupation of some size and duration.

BROADGATE (*=Information from the Accessions Register only.)

Norton: There are fifteen Imperial bronzes in the Norton Collection at Rougemont House which have 'Broadgate Area' as their provenance. All are very worn.

				A.D.
Vespasian.	*As.*	R) Fig. L.	↓ 25 mm	69–79
Vespasian.	*As.*	R) fig. L.	↓ 25 mm	69–79
Domitian.	*As.*	R) fig. R.	↑ 25 mm	81–96
Trajan.	*Dup.*	R) SPQR [ ] $\frac{\mathrm{I}}{\text{FORT RED}}$ figure seated l. *RIC 653*	↓ 26 mm	114–117
Trajan.	*As.*	R) Victory ? L.	↙ 25 mm	98–117
Trajan.	*As.*	Illegible	25 mm	98–117
Hadrian.	*Sest.*	Illegible	29 mm	117–138
Hadrian.	*As.*	R) fig. L.	↓ 25 mm	117–138
Aelius.	*Sest.*	O) AELIVS CAESAR, R) ill.	↑ or ↓ 30 mm	136–138
A. Pius.	*Sest.*	R) Salus L.	↑ 30 mm	138–161
Philip II.	*Sest.*	R) PMTRPV [ ] cos [ ] Mars with spear and trophy	↑ 28 mm	246–49
Gallienus provincial Ae.		R) fig. seated L.	↓ 22 mm	253–68
Mid (3.	*As.*	R) fig. L. at altar	↑ 24×22 mm	240–270
Mid (3.	provincial Ae. 28	R) Cybele	↓	240–270
Tetrarchy.	*Follis.*	R) GENIO POPULI ROMAN $\underline{\quad}^{\mathrm{I}}$	↑ 25 mm	297–306

1874 GAS MAIN

The Accessions Register records some details of coins found during the laying of a new gas main at the entrance to Broadgate in June, 1874, some of which may still be identified within the museum collection.

Domitian.	*Sest.*	*RIC* 284	↓ 31 mm		85
Trajan.	*As.*	R) fig. seated L.	↓ 26 mm		198–117
A. Pius.	*Sest.*	R) fig. L.	↓ 30 mm		138–161
Claudius II.	*Ant.*	R) [LAETIT]IA AVG	↑ 18×16 mm		271–73
*Tetricus I.	*Ant.*	O) IMP. C. TETRICVS[] R) Spes?			271–73
*Tetricus I.	*Ant.*	Illegible			271–73
*Barbarous radiate.		R) fig. with palm	↖ 17×13 mm		270–85
*Constans.		R) GLORIA EXERCITVS 2+2			333–35
*Constantinopolis.					330–35
*Valentinian I		R) GLORIA ROMANORVM			364–75
Valens.		R) SECVRITAS REIPVBLICAE.	↓ 17 mm		364–78

1913.   CORNER OF BROADGATE/CLOSE

Constans.	O) DN CONSTANS PF AVG			
	R) VOT/XX/MVLT/XX $\frac{\text{I}}{\text{III}}$	↑ 15 mm		341–46

1923   BROADGATE

Tetricus I. Barbarous copy.	R) Laetitia type	↓ 16×14 mm	271–80

PROBABLY 1810.   BROADGATE/MILK LANE

A. Pius.	*Sest.*	*RIC* 547	↓ 32 mm	139
Theodora.	*Ae3.*	*HK* 120	↓ 15 mm	337–41

HIGH STREET/SOUTH STREET CROSS ROADS

1883.   SITE OF BROCK'S SHOP

Antonia. Dup.		as *RIC* (Claudius) 82, very worn	↘ 27 mm	41–45
Nero.	*As.*	*RIC* 329	↓ 25 mm	61–68
Vespasian.	*As.*	*RIC* 528	↓ 27 mm	72–73
Vespasian.	*Sest.*	*RIC* 752	↓ 31 mm	77–78
Vespasian.	*As.*	O)]ASIAN[ ]AVG R) ill. Victory L.	↓ 26 mm	69–79
Trajan.	*Den.*	O) mostly flaked away. R) COS V PP SPQR OPT[ ] fig. seated L.	↓ 18 mm	103–112
Trajan.	*As.*	Illegible.	↑ or ↓ 25 mm	98–117
*Philip I.	*Ant.*	O) IMP CAESAR PHILIPPVS AVG R) PM TRP COS III fig. seated L. RIC?		248
Valens.	*Ae3.*	R) ill. Emp. dragging captive	↓ 17 mm	364–78
Illegible	(4 Bronze			

c. 1906.   HIGH STREET/SOUTH STREET

Vespasian.	*Au.*	*RIC* 123	↓ 20 mm	75–79

NATIONAL WESTMINSTER BANK (opposite Guildhall) 1882.

*Nero.	Ae2.	R) Winged Victory		61–68
Probus.	Ant.	RIC 116	↑ 22 mm	277–282
* ?	Ant.	O) bust with spiked crown R) square with crossed lines and dot in each compartment of square. ? copy of Claudius II, RIC 259 ff.?		
*Magnentius?	Ae.	O) soldier with victory and labarum in galley		350–3

*Julian ? Ae. R) SECVRITAS $\left(\frac{OF|}{LVG}\right)$

N.B. must be later if rev. is correctly described. 364–67

*Valentinian. Ae. R) GLORIA ROMANORVM $\left(\frac{OF/II}{//////}\right)$ 364–75

*Valens. Ae. R) GLORIA ROMANORVM $\left(\frac{OF////}{//////}\right)$ 364–75

DEANERY 1871.

Vespasian.	As.	RIC 766	↓ 27 mm	77–78

CLOSE 1891, ETC.

'below the passage of Mr Mackie's house. 9/7/91'.

Faustina II. plated Den. O) FAVSTINA AVG.
    bust r. draped.

    RIC ——R) PAX AVG Pax std. l.
    with O.B. ↓ 18 mm 161–75

"EXCAVATIONS AT THE BASE OF THE SOUTH TOWER OF THE CATHEDRAL 9 ft–10 ft DEEP. JUNE 1906."

*Tetricus II O) C PIV ESV TETRICVS CAES 271–73

Crispus. RIC 168 $\left(\frac{C|R}{PLG}\right)$ ↓ 20 mm 322–23

3. THE HOARD OF 1715

by N. Shiel

J. G. Milne (1948, 219–23) provides what appears to be the only recent account of the large hoard of third-century Roman coins which was found in Exeter in 1715. He reproduces contemporary, or near contemporary, allusions to the find from Thomas Hearnes' *Collections*[1] and Wm. Stukeley's *Itinerarium Curiosum*.[2] He also gives in full the Latin account of its discovery and dispersal, which was written by Mr Reynolds, the local schoolmaster who acquired some of the coins for himself. This manuscript account together with his portion of the hoard, was given by Reynolds to the

Dean and Chapter of Exeter Cathedral in whose possession they remain. Apart from these coins, of which Milne gives only a brief summary by number of specimens per reign, there are seventeen coins in the Heberden Coin Room, Oxford, which he shows to have come from this hoard. All this remains but a small fraction of a hoard which was said to have originally consisted of about half a bushel of coins. Reynolds' account of the fate of these makes it clear that there is little chance of ever putting together a great deal more of the hoard:

Hos nummos quum invenerunt opinantes fuisse thesaurum, certatim cupide rapiebant ad se operarii et aliqui ex plebe, qui praetereuntes illuc confluxerunt; sed sentientes illico nullo illos ex usu esse pro nummo, plena manu dederunt largiter atque alienarunt, esse deputantes nullius pretii, et magnum eorum numerum vilissimis rebus vendiderunt.

This account goes on to describe the efforts of various local men, with an interest in antiquities, to buy up specimens, and Reynolds' own portion of the hoard was obtained from a variety of people. Not surprisingly for coins obtained in this way, they are nearly all different and thereby misleading as a guide to the frequency of types within the hoard as a whole.

There is in the collection of the Rougemont House Museum, Exeter, a group of coins which is strikingly similar to those which Reynolds gave to the Cathedral. It is not certain that they also come from the hoard of 1715 but the circumstantial evidence is very strong. These coins are part of a very large collection of Roman coins, the majority of which are Exeter finds, which was loaned to the Museum in 1881 and finally donated in 1902 by W. J. J. Norton. A study of the family papers has shown that the bulk of this collection had been handed down from Norton's forebear, Alexander Jenkins (1737–1825), the well-known local antiquary. That a collection with such a well-established pedigree should contain a group of *antoniniani* ranging from Gordian III to Postumus, all of very similar appearance, both to each other and to those in the Chapter Library, which certainly come from the hoard, and with each coin a different variety, makes it extremely probable that this is another parcel of selected coins from the 1715 find.

The nature of the concealment was reasonably well documented by Reynolds. It was found by workmen excavating a cellar in a bakehouse in the Cathedral Close near the gate of Saint Catherine's (see p. 20):

'*Hi operarii . . . effracto de coegmentis lapidum pavimento, soloque ad digiti pollicis crassitudinem novies revulso, ad alterum pavimentum lapideum pervenerunt. Eo quoque effracto, et terra sesquipede exhausta, ad tertium, sed de calce et arena, pavimentum pervenerunt. Sub hoc etiam quum penetrarant duos pedes, hos offenderunt nummos . . . .*'

This location some two feet below what may have been a Roman floor-level and the fact that the coins were in a leaden container shows this to have been what Milne calls a 'concealment hoard'. Discounting the Claudian copies associated with the hoard (one of which is in the Chapter Library and one at Oxford), which may have become associated afterwards, the range of extant coins is from Severus to Postumus save for one *denarius* of Trajan. Of the previously cited early allusions to the find only Hearnes' entry for 26 Sept. 1717 expands on this in talking of a range 'from Antoninus Pius to Gallienus.' Undoubtedly the majority of the hoard consisted of mid third-century coins and represented a cross-section of the coinage in use at that time rather than an accumulation made over several generations. The latest surviving coins date to the early 260s. Given the considerable element of chance that has dictated the nature of this surviving portion, it would seem reasonable to suggest the mid 260s as a probable deposition date. Milne's acceptance of Reynolds' observations on the reason why the hoard was hidden and never recovered seems right. There is nothing to suggest any reason specific to Exeter at this time which was, in any case, a period of high incidence of hoarding generally.

Below are listed all the coins which remain in Exeter followed by a summary of those in Oxford and a list of the numbers per reign in all these groups.

Summary by Reign

Trajan	1	T. Decius	6
Severus	5	Her. Etruscilla	1
Caracalla	2	Her. Etruscus	5
Geta	2	Hostilian	1
J. Dumna	1	Treb. Gallus	13
Elagabalus	6	Volusian	11
J. Paula	1	Aemilianus	1
J. Soemias	1	Valerian I	22
J. Maesa	2	Mariniana	1
Sev. Alexander	6	Gallienus (J)	11
J. Mamaea	2	Gallienus (S)	109
Maximinus	2	Salonina (J)	4
Gordian III	24	Salonina (S)	9
Philip I	15	Valerian II	5
Philip II	4	Saloninus	2
Ot. Severa	4	Postumus	33

plus one Claudian copy at Exeter and one at Oxford supposedly from this hoard.

THE COINS

(Cathedral Library coins prefixed C, Rougemont House coins R)

RIC

Trajan (98–117)

C1	Denarius	SPQR OPTIMO PRINCIPI
		⎯⎯⎯⎯⎯⎯⎯⎯
		VIA TRAIANA	↓ 17 mm	267

Septimius Severus (193–211)

C2	Denarius	[PACI] AETERNAE	↓ 15 mm	118
C3	Denarius	SALVS	↑ 17 mm	119
C4	Denarius	PM TRP VIII COS II PP	↓ 17 mm	150
C5	Denarius	PM TRP XVII COS III PP	↓ 20×18 mm	232
C6	Denarius	FVNDAT//PAC//S (doublestruck)	↓ 20×19 mm	265

Caracalla (198–217)

C7	Denarius	PRINCIP IVVENTVTIS (pierced)	↑ 15 mm	13
C8	Denarius	LIBERALITAS AVGG V	↑ 18 mm	215a

Geta (209–212)

C9	Denarius	SECVRIT IMPERII	↑ 19 mm	20
C10	Denarius	PONTIF COS	↑ 18 mm	346

Julia Domna

C11	Denarius	DIANAE LVCIFERAE	↓ 16 mm	548

Elagabalus (218–222)

C12	Denarius	PM TRP III COS III PP	↓ 17 mm	29
C13	Denarius	PM TRP IIII COS III PP $\left(\dfrac{\quad^{*}|\quad}{}\right)$	↓ 19 mm	40
C14	Denarius	INVICTVS SACERDOS AVG	↑ 17 mm	88
C15	Denarius	LIBERALITAS AVG II	↓ 18 mm	99
C16	Denarius	VICTORIA AVG	↓ 17 mm	160

Julia Paula

C17	Denärius	CONCORDIA	↑ 20×17 mm	211

Julia Soemias

C18	Denarius	VENVS CAELESTIS	↑ 19 mm	243

Julia Maesa

C19	Denarius	PVDICITIA	↑ 17 mm	268
C20	Denarius	SAECVLI FELICITAS	↑ 17 mm	271

Severus Alexander (222–235)

C21	Denarius	PM TRP II COS PP	↓ 19 mm	19
C22	Denarius	PM TRP VIII COS III PP	↑ 19 mm	92
C23	Denarius	ANNONA AVG	↑ 18 mm	133
C24	Denarius	VIRTVS AVG	↑ 18 mm	226
C25	Denarius	PROVIDENTIA AVG	↓ 18 mm	296
C26	Denarius	O) IMP SEV ALEXAND AVG bust r. laur. R) PM TRP VIII COS III PP Jupiter standing l. with thunderbolt and sceptre, infant before	↓ 18 mm	—

Julia Mamaea

C27	Denarius	FELICITAS PVBLICA	↑ 20 mm	335
C28	Denarius	IVNO CONSERVATRIX	↓ 17 mm	343

Maximinus I (235–238)

C29	Denarius	PAX AVGVSTI	↑ 19 mm	12
C30	Denarius	SALVS AVGVSTI	↓ 20 mm	14

Gordian III (238–244)

C31	Antoninianus	LIBERALITAS AVG II	↑ 22 mm	36
C32	Antoninianus	PM TRP II COS PP	↓ 22 mm	37
C33	Antoninianus	AEQVITAS AVG	↓ 22 mm	63
C34	Antoninianus	ROMAE AETERNAE	↓ 21 mm	70
R35	Antoninianus	IOVI STATORI	↓ 22 mm	84
R36	Antoninianus	LAETITIA AVG N	↑ 22 mm	86
C37	Antoninianus	PM TRP IIII COS II PP	↓ 21 mm	88
C38	Antoninianus	PM TRP IIII COS II PP	↓ 22 mm	92
C39	Antoninianus	PM TRP V COS II PP	↑ 23 mm	93
C40	Antoninianus	PM TRP VI COS II PP	↑ 22 mm	94
C41	Antoninianus	VIRTVTI AVGVSTI	↑ 21 mm	95

R42	Antoninianus	VIRTVTI AVGVSTI	↗ 22 mm	95
C43	Antoninianus	IOVI STATORI	↓ 21 mm	136
C44	Antoninianus	FORTUNA REDVX	↑ 20 mm	144
C45	Antoninianus	PROVID AVG	↓ 22 mm	148
C46	Antoninianus	PROVIDENTIA AVG	↓ 21 mm	150
C47	Antoninianus	SECVRIT PERPET	↑ 20 mm	152
C48	Antoninianus	FIDES MILITVM	↓ 22 mm	209
R49	Antoninianus	FORTVNA REDVX	↙ 22 mm	210
C50	Antoninianus	PAX AVGVSTI	↑ 24×19 mm	215

Philip I (244–249)

C51	Antoninianus	PM TRP II COS PP	↑ 20 mm	2
R52	Antoninianus	TRANQVILLITAS AVGG	↙ 21 mm	9
C53	Antoninianus	SAECVLARES AVGG $\left(\frac{\mathrm{I}}{\mathrm{V}}\right)$	↓ 23 mm	19
C54	Antoninianus	ADVENTVS AVGG	↑ 21 mm	266
R55	Antoninianus	ANNONA AVGG	↗ 21 mm	280
C56	Antoninianus	FELICITAS TEMP	↑ 20 mm	31
C57	Antoninianus	FIDES MILITVM	↑ 21 mm	346
C58	Antoninianus	PAX AETERNA	↓ 20 mm	42
R59	Antoninianus	ROMAE AETERNAE	↓ 22 mm	44
C60	Antoninianus	ROMAE AETERNAE	↑ 22 mm	446
C61	Antoninianus	AETERNITAS AVGG	↓ 21 mm	58
C62	Antoninianus	PM TRP VI COS PP	↑ 22 mm	79
R63	Antoninianus	PM TRP III COS PP	↑ 22 mm	105

Philip II (247–249)

C64	Antoninianus	PRINCIPI IVVENT	↑ 22 mm	216c
R65	Antoninianus	PRINCIPI IVVENT	↑ 22 mm	218
R66	Antoninianus	PAX AETERNA	↑ 22 mm	231

Otacilia Severa

R67	Antoninianus	SAECVLARES AVGG $\left(\frac{\mathrm{I}}{\mathrm{I}\,\mathrm{I}\,\mathrm{I}\,\mathrm{I}}\right)$	↗ 22 mm	116b
R68	Antoninianus	PVDICITIA AVG	↓ 22 mm	123c
C69	Antoninianus	PVDICITIA AVG	↓ 22 mm	123c
R70	Antoninianus	IVNO CONSERVAT	↓ 22 mm	127

Trajan Decius (249–251)

C71	Antoninianus	GENIVS EXERCITVS ILLVRICIANI	↓ 21 m	46
C72	Antoninianus	ABVNDANTIA AVG	↑ 22 mm	106
C73	Antoninianus	ADVENTVS AVG	↓ 20 mm	116
C74	Antoninianus	DACIA	↑ 21 mm	12b
C75	Antoninianus	GENIVS EXERC ILLVRICIANI	↓ 21 mm	16c
R76	Antoninianus	GENIVS EXERCITVS ILLVRICIANI	↙ 22 mm	18

Her. Etruscilla

| C77 | Antoninianus | PVDICITIA AVG | ↑ 21 mm | 586 |

Her. Etruscus (251)

C78	Antoninianus	PIETAS AVGG	↓ 20 mm	142b
R79	Antoninianus	PIETAS AVGG	↑ 22 mm	142b
R80	Antoninianus	PIETAS AVGVSTORVM	↓ 20 mm	143
C81	Antoninianus	SPES PVBLICA	↙ 24×19 mm	149

Hostilian (251)

C82	Antoninianus	PIETAS AVGG	21 mm	178b

Trebonianus Gallus (251–253)

C83	Antoninianus	APOLL SALVTARI	↓ 21 mm	32
R84	Antoninianus	APOLL SALVTARI	↓ 20 mm	32
C85	Antoninianus	FELICITAS PVBLICA	↓ 21×20 mm	33
C86	Antoninianus	LIBERTAS AVGG	↓ 20 mm	39
C87	Antoninianus	LIBERTAS AVGG	↑ 20 mm	39
C88	Antoninianus	PIETAS AVGG (—│*—)	↑ 20 mm	42
R89	Antoninianus	LIBERTAS PVBLICA	↗ 21 mm	70
R90	Antoninianus	PAX AETERNA	↑ 20 mm	71
C91	Antoninianus	PAX AETERNA	↓ 22 mm	71
R92	Antoninianus	PIETAS AVGG	↑ 21 mm	72
R93	Antoninianus	IVNO MARTIALIS	↑ 20 mm	83
C94	Antoninianus	PAX AVGVS	↓ 22 mm	86

Volusian (251–253)

R95	Antoninianus	PM TRP IIII COS II	↓ 20 mm	140
C96	Antoninianus	PM TRP IIII COS III	↑ 21 mm	141
C97	Antoninianus	CONCORDIA AVGG	↑ 21 mm	167
R98	Antoninianus	CONCORDIA AVGG	↑ 21 mm	167
R99	Antoninianus	CONCORDIA AVGG	↗ 21 mm	169
C100	Antoninianus	IVNONI MARTIALI	↓ 20 mm	172
R101	Antoninianus	PAX AVGG	↑ 20 mm	179
R102	Antoninianus	PIETAS AVGG	↑ 21 mm	182
C103	Antoninianus	VIRTVS AVGG	↑ 21 mm	186
C104	Antoninianus	FELICITAS PVBL	↓ 23×20 mm	205

Aemilianus (253)

C105	Antoninianus	MARTI PACIF	↑ 22×20 mm	15

Valerian I (253–260)

C106	Antoninianus	DEO VOLKANO (pierced)	↑ 22 mm	5
C107	Antoninianus	ORIENS AVGG	↑ 22 mm	12
R108	Antoninianus	ORIENS AVGG	↑ 22 mm	13
C109	Antoninianus	ANNONA AVGG	↑ 22×20 mm	69
R110	Antoninianus	APOLLINI CONSERVAT	↑ 20 mm	71
C111	Antoninianus	APOLLINI PROPVG	↓ 21 mm	75
R112	Antoninianus	CONSERVAT AVGG (—Q│—)	↓ 19 mm	84
C113	Antoninianus	FELICITAS AVGG	↓ 19 mm	87

C114	Antoninianus	FELICITAS AVGG	↑	20 mm	87
R115	Antoninianus	FIDES MILITVM	↑	22 mm	89
R116	Antoninianus	IOVI CONSERVATORI	↑	20 mm	92
R117	Antoninianus	IOVI CONSERVA	↑	19 mm	92
R118	Antoninianus	IOVI CONSERVAT	↓	19 mm	93
C119	Antoninianus	ORIENS AVGG	↓	20 mm	107
C120	Antoninianus	RESTITVTOR ORBIS	↓	19 mm	117
R121	Antoninianus	VICTORIA AVGG	↑	20 mm	125
C122	Antoninianus	VICTORIA AVGG	↑	20 mm	126
R123	Antoninianus	VICTORIA AVGG	↑	20 mm	128
C124	Antoninianus	FIDES MILITVM	↓	21 mm	241
R125	Antoninianus	RESTITVT ORIENTIS	↓	22 mm	286
R126	Antoninianus	RESTITVT ORIENTIS	↓	20 mm	287
R127	Antoninianus	VIRTVS AVGG	↓	20 mm	292

Mariniana

| C128 | Antoninianus | CONSECRATIO | ↑ | 20 mm | 6 |

Gallienus (Joint Reign) (253–260)

R129	Antoninianus	DEO MARTI	↑	20 mm	10
R130	Antoninianus	GERMANICVS MAX V	↓	20 mm	18
R131	Antoninianus	VICT GERMANICA	↓	20 mm	44
R132	Antoninianus	VICT GERMANICA	↓	20 mm	49
C133	Antoninianus	PM TRP IIII COS II	↓	21×18 mm	118
R134	Antoninianus	IOVI CONSERVA	↓	20 mm	143
R135	Antoninianus	PROVIDENTIA AVGG	↓	20 mm	159
C136	Antoninianus	VIRTVS AVGG	↑	20 mm	456
C137	Antoninianus	O) GALLIENVS AVG bust r. rad. cuirassed R) LAETITIA AVGG $\left(\dfrac{\ \mid\ }{}\right)$ Laet. std. l. wreath & baton	↓	18 mm	
C138	Antoninianus	O) IMP GALLIENVS AVG bust r. rad & cuirassed. R) PAX AVGG $\left(\dfrac{7\mid}{}\right)$ Pax std l. & olive branch & patera	↑	20 mm	

Gallienvs (Sole Reign) (260–268)

C139	Antoninianus	PM TRP VII COS IIII PP	↓	20 mm	152
C140	Antoninianus	ABVNDANTIA AVG $\left(\dfrac{B\mid}{}\right)$	↑	19×18 mm	157
C141	Antoninianus	ABVNDANTIA AVG $\left(\dfrac{B\mid}{}\right)$	↑	18 mm	157
C142	Antoninianus	AEQVITAS AVG $\left(\dfrac{\mid VI}{}\right)$	↑	20 mm	159
C143	Antoninianus	AEQVITAS AVG $\left(\dfrac{\mid VI}{}\right)$	↑	22×18 mm	159
C144	Antoninianus	AETERNITAS AVG	↓	22×18 mm	160
C145	Antoninianus	ANNONA AVG	↑	20 mm	162
C146	Antoninianus	ANNONA AVG	↓	19 mm	162
C147	Antoninianus	APOLLINI CONS AVG $\left(\dfrac{\mid}{Z}\right)$	↓	20 mm	164

C148	Antoninianus	APOLLINI CONS AVG $\left(\frac{\mid}{}\right)$	↓	20 mm	165
R149	Antoninianus	APOLLINI CONSER	↓	19 mm	168
C150	Antoninianus	DIANAE CONS AVG $\left(\frac{\mid}{X}\right)$ stag. l.;	↓	21×20 mm	179
C152	Antoninianus	DIANAE CONS AVG antelope r	↑	16 mm	180
C153	Antoninianus	DIANAE CONS AVG antelope l	↓	20 mm	180
C154	Antoninianus	DIANAE CONS AVG antelope l	↓	19 mm	180
C155	Antoninianus	DIANAE CONS AVG antelope l	↓	22×19 mm	180
C156	Antoninianus	DIANAE CONS AVG antelope l	↓	20×17 mm	180
C157	Antoninianus	DIANAE CONS AVG antelope l	↑	18×15 mm	180
C158	Antoninianus	DIANAE CONS AVG antelope l	←	17 mm	180
C159	Antoninianus	DIANAE CONS AVG antelope l	↑	17 mm	180
C160	Antoninianus	DIANAE CONS AVG antelope l	↓	19×17 mm	181
R161	Antoninianus	DIANAE CONS AVG antelope l	↓	20 mm	181
C162	Antoninianus	DIANAE CONS AVG antelope l	↑	19 mm	181
C163	Antoninianus	DIANAE CONS AVG antelope l	↑	19 mm	181
C164	Antoninianus	FELICIT AVG $\left(\frac{P\mid}{}\right)$	↓	20 mm	191
C165	Antoninianus	FIDES MILITVM $\left(\frac{\mid N}{}\right)$	↑	22×18 mm	192a
C166	Antoninianus	FIDES MILITVM $\left(\frac{\mid N}{}\right)$	↑	18 mm	192a
C167	Antoninianus	FORTUNA REDVX	↓	18 mm	193
R168	Antoninianus	FORTVNA REDVX	↑	20 mm	193
C169	Antoninianus	FORTUNA REDVX	↓	19 mm	193
C170	Antoninianus	INDVLGENTIA AVG $\left(\frac{\mid X}{}\right)$	↓	20 mm	206
C171	Antoninianus	IOVI CONS AVG $\left(\frac{\mid}{S}\right)$	↓	20 mm	207
C172	Antoninianus	IOVI CONS AVG $\left(\frac{\mid}{S}\right)$	↓	20 mm	207
C173	Antoninianus	IOVI CONS AVG $\left(\frac{\mid}{S}\right)$	↑	19 mm	207
C174	Antoninianus	IOVI CONSERVAT	↗	19×16 mm	210
C175	Antoninianus	IOVI PROPVGNAT $\left(\frac{X\mid I}{}\right)$	↓	17 mm	214
C176	Antoninianus	IOVI PROPVGNAT $\left(\frac{X\mid I}{}\right)$	↓	18 mm	214
C177	Antoninianus	IOVI VLTORI $\left(\frac{S\mid}{}\right)$	↓	21 mm	221
C178	Antoninianus	IOVI VLTORI $\left(\frac{S\mid}{}\right)$	↑	20 mm	221
C179	Antoninianus	LAETITIA AVG $\left(\frac{\mid}{}\right)$	↑	20 mm	226
C180	Antoninianus	LAETITIA AVG $\left(\frac{\mid V}{}\right)$	↑	20×17 mm	226
C181	Antoninianus	LIBERAL AVG $\left(\frac{S\mid}{}\right)$	↗	17 mm	227
C182	Antoninianus	LIBERO P CONS AVG $\left(\frac{\mid}{B}\right)$ panther l.	↑	20 mm	230
C183	Antoninianus	MARTI PACIFERO $\left(\frac{P\mid}{}\right)$	↙	20 mm	236

C184	Antoninianus	MARTI PACIFERO ($\frac{P|}{\quad}$)	→	19 mm	236
C185	Antoninianus	ORIENS AVG ($\frac{|}{\quad}$)	↓	18 mm	249
C186	Antoninianus	ORIENS AVG ($\frac{|}{\quad}$)	↓	18 mm	249
C187	Antoninianus	ORIENS AVG ($\frac{|}{\quad}$)	↓	20 mm	249
C188	Antoninianus	ORIENS AVG ($\frac{|}{\quad}$)	↑	19 mm	250
C189	Antoninianus	PAX AETERN AVG ($\frac{|Z}{\quad}$)	↑	18 mm	253
C190	Antoninianus	PAX AETERN AVG ($\frac{|Z}{\quad}$)	↓	21 mm	253
R191	Antoninianus	PAX AVG ($\frac{|S}{\quad}$)	↓	19 mm	256
C192	Antoninianus	PAX AVG ($\frac{|R}{\quad}$)	↑	19 mm	256
C193	Antoninianus	PAX AVG ($\frac{|}{S}$)	↑	21 mm	256
C194	Antoninianus	PAX AVG ($\frac{|}{S}$)	↓	22 mm	256
C195	Antoninianus	PAX AVG ($\frac{|}{S}$)	↑	18 mm	256
C196	Antoninianus	PAX AVG ($\frac{|}{S}$)	↑	15 mm	256
C197	Antoninianus	PAX AVG ($\frac{|}{S}$)	↑	21×18 mm	256
C198	Antoninianus	[PAX] PVBLICA	↑	18 mm	260
C199	Antoninianus	[PROV]ID AVG ($\frac{|X}{\quad}$)	↓	23×20 mm	267
C200	Antoninianus	PROVID AVG ($\frac{|X}{\quad}$)	↓	19×14 mm	267
C201	Antoninianus	PROVID AVG ($\frac{|X}{\quad}$)	↑	21×18 mm	267
C202	Antoninianus	SALVS AVG ($\frac{|R}{\quad}$)	↖	20 mm	274a
C203	Antoninianus	SALVS AVG ($\frac{|R}{\quad}$)	↑	20 mm	274a
C204	Antoninianus	SALVS AVG ($\frac{|R}{\quad}$)	↓	19 mm	274a
C205	Antoninianus	SECVRIT ORBIS	↑	19 mm	278
C206	Antoninianus	SECVRIT PERPET ($\frac{|''}{\quad}$)	↑	20 mm	280
C207	Antoninianus	SOLI CONS AVG ($\frac{|}{A}$)	↑	22 mm	283
C208	Antoninianus	SOLI CONS AVG ($\frac{|}{XL}$)	↓	18 mm	285
C209	Antoninianus	O) GALLIENVS AVG bust r. rad.			287 var.
		R) VBERITAS AVG ($\frac{|}{\quad}$)	↗	22×17 mm	
C210	Antoninianus	VICTORIA AVG ($\frac{Z|}{\quad}$)	↓	21×18 mm	299
R211	Antoninianus	VICTORIA AVG III	↑	20 mm	305

C212	Antoninianus	VIRTVS AVG ($\frac{\;\mid\;}{}$)	↑	20 mm	317
R213	Antoninianus	VIRTVS AVG ($\frac{\;\mid\;}{}$)	↗	22 mm	324
C214	Antoninianus	VIRTVS AVG ($\frac{\;\mid\;}{}$)	↑	20 mm	325
C215	Antoninianus	VIRTVS AVGVSTI ($\frac{X\mid}{}$)	↑	19 mm	331
R216	Antoninianus	PM TRP VII COS ($\frac{\;\mid\;}{}$)	↑	20 mm	456
C217	Antoninianus	PM TRP VII COS ($\frac{\mid}{MP}$)	↓	20 mm	460
C218	Antoninianus	CONCOR AVG ($\frac{\mid}{MT}$)	↓	21×17 mm	471
R219	Antoninianus	DIANA FELIX ($\frac{\mid}{}$)	↗	20 mm	473
R220	Antoninianus	FELICIT AVG ($\frac{\mid P}{}$)	↓	20 mm	474
C221	Antoninianus	FIDES MILIT ($\frac{\mid}{MP}$)	↓	18 mm	481
C222	Antoninianus	FORT REDVX ($\frac{\mid}{MS}$)	↑	20 mm	483
R223	Antoninianus	LAETITIA AVG ($\frac{\;\mid\;}{}$)	↑	20 mm	489
R224	Antoninianus	ORIENS AVG ($\frac{\;\mid\;}{}$)	↑	20 mm	495
C225	Antoninianus	[PIET]AS AVG ($\frac{\;\mid\;}{}$)	↓	19 mm	507
C226	Antoninianus	PROVID AVG ($\frac{\mid}{MP}$)	↓	20 mm	508a
R227	Antoninianus	SALVS AVG ($\frac{\mid}{MP}$)	↓	20 mm	511
C228	Antoninianus	SALVS AVG ($\frac{\mid}{MP}$)	↓	21 mm	511b
R229	Antoninianus	VIRTVS AVG ($\frac{*\mid}{}$)	↖	22 mm	534
R230	Antoninianus	VIRTVS AVG ($\frac{\;\mid\;}{}$)	↓	19 mm	534
C231	Antoninianus	FORTVNA RED ($\frac{\;\mid\;}{}$)	↓	19 mm	572
R232	Antoninianus	VBERITAS AVG ($\frac{\;\mid\;}{}$)	↑	20 mm	585
R233	Antoninianus	VBERITAS AVG ($\frac{\;\mid\;}{}$)	↙	20 mm	585
R234	Antoninianus	VICTORIA AET ($\frac{\;\mid\;}{}$)	↓	20 mm	586
R235	Antoninianus	VIRTVS AVG ($\frac{\mid}{PXV}$)	↓	21 mm	612
R236	Antoninianus	AEQVITAS AVG ($\frac{\;\mid\;}{}$)	↓	21 mm	627
C237	Antoninianus	O) IMP GALLIENVS AVG bust r. rad R) LIBERTAS AVG ($\frac{\mid XI}{}$) Libertas stg. l.	↑	19 mm	—

C238	Antoninianus	O) GALLIENVS AVG bust r. rad		
		R) DIANAE CONS AVG $\left(\dfrac{|}{\quad}\right)$ Hippocamp r.	↓ 20 mm	—
C239	Antoninianus	O) GALLIENVS AVG bust r. rad		
		R) VBERITAS AVG Libertas stg l. & grapes & cornu	↓ 20 mm	—
C240	Antoninianus	O) GALLIENVS AVG bust r. rad		
		R) SECVRITAS AET Securitas stg with baton leaning on column	↓ 20 × 16 mm	
C241	Antoninianus	O) GALLIENVS AVG bust r. rad		
		R) VICTORIA AVG Victory seated 1 on pile of arms	↓ 21 mm	—
C242	Antoninianus	O) GALLIENVS AVG bust r. rad		
		R) SECVRITAS AVG Securitas as C240	↓ 19 mm	—
C243	Antoninianus	R) [ ] AVG $\left(\dfrac{|}{P}\right)$ fig. 1	22 mm	?
C244	Antoninianus	R) [ ] AVG $\left(\dfrac{|}{\quad}\right)$ fig. 1 & tr. sceptre	↓ 21 mm	?

Salonina (Joint Reign)

C245	Antoninianus	DEAE SEGETIAE	↓ 23 × 20 mm	5
C246	Antoninianus	VENVS VICTRIX	↑ 21 mm	8

Salonina (Sole Reign)

R247	Antoninianus	FIDES MILITVM	↑ 22 mm	7
C248	Antoninianus	IVNO REGINA	↓ 20 mm	11
R249	Antoninianus	IVNO REGINA	↓ 20 mm	12
R250	Antoninianus	PVDICITIA	↓ 21 mm	25
R251	Antoninianus	VENVS GENETRIX	↓ 20 mm	30
R252	Antoninianus	FECVNDITAS AVG	↓ 20 mm	35
C253	Antoninianus	VESTA	↓ 22 mm	45
R254	Antoninianus	PIETAS AVG	↓ 20 mm	64
R255	Antoninianus	VENVS VICT	↓ 20 mm	66

Valerian II (Caesar 256–258)

R256	Antoninianus	IOVI CRESCENTI	↓ 20 mm	3
C257	Antoninianus	IOVI CRESCENTI	↑ 24 × 20 mm	3
R258	Antoninianus	CONSACRATIO	↑ 22 mm	9
C259	Antoninianus	IOVI CRESCENTI	↑ 19 mm	13
R260	Antoninianus	PRINC IVVENTVTIS	↓ 22 mm	49

Saloninus (Caesar, 258–259)

C261	Antoninianus	PIETAS AVG	↓ 21 × 18 mm	9
R262	Antoninianus	SPES PVBLICA	↓ 20 mm	13

Postumus (259–268)

C263	Antoninianus	COS IIII Victory r.	↑	21 mm	52
C264	Antoninianus	PM TRP COS II PP	↓	22 mm	54
R265	Antoninianus	PM TRP COS II PP	↓	22 mm	54
R266	Antoninianus	PM TRP IIII COS III PP	↓	21 mm	57
C267	Antoninianus	FELICITAS AVG	↑	21 mm	58
R268	Antoninianus	FELICITAS AVG	↓	22 mm	58
R269	Antoninianus	FELICITAS AVG	↑	22 mm	58
C270	Antoninianus	FIDES MILITVM	↑	22 mm	59
R271	Antoninianus	FIDES MILITVM	↑	21 mm	59
C272	Antoninianus	FORTVNA AVG	↓	20 mm	60
R273	Antoninianus	HERC DEVSONIENSI	↙	20 mm	64
R274	Antoninianus	HERC PACIFERO	↑	22 mm	67
C275	Antoninianus	HERC PACIFERO	↓	22 mm	67
C276	Antoninianus	LAETITIA $\left(\frac{\mid}{\text{AVG}}\right)$	↓	21 mm	73
R277	Antoninianus	LAETITIA $\left(\frac{\mid}{\text{AVG}}\right)$	↑	22 mm	73
C278	Antoninianus	MINER FAVTR	↓	23 mm	74
R279	Antoninianus	MONETA AVG	↑	22 mm	75
C280	Antoninianus	MONETA AVG	↓	22 × 30 mm	75
C281	Antoninianus	ORIENS AVG	↑	20 mm	77
C282	Antoninianus	PAX AVG	↑	21 mm	78
R283	Antoninianus	PAX AVG	↓	21 mm	78
R284	Antoninianus	PROVIDENTIA AVG	↗	20 mm	80
C285	Antoninianus	PROVIDENTIA AVG	↑	21 mm	81
C286	Antoninianus	SAECVLI FELICITAS	↓	20 mm	83
C287	Antoninianus	SALVS AVG	↑	20 mm	86
R288	Antoninianus	SALVS PROVINCIARVM	↑	21 mm	87
C289	Antoninianus	SALVS PROVINCIARVM	↑	22 mm	87
C290	Antoninianus	VICTORIA AVG	↓	23 mm	89
R291	Antoninianus	VIRTVS AVG	↙	21 mm	93
C292	Antoninianus	VIRTVS AVG	↓	21 mm	93
C293	Antoninianus	IOVI CONSERVATORI	↑	21 mm	308
C294	Antoninianus	IOVI STATORI	↓	20 mm	309
C295	Antoninianus	IOVI VICTORI	↑	20 mm	311

Coins at Oxford

	RIC
Elagabalus	68.
Gordian III	35, 88, 89, 151.
Philip I	41, 44.
Philip II	218.
Her. Etruscus	147.
Treb. Gallus	72.
Volusian	182.
Gallienus	(Joint) 29; (Sole) 155, 182.
Salonina	(Joint) 7; (Sole) 39.

NOTES

1. (Oxford Historical Society Edition) vol. V, p. 318 for 1 Oct. 1716; vol. VI, p. 93 for 26 Sept. 1717; vol. VI, p. 135 for 1 Feb. 1718.

2. 1724 ed. p. 151. N.B. Even by the 1723 edition, the date of Stukeley's visit to Exeter, a certain amount of confusion had arisen over the circumstances of the find. He records them as found 'two years ago (*sc.* 1721) near St Martins' Church' and records some being in the possession of Dr Musgrave and Mr Loudham as well as Reynolds. Shortt (Shortt, 1840, p. vi), transmits this in such a way as to suggest two hoards: 'a peck of coins had been found under St Martins' Church, and many hundreds in Catherine Lane adjoining.' This seems the result of a proliferation of accounts of the 1715 find circulating by the time of Stukeley's visit.

X. THE POTTERY

1. DECORATED SAMIAN

by G. B. Dannell

Fig. 58.

(1) Dr. 29. Too little for secure identification, but the MVRRANVS workshop has all the detail (Knorr, 1952, Taf. 44A, for spirals, tendril binding and striated rods).

   14: 1151; Period 1A (construction). *c.* 50–65, S. Gaulish.

(2) Dr. 30. A neat double-bordered ovolo with straight tongue to the left ending in an eight-petalled rosette. The two petals on the right-hand side of the rosette are defective and faint. The others have clipped ends. Winding scrolls above a panel of leaf decoration. The scroll ends in narrow palm leaves and has small birds, 0.2261B type, on the ground. This may be the FRONTINVS ovolo in its earliest form (see no. 10).

   9: 68D; Period 1A (construction). *c.* 60–75, S. Gaulish.

(3) Dr. 29. The dog in the wreath is Hermet 31 (Pl. 26), which is shown together by the lion 0.1417 and bear 0.1614 (Pl. 66.25).

   17: 537; Period 1B (construction). *c.* 50–65, S. Gaulish.

(4) Dr. 37. Panel decoration with a Diana and hare, winged figure, 0.274 and two geese, 0.2220 and 2257. FRONTINVS' style; he uses the geese (Knorr, 1952, Taf. 25A) and winged figure (Hermet, 1934, Pl. 85.2). The leaf is on a Dr. 37 with his ovolo (Knorr, 1919, Taf. 94D). Vessels in this style are also found at Pompeii (Atkinson, 1914, Pl. VII have the leaf and geese).

   1: 9EB1; Period 2A (construction). *c.* 75–90, S. Gaulish.

5) Dr. 29. A small bowl with very blurred decoration. The tightly packed motifs are similar to the design of BASSVS and COELVS. They use the scroll terminal and frilled leaf (Knorr, 1919, Taf. 13C as Knorr, 1952, Taf. 10E). The leaf ornament is used on a Dr. 29 from Wiesbaden (Knorr, 1919, Taf. 13L) but I cannot identify the contents of the medallion.

   14: 1138; Period 2A (construction). *c.* 60–75, S. Gaulish.

(6) Dr. 29, stamped [OF MO]DES+ (no. 9). Upper zone of small leaf motif as on a Dr. 29 from London (Knorr, 1952, Taf. 42A). The lower zone has wreathed medallions with a compound rosette and a small winged figure, 0.406 (note the lack of feet), separated by upright 'dividers'. These are made from two of the leaf motifs from the upper zone, bound by a small medalion containing a six-pointed hollow-centred rosette. 0.406 is used on a Dr. 29 by MODESTVS from Silchester (May, 1916, Pl. VIIIA).

   22: 2126; Period 2A (construction). *c.* 50–65, S. Gaulish.

(7) Dr. 29 (burnt). A small bowl with design made from motifs common in the Flavian period. SABINVS and VITALIS used similar pendants (Knorr, 1919, Taf. 69. 21 and 84.15).

   13: 1409B–D; Period 2A (cosntruction). *c.* 75–90, S. Gaulish.

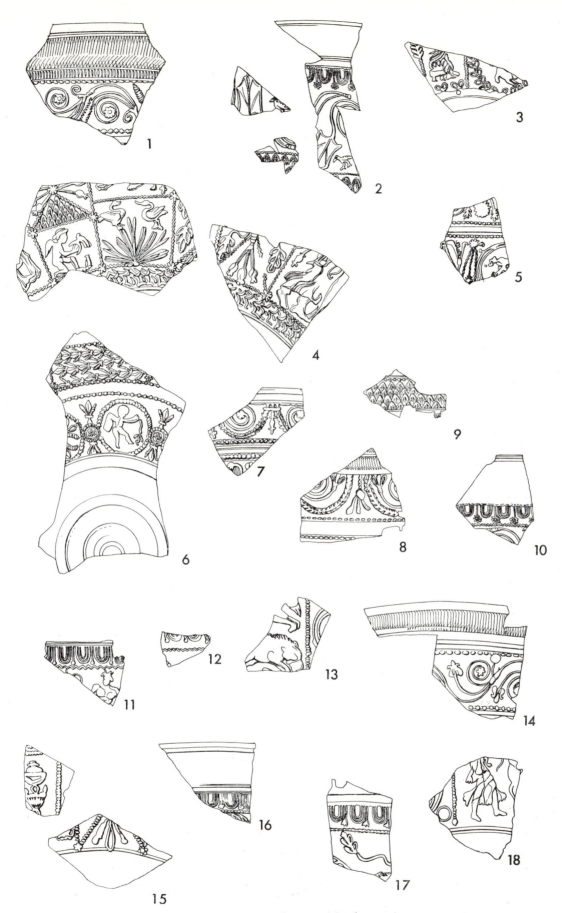

Fig. 58. Decorated samian (scale 1 : 2).

(8)   Dr. 29. Perhaps the work of PASSENVS who used the wreathed festoon and small leaf motif (Knorr, 1952, Taf. 49.D and unpublished from the Musée Fenaille, Rodez, and Knorr, 1919, Taf. 62.43).

14: 1137; Period 2A (construction).   c. 70–85, S. Gaulish.

(9)   Dr. 29. Sharp pinnate leaves.

14: 1137; Period 2A (construction).   Probably pre-Flavian, S. Gaulish.

(10) Dr. 37. The same ovolo as No. 2 but much more worn. In this form it is very close to that of FRONTINVS.

13: 1409B–D; Period 2A (construction).   c. 70–90, S. Gaulish.

(11) Dr. 37 (burnt). Rogers' ovolo B76 ascribed to ARCANVS and GEMINVS.

8: 49A; course of Period 2A.   c. 120–140, C. Gaulish.

(12) Dr. 37. Small scrap in what appears to be Montans fabric. The ovolo is not illustrated by Dr Grace Simpson in her recent paper (1976, 244–73).

9: 39A; early second century.

(13) Dr. 37. Boar, o.1696F. The paste and colouration suggest a Hadrianic–Antonine date.

9: 38G5; mid to late second century.   c. 130–150, C. Gaulish.

(14) Dr. 29. A late vessel with an everted rim and, almost, a bead lip (cf. Knorr, 1952, Taf. 5D by PATRICVS).

1: 10EB; Period 2B (construction).   c. 75–90, S. Gaulish.

(15) Dr. 37. Two pieces probably from the same bowl. The leaf is Rogers' G76, and the candelabrum, his Q10.

17: 36; Period 2B (construction).   c. 140–160, C. Gaulish.

(16) Dr. 37. Blurred ovolo.

14: 1082; Period 2B (construction).   c. 100–120, Martres de Veyre.

(17) Dr. 37. There is a similar design from Holt (Grimes, 1930, Fig. 37.42).

12: 1092; course of Period 2B.   c. 75–95, S. Gaulish.

(18) Diana, o.106 on an Antonine vessel.

Mid or late second- to mid third-century ditch deposits on the north-west side of the street (see pp. 97–8).   Antonine.

2. SAMIAN STAMPS

by Brenda M. Dickinson

(1)   Albanus 1b 27g **OFALBANI** La Graufesenque.[1] The die for this stamp became broken at one or both ends and continued in use. Most examples come from the broken version, including ones from Rheingönheim and Verulamium (Period II, before A.D. 75), but the original version (1b) occurs three times at the Nijmegen fortress, i.e. after A.D. 70. There is no reason to suppose that either of the stamps was used in the pre-Flavian period, though as some of his stamps are earlier, dating c. 65–80 is best for the original version. Period 2B (construction); 13: 1405.

(2) Aquitanus 2b 15/17 or 18 OFAQV[ITAN] La Graufesenque.² This stamp, always on dishes, appears three times in Period I at Zwammerdam and once in the Colchester Pottery Shop I. *c.* 50–65.

Trodden into natural under road south of the baths.

(3) Flavinus i Incomplete 1 cup of uncertain form FLAV[Montans.² The lettering makes this almost certainly a stamp of Flavinus, and the fabric supports origin at Montans. His other stamps are on forms Curle 15 and 23, so he is likely to have been one of the Montans potters who, like Chresimus and Felicio iii, worked in the second century. The work of several of these potters appears in Antonine Scotland, *c.* 115–145.

Period 2B (construction); 18: 33.

(4) Gabrillus i 1a 18/31R or 31R CABRILLIMA Lezoux.³ There is very little dating evidence for this potter, but his forms (18/31, 18/31R, 27 and possibly 42) suggest Hadrianic-Antonine activity.

Graveyard levels.

(5) Iolius 1a 27g IOLII La Graufesenque.³ Only five examples of this stamp are known, all on form 27g. The one complete cup (unprovenanced at Amiens) suggests a Flavian or Flavian-Trajanic date.

Period 2A (construction); 13: 1409B–D.

(6) Iucundus ii 16a 27g IVCVNDV La Graufesenque.¹ Iucundus's record is basically Flavian, but this stamp has been recorded from the pre-Flavian cemeteries at Nijmegen. There is also one example from Hofheim. *c.* 65–90.

Period 2A (construction); 14: 1137.

(7) Iustus ii 2b 31 IVST[I]MA Lezoux.¹ This stamp occurs at northern sites associated with Period 1B on Hadrian's Wall, and there are two examples from the Pudding Pan Rock wreck. *c.* 160–190.

Graveyard levels.

(8) Latinus i 1a 27 LATIMI Les Martres-de-Veyre.² There is no dating evidence for this particular stamp, but his range of forms and fabrics, including form 33a, suggests the Trajanic or early-Hadrianic period.

Course of Period 2A; 8: 29G2.

(9) Modestus i 2g 29 [OFMO]DESTI La Graufesenque² (see p. 180, no. 6). This stamp was used almost exclusively on form 29, and occurs in the group from the Cirencester fort ditch. *c.* 55–65.

Period 2A (construction); 22: 2126.

(10) Montanus i 7c or c′ 18 MONT[ANI] or MONT[AN] La Graufesenque.² There is no site dating for the die in its original form, but there is one stamp on form 16. Examples from the broken version occur at Camulodunum and the Gloucester Kingsholm site, but also at Caerleon and Chester. Montanus's stamps are relatively common at Vespasianic foundations, but also appear in one of the Colchester pottery shops. *c.* 60–75.

Period 2A (construction); 13: 1409B–D.

(11) Murranus 10b 29 [OF.MV]RRA La Graufesenque.² The stamp does not occur in dated contexts. It is always on form 29, and the associated decoration is of the period *c.* 45–60.

Period 1A (construction); 1: 61B.

(12)   Pateratus 3a 33 PΛTIIRΛTIM Lezoux.[2] One of Pateratus's less common stamps, which has not been noted in a dated context. His other stamps occur at such sites as Birdoswald, Chesterholm and (probably) Chester-le-Street, but also in the Castleford Pottery Shop of A.D. 140–150 and occasionally on forms 18/31R and 27. c. A.D. 140–175.

Mid or late second- to mid third-century ditch deposits on north-west side of the street, (see pp. 97–8).

(13)   Secundus ii 8b 29 [OFSECVN̄D La Graufesenque.[2] There is no evidence for the use of this stamp in the pre-Flavian period, though Secundus must have begun work before A.D. 70. It occurs at such sites as Brough-on-Humber, Castleford, York and the Nijmegen fortress, and is common on form 29. c. 70–85.

Period 2B (construction); 13: 1405.

(14)   Secundus ii 8f 18 OFSECV̄ND La Graufesenque.[2] This stamp was nearly always used on dishes. It occurs at Rheingönheim. c. 65–90.

Period 2A (construction); 13: 1409.

(15)   Viducus ii 5b 18/31 VIDV[CVꟃ F] Les Martres-de-Veyre.[2] There is no dating evidence for this stamp, but others of his appear in the groups from the London Second Fire, and there is one example from Malton. c. 105–125.

Period 2B (construction); 13: 1402.

(16)   An illiterate stamp on form 24 [V]ꟃ III La Graufesenque. The stamp is not known from dated contexts, but this form is invariably pre-Flavian.

Period 1A (construction); 9: 68D.

(17)   An eight-petalled rosette on form Curle 23 Lezoux.[3] Rosette stamps of this kind were in common use at Lezoux in the Antonine period on a small number of forms. This particular piece seems to belong to the earlier half of the period.

? Period 2B (construction); 8: gully 5.

(18)   An unidentified stamp on form 29]II La Graufesenque.[3] Neronian, to judge by the fabric and glaze.

Period 1A (construction); 4: F.63.

NOTES

1. Stamp attested at the pottery in question.
2. Other stamps of the same potter attested at the pottery in question.
3. Assigned to the pottery on form, fabric, etc.

3. LAMPS

by D. M. Bailey

Fragments from five lamps are described in the catalogue below. All are mould-made volute-lamps of Loeschcke Type I or Type IV (Loeschcke, 1919). Unless the nozzle survives, it is not always possible to distinguish these types one from the other. The Shoulder-forms mentioned in the catalogue-entries are those illustrated by Loeschcke. Loeschcke Type I and IV lamps were first devised in Italy during the reign of Augustus, and they were swiftly copied in lamp work-shops throughout the Empire. None of the Exeter lamps is Italian, and, although there is good evidence for lamp-production in Britain before the Flavian period, notably at Colchester, it seems unlikely that any of these lamps were made in this country. Their fabrics are not very close to that of the products of the Roman settlements on the Rhine, and it seems very probable that they come from Central Gaul, mostly, if not entirely from the neighbourhood of Lyons (for Lyons Ware, see Greene, 1972, 1–2). Loeschcke Types I and IV were comparatively long-lived types, and close dating is not possible in most cases. The dates given here would seem to cover the most likely period of production of the individual lamps, and the context dates are useful for refining these periods. However, if they are of Lyons Ware, a date after A.D. 70 would be unusual, and after A.D. 80, surprising (Greene, 1972, 2).

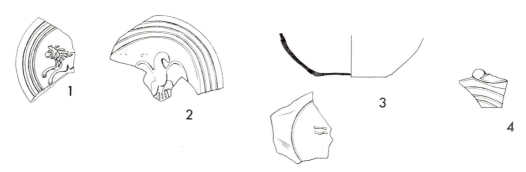

Fig. 59. Lamps (scale 1 : 2).

Catalogue (Fig. 59).

(1) (1: 61C). L. 4.5 mm. Loeschcke Type I or IV; Shoulder-form I. Fr. Discus: lion to left. *C.* A.D. 40–70. Context date: Period 1A (construction), *c.* 60–65. Compare Loeschcke Lamps 211–221 (Loeschcke Type I) and 492–6 (Loeschcke Type IV) from Vindonissa, and made at that site: Bailey, forthcoming, Q952 (Loeschcke Type IV), made in Campania; Vegas, 1966, Lamp 209 (Loeschcke Type IV), of the middle of the first century A.D.

(2) (4: 56B). W. 6.5 cm. Loeschcke Type I or IV; Shoulder-form I/III a. Rear-top, and some non-joining body frr; one small alien fr. Discus: eagle displayed, head to its left, left foot raised.

Pale yellow-buff clay, very soft, details much worn; traces of a darker slip.

c. A.D. 40–80. Context date: Period 1A (construction) *c.* 60–65. There are a great many parallels to this figure-type, from lamp factories all over the Empire (several are listed in Bailey, forthcoming). It occurs on lamps of Loeschcke Types I, III, IV, V and VIII. Most of the examples from the north-western Provinces appear to be of Loeschcke Type I, and include Merrifield, 1965, pl. 123 from a mid-first century A.D. context, and Loeschcke, 1919, Lamps 281–4, from Vindonissa.

(3) (12: 1161A). W. 6.0 cm. Loeschcke Type I or IV, probably the latter. Base and lower body frr; slightly-raised, flat base, with a mouldmark of two short parallel relief lines (mouldmarks were probably a control device used in the workshop to monitor the products of a particular mould).

Yellow-buff clay; yellow-brown slip.

c. A.D. 40–80. Context date: Period 1A (construction) *c.* 60–65.

(4) (1: fill of gully 4). L. 2.6 cm. Loeschcke Type I or IV, probably the former; Shoulder-form I/IIIa.

Shoulder fr. with part of volute.

Yellow-buff clay; orange-brown slip.

c. A.D. 40–80. Context date: Period 2A (construction) *c.* 80.

(5) (Unstratified). L. 3.7 cm. Loeschcke Type I or IV, probably the former; Shoulder-form I ?
Shoulder fr., with part of volute.

Pale buff clay; pink-purplish slip (Lyons fabric ?).

c. A.D. 40–70.

4. THE COARSE POTTERY

A. INTRODUCTION

The Cathedral Close sites produced about 150 kg of pottery from Roman levels; a much smaller
quantity of Roman pottery was recovered from later graveyard levels. Catalogues of the pottery
submitted to specialists are published in full below according to the contexts of individual sherds
and vessels. Publication of the remaining material is more cursory. Work is in progress at present
on a type-series of vessels within the fabric-types so far identified. When this is completed, it
will be possible to list the bulk of the pottery economically and with very little illustration, but
as the moment, without a type-series, full publication is not feasible.

Five groups of pottery have been judged to be of special importance (groups from Periods 1A,
1B and 2A (construction) (Figs. 60–4, 1–137), and two fourth-century groups (Figs. 67–8, 208–30
and 69, 231–5)). Most of the drawable vessels within these groups are published below, together
with tables which supply an estimate of the number of vessels in different fabrics.[1] The weight of
sherds is also included; when comparing fabrics with a similar range of forms (e.g. fabrics
31, 40, 81, 125, 190), this figure seems more likely to give a reliable estimate of quantity than
a reckoning of the number of vessels represented by a pile of sherds.

The remaining groups contain large quantities of residual pottery and only those vessels which
are thought to be broadly contemporary with the date of a deposit or of special interest are
published. Parallels for individual vessels are not usually quoted unless they throw light on the
dating of a deposit when other evidence is lacking. Most of the fabrics have been described by
reference to a type-series (pp. 191–5) which has already been employed in the publication of
pottery from Exeter (i.e. in Jarvis and Maxfield, 1975; Bidwell, 1977; Darling, 1977). Certain new
types have been added to the series and a few of the descriptions have been corrected. Variations
of colour and finish in the case of individual vessels are not described.

First-century pottery at Exeter (*Tables 8 and 9*):

Some discussion of the sources and significance of the first-century pottery from Exeter has
already been published (see above). As yet only a little work has been done on tracing the sources
of the pottery and not a great deal can be added to the previous discussions. However some
evidence for the importance of the local industries at Exeter has been recovered recently. Sherds of
fabric *190* have been recovered from the fort at Okehampton (see p. 18, n. 18). From an unpublished site at Carvossa, Probus (near Falmouth, Cornwall, a site some 90 km west of Exeter)
large numbers of flagons, predominantly in fabric 440, have been recovered, together with some
vessels in fabric *190*.[2] Unfortunately few of the vessels were excavated from stratified contexts
on the site and since the forms recovered can be shown to have continued in production after
the end of the military period at Exeter, it is impossible to determine whether their importation
to Carvossa took place before or after *c.* 75.

These two finds of pottery are the first indications of the role Exeter played in supplying the
Roman army in the South-West, and perhaps also other civilian settlements in the post-military
period.

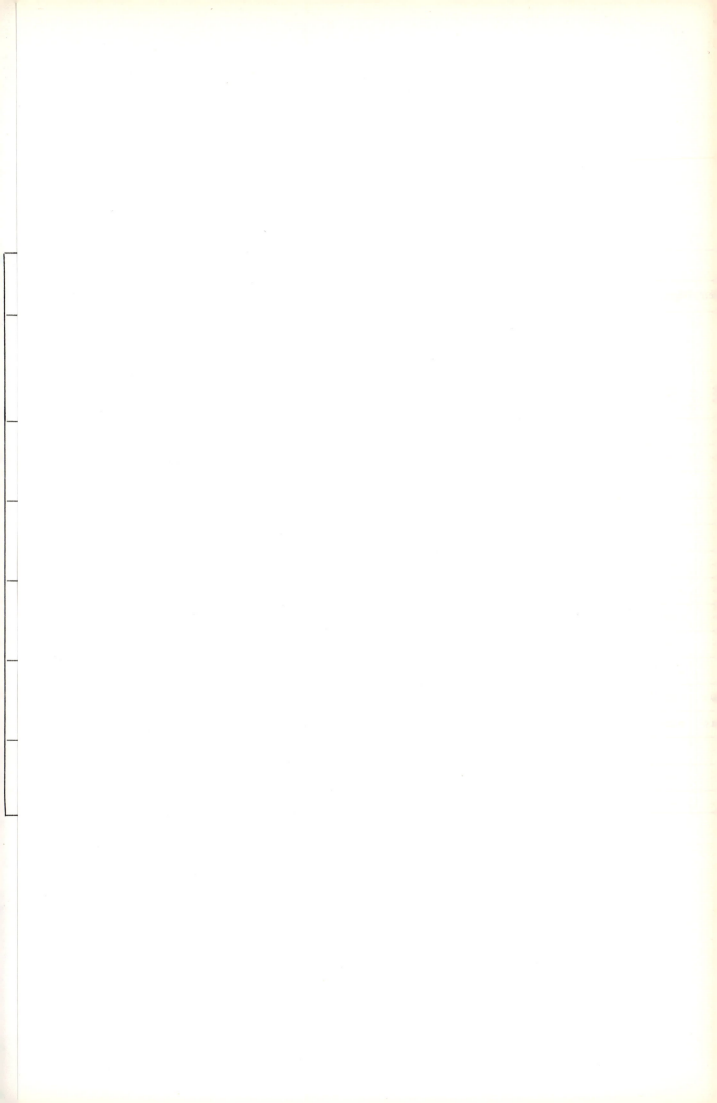

African body	African handles	Cam. 186 rim/handle	Cam. 186 body	Carrot body	Algerian Dr 30	Dressel 2–4 body	Richborough 527 body	Rhodian	Unidentified	Remarks
—	—	1	—	—	—	—	—	1	1	Rhodian handle fr.; Cam. 186, spike, handle
—	—	1	1	—	—	—	—	1	2	Neck and rim, Cam. 186B, South Spanish,? Cadiz (fig. 61, no. 42).
—	—	1	4v +5	1	—	—	1	4	6	Dr 20 handle stamped CS[
—	—	—	1	—	—	—	—	—	—	
—	—	—	—	—	—	—	—	—	1	
—	—	—	—	—	—	—	—	—	—	
—	—	—	1	—	—	—	—	—	16	
—	—	—	—	—	—	—	—	—	—	
—	—	—	—	—	—	—	—	—	1	
—	—	—	—	—	—	—	—	—	—	
9	1	—	—	—	2	1	—	—	—	Dr 30, many fr. of one vessel (Fig. 67, 208). Two Algerian sh. from one v.
4	—	—	—	—	—	—	—	—	—	
13	—	—	2	—	1	1	—	—	12	Five sh. in ? late Palestinian fabric.
26	1	3	10 +4v	1	3	2	1	6	39	

ntifications (by D. P. S. Peacock).

Table 8: Summary of Table 9 (percentages)

	Native	Locally-produced	BB1	Other south-western products	Southern British	Continental
1.	0.67	13.33	24.00	18.01	2.67	41.33
2.	0.3	14.32	17.91	18.82	5.37	43.26
3.	0.97	20.38	14.56	22.32	10.68	32.03
4.	4.1	18.73	20.85	22.81	5.58	30.18
5.	0.63	12.58	30.76	20.3	8.19	27.67

Significance of individual first-century groups:

Period 1A (construction) (Figs. 60–1, 1–30): this group dates to *c.* 60–65. It is of particular importance because it is the largest (150 vessels) and perhaps also the earliest group recovered from the occupation period of the fortress. The contents of the group show that although the local industries were well established, the bulk of the pottery-supply drew on sources elsewhere in the South-West. Manufacturing centres elsewhere in southern Britain contributed little. Continental imports occur in large numbers but, apart from a few flagons of uncertain origin, comprise types which would be found on any military site in Britain at this period. The only remarkable feature of these imports is the absence of *terra nigra* and imitation *terra nigra;* a glance at the later groups in Table 9 will show that in a group of this size a few such vessels ought to be represented. Their absence tends to confirm one of the explanations put forward by V. Rigby (see p. 190) for the limited range of Gallo-Belgic imports supplied to the army in South-West England and South Wales ". . . almost no Gallic-Belgic wares were reaching the South-West and South Wales before A.D. 60–65".

Period 1B (construction) (Fig. 61, 31–48) and miscellaneous late fortress deposits: deposits associated with Period 1B (construction) are contemporary with the disbandment of the fortress (*c.* 75). For the sake of comparison and amplification a number of groups associated with the demolition of buildings within the fortress and the establishment to its south-east or with late military occupation (associated with early Flavian samian) have been included in Tables 8 and 9. In these deposits *terra nigra* and imitation *terra nigra* occur in some quantity. Deposits specifically associated with the demolition of the fortress have produced sherds of fabric *125,* a fabric which is absent from all earlier contexts.

Period 2A (construction) (Figs. 62–4): this assemblage is estimated to comprise some 609 vessels and is the largest first-century group so far recovered from Exeter. The terminal date of the group is fixed at *c.* 80, although the deposits from which many of the vessels were recovered probably accumulated on the site over a period of some years (see p. 87). The presence of pre-Flavian samian and fine wares suggests that some of the coarse wares are likely to be residual.

In this group are represented all but one of the fabric-types and categories listed in Table 9. The exception is mica-coated ware, the earliest context for which at Exeter is the fill of the fortress ditch. The group forms the earliest known context for fabric 130 and for a cornice-rim beaker of Swan's variety 1 (Fig. 62, 62). It also forms the earliest context for an important black-burnished ware type, the flat-rimmed bowl (Fig. 64, 115–117); these prototypes of Gillam 220 and 306 have been discussed in Gillam, 1976, 67–8 and Bidwell, 1977, 191.

A group from the filling of the fortress ditch at Rack Street (excavated in 1975) has been included in Table 9 for comparison. There were a total of 38 samian vessels in the group, the latest decorated examples dating from c. 80. The remainder of the samian, both plain and decorated, was exclusively Flavian; *terra nigra* and pre-Flavian fine wares were absent. This group was recovered from a heap of domestic rubbish mixed with many food-bones and shells, which only partly filled the ditch (see p. 6); it contained no obviously residual pottery. The only Continental imports are samian and amphorae (and possibly mortaria). The flagons in fabric *406* are no longer present, although there are still flagons with a red body and a white slip (fabric *451*). Mica-coated wares make their first appearance. Products of the local industries are still well represented (fabrics *190, 191, 371, 435, 440*). The wheel-thrown micaceous ware (fabric *125*) is now present in larger quantities than the handmade version (fabric *81*). The overall proportion of black-burnished ware to other South-Western and local fabrics is somewhat higher than in other groups of the period c. 80–100 at Exeter (Bidwell, 1977, 189, 193).

Fourth-century pottery:

Two fourth-century groups have been published as fully as possible because they are amongst the latest recovered from Exeter:

(i) from the *insula* north-east of the *basilica* and *forum* (Figs. 67–8, 208–30). This group dates to after c. 337 but contains some residual material. Its composition is not typical for the period; there are many more amphorae and fine wares than in other contemporary groups.

(ii) course of Period 3A, material from the ditch and its recut (26: 168) north-east of the *basilica* and *forum* (Fig. 69, 231–5).

In the fourth century at Exeter, as throughout most of Western Britain, the pottery market was dominated by the black-burnished ware industry. The only other coarse ware of any importance was fabric *5*.

It may eventually be possible to show that Exeter and other south-western sites had a pattern of pottery imports which differed significantly from that of sites further to the east. Fragments of North African amphorae occur quite commonly on most excavations in Exeter. They usually come from accumulations of post-Roman dark soil or occur residually in mediaeval or later features. Where stratified, their contexts can be shown to date to after c. 350 except in the case of the group discussed above, which only has a *terminus post quem* of c. 337. Some large sites to the east with large amounts of later fourth-century material have apparently failed to produce any North African amphorae (e.g. Portchester, M. Fulford in Cunliffe, 1975, and Cirencester, information V. Rigby, although one site has produced a possible example of a Palestinian amphora), so their relative commonness at Exeter may be significant.

Another imported ware which appears to be commoner at Exeter than at other sites further to the east is *céramique à l'éponge*. Two vessels of this type have already been published from Exeter, although neither was attributed to the correct source (Fox, 1952, 65 and Pl. XD, thought to be a 'Gaulish product, probably of the early first century A.D.' cf. Raimbault, 1973, Fig. 1; Greenfield, 1964, 345, no. 11, from a post-Roman context, possibly a variant of Raimbault, 1973, Form II, type B). Although *céramique à l'éponge* has been recovered from other sites to the east, the estimated total of at least thirty vessels from Exeter represents an exceptionally high figure.[3]

NOTES

1. The estimation of the minimum number of vessels represented in a group is a somewhat subjective process. I have therefore made my own count of the number of vessels represented by sherds of samian, amphorae, etc., in Tables 8 and 9, and inevitably my results sometimes differ from those in the catalogues contributed by specialists.

2. I am grateful to Mrs H. Miles for showing me the material from the site. For the site see Douch and Beard, 1970, 93–7.

3. See Fulford, 1977, 77 where 34 vessels are listed from 16 sites in Britain. Two sherds were recovered from the villa at Holcombe, Devon (nos. 252 and 476, unpublished, both from plough-soil).

B. COLOUR-COATED WARES (POST FLAVIAN)
by Vivien G. Swan

The total amount of colour-coated material from the site is relatively small and, chronologically, is fairly evenly spread from the late first to the end of the fourth century; however wares were drawn from a wider variety of sources during the third and fourth centuries. A large proportion of the material occurs residually in later Roman or post-Roman deposits, and for this reason in some cases dating is uncertain where the form and fabric combinations are not recorded elsewhere; indeed, as yet, comparatively little pottery has been published for the area, and even at a notable exception, the Holcome villa (Pollard, 1974), the third- and fourth-century wares were largely unstratified.

Two varieties of rough-cast beakers are present; the first occurs in some quantity (22 sherds); the second is known only in small amounts from residual contexts, but probably dates to the second century A.D.

The former variety seems worth discussing in detail, in the hope that it may be recognised elsewhere in the future and that more evidence of its date, distribution and source may emerge. The fabric is fine, ranging from brick red or orange to pinkish-brown (less commonly), sometimes with a grey core, and with sparse, small inclusions of yellow mica sometimes visible. The colour-coat, which ranges from dark grey or brown to black, is occasionally lustrous, but normally matt. A few oxidised vessels occur in an orange or light brown slip. No complete beaker form is known but vessels were probably either bag-shaped, or less commonly, indented with a grooved or double cornice-rim and a single shoulder-groove above the pelleted-clay rough-cast decoration, which covered the rest of the body, including the underside of the base. Often diagonal 'wipe-marks' are visible on the exterior immediately below the rim and overlying the usual horizontal 'throwing' marks. Their earliest occurrence on the site is in a Period 2A (construction) context (Fig. 62, no. 62), but they were probably current until the middle of the second century, and sherds appear residually thereafter. A beaker from the same source was published from Holcombe (Pollard, 1974, Fig. 15, no. 24), but until more examples are recorded elsewhere it is impossible to tell whether they arrived via the Fosse Way, along the south coast, or were produced locally.

The great importance of the Fosse Way as a trade route is attested by the occurrence of Nene Valley colour-coated wares (10 sherds): the very slender evidence available (from both this site and others in Exeter) suggests such trade falls prominently within the second and third centuries, and was no doubt smothered by the emergence of the Oxfordshire colour-coated wares (and to a lesser extent the New Forest wares) in the late third and fourth centuries; the products of these two industries are present in almost equal proportions (New Forest—13 sherds, Oxfordshire—15 sherds), stressing, as at Holcombe, the strength of the Oxfordshire industries, even when trading from a situation less advantageous from the point of view of transport. A range of Continental imports spanning the first to fourth centuries, serves to emphasise Exeter's near-coastal situation and wide trade contacts: these include Flavian-Trajanic colour-coated beakers from Lezoux (4 sherds), colour-coated beakers of the late second–third century, from the same source (7 sherds), Rhenish ware (6 sherds), and *céramique à l'éponge* from N.W. France (2 sherds).

C. THE GALLO-BELGIC IMPORTS FROM EXETER—A SUMMARY
by V. Rigby

The total collection from Exeter is fairly large, comprising sherds from about 50 different vessels. The position of Exeter beyond the main distribution area of G.B. imports, south and east of a line from the Humber to the Solent, combined with a date for the establishment of the fortress between A.D. 50 and 60 on a site with no previous occupation make the collection highly significant.

Of the 50 vessels, all but one are in TN, the exception being a platter sherd in what is probably TR 2, since it is pale pink in colour (for the classification of the fabrics, see Rigby, 1973, 1, 11). The range of forms is restricted to three of the most common, widely found and latest types in Britain—the platter forms 8(4) and 16 (35+) ,and the cup form 58 (6) (for the classification of the forms, see Hawkes and Hull, 1947, 221). Finds from York, Malton, Catterick, Corbridge and Camelon show that TN was still in use c. 70–85, but the forms were restricted to just 16 and 58; however both were being imported in the pre-Flavian period also for they occur in pit-groups pre-dating the Boudiccan destruction at Camulodunum (excavations in 1970 by Mrs R. Niblett). The examples of form 8 are typologically late, being those imported after c. 50 rather than before that date, and were no longer being imported by c. 70. The style of the illiterate mark on one example suggests that they were all from the same source as almost identical platters of form 8 found at Southampton (Cotton and Gathercole, 1958, fig. 191, no. 1). It seems likely that they were imported directly rather than via Camulodunum since the stamps from Exeter, Topsham, Southampton and Nanstallon are not paralleled at Camulodunum. Before c. 60/1, Camulodunum appears to have been the main distribution point for G.B. imports for not only is the stamp-list greater than that for the rest of Britain but most stamps found on other sites are paralleled in some way at Camulodunum.

In addition to the common forms, there is a unique cup which is a cross between form 58 and the bowl form 46, with a vestigial and absolutely useless foot-ring (Museum no. 9447975; Fig. 69, no. 247). Due in particular to its foot-ring the cup is unparalleled although it is possible that body and flange sherds if found alone could have been wrongly classified as form 58. Its relationship to forms 58 and 46 and the technique of its moulded foot-ring, a later characteristic on platters, suggest that it is Neronian—early Flavian.

Although the stamps are from different dies, the examples of forms 16 and 58 show a marked similarity to those from Topsham (Jarvis and Maxfield, 1976, 232). They appear to have been imported at the same time, from the same sources. One of the sources may have been fairly 'local' to judge from the poor quality of the finish of some vessels and the presence on both sites of distorted 'seconds'. The particular fabric concerned, although it is almost iron-free and typically fine-grained, has more grey ferrous inclusions than is usual for TN, while the quality of the colour and the finish are below standard. However, other factors could have been involved and resulted in the use of poorly prepared clay or a different source of clay to make up just one quota, and someone could have been passing off 'seconds' as perfect goods to make up the numbers.

Even allowing for the presence of examples of TR and platters of form 8, as a whole, the collection suggests that it belongs to the period after 55, and that the greatest period of import occurred after 65 when the only cup and platter forms available were forms 86 and 58. A much wider range of cup and platter forms in TN and TR occurs in pre-Flavian contexts, on both civilian and military sites, within the main distribution areas than is present at Exeter. In addition, these sites have produced examples of butt-beakers, form 112, in TR 3, girth beakers, forms 82 and 84, also in TR 3, and some even include pedestal beakers of forms 74, 75 or 76, in TR 1 (A), all of which are absent from Exeter.

The causes may not be solely chronological for, as it stands, the distribution of G.B. imports suggests that supplies to sections of the Roman army in the South-West and South Wales differed from those to sections stationed in the east in the pre-Flavian period (Rigby, 1977, fig. 1). If the existing finds are representative, then either almost no G.B. wares were reaching the South-West and South Wales in the period before 60/5, or else only a deliberately limited range of forms, primarily 16 and 58, with the bowls 46 and 50, exclusively in TN, was being brought in (cf. p. 187). There are exceptions to the overall pattern, the platters of form 8 at Exeter, platters of forms 4 and 8 at Hamworthy, while a platter of form 14 reached Caerleon and a cup, form 58, in TR 2 reached Cirencester. It remains to be seen whether or not the exceptions indicate that a wider range of forms and fabrics did reach units in the South-West in particular. Whatever happens, the collection of G.B. wares from Exeter will remain significant.

NOTES FOR TABLE 10

1. v=vessels. Where a number of sherds are obviously from the same vessel the number of vessels is quoted.
2. African amphorae all in North Tunisian Fabric.
3. Camulodunum 186 probably made in Cadiz area.
4. Algerian Dressel 30. For parallels see Panella, 1972, 99.
5. Richborough 527 to be discussed in Peacock, forthcoming.
6. Rhodian fabrics are of a type probably made at Rhodes (Peacock fabric 1, in Peacock, forthcoming).

D. FABRIC TYPE-SERIES

Summary of types:

'Native': *3, 5, 10, 14.*
Locally-produced wares: *101, 190, 191, 371.*
Black-burnished ware: *31, 40, 60.*
Micaceous grey wares: *81, 125.*
Other grey wares: *110, 130, 151.*
Butt-beakers: *220.*
Imitation *terra nigra: 372–6.*
Flagons: *401, 405, 406, 407, 435, 440, 451.*

Introduction:

A type-series has been devised for fabrics from Exeter which are not otherwise known by familiar names; most of these probably originated in South-West England. If fabrics are well-known types, such as Severn Valley ware, the familiar names are used and they are excluded from the type series. The only exception to this rule is black-burnished ware, which, at Exeter, includes vessels in at least three different fabrics; these have been given numbers within the type-series.

Fabric Type Series:

'Native' wares: these comprise a series of at least four fabrics which are thought to be of relatively local origin, although probably not produced in the immediate vicinity of Exeter. For the most part vessels produced in these fabrics are crude copies of black-burnished ware types, although some early vessels may well represent the continuation of a South-Western pre-Roman ceramic tradition. The fabrics have been called 'native' because they are likely to have originated in south or central Devon, in areas where Romanisation was little advanced and where, on present evidence, there was an almost total dependence on local pottery supplies during the third and fourth centuries, even to the virtual exclusion of black-burnished ware (e.g. Masson Phillips, 1966, 18–23).

3. Visible inclusions: hard black angular inclusions of irregular size; soft black rounded inclusions of irregular size (?shillet). Dark grey, sometimes with buff surfaces which take a smooth burnish. Apparently both wheel-thrown and hand-made vessels. Date range: first and early second century.

5. Visible inclusions: frequent rounded and angular quartz grits; frequent black mica plates; occasional white or buff soft non-calcareous inclusions. Colour varies from light grey to very dark grey. Overall feel: quite sandy. All vessels wheel-thrown, except storage jars. This is the most common fabric in this group. The range of forms tallies well with vessels found on sites in south Devon (e.g. Mount Batten, Plymouth (Clarke, 1971, Figs. 7, 8) Stoke Gabriel (Masson Phillips, 1966, 1–23) and Clanacombe (Greene and Greene, 1970, 130–6)), all in our fabric 5. Thin-sectioning indicated that a sherd in this fabric at Stoke Gabriel contained inclusions derived either from

crushed granite or river sand not too far removed from the granite (Masson Phillips, 1966, 23); since the primary distribution area is in south Devon, the granitic inclusions are probably derived from Dartmoor. Date range: sherds from first-century contexts, but very little until the early third century; continues through to the late fourth century.

10.   Visible inclusions: frequent large black rounded inclusions; white calcareous inclusions of irregular size (?shell). Dark grey surfaces, lighter grey interior. Crude hand-made vessels. Date range: (?) first century only.

14.   Visible inclusions: frequent shell fragments up to 5 mm across; very occasional ferrous inclusions. Overall feel: quite hard, but surfaces have slightly 'soapy' feel. Dark grey surfaces, mid-grey interior. Date range: late third century onwards.

Locally-produced wares: three fabrics from first-century contexts at Exeter appear to represent the products of a single industry for the following reasons:

(i)   similar treatment and techniques: vessels are all wheel-thrown and very competently potted. Decoration is confined to shallow cordons or grooves (e.g. Fig. 64, 114) or, very rarely, single burnished lines around the circumference of the vessel (e.g. Fig. 64, 113). Overall burnishing of the exterior surfaces was not carried out.

(ii)   similar range of forms: some forms are common to two of the fabrics and at least one to all three (e.g. Fig. 61, 35 (*371*); Fig. 63, 89 (*100*), 90 (*190*)). The forms are generally 'Belgic' in character, although there are copies of Pompeian Red platters. The absence of black-burnished ware copies is particularly notable.

(iii)   similarity of fabrics: in general the three fabrics are easily distinguishable, but, as far as can be seen, the inclusions are broadly similar in the case of fabrics *190* and *191*; fabric *371* has few visible inclusions.

The very close resemblance of fabric *191*, especially in the case of mortaria, to the fabric of tiles found in legionary contexts points to a common production source. Evidence for the location of an early tile industry on the east side of the fortress has been recovered (see p. 148). In addition, a Saxo-Norman pottery kiln (Fox and Dunning, 1957, 53f, originally thought to be thirteenth century in date, but recently redated by J. Allen) was excavated in this area in 1931; the fabrics of its products are indistinguishable from fabrics *190* and *191*.

The tile-kilns can be shown to have been operated by legionary craftsmen (see p. 13) and it is likely that production of vessels in these fabrics was nothing more than another aspect of the same industry. Present evidence indicates that production continued well into the Flavian period; this may perhaps represent the activity of a veteran potter who remained at Exeter after the departure of the legion in *c.* 75.

During the first half of the second century vessels in a fourth fabric, *101*, began to play an important part in the pottery supply at Exeter. This fabric often resembles fabric *190*, although it tends to be much more variable in texture; it comprises a range of forms which is dominated by copies of black-burnished ware vessels.

190.   Visible inclusions: very frequent angular quartz grits up to 2 mm across; occasional ferrous inclusions up to 5 mm across; occasional grey grits up to 2 mm across. This is a heavily-gritted fabric and its exterior surfaces have a 'pimply' feel. Vessels are usually fired at a high temperature, to judge from the relative hardness of the fabric, and range in colour from mid to dark grey, although occasionally the vessels are oxidised. A very few (?late) examples are mica-dusted.

191.   Visible inclusions: as fabric *190* but much less heavily gritted. Vessels in this fabric are larger and less carefully finished than those in fabric *190*; they appear generally to have been fired at the same temperature as tiles, often resembling them in the degree of hardness and texture, although vessels which are light-buff in colour are common.

371. Visible inclusions: cindery black inclusions up to 3 mm in length, presumably burnt ferrous particles; occasional small hard black grits. Rather sandy in texture with mid grey surfaces and interior but sometimes a lighter coloured interior.

101. Similar to *190* but more variable in texture.

Black-burnished wares:[1] there are two major black-burnished ware (BB1) fabrics, *31* and *40*, at Exeter; a further fabric, *60*, is merely a sub-division of *40*. The essential characteristics of the two fabrics and their relative importance in the first century have already been discussed and nothing can be usefully added to these observations at present (Bidwell in Jarvis and Maxfield, 1975, and Bidwell, 1977). In the second century the relative quantity of fabric *31* diminishes markedly and fabric *40* is supplemented by fabric *60*. However by the middle of the fourth century at the latest the only black-burnished ware at Exeter is fabric *31*. It should be noted that the three black-burnished ware fabrics described here may well embrace the products of more than three centres.

31. Visible inclusions: very frequent quartz grits up to 2 mm in length; very occasional rounded fragments of slate, shale or shillet up to 5 mm across. This represents the coarsest of the black-burnished ware fabrics. Date range: throughout the Roman period.

40. Visible inclusions: occasional small quartz grits; occasional soft white non-calcareous inclusions (c.f. erroneous description in Jarvis and Maxfield, 1975, 236); very occasional flint fragments up to 8 mm across. Overall feel: quite fine, slightly sandy. The fabric is much more variable than *31*. Vessels in this fabric are covered by a black slip, the presence of which is always obvious on semi-closed forms like cooking-pots where smears and wipe-marks can always be seen at the edge of the slipped area below the interior of the rim. Date range: mid first to mid fourth century at the latest.

60. A finer version of *40*. Vessels are comparatively thin-walled and neatly finished; where burnished the surfaces have an almost silky feel. Some of the vessels in this fabric appear to be wheel-thrown although the majority are certainly hand-made. Date range: early second to late second or early third century.

Micaceous grey wares: these appear to be South-Western products since they copy black-burnished ware forms well before the end of the first century. No evidence has been recovered to suggest more precise locations for these industries.

81. Visible inclusions: scattered small quartz grits; very occasional ferrous inclusions up to 3 mm across; micaceous surfaces but no visible mica plates. Vessels fired at a high temperature in most cases to judge from their hardness; colour varies from light buff to dark grey, but usually mid-grey exterior surfaces often with buff interiors. Very narrow range of forms, all of them hand-made (indeed were it not for the fabric, a fine, good quality grey-ware, this fabric could be classified as a black-burnished ware). Copies of black-burnished ware types. Date range: exclusively first century.

125. Visible inclusions: as *81*. Fabric and finish similar to *81*, but many of the vessels appear to have been fired at a lower temperature. All vessels wheel-thrown. The first appearance of this fabric at Exeter in the early Flavian period coincides with a diminution in the quantity of fabric *81* from contemporary deposits. This confirms what is suggested by the similarities of these two fabrics—that fabric *125* represents a more sophisticated product from the same source as fabric *81*. Date range: early Flavian to early third century.

Other wares:

Other grey wares:

110. Visible inclusions: occasional small quartz grits and small ?slate fragments. Exterior surfaces usually reduced to a dark grey tone; slightly soapy or greasy feel. Hard fabric sometimes with a grey-brown core. Date range: third and fourth centuries.

130.   No visible inclusions apart from very occasional small quartz grits. Varies in colour from very light grey to mid grey; apparently fired to a high temperature. Forms include large rouletted beakers and samian imitations. Date range: early Flavian to early second century (?or later).

151.   Visible inclusions: occasional ferrous inclusions up to 3 mm across; very occasional soft white non-calcareous inclusions. This is a fairly soft sandy fabric with micaceous surfaces but no visible mica plates. Vessels in this fabric are always wheel-thrown and comprise primarily a range of 'Belgic' forms although black-burnished ware influence can be detected, e.g. in the case of lattice decorations on cooking-pots. Date range: mid first century to late second century.

Imitation Terra Nigra (ITN): Five fabrics have been distinguished so far. They are likely to represent the products of a variety of industries, one fairly local perhaps, the others possibly located on the Continent. V. Rigby has examined two of the fabrics and her comments are included in the fabric descriptions below.

372.   'The fabric closely resembles TN, having a pale grey fine-grained sandy paste and dark blue-grey surface. However the burnished finish is not quite right for TN. Possibly from a fairly local source' (V.R.). This is the most common ITN fabric at Exeter; the majority of vessels are jars.

373.   A comparatively soft fine sandy micaceous ware occasionally with white mica plates. Usually light to mid grey, sometimes with a reddish-buff exterior under black (?slipped) surfaces. The second most common ITN fabric at Exeter; the most common form seems to be a small biconical beaker with a foot-ring.

374.   'Good quality copy. Brown fine-grained paste. Possibly an import from Gaul' (V.R.). Takes a highly burnished finish. Broadly similar to 373, but distinguishable from it by the complete absence of mica.

375.   Fairly coarse-grained fabric with occasional specks of mica or quartz. Grey or sometimes light buff interiors with dark grey surfaces treated with a very rough facetted polish. Thicker and cruder than most ITN.

376.   Dense dark grey fabric with no visible inclusions. Surfaces take a smooth polish.

Butt-beakers:

220.   Hard slightly sandy buff fabric; very occasional quartz and ferrous inclusions. Camulodunum form 113 only (Hawkes and Hull, 1947, 238–9). Probably a Colchester product.

Flagon fabrics:

Apart from the fabrics listed below, a few flagons in fabric *190* have been found.

435.   Light buff to pinkish red fabric with occasional ferrous inclusions; sometimes slightly micaceous. This classification probably includes the products of more than one source since the range of forms is very wide. Nevertheless the majority are likely to represent the products of a local industry. Date range: first and second century.

440.   Light buff to red sandy fabric with fairly frequent small hard dark grey inclusions. A distinctive fabric with a limited range of forms, examples of which were associated with the probable kiln in Bartholomew Street (see p. 12). Date range: first century.

406.   Frequent small ferrous inclusions. Off-white to pink fabric sometimes with a blue-grey core. Firing seems to be very variable with some quite soft examples and many others almost as hard as stoneware. Well-made thin-walled vessels usually with a carefully smoothed exterior with many horizontal red-brown streaks caused by smearing of the ferrous inclusions.[2] Date range first century, probably not current after the departure of the legion *c.* 75.

451. Red-buff fabric with white slip. Very variable in range of texture and inclusions; probably represents the products of more than one source. Date range: mid first to late second century.

Continental (?):

401. Off-white dense sandy body (?) grog and ferrous inclusions, which, because of a high firing temperature, form small unintended spots of glaze on the exterior surfaces. Rare. Date range belongs exclusively to the fortress period.

405. White-cream 'pipe-clay' fabric with very occasional ferrous incusions. Vessels often have an interior slip, olive to dark grey in colour. Date range: belongs exclusively to the fortress period.

407. Very hard off-white sandy fabric with scattered quartz grits. The surfaces are usually smoothed but when left rough they have a very 'pimply' feel. Both flagons and small jars have been recorded in this fabric. Rare. Date range: belongs exclusively to the fortress period.

NOTES

1. The term 'black-burnished ware' has been used in the sense proposed by R. A. H. Farrar (1973, 68), and not according to the definition employed by G. Webster (1976, 12), which applies only to 'distinctive forms of cooking. pots, dishes and bowls made from *c*. A.D. 120'.

2. M. Darling (1977, 67-8) has suggested that these vessels could be products of the Corfe Mullen kiln (Calkin, 1935, 42f.). The fabric of the flagons from Corfe Mullen and Exeter are similar, both having a whitish body with many ferrous inclusions, and Mrs K. Hartley has drawn attention to a mortarium from Exeter (Fig. 61, no. 41) which is reminiscent of Corfe Mullen products. Nevertheless the Corfe Mullen flagons are much more clumsily made than the Exeter examples and have much softer fabrics. It is doubtful whether fabric *406* represents the products of the Corfe Mullen kiln.

E. CATALOGUE OF THE COARSE POTTERY

with contributions by K. T. Greene, K. Hartley, D. P. S. Peacock, V. Rigby and V. G. Swan.

Period 1A (construction) (c. 60–65) (Fig. 60):
(In the following catalogue details of context are preceded by fabric numbers where appropriate).

Amphora.
(1) Rim of Dressel 20, 1: F.34.

Flagons.
(2) Roughly-wiped exterior, *401*, 12: 1161B. (3) *405*, 12: 1161A. (4) Thin greyish-white slip on exterior, *451*, 4: 56B (trodden into surface). (5) Soft fabric, possibly underfired, *435*, 14: 1151. (6) *440*, 1: F.34. (7) *406*, 5: 31G. (8) *406*, 4: 56C.

Jars.
(9) *190*, 12: 1163. (10) *190*, 14: 1151. (11) Roughly burnished exterior, *151*, 12: 1161A. (12) Carefully wheel-burnished mid-grey exterior, *151*, f. 65. (13) Finish similar to no. 12, *151*, 14: 1144. (14) *371*, 4: 56B. (15) *31*, 8: 49G2. (16) *40*, 12: 1161A.

Cooking-pots.
(17) *190*, 12: 1160 (18) Vessel large enough for use as storage-jar, *31*, 7: 32H. (19) *31*, 1: f.34. (20) *31*, 1: f.34. (21) The unburnished zone has been wiped before the application of decoration, *40*, 1: 9EC. (22), *40*, 1: f.34.

Bowl.
(23) *151*, 1: f.34.

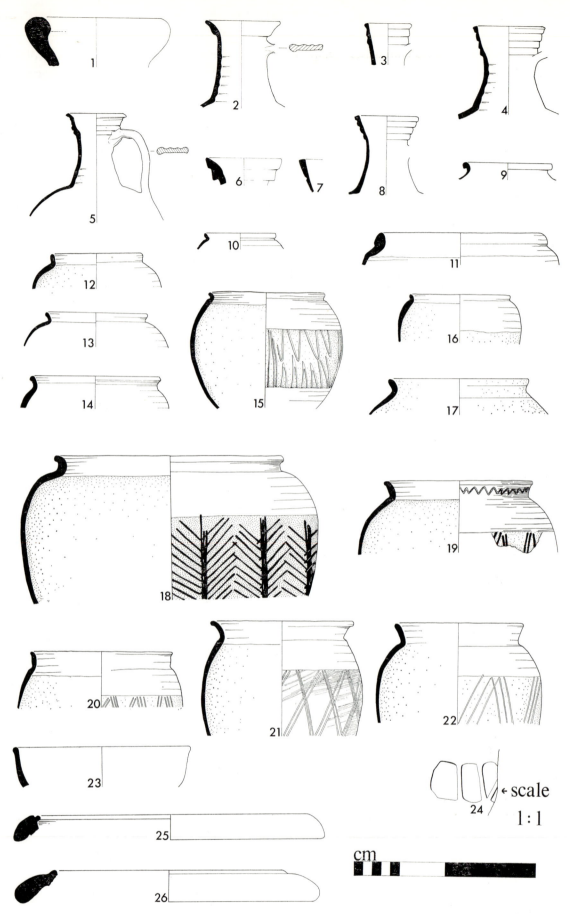

Fig. 60. Coarse pottery, Period 1A (construction) (scale 1 : 4, except stamp, 1 : 1).

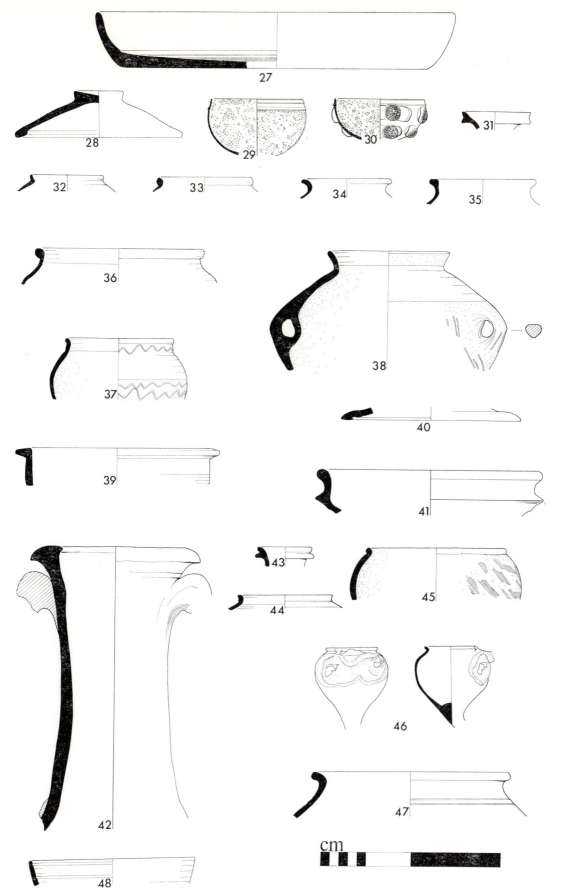

Fig. 61. Coarse pottery, Periods 1A (construction) (27–30) and 1B (construction) (31–48) (scale 1 : 4).

Mortaria (K.H.).

(24) A flange fragment, burnt black throughout. The fragmentary potter's stamp impressed diagonally along the flange reads LV[. This stamp is from one of two dies giving LVGVDV, which is used alone (i.e. without a corresponding potter's namestamp), and it is undoubtedly an abbreviation for the placename Lugudunum like the counterstamps of such potters as Albinus and Ripanus. Although these stamp-types cannot be associated with any individual potter the mortaria were clearly made in the same area as those with F. LVGVDV and LVGD.F counterstamps, and there is abundant evidence to show that this site lies between Verulamium and London (for discussion of this placename, see Frere, 1972, 371–2). The potters using these counterstamps can be dated to the first-century and there is every reason to believe that the mortaria concerned were made within the period A.D. 60–95. 7: 44A.

(25) A mortarium in bright orange-brown fabric, basically fine-textured but tempered with much tiny grit. It was probably made locally (the fabric resembles that of tiles used in the bath-house, see p. 148–51, P.B.). I know of no closely-dated parallel but it would fit with a date in the pre-Flavian period. 12: 1160.

(26) A mortarium in very hard white fabric with buff slip. This is an unusual mortarium from a source either in Southern England or the Continent. It would fit well with manufacture in the period A.D. 50–65 when a wide range of mortaria were being made on an equally wide range of sites before the major potteries of the Flavian period were established. 'Pit' 29, post-pit of building south of road and pre-dating construction of baths.

Flange fragment in brownish-cream fabric. (Probably made by Group 1 potters in Dore and Greene, 1977, 5–17). 12: 1162.

A mortarium in brownish-pink fabric fired to cream at the surfaces, with traces of concentric scoring on the inside. South-Eastern England or Gaul. 16: 1534.

Four fragments (two adjoining), probably all from the same well-worn mortarium in fine, soft yellowish-cream fabric with concentric scoring and flint grit. Made in South-Eastern England or Gaul, A.D. 55–100. 9: 68D.

Three joining body fragments from a mortarium in hard, cream fabric with brownish-pink core and much tiny trituration grit. Indeterminate. 15: 1186.

Three body fragments (two joining), probably all from a very worn mortarium which had been riveted, in pinkish-brown fabric fired to cream at the surface. Made in South-Eastern England or Gaul, A.D. 55–100. See Dore and Greene, 1977, 5–17 for comments on the two groups of potters who produced this type of fabric. 8: 49G1.

Dish.

(27) Imitation of a Pompeian Red platter, *191*, 17: 75.

Lid.

(28) *371*, 8: 49G1.

Fine wares (K.G.).

(29) Four sherds from a Lyons cup (Greene, 1972, type 1.5). 1: F.34.

(30) Lyons cup (Greene, 1972, type 5.2). 1: 61B.

Lyons cup (Greene, 1972, type 1.–). 1: F.34.

Small sherd from Lyons beaker (Greene, 1972, type 20.–.). 1: 9EC3.

Sherds from two Lyons beakers (Greene, 1972, type 20.–.). 4: 56B and 9: 68D.

Two sherds from same beaker. Central Gaulish (small version of Greene, 1972, Fig. 7, no. 3). 1: 61B.

Sherd from lower wall of Central Gaulish glazed ware flagon (Greene, 1972, Fig. 10. 2; Déchelette form 60). 1: 9EC.

Period 1B (construction) (c. 75), pottery sealed below mortar floor in former tepidarium. (Fig. 61).

Flagon.

(31) *440*, 23: 2152.

Jars.

(32) Carefully wheel-burnished grey exterior, *190*, 17: 537. (33) *190*, 23: 2152. (34) *371*, 23: 2152. (35) *371*, 17: 537. (36) *151*, 17: 537. (37) Appears to have been handmade, *151*, 23: 2154.

Other coarse wares.

(38) *81*, 17: 537. (39) *151*, 17: 537. (40) *371*, 17: 537.

Mortaria (K.H.).

(41) A mortarium of unusual form in hard, cream fabric with greyish core. It is reminiscent of the curious mortaria made at Corfe Mullen in Dorset in the mid-first century. The wall-sided type to which it is allied was being superseded by flanged forms in the period A.D. 50–60, and it is very unlikely that any were still being made in A.D. 65. 23: 2152.

Flange fragment in brownish cream fabric. Probably first century. South-Eastern England or Gaul. 23: 2154.

Terra Nigra (V.R.).

Wall sherd in TN. Buff smooth paste; blue-grey surfaces, polished interior, matt exterior (Form 16, *c*. A.D. 45–85). 23: 2152.

Rim sherd in T.N. Heavily burnt and discoloured (form as above). 23: 2154.

Sherd from a bowl. 23: 2154.

Imitation Terra Nigra.

Sherd from bowl, or more probably a platter, sharply carinated with an incised concentric line on the floor of the vessel; burnt *376*. 23: 2154.

Sherd apparently from same form as above, but no incised groove *376*. 17: 537.

Sherd probably from a jar, perhaps as Fig. 63, 97. *372*. 17: 537.

Fine Wares (K.G.).

Base sherds from two Lyons beakers (Greene, 1972, type 20.–.).

Period 1B (construction) (c. 75), miscellaneous deposits.

Amphora.

(42) Neck and rim as Camulodunum 186B (Hawkes and Hull, 1947), Southern Spanish,? Cadiz; fragments built into Period 1B wall forming probable south-east wall of fuel-store of north-east *caldarium* furnace-house.

Flagon.

(43) Red body with thick white slip, *451*, 8: gly. 7B.

Jars.

(44) Both the finish and general appearance of this vessel are similar to an example from Topsham, dated *c.* 50/55–70/75 (Jarvis and Maxfield, 1975, Fig. 11, 18), although the profile of the rim is slightly different. The Topsham vessel has a zone of rusticated decoration below the groove on its shoulder, ?*371*, 4: gly. 8. (45) Roughly-made vessel with a wiped exterior, *10*, 4: gly. 8. (46) Part of a triple vase of unusual form; grey-buff fabric. The lower part of the surviving container is elongated to form a stem which must have been attached to a central base, 4: gly. 8. (47) *371*, 4: gly. 8.

Bowl or dish.

(48) Form possibly as R.C.H.M., 1970, 577, no. 22, *40*, 4: gly. 8.

Terra Nigra (V.R.).

Base sherd in T.N., bluish-white paste: finish as Form 58 cup from Period 2A (construction) (Fig. 64, 128), 8: 49F2.

Mortaria (K.H.).

A rim fragment from a mortarium in fine cream fabric. This wall-sided type was common in Britain in the Claudian period, and they were probably not made later than A.D. 55/60 though many would, of course, continue in use after this date. 4: gly. 8.

Body fragment. Indeterminate. 6: 52G.

Body fragment in very hard, off-white fabric with buff slip and opaque white and transparent grit. Indeterminate. 8: 49F1.

Period 2A (construction) (c. 80). (Fig. 62–4):

* signifies that a vessel comes from a deposit mostly or wholly composed of furnace-ash.

Amphorae.

(49) 14: 1137. (50) 1: 10ED.

Flagons.

(*51) *440*, 13: 1409B–D. (52) *406*, 1: 10EC. (53) *435*, 1: 9EB. (*54) *435*, 1: 9EB1. (55) *435*, 14: 1137. (56) *440*, 17: 43. (*57) *440*, 13: 1409B–D. (58) *440*, 1: 10EC. (59) *40*, 1: 9EA. (60) *40*, 1: 9EA.

Beakers.

(*61) *407*, 1: 9EB1. (62) 'Rough-cast cornice-rim beaker with light brown oxidised slip: variety 1 (see p. 189). End of first to mid second century A.D.' (V.S.) 8: gly. 6.

Jars.

(63) *373*, 14: 1137. (64) Possibly from a pear-shaped jar (Brailsford, 1958, no. 7). *40*, 14: 1137. (*65) *371*, 12: 1139. (66) *371*, 14: 1135. (*67) *371*, 12: 1139, 13: 1409B–D. (*68) *151*, 13: 1409B–D. (69) *40*, 16: 1518. (*70) *40*, 14: 1148. (*71) *31*, 1: 9EB. (*72) *31*, 13: 1409B–D. (73) *40*, 16: 1514. (*74) Cf. Brailsford, 1958, no. 2, *40*, 13: 1409B–D. (75) The only example of Brailsford's type 12 so far recorded from Exeter (Brailsford, 1958, Fig. 1), *40*, 14: 1137.

Cooking -pots.

(*76) *40*, 13: 1409B–D. (*77) *40*, 13: 1409B–D. (78) *40*, 4: 46B. (*79) *40*, 1: f.51. (*80) Possibly from a vessel with countersunk-lug handles, *40*, 1: 9EB. (81) *40*, 16: 1524. (*82) *81*, 13: 1409B–D. (*83), *81*, 13: 1409B–D. (84) *81*, 9: gly. 11. (*85) *40*, 13: 1409B–D. (*86) *40*, 13: 1409B–D. (87) *151*, 14: 1137. (88) *151*, 16: 1521. (89) *371*, 22: 2139. (*90) *190*, 13:

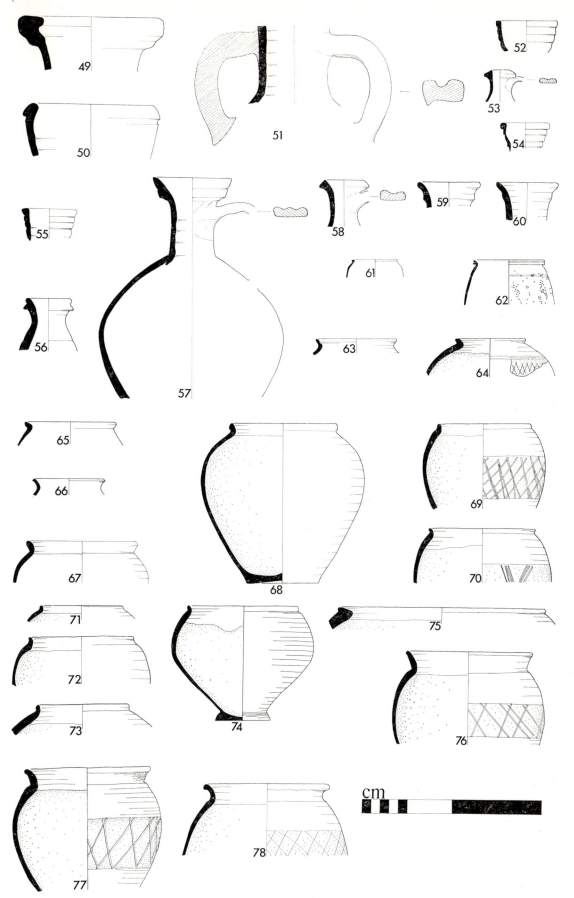

Fig. 62. Coarse pottery, Period 2A (construction) (scale 1 : 4).

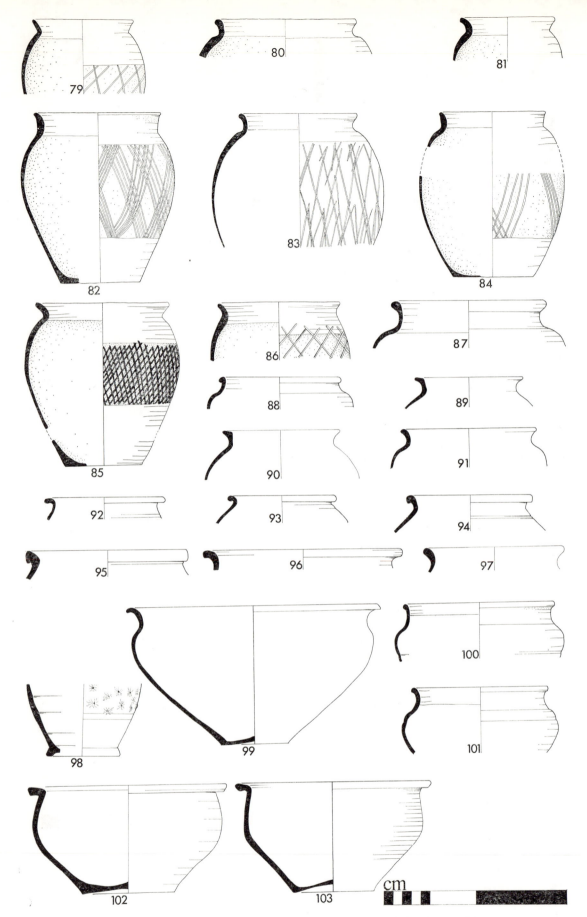

Fig. 63. Coarse pottery, Period 2A (construction) (scale 1 : 4).

1409B–D. (91) *190*, 16: 1514. (92) *190*, 14: 1137. (93) *371*, 14: 1137. (94) *371*, 16: 1524. (*95) *191*, 1: 9EB1. (96) Possibly a storage-jar, *125*, 22: 2139.

Miscellaneous.

(97) *372*, 16: 1514. (98) Base of a rusticated jar with a foot-ring; fine sandy mid-grey fabric, 16: 1518.

Bowls.

(99) *190*, 17: 534. (*100) *151*, 1: 9EB1. (*101) *151*, 13: 1409B–D. (102) *151*, 18: 61. (*103) *151*, 13: 1409B–D. (104) *151*, 4: under gly 1. (105) *190*, 4: 36A. (*106) Possibly a lid, *371*, 1: 9EB1.

Terra nigra bowl (V.R.).

(*107) Sherd from a carinated bowl decorated with a band of rouletting. Although the fabric falls within the broad definition of TN, it is not the variety used for cups and platters. It most closely resembles the range of fabrics used for small jars and beakers, Holwerda types 26, 27 and 74, some of which are decorated with bands of rouletting.

Military sites in South Wales have produced copies of samian form 29 and 37 in well-finished imitation TN, usually decorated with bands of rouletting; no systematic search has been undertaken, but the sites are Usk, Caerleon, Caerwent and Chester. Such rouletted bowls appear to be common at sites on the upper Rhine, but in oxidised imitation samian fabrics. 13: 1409B–D.

Bowls

(108) Probably a copy of samian Dr. 29 in a sandy red fabric with a thick white-cream slip. Rouletted exterior. No other examples known from Exeter; the fabric appears to be quite different from that of the white-slipped flagons in fabric *451*, 16: 1521. (*109) Copy of samian Dr. 29; there is a faint scribed circle on the floor of the vessel, as with its prototype, *151*, 13: 1409B–D. (*110) *151*, 13: 1409B–D. (*111) *371*, 18: 65. (112) *371*, 12: 1138. (*113) *371*, 1: 9EB1. (*114) *190*, 13: 1409B–D. (115) *40*, 23: 2126. (116) *40*, 8: gly. 6. (117) Flat-rimmed dish; a few flat-rimmed dishes in fabric *40* have been recovered recently from contexts at Exeter which date to before *c.* 100 (see no. 115 above and Bidwell, 1977, Fig. 13.2, 23–9), *31*, 8: gly. 6. (*118) *40*, 13: 1409B–D. (119) *40*, 16: 1512. (*120) *40*, 1: 9EB1. (121) *40*, 1: 10ED. (122) *40*, 14: 1137. (123) *151*, 12: 1139. (*124) *31*, 1: 9EB1. (*125) *40*, 13: 1409B –D.

Mortaria (K.H.).

(126) A spout fragment and a bead and flange fragment (unstratified) probably from the same vessel, in fine-textured, pinkish-brown fabric. Although fragmentary, sufficient survives to demonstrate that this mortarium was made in an unlocated pottery situated in Gallia Lugdunensis or Gallia Narbonensis. Several of the potters who made mortaria of this distinctive type are known but only one, Primus, is attested in Britain (Priamus is also recorded but this could perhaps refer to the same potter). The date of their activity is uncertain but one recorded from Wroxeter was described as from a deposit earlier than the middle of the second century (Bushe-Fox, 1916, Fig. 3, no. 51 and p. 60). 4: 12C1 (spout fragment).

*A flange and bead fragment in hard cream fabric with flint grit. South-Eastern England or Gaul. First century (possibly Group 1 in Dore and Greene, 1977, 5–17). 13: 1409B–D.

*Body fragment in hard cream fabric. South eastern England or Gaul. First century. 13: 1409B–D.

Body fragments, worn. Probably first-century. South-Eastern England or Gaul. 14: 1137.

*A mortarium in slightly sandy cream fabric with orangy-buff slip. Indeterminate. 13: 1409B–D.

Sherds from at least two mortaria, both indeterminate. 14: 1137.

Cup:

(*127) *151*, 13: 1409B–D.

Terra Nigra (V.R.).

(128) Flanged bowl with stamp: 'ΛTEIO'. A central stamp within an incised circle on a shallow cup, form 58, in TN. Bluish-white fine-grained paste with sparse white and grey grits, variegated dove-grey surfaces, polished interior and carelessly finished exterior below the flange. The cup is a distorted second, the lip is uneven and the flange droops unevenly; it is more than usually poorly finished for an import. The foot-ring was made separately and then luted onto the bowl. The letters of the die were so crudely cut that the reading is uncertain, but is possibly ATEIO, for stamps bearing different versions of the name Aetius or Ateius are fairly common on the Continent and have been found in Britain also. No other stamps from this particular die have been identified; the closest is on a small carinated cup, form 56, found in a Claudio-Neronian pit group at Colchester, during the excavation of 1970 (directed by Mrs R. Niblett). However there appear to have been several different potters of the same name working from the late Augustan to the early Flavian periods. At least one worked at La Prosne, Marne, near Rheims, but it is not possible to say if this is from that pottery.

The cup is typologically late. The offset on the inside below the lip has been replaced by a crudely burnished groove, while the proportions, with a wide mouth and shallow depth, are also typical of late Neronian-Flavian examples. The fabric and finish, although not the proportions, closely resemble examples from the nearby site at Topsham, one of which has a different stamp but which is from an equally crudely cut die (Jarvis and Maxfield, 1975 Figs. 10, 11 & 17). Although the stamps are different, there is little doubt that they are from the same source, which may even be 'local', since the group from Topsham also includes seconds, fissured and distorted in the firing process. 1: 10ED.

(*129) Base sherds from a hemispherical bowl with a tall functional foot-ring, possibly form 58, in TN. The fabric and finish are like the stamped cup (no. 128 above), with a poor, dull finish. Not stamped. *c.* A.D. 45–75. 1: F.51.

(130) Rim sherd in TN. Buff fine-grained paste; blue-black micaceous surfaces; worn, but traces of a polished finish survive. 22: 2135.

(*131) Rim sherd in TN. Heavily burnt and discoloured. 4: 46B1 and C.

(132) Rim sherd in TN. Buff fine-grained paste; blue-grey surfaces, with a polished internal and matt external finish. 14: 1135.

(*133) Rim sherd in TN. Bluish-white fine-grained paste with fine grey inclusions; dove grey surfaces; polished interior finish, poorly finished-off streaky exterior. Local' 1: 9EB1.

Cups of form 58, *c.* A.D. 45–75:

Rim sherd in good quality TN. Pale buff smooth paste; very dark blue-grey surfaces with a facetted polished finish. From a Period 3A (construction) feature (3: F.92), but a body-sherd, probably from the same cup, came from 1: 10ED, through which 3: F.92 was cut. Two body sherds from below the line of the flange in TN. As with the above example, the exterior has a lighter blue-grey and less glossy finish. 14: 1137.

Platters of form 16, c. A.D. 45–85:

Rim sherd in TN. Bluish-white fine-grained sandy paste; metallic pale blue-grey surfaces with a facetted polished finish. 14: 1137.

Rim sliver as example above. 22: 2139.

Wall and base sherds in TN. Pale buff fine-grained paste, with some grey inclusions; dark blue-grey surfaces, highly polished interior, smoothed exterior. Two concentric circles incised on the upper surface of the base. The platter is in good condition and the foot-ring looks relatively unused. 14: 1137.

Wall sherd in TN. White fine-grained paste; dove grey surfaces with a polished finish; an unusually pale variety of TN. 14: 1137.

Miscellaneous Bowl sherds:

Body sherd from a large rounded bowl, possibly form 46, in TN. Hard dense pale grey paste; dark blue-grey surfaces; the darker interior surface has a highly polished finish, the exterior shades light to dark and has a less glossy finish. c. A.D. 50–75. 22: 2126.

Sherd from a platter or a bowl in TN. The fabric and finish are like those of the cup from F.92 and 10ED (see above). 1: 10ED.

Other forms:

*Body sherds from a small beaker, probably with a sharply carinated shoulder, similar to form 120, in very thin, 'eggshell' TN. The fabric is fine-grained, sand-free and dark-grey in colour; the surfaces are a dense grey-black, the exterior having a patchy highly polished finish.

An import, probably from the Rhineland or possibly Bavay. Compared to platters and cups in TN and TR, beakers in TN are comparatively rare and examples with potters' stamps on the underside of the base or on the side, even rarer. There are two from Southwark and one from Chichester, with virtually illegible stamps due to the small size of the die face. Pre-Flavian or early Flavian. 13: 1409B–D.

Platters of form 17 in Pompeian Red ware.

Matching base sherds from a platter in a variety of Pompeian Red ware. Cream fine-grained sand-free micaceous ware; thick coral-red slip on the upper surface only. The upper surface is decorated with groups of concentric incised circles. Platters of this form occur in at least six different varieties of so-called Pompeian redware. The paste varies from a coarse-grained gritty texture, like B.B.1, to a smooth sand-free texture, like this piece. The finish of the lower exterior surfaces differ, some are covered with a thick pale slip, others are not, but they all have a similar thick red glossy slip on the interior, upper surface only. Most, if not all, the varieties occur at Camulodunum, although some varieties may eventually show different regional distributions when there is more evidence (Hawkes and Hull, 1947, 201). (P.B: These sherds appear to be in Peacock's Fabric 3 (1977, 154) which probably comes from the Auvernes of Central France, perhaps more specifically from Lezoux.)

Lids.

(134) *190*, 16: 1514. (135) *151*, 18: 60. (136) *81*, 14: 1137.

Imitation Terra Nigra (ITN):

Sherds from a bowl *375*. 1: 10ED, with a foot-ring.

*Sherds from two bowls, or more probably platters, with sharp carinations; the floor of one vessel has a pair of concentric lines incised near the carination *376*. Both from 1: 9EB1.

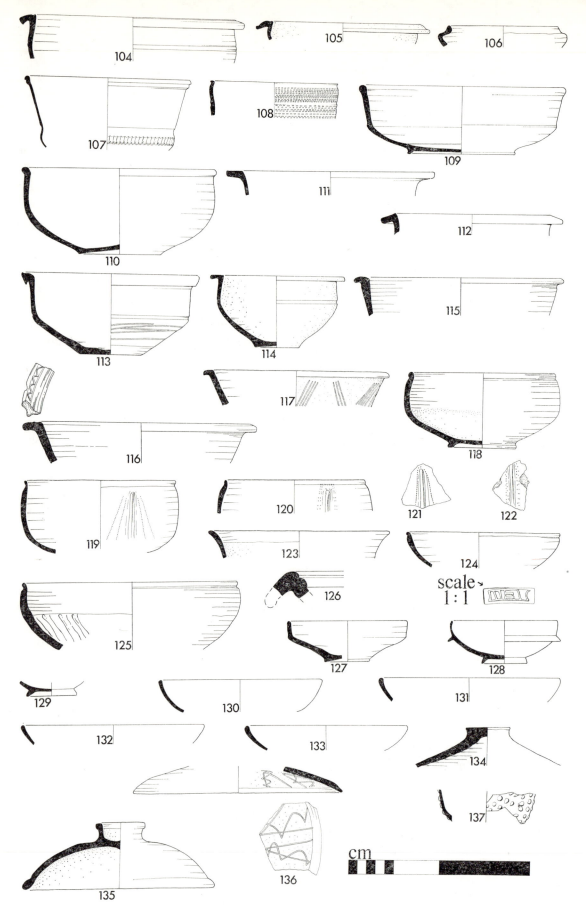

scale
1 : 1

cm

Fig. 64. Coarse pottery, Period 2A (construction) (scale 1 : 4).

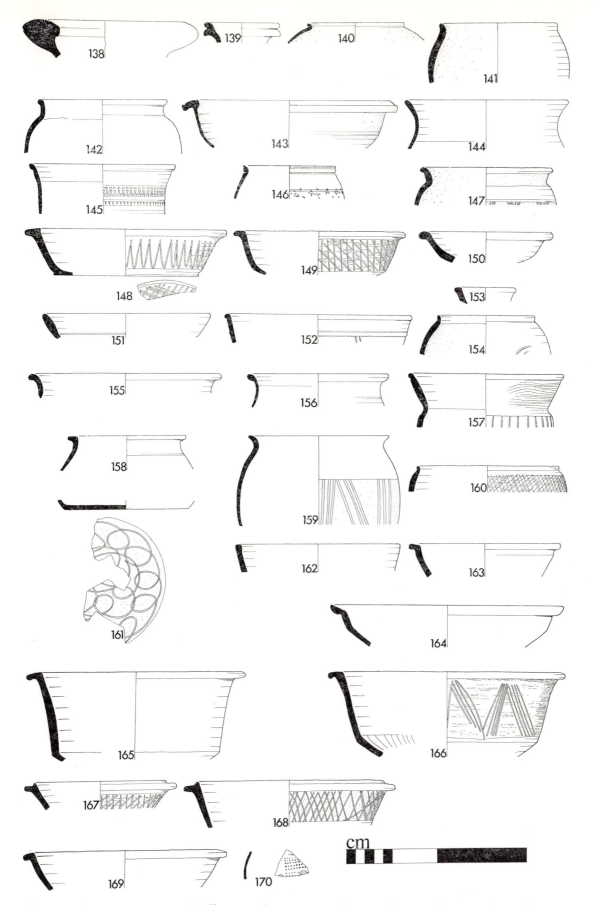

Fig. 65. Coarse pottery, miscellaneous first century deposits (138–145); Period 2A deposits (146–152); Period 2B (construction) (153–170) (scale 1 : 4).

Rim of jar similar in form to No. 128. *372*. 22: 2126.

*Base and body sherd from jar *372*. 14: 1148.

*Sherd from jar *372*. 1: F.51.

Sherd from a small closed form decorated with a band of rouletting on an unpolished zone *373*, 14: 1137.

Sherd from a closed form *373*, 12: 1139.

*Sherd from a bowl or platter *373*, 13: 1409B–D.

Sherd from a bowl or platter *374*, 1: 10ED.

*Sherd from a closed form *374*, 4: 46B1 and C.

Fine Wares (K.G.):

Lyons beaker, rouletted; Greene, 1972, Fig. 3, 26. 1: 10EC.

? Burnt body sherd of Lyons beaker; Greene, 1972, Fig. 2, 20.– (or badly fired imitation) (8: gly. 7A).

Rim of Lyons beaker; Greene, 1972, 20.3 or .5. 1: 10EC.

(*137) ? sherd of Central Gaulish colour-coated ware; form uncertain, but a beaker. 1: 9EB1.

Three joining sherds of a Central Gaulish glazed beaker; Greene, 1972, Fig. 12, 16. The barbotine dots are much larger than usual. 14: 1136.

*Small sherd of Central Gaulish glazed beaker; Greene, 1972, Fig. 12, 13. 18: 65.

Two joining sherds, Lyons cup; Greene, 1972, Fig. 2, 5.2. Parts of adjacent leaves survive. 1: 10ED.

Rim of Lyons cup; Greene, 1972, Fig. 1, 1.2. Uncommon. 1: 10EC.

Lyons cup rim which could come from a number of forms, both rough-cast and decorated by other means. 1: 10EC.

Lyons cup base; Greene, 1972, Fig. 2, 5.2. Fragment of decoration remains. 1: 10EC.

Lyons cup base, not rough-cast and therefore a decorated form. 8: gly. 7A.

Miscellaneous first-century deposits (Fig. 65).

Amphora.

(138) 9: 39D. This deposit may well be broadly contemporary with Period 2A (construction).

Miscellaneous coarse wares (all from 9: 39D).

(139) *451.* (140) *190.* (141) Clumsily finished vessel with roughly-burnished exterior surfaces, *3.* (142) *190.* (143) *190.* (144) *151.* (145) *151.*

Terra Nigra (V.R.).

Body sherd from a cup, probably form 58 (*c.* A.D. 45–75) in TN. Buff fine-grained paste; blue-grey surfaces, with a polished internal and matt external finish. 9: 49E.

Mortaria (K.H.).

Two body fragments from two different mortaria, both worn, in cream fabric with flint grit, one with some concentric scoring surviving. First or less probably second century. 9: 39A.

Deposits in the course of Period 2A (c. 80 to late Antonine).

Miscellaneous coarse wares.

(146) Rough-cast black-coated beaker; variety 1. Fragments of another. (V.S.) 8: 29H2. (147) *3*, 8: 29GI. (148) *101*, 8: 29GI. (149) *40*, 8: 29HI. (150) *151*, 8: 29HI. (151) Copy in ITN of Camulodunum Form 2 platter (Hawkes and Hull, 1947, 216). This type is normally pre-Claudian, *376*, fill of post-hole at north-east end of enclosure south-east of *basilica*. (152) Copy of Dr 37; two incised lines below cordon may represent part of a crude ovolo, *125*, 8: 29HI.

Mortaria (K.H.).

A rim in fine yellowish cream fabric closely paralleled in form and fabric with one recorded from Richborough (Bushe-Fox, 1949, Pl. XCV, no. 500) from a deposit dated A.D. 90–125. 8: 49A.

Two body fragments. Nondescript. 8: 49A.

Flange from a mortarium in cream fabric with thick pink core. This mortarium, though not identical, is probably from the same pottery as one recorded from Richborough (Bushe-Fox, 1949, Pl. XCV, no. 500). Mortaria of this general type are common in southern England and must have been made either in Southern England or in Gaul. This example is more likely to be second century than first century in date. 8: 29HI.

Flange and body fragment. South-East England or Gaul. First century. 8: 29HI.

Flange fragment in brownish cream fabric. South-eastern England or Gaul. Possibly early second century. 8: 29HI.

Three body fragments from two vessels, two pieces joining. South-Eastern England or Gaul. (a) Probably first century. (b) First or second century. 8: 29HI.

Flange and body fragments from three mortaria in brown or pinkish brown fabric. Indeterminate. All. 8: 29HI.

Period 2B (construction) (late Antonine).

Flagon or flask.

(153) *151*, 12: 1113.

Jars.

(154) Part of a shallow circular depression survives on the body of the pot, which may represent part of an eye-brow motif (cf. Bidwell, 1977, 190); however it is possible that this feature was associated with a handle, *40*, 4: fill of gly. 1.

Cooking-pots.

(155) *40*, 17: 36. (156) *101*, 18: 33. (157) *125*, 42, lime-storage pit in the *forum*-courtyard. (158) *371*, 4: fill of gly. 1. (159) *125*, 18: 33.

Bowls and dishes.

(160) *40*, 4: fill of gly. 1. (161) Base of plain-rimmed dish?, *31*, 4: fill of gly. 1. (162) *125*, 17: 36. (163) *101*, 17: 36. (164) *151*, 17: 36. (165) *40*, 13: 1403. (166) *40*, 13: 1402. (167) *151*, 4: fill of gly. 1. (168) There are slight traces of the base (or possibly a chamfer) at the bottom of the illustrated sherd, *40*, 17: 36. These two flanged dishes are typical of several, in both black-burnished and other fabrics, which have been recovered from deposits at Exeter dating to before the end of the second century. They can easily be distinguished from the fully-developed flanged-bowl type (Gillam, 1970, no. 228) by their shallow depth and by the

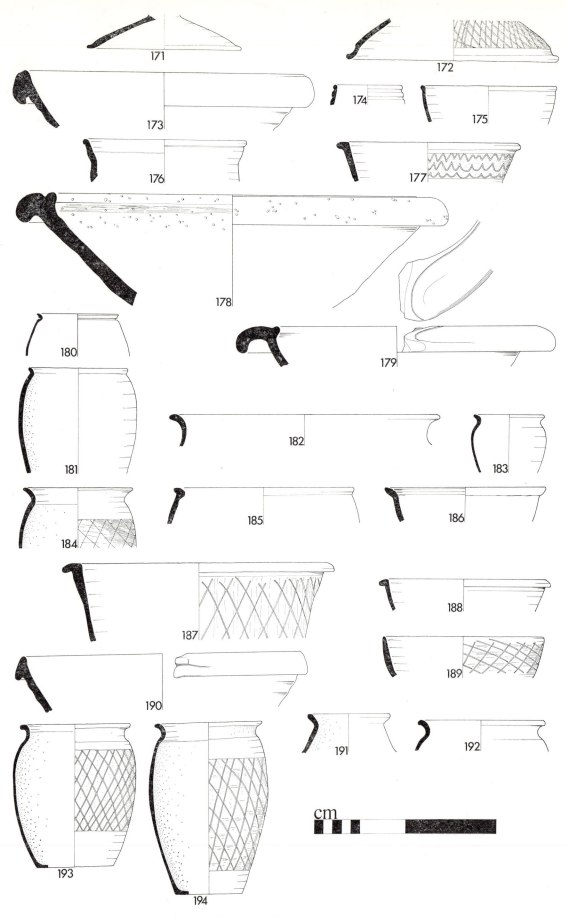

Fig. 66. Coarse pottery, Period 2B (construction) (171–2); second-century deposits south-east of the *forum* (173–179); mid or late second- to mid third-century ditch deposits on north-west side of road (180); Period 2B deposits (181–190); Period 2C (construction) (191–4) (scale 1 : 4).

frequent presence of lattice decoration. It is clear that they were introduced before the 'incipient' flanged bowls (Gillam, 1970, nos. 227 and 314), now thought to have come on the market 'towards the very end of the second century' (Gillam, 1976, 68 and 70). They may represent a development of a late first-century black-burnished ware type (Fig. 64, 115–7 and Bidwell, 1977, Fig. 13.2, 23–9). Other early flanged bowls or dishes are known from South-Western sites: Camerton, Wedlake, 1958, Fig. 44, 471, from a context dated *c.* A.D. 150–200; Cirencester, undecorated, from a group with Trajanic-Hadrianic samian (CIR 61, Site C, Tr. V (29), no. 2, information from V. Rigby); from the enclosure ditch underlying the Holcombe villa (Pollard, 1974, Fig. 15, 33 and Fig. 16, 56–7, where these are taken to indicate a *terminus post quem* of *c.* A.D. 180 although none of the samian from the deposit is later than *c.* A.D. 150). At Seaton, Devon, gully 26 produced a group of pottery thought to date to the late first century (Miles, 1977, Fig. 12, nos. 1–11, 13, 15–17). The group included the upper part of a flanged dish or bowl (Miles, 1977, Fig. 12, no. 6), which has a profile similar to that of the common late flanged-bowl type (Gillam, 1970, no. 228). It is difficult to accept this vessel as a representative of the earlier flanged-dish type; the group with which it was associated appears to be contaminated by intrusive material, since it also contains a plain-rimmed dish of normal late second-century aspect (Miles, 1977, 130, no. 16). (169) *60*, 17: 36.

Miscellaneous coarse wares.

(170) Sherd from a poppy-head beaker; hard fine fabric with light-grey smoothed exterior surface and barbotine dots of grey clay; rare at Exeter, 17: 36. (171) *31*, 13: 1403. (172) *151*, 12: IIII.

Fine wares (K.G.).

Lyons cup or beaker. Foundations of wall blocking north-west end of passage leading from road.

Fine wares (V.S.).

Sherd of flagon or beaker in hard fine cream-buff fabric with irridescent dark-grey brown slip: Nene Valley: mid second century A.D. onwards. 12: 1105.

Mortaria (K.H.).

Flange from a mortarium in very hard fabric fired to a dark grey almost throughout but clearly intended to be cream with buff slip. Source unknown. First or second century. 4: fill of gly. 1.

(173) A very weathered fragment from a mortarium in hard brownish cream fabric with pink core. This is probably an import, perhaps from the Rhineland. Dating evidence is lacking, but I would expect it to have been made in the late second or first half of the third century. 18: 33.

Body fragment. South-Eastern England or Gaul. Probably first century. 1: 10EB1.

Second-century deposits south-east of the forum.

Miscellaneous coarse wares.

(174) *101?*, 9: 38G7. (175) *40*, 9: 38G6. (176) *151*, 9: 38G3. (177) *60*, 9: 38G5.

Fine wares (V.S.).

Two bases of rough-cast beakers with black slip: variety 1 (see p. 189). 9: 38G5 and 29: 233. Colour-coated beaker sherd; fine pale brown fabric with visible platelets of mica, matt dark brown slip: probably Lezoux in origin. 9: 38G5.

Mortaria (K.H.).

(178) A well-worn mortarium in hard, yellowish-cream fabric with flint grit and concentric scoring on the inside and with some flint grit on the flange. Made in South-Eastern England or Gaul in the first or early second century. 9: 38G5.

(179) A mortarium of form Gillam 238 in hard, cream fabric with flint grit combined with concentric scoring on the inside and on the flange. Made in South-Eastern England or Gaul, A.D. 70–100. See Dore and Greene, 1977, 5–17 for comments on the Group 2 potters who used this form. 25: 31.

Mid or late second- to mid third-century ditch deposits on north-east side of road (see p. 97):

Fine wares (V.S.).
Rough-cast beaker; dark grey slip; variety 1 (see p. 189).

(180) Two sherds from a beaker in hard fine deep buff fabric with lustrous brown slip: cf. Gillam, 1970, type 86; Nene Valley, mid second to early third century.
Scraps from two beakers, one in fine cream fabric, the other in fine buff fabric; both with a dark brown slip. Probably Nene Valley, mid second century onwards.

Mortaria (K.H.).
Body fragment in reddish-brown fabric, probably made in South-West England. Indeterminate.

Deposits in the course of Period 2B (late Antonine to last quarter of third century).

Beaker.
(181) Probably originally handled, *40*, 26: 218.

Cooking-pots:
(182) Large enough for use as storage-jar, *125*, 17: 25. (183) *101*, 26: 218. (184) *60*, 26: 218. (185) *125*, 28: 276.

Bowls and dishes.
(186) Wheel-thrown bowl or dish. Fabric contains frequent white non-calcareous grits of irregular size, scattered hard black and brown grits, and scattered quartz grits. Mid brown external colour. This fabric is identical in appearance to Cornish wares with inclusions which have been derived from the weathering of gabbro (see Peacock, 1969, 57–8; I am grateful to H. Miles for confirming the identification of this fabric). This vessel probably derives from a series of bowls and dishes, which are often decorated with cordons and frequently have rims grooved for lids; they were established in Cornwall by the end of the first century A.D. at the latest, as is shown by their presence at St Mawgan-in-Pyder (Murray-Thriepland, 1956, 66, Type R). For a close parallel, from Porth Godrevy, Gwithian see Fowler, 1962, Fig. 11, 46. 28: 222. (187) *31*, 17: 35. (188) *110*, 17: 25 (189) *40*, 12: 1039.

Fine wares (V.S.).
Base of beaker in very hard miscaceous orange-buff fabric with lustrous dark grey slip: Lezoux: late second to mid third century A.D. 12: 1039.

Third-century deposits south-east of the forum:

Fine wares (V.S.).
Fragments of four rough-cast beakers with black slip: variety 1. From 9: 38E1, 38E2, 38F3, pit 12.

Base of beaker in fine deep buff fabric with matt dark brown slip: rough-cast decoration including particles on under side of the base; possibly of Lezoux origin: late first to early second century A.D. 9: 38F1.

Everted-rim beaker in hard fine light brown-grey fabric with matt black slip: source unknown. 9: 38F1.

Body sherd of beaker in hard fine pale buff fabric with thick lustrous slip, orange-brown on exterior and dark grey on interior: Nene Valley: mid second to third century A.D. 9: 38F1.

Mortaria (K.H.).

(190) A mortarium in very hard cream fabric with a few quartz trituration grits. This type was first made in the second half of the second century but production continued well into the third century. This example has an unusual spout. It is probably an import from the Rhineland (cf. Cunliffe, 1971, Vol. 2, Fig. 11, No. 293.1). 9: 38F3.

Flange fragment in hard cream fabric. Indeterminate. 9: 38F2.

A well-worn body fragment. South-Eastern England or Gaul. Probably first century. 9: F.50.

Period 2C (construction) (last quarter of the third century).

Beaker.

(191) Beaker with funnel-shaped neck and everted rim. Brown fabric with gabbro inclusions (as No. 186). This neck can be paralleled by an unpublished vessel from Carvossa, Probus (for the site, see Douch and Beard, 1970, 93–7), which likewise has the beginning of a cordon at the base of the neck. They probably both come from rather crude copies of butt-beakers; the site at Carvossa has produced a number of such copies, all in a ware with gabbro inclusions, and the majority much finer than our example. 17: 515.

Cooking-pots.

(192) *101*, 17: 515. (193) *101*, 28: 209. (194) *40*, 17: 1.

Bowls and dishes.

(195) *101*, 28: 209. (196) *60*, 17: 1. (197) Dish with a flange and what appears to be a sagging rather than a chamfered base, *40*, 28: 209. (198) *40*, 20: 527. (199) *101*, 17: 515. (200) *31*, 28: 216. (201) *14*, 17: 1.

Fine wares (K.G.).

Lyons Beaker, Greene, 1972, Fig. 3, 26. 17: 1.

Fine wares (V.S.).

Base of beaker in fine white-buff fabric with dark brown-black slip: probably Nene Valley: mid second century onwards. 17: 515.

Rim of fine colour-coated beaker: source unknown: late first or second century A.D.; residual. 4: 10A.

Rough-cast colour-coated beaker sherds, one scrap oxidised, 28: 21, two scraps with reduced surfaces: variety 1 (see p. 189), residual. 17: 1.

Cornice-rim black colour-coated beaker; variety 1 (see p. 189). 28: 209.

Mortaria (K.H.).

A mortarium in hard cream fabric with flint grit, made in Southern England or on the Continent at an uncertain date in the late first or second century. 19: 519.

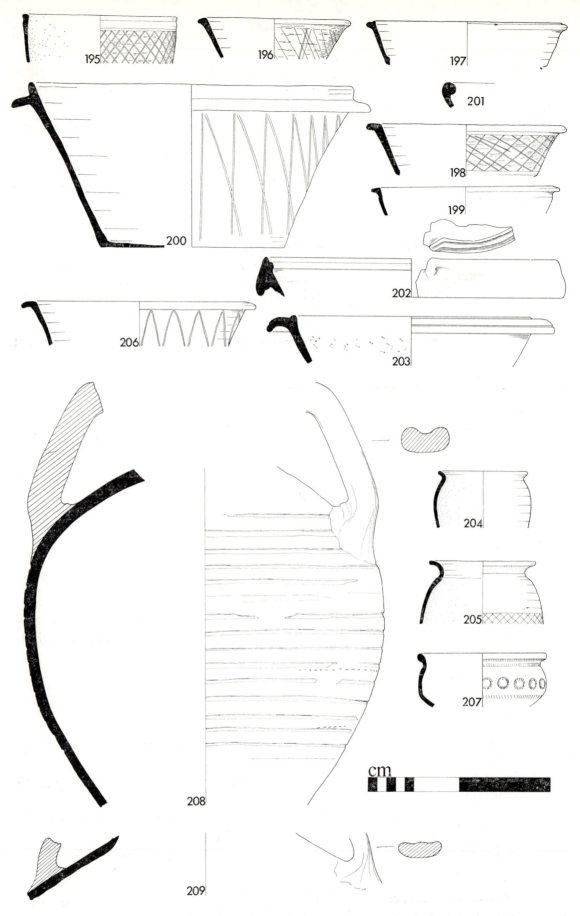

Fig. 67. Coarse pottery, Period 2C (construction) 195–203); Period 2C deposits (204–6); Period 3A (construction) (207); fourth-century deposits from *insula* north-east of *forum* (208–9) (scale 1 : 4).

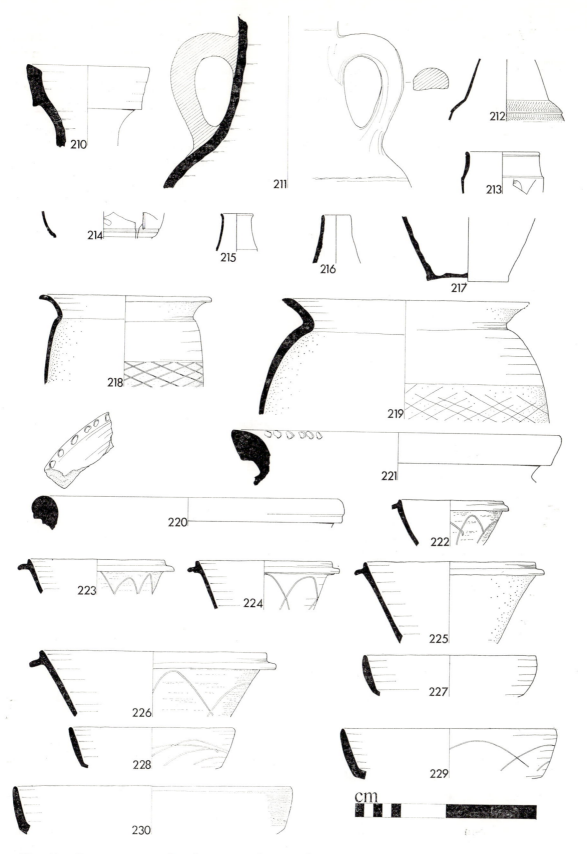

Fig. 68. Coarse pottery, fourth-century deposits from *insula* north-east of *forum* (scale 1 : 4).

(202) A wall-sided mortarium in fine-textured, hard, pale brown fabric and drab brownish buff slip; abundant quartz trituration grit. The bead has been broken and turned out to form the spout. This type of mortarium was first made in the second half of the second century but production continued until at least the middle of the third century. This example is likely to be an import from the Rhineland where it was a common form. 17: 1.

(203) A mortarium, burnt throughout, in a brown fabric with red-brown slip; the trituration grit includes some quartz and dark grits. This mortarium can be attributed to the kilns at Shepton Mallet. These kilns were active in the second century but cannot be closely dated. The Antonine period is perhaps the most likely date for them, but some of their rim-profiles look earlier. The paucity of their products on sites in the South-West suggests that their activity is unlikely to have been prolonged. 28: 209.

Course of Period 2C (last quarter of the third century to c. 340/350).

Miscellaneous coarse wares.

(204) *5*, 28: 178, (205) *31*, 28: 197. (206) *31*, 243, hearth inside 'shop'.

Fine wares (V.S.).

Sherds from two black colour-coated beakers, one indented and rough-cast, the other with a cornice rim: variety 1 (see p. 189). Both 28: 191.

Colour-coated beaker, probably rough-cast: variety 1 (see p. 189) end of first to mid second century. 28: 181.

Sherd of colour-coated beaker or flagon: source unknown; not closely datable. 28: 195.

Period 3A (construction) (c. 340/350).

Fine wares (V.S.).

(207) Abraded, fine, micaceous, pinky-buff bowl with bright red colour-coat; rouletted and impressed with roulette-stamp decoration; an Oxfordshire product: cf. Cunliffe, 1975, Type 36, *c.* A.D. 340/350 onwards. 1: 8.

Sherd of New Forest imitation samian. 19: 516.

Fourth-century pot from the insula north-east of the forum (all 24: 14 except where stated):

Amphorae

(208) Body of Dressel 30 with deeply grooved exterior.

(209) Shoulder and handle of North African amphora.

(210) North African (Algerian) amphora rim.

(211) North African amphora neck with handles. A line has been pecked around the base of the neck, presumably to help with its removal for subsequent re-use of the body.

Fine wares (V.S.).

(212) Rouletted, pentice-moulded, funnel-mouthed beaker in a medium to fine browny-orange fabric with rich chocolate slip. This vessel emanates from a major factory, as yet unlocated, but probably lying in Oxfordshire or Gloucester and supplying most of Central-Southern and South-West England with colour-coated beakers, mostly globular or pentice-moulded, often rouletted, as here, or decorated with crude figures or overlapping scales *en barbotine*, as occurs elsewhere at Exeter cf. Cunliffe, 1975, Fig. 171, Type 15.2; late third to mid fourth century A.D.

Colour-coated beaker: probably from the same source.

(213) Indented beaker: very hard fine blue-grey fabric with lustrous plum-coloured slip. New Forest: probably late third to mid fourth century; those produced later in the fourth century tend to have a darker, more matt slip.

Two sherds from a colour-coated beaker or flagon with white painted decoration: probably New Forest: late third to third quarter of fourth century.

Colour-coated sherd: probably Nene Valley: mid second century and onwards.

Base of Rhenish ware beaker: late second to third century.

Abraded sherd of Oxfordshire colour-coated ware: third to fourth century.

Body sherds of two separate beakers in fine light orange-buff fabric with visible platelets of yellow mica and a matt dark brown-black slip: fine vertical lines *en barbotine* forming the lower part of 'hair-pin' decoration: Lezoux source: Flavian to Trajanic: cf. Down and Rule, 1971, Fig. 5, 22, no. 89b.

Sherd in fairly fine creamy yellow fabric with slightly glossy pale yellow slip: form not identifiable: probably *céramique à l'éponge* (Raimbault, 1973): probably fourth century.

(214) Two fragments of the same or similar globular beakers in a fairly fine, bright orange-red slip on a very smooth exterior surface: incised 'cut-glass' decoration in the form of vertical lines (perhaps dividing panels) and part of a diagonal 'petal' or 'leaf'; possibly an imitation of late samian or Argonne 'cut glass' decorated globular beakers (Déchelette, 1904, Pl. V.2. or Chenet, 1941, Pl. XVI, 333). This interesting type has not previously been defined in Britain and it is possible that, in view of Exeter's trade contacts, its source may well lie somewhere in Gaul; probably third or fourth century.

Other coarse wares.

(215) Rim of beaker with groove at base of neck. Hard slightly sandy fine light red fabric with thin brick-red slip. Source unknown.

(216) Neck of flagon (?). Highly micaceous, slightly soapy red-buff ware. Sherds from at least two other vessels in a similar fabric from this deposit. Source unknown.

(217) Base of a jar in a hard brick-red fabric with frequent gold mica plates and occasional quartz grits. The interior shows prominent wheel-throwing rills with a deep groove at the junction of the wall and base. The underside of the base has whorls which have resulted from detaching it from the wheel with a wire. The exterior of the vessel has not been smoothed or burnished. In spite of the inclusion of gold mica plates in its fabric a Cornish origin for this fabric can be ruled out since its general appearance and feel are quite different from those of contemporary locally-produced wares. A Continental source is likely.

Cooking-pots.

(218–9) *31*

Storage-jars.

(220–1) *101.*

Bowls and dishes.

(222–30) *31.*

Fine wares from layer below fourth-century deposits (K.G.).

Sherd from a Lyons cup; Greene, 1972, Fig. 1, 3. 24: 19.

Sherd from a carinated vessel, Central Gaulish glazed ware: perhaps Greene, 1972, Fig. 11, 11. 24: 19.

Course of Period 3A (c. 340/350 *to no later than the mid fifth century*).

Miscellaneous coarse wares.

(231) *110*, 28: F.168–1.

(232) Sherd from black-burnished ware vessel with a combed exterior. There is no doubt that this is a black-burnished ware fabric (type *31*) but its decoration is very unusual. The combing appears to run vertically, although with a hand-made sherd it is difficult to be certain about this. Possible models for this vessel may have been late-Roman shell-gritted wares, some of which had horizontal combed decoration. These penetrated into South-West England in small quantities, apparently during the second half of the fourth century A.D.; the nearest find-spot to Exeter is at Holcombe, Uplyme, where there is a fragment of a jar (Exeter Museum, unpublished). There is a clumsy black-burnished ware imitation of this type of vessel from Cirencester, with diagonal combing on the body (unpublished, CIR 68, Site H, Tr. 3. L.1 (unstratified) information V. Rigby). *31*. 28: F.168–1.

(233) *101*, 28: F.168–1. (234) *31*, 28: F. 168–1. (235) Bowl in a fine light buff fabric with a hole 12 mm in diameter pierced through wall before firing. 2104, robber-trench of Period 3A stylobate wall crossing south-east end of the *basilica*.

Fine wares (V.S.).

Sherd of bowl in hard fine orange micaceous fabric with blue-grey core and bright red slip: Oxfordshire; late third to late fourth century A.D. 2104, fill of robber trench of Period 3A wall crossing *basilica* nave. Cornice-rim black colour-coated beaker; variety 1 (see p. 189) residual. 28: F.168–1.

Pottery occurring residually in later features:

(236) Double-handled flagon in a hard thin cream fabric (probably *406*).

(237) Jar with shallow cordon below rim: the shoulder of the vessel is mica-dusted *190*.

(238) Jar with small everted rim and one surviving handle. This vessel does not appear to belong to Gillam's class of 'beakers of cooking-pot form with handles' (Gillam, 19770, 64–6; Gillam, 1976, 66 and Fig. 2, 23–9), since its profile is too globular. It is reminscent of the double-handled beakers which were produced in grey ware by the New Forest kilns (Fulford, 1975, Fig. 34, Type 36). A few examples of this type were found in black-burnished ware at Portchester (Cunliffe, 1975, 361, Type 175.4). *31*.

(239) Storage jar with small holes pierced through rim. The rim is not burnished but its fabric is identical to *31*.

(240) Base of a tankard in Severn Valley ware; hard orange micaceous fabric; rare at Exeter.

Fine wares (K.G.).

Two sherds from different Lyons cups; Greene, 1972, Fig. 1.1, Sherds from the same Lyons rouletted beaker (?); Greene, 1972, Fig. 3, 26. Three joining sherds from lower wall of Central Gaulish glazed ware flagon, Déchelette 60; Greene, 1972, Fig. 10, 2.

Post-Flavian colour-coated vessels (V.S.).

(241) *New Forest hard fine colour-coated ware:* from a flagon with painted decoration within incised concentric circles (late third to mid fourth century).

Also sherds from five vessels including three indented beakers, one with traces of a panel of 'Christmas tree' decoration: cf. Cunliffe, 1975, Fig. 172, Type 19, 1–5, early to mid fourth century.

New Forest red colour-coated imitation samian bowls (fourth century): five examples, including one sherd from a mortarium.

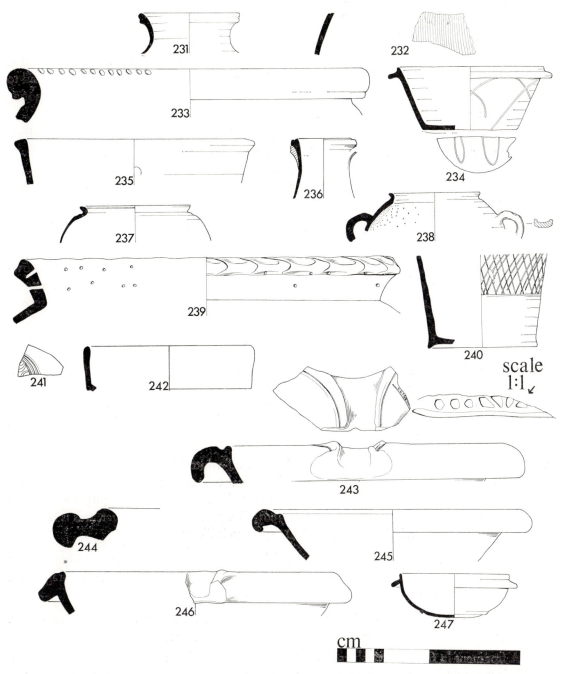

Fig. 69. Period 3A deposits (231–5); material from graveyard levels (236–46); a *Terra Nigra* bowl from the site of the Telephone Exchange, Musgrave Row (247) (scale 1 : 4).

(242) *Oxfordshire red colour-coated ware:* imitation mortarium Dr. 45 (fourth century). Also nine other sherds in this ware including two more mortaria, a beaker, a flagon with white painted scroll decoration, a sherd from either a beaker or a flagon, a carinated, rouletted bowl and a bowl imitating a samian Dr. 31R.

One sherd probably from an Oxfordshire product as above.

A sherd from a vessel in the same fabric as Fig. 68, 216.

Rhenish ware: fragments from five beakers, one indented with white painted decoration (probably a 'motto beaker', third century) and three indented and rouletted (late second to mid third century). Lezoux colour-coated beakers: six examples, one with barbotine decoration, probably as Gillam, 1970, Type 48. (All late second to early third century.)

Céramique à l'éponge: sherd, probably from a bowl in fine pale yellow fabric: glossy yellow slip mottled browny-orange (see Raimbault, 1973, and Fulford, 1977, 45–7).

Nene Valley colour-coated ware (mid second to fourth century): three unrecognisable vessels, one with white painted decoration (third century onwards) and a barbotine-decorated beaker (mid second to third century).

Rough-cast colour-coated beakers, variety 1 (see p. 189; late first to mid second century); three vessels.

Two sherds from a cornice-rim beaker in a deep pinkish-buff fabric with a glossy yellow-orange slip and clay pellet rough-cast decoration; one sherd has mortar adhering to it. This comprises the second variety of rough-cast beaker (see p. 189); probably second century.

Mortaria (K.H.).

(243) A mortarium in pale brown fabric fired to cream at the surface, with a few flint grits surviving. This mortarium is of the type made by potters like Buccus and Paullus who worked *c.* A.D. 55–85 in South-Eastern England or Gaul (see Dore and Greene, 1977, 5–17 for comments on these potters). Part of the border of a potter's stamp is preserved on this mortarium but it is from an unknown die.

(244) The flange from a very large mortarium in hard, off-white fabric from an unknown source possibly in the Rhineland. Mortaria of this general type and size are so rarely found that as yet they can only be dated by the context in which they occur. A roughly similar mortarium is recorded from Colchester (Hull, 1963, Fig. 5, no. 8). If, however, this is from the Rhineland, a date within the period A.D. 150–240 is likely.

(245) A worn mortarium in fine cream fabric with inky blue core, tempered with gritty particles; the trituration grit includes quartz and opaque white and probably brown fragments. Probably made in the south of England, *c.* A.D. 110–150.

(246) A mortarium in pale brownish cream fabric with quartz grit, from an unknown source. This is possibly an import from the Rhineland made in the period A.D. 150–240.

A fragment in fine, brownish cream fabric. I am not certain that this is a mortarium but if it is it would have to be from the deep flange of form Gillam 236 (see Dore and Greene, 1977, 8 for comments on this type). First century, probably A.D. 55–85.

A mortarium of form Gillam 238, made *c.* A.D. 70–100 in South-Eastern England or Gaul. Two other fragments of the same type.

Body fragment in brownish cream fabric with drab slip and crystalline grit. Made in kilns at or near Oxford, A.D. 100–400.

Flange fragment in hard, white fabric with pink core and buff slip.

Indeterminate. South-Eastern England or Continent.

Bead and body fragment. South-Eastern England or Gaul. First century.

Fragments from at least five indeterminate mortaria.

A TN cup from the site of the telephone exchange, Musgrave Row (V.R.).

(247) A hemispherical cup or bowl with a straight flange and a shallow moulded foot-ring; a cross between forms 46 and 58, in TN. Soft fine-grained sand-free greyish-white paste, with a rather large number of fairly coarse white grog and grey ferrous inclusions, as well as voids caused by leaching, suggesting calcarous or vegetable inclusions also. The surfaces are in very poor condition due to wear and they have flaked and laminated so that little of the original finish survives, just patches of streaky blue-grey colour. The piece was not stamped, nor decorated on the inside of the base.

At present the cup is unique although small sherds may have been wrongly classified as form 58 previously. Its most notable feature is the shallow moulded foot-ring placed too high on the wall to be functional, and moulded on the cup, not made separately and then applied, which is the standard technique for cups.

The fabric is of poor quality, but does not have to be discarded as a local copy for that reason; half the product of one potter known to have worked in Gaul, probably in the Rheims area, Benois, deteriorate in just this manner, having an unusually high count of inclusions and voids, possibly a result of badly prepared clay and the inherent characteristics in the clay itself. Not all of his products were in this particular clay, which may indicate that he worked at more than one site, and may even have moved to Britain. A number of TN seconds from Exeter and Topsham with an unusually large quantity of inclusions in their fabric may well have originated from the same source, which could just be 'local', rather than situated in the traditional areas from which Gallo-Belgic wares were originally imported.

Probably Neronian or early Flavian.

Exeter Museums Acc. No. 9447975.

XI. GLASS (INCLUDING MATERIAL FROM ALL OTHER EXETER SITES EXCAVATED BETWEEN 1971 AND 1976)

by D. Charlesworth

The great bulk of the material from Exeter is natural green glass, 'bottle glass', which was used from the first to the early fourth centuries for large numbers of free-blown and mould-blown vessels. This is not listed *in toto*, and only the identifiable fragments, which probably represent about 30% of the total number of vessels, are discussed. The few pieces of good-quality glass all merit discussion.

Vessels.

(A) *Bowls and beakers.* Fig. 70.

1. GS71, F160 (fourth century). Rim fragment in good colourless glass with one half of a cut handle; the straight side of the bowl has an open-based square cut in relief on it; polished on both surfaces.

2. Cathedral Close, graveyard levels. Fragment from the side of a vessel with relief-cut decoration, complete heart-shaped leaf, part of a circle with a radial design and the angle of another shape cut in relief, polished.

These two fragments have a style of decoration used in the first century A.D. on a number of high-quality colourless bowls and beakers. Examples in Britain include a beaker fragment from Leadenhall Street, London (Wheeler, 1930, 122, fig. 42, 7), Caerwent (Boon, 1972–3, 118–9, Fig. 2, 22, a shallow vessel which could have had cut handles) and a fragment of Hadrianic date from Caerleon (Boon, 1972–3, 118). There are tall beakers found at Köln (Fremersdorf, 1967, T30, 31, a flask (T29) and a plain *scyphos* with cut handles of the same type as at Exeter (T21)). Examples of *scyphoi*, with a different type of handle but with relief-cut decoration, which can be dated to the first century A.D. were found at Syphnos (Brock and Macworth Young, 1949, 90 and Pl. 33, 34) and at Pompeii (Brock and Macworth Young, 1949, 91), the first with an elaborate design of a hypocamp and a griffon each ridden by a cupid, the second with leaf-shapes. Undecorated *scyphoi* with handles of the same type as the half-handle from Exeter include a nearly complete example from a Flavian pit in London (Noel-Hume, 1950, vii), a deeper vessel used as a wine-glass, depicted on a wall-painting from Pompeii (Maiuri, 1957, xxii), two handle fragments and a base from York, which seem to be from a similar vessel (R.C.H.M., 1962, 136 and Fig. 88) and an undated vessel from Merida near Badajoz (Price, 1973, 76, Fig. 2, 2). The type goes back to at least 30 B.C., the date of the Antikythera shipwreck, where a handle-fragment of this type was found (Weinberg, 1965, 3, 33). By the mid first century many *scyphoi* were produced in mould-blown glass either plain or decorated (Isings, 1959, form 39).

3. VS74, F.606–10 (Antonine). Fragment of a shallow bowl, probably cast in a mould, totally covered in heavy iridescent weathering, but seems to be dark green; plain rim with a wheel-cut line on the inside, both surfaces polished.

These bowls are comparatively rare in Britain as they are luxury glass produced in the early to mid first century. Some fragments were found at Camulodunum (Hawkes and Hull, 1947, 300–1; Isings, 1959, Form 18).

4. VS74, F.280 (fourth century) but almost certainly originating from F.362 (late Neronian). Rim fragments of a small bowl, probably cast in a mould, emerald green, outsplayed possibly to form the seating for a lid-polished. Mid first century.

5. VS74, unstratified. May be base of the same vessel as no. 4, foot-ring.

   BS74, unstratified. Fragments from at least two blown vessels, emerald green, broad cut line below the rim, narrow cut line lower on the body. Mid first century (Isings, Form 12).

6. Cathedral Close, 13: 1405 (Period 2B (construction)). Fragments of a similar bowl in deep blue glass.

These small bowls are widely distributed in the western provinces of the Empire on mid first-century sites. Some, like this, are in good-quality coloured metal, others in bottle glass. Sites in Britain where such bowls have been found include Camulodunum (Hawkes and Hull, 1947, 302–3), Richborough (Bushe-Fox, 1926, 48 Pl. XIX), London, York and an unusual example with ribbing on the lower side and base from Fore Street, Exeter (Fox, 1952, 109).

   VS74. F.367–4 (late second century). A colourless fragment with a broad cut line may be of this type, but the metal is unusual.

   BS74, unstratified. Fragment of deep blue glass flashed on opaque white. This may be from a small bowl of the same shape as nos. 5 and 6 above. The use of two layered or flashed colours is known in the early to mid first century for plain vessels and also for elaborate cameo-cut glass like the Portland vase. Then the white is generally the outer layer. Plain fragments have been published from Camulodunum (Hawkes and Hull, 1947, 297) but they are not common. There is also one cameo-cut fragment recently found in Southark (Wilson, 1976, 352, Pl. xxxi B).

   GS71, F.394 (third or fourth century). Rim fragment of a small bowl in millefiori, green flecked with opaque yellow. Mid first century.

7. GS71, F.420 (fourth century). Folded rim of a small bowl, blown emerald-green glass. Probably Isings Form 44. Mid first century. VS74 (unstratified). Similar in green glass.

   GS71, F.547 (fortress levels). Millefiori, pillar-moulded bowl, green flecked with yellow, melted in fire, RS75, F.240–11 (pre-Flavian): fragment of base in amber glass. Cathedral Close, 14: 1137 (Period 2A (construction)): another amber fragment.

8. Cathedral Close, 14: 1137 (Period 2A (construction)). Pillar-moulded bowl in natural green bottle glass.

   Other examples in natural green bottle glass:
GS71, L.395 (late first century); L.419 (late first century); L.404 (late first century); F.486 (fourth century); L.415 (third century); F.422 (fourth century); HL74. F.2–2 (second century); FG73. F.26 (first century). Isings Form 3.

The pillar-moulded bowl is one of the most easily identified types, even from small fragments. It is copied from metal-work and first appears late in the first century B.C. The millefiori bowls are not common after the mid first century and manufacture probably ceased then, but the coloured monochrome bowls are frequently found in Flavian contexts and the natural green glass pillar-moulded bowl, introduced for the mass-market, appears in the mid first century and continues until the end of the century at least.

   GS71, L.44 (second or third century). Small fragments of a slightly concave-sided beaker in good colourless glass, rim rounded at the tip, horizontal trail at juncton of the rim and side, fragments of pushed-in base ring and slightly concave base. c. 70–200.

9. GS71, F.409 (second century). Fragment from the side of a colourless beaker, slightly concave with upper group of three, lower of two cut lines.

These two examples are possibly from carinated beakers with a high foot similar to those from Crundale (Charlesworth, 1959, 49, Pl. II, 2) or Hardknott.

GS71, F.377 (second century). Colourless fragment with a trail below the angle of the side with the base. Possibly second-century and of the same type as two fragmentary bowls from Housesteads (Charlesworth, 1971, 34, Fig. 2 and 3).

10. GS71, F.376 (early second century). Rim of a beaker or bowl, knocked off and ground, with part of the convex side, signs of wheel-polishing, iridescent weathering.

11. HS73. L.41 (Antonine). Good-quality colourless-glass beaker-rim, slightly everted with ground moulding, white weathering, *c.* 70–120 from a facet-cut beaker, probably Isings form 21.

12. Cathedral Close (7: 32H (Period 1A (construction)). Fragment from the side of a beaker, colourless glass, closed diaper of facets, the bottom row and part of one preserved above, smooth polished surface below. Probably Isings form 21.

There are many minor variations of these facet-cut beakers, some moulded and some free-blown It is not possible from these small fragments to restore the vessels.

13. Cathedral Close, 24: 14 (*c.* A.D. 337). Colourless beaker rim, tip ground smooth, thin cut line below, *c.* 70–200.

14. Cathedral Close, 13: 1401 (Period 2B (construction)). Colourless beaker rim, slightly everted edge ground smooth, straight side with two cut lines. Probably second century.

15. Cathedral Close 18: 33 (Period 2B (construction)). Fragments of a colourless beaker, dulled and scratched, rim slightly everted, edge ground, straight side with a group of three cut lines. Probably second century.

TS73, L.577 (second century). Another fragment with three cut lines.

16. GS71, L.44 (second or third century). Rim of colourless beaker, slightly outsplayed, rounded at the tip, straight undecorated side, later first to third century.

17. GS71, L.44 (second or third century). Rim of colourless beaker, ground with two broad wheel-cut lines below, sides may be indented. Late first to third century.

18. Cathedral Close, (18: 33 Period 2B (construction)). Fragment of a colourless indented beaker. Late first to third century. Isings form 32 and 35.

TS72, F.384–5 (fourth century). Fragment of a colourless indented beaker and three or four other vessels in nearly colourless glass.

19. Cathedral Close, graveyard levels. Double concentric-coil base-ring, colourless glass, second and third century. Isings form 85b. (Charlesworth, 1971, 34, Nos. 4, 5 and 6).

20. GS71. F.654 (fourth century). Centre ring-fragment of a double-coil base-ring. Second to third century.

Cathedral Close, graveyard levels. Small bowl in thin streaky colourless metal, knocked-off unworked rim, short side curving in to base. Late fourth century.

This seems quite out of place in the assemblage of mid first- to third-century glass. It is the only piece showing the characteristics of the later fourth century, a thin poor-quality glass, associated with the knocked-off, unworked rim. It is not impossible that it is an earlier vessel for there is poor-quality glass at all periods, but the fragment, like 21 below, is more readily comparable with fourth century bowls, Isings form 96, for example, from the late cemetery at Mayen (Habery, 1942, 439F), than with earlier glass. There is also a fragmentary fourth-century unguent-flask, Fig. 71, 39.

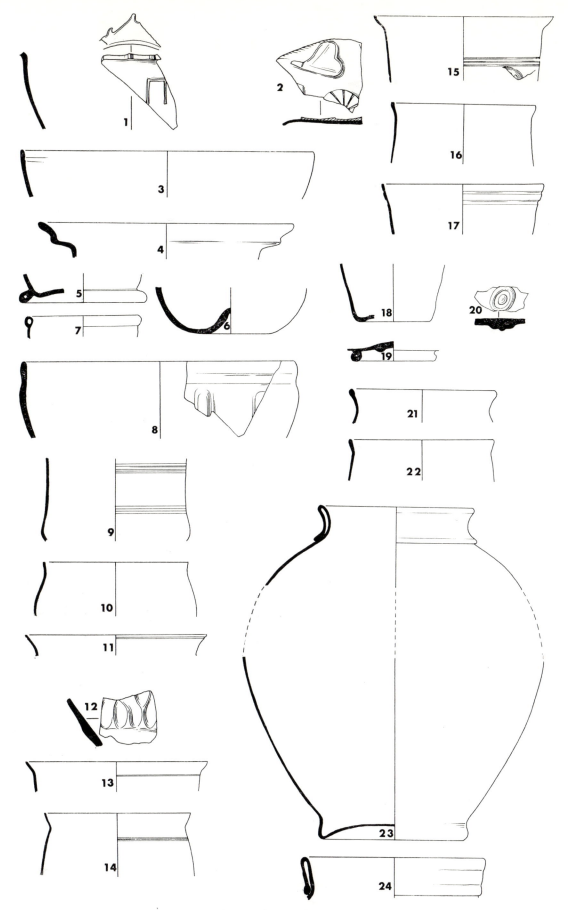

Fig. 70. Glass (scale 1 : 4).

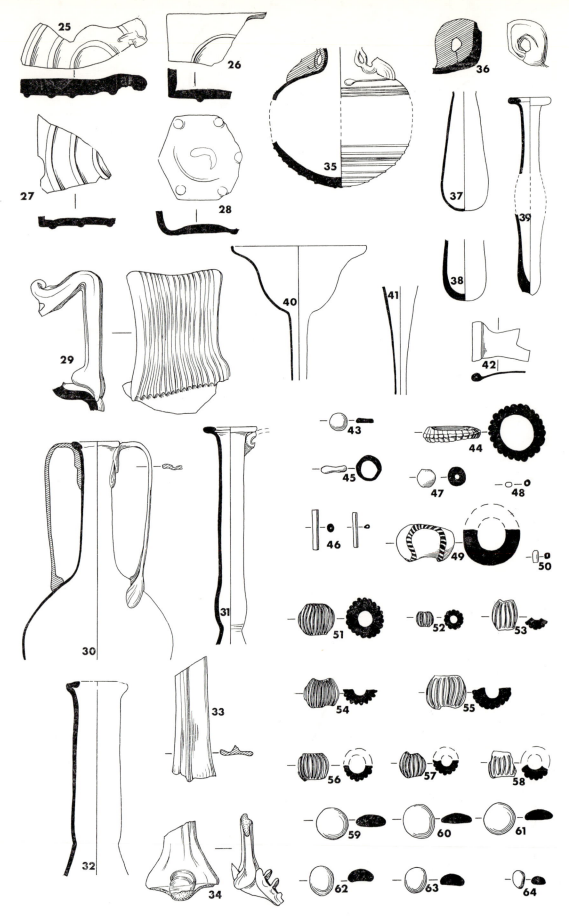

Fig. 71. Glass (scale 1 : 4).

21. TS72, L.445 (fourth century). Rounded rim, poor-quality yellowish-green glass from a beaker. Late fourth century.

22. BFW73, F.76 (fourth century). Rounded slightly everted rim in streaky colourless glass, some bubbles.

It is impossible to be certain from a fragment, but as in the case of the example from the Cathedral Close it seems probable that these are late rims. A group of late fourth- or early fifth-century glass from Burgh Castle included both funnel-shaped beakers and beakers on a stem with this type of rim (Harden, 1969, 76, Pl. IXE).

23. VS74, F.362 (late Neronian). Deep bowl or jar, folded hollow tubular rim, bulbous almost globular body with an open pushed-in base ring. Isings form 67c. c. 60–130.

24. TS72, F.3–4 (c. 80–100). Rim-fragment from a similar vessel, blue green.

The ribbed version of this shape is perhaps more common than the plain. It seems to be confined to the north-west provinces. Recent finds in dated contexts include examples from Fishbourne period 1 (Cunliffe, 1971, 355, No.79) and Verulamium, seven examples, dated c. 60–105.

Fig. 71, 42, 17: 22 (Course of Period 2B). Flat fragment of green glass with a folded edge.

This is probably a piece of crown glass and has therefore been discussed with the window glass, but as identification is not certain it seems reasonable to repeat it here to indicate the other possibility, that it is from the outsplayed rim of a plate of shallow bowl, Isings form 97a, second to third century.

(B) Bottles.

Fig. 71.

These vessels are imported as containers and later re-used for general domestic purposes or even as cinerary urns. The most important fragments are the marked bases as it will eventually be possible to trace them to their point of origin. The bottles are generally blown in a mould, the majority square-bodied, but hexagonal, octagonal and cylindrical bottles are found. The metal is natural green or blue-green glass, used also for many kinds of vessel, particularly containers. The bottles become common in the early 70's, but they were produced earlier (Charlesworth, 1966, 26–40).

TS72, L.513 (second century). Part of a square bottle base with three concentric circles.

25. GS71, F.411 (fortress levels). Part of a square bottle base with three concentric circles, one edge partly fused in fire.

GS71, L.409 (second or third century). Another also with three concentric circles.

26. GS71, F.401 (third or fourth century). Angle of the base of a square bottle with part of a moulded marking, part only of one circle remaining.

27. GS71, F.122 (fortress levels). Part of a base with three concentric circles.

28. Cathedral Close, unstratified. Almost complete base of a hexagonal bottle, moulded dot at each corner, also a central circle partly obscured by the pontil mark.

29. TS72, Residual in mediaeval pit. Complete multi-ribbed handle and part of shoulder of a square bottle.

GS71, F.140 (fortress levels). Part of angle of square bottle.

Cathedral Close, graveyard levels, similar.

Cathedral Close, 16: 1532, Period 1A (construction), similar.

VS74, F.606 (Antonine). Part of a multi-ribbed handle.

TS72, L.577 (second century). Similar.

RS75, F.363-2 (Antonine). Shoulder.

TS72, F.402 (second century). Fragment of the edge of the base of a cylindrical bottle.

Other fragments:

Cathedral Close: 15: 1185; 4: 46B1 and C; 4: 36D; 22: 2139—all Period 2A (construction).

GS71, F.116 (third century); unstratified examples.

TS72, L.921 (probably third century; F.384 (fourth century); F.933 (second century); F.3–3 (c. A.D. 80–100); L.502 (second century); L.903 (second century); F.538 (fourth century). HS73, F.98–5 (Antonine); L.122 and 123 (Antonine).

BFW73, Pit 21 (fourth century). VS74 F.280 (fourth century); F.606, at least three vessels (Antonine); F.315-4 (fourth century); F.368 (early Flavian). SG74, F.1 (pre-Flavian). RS75, F.270 (third century); F.311 (fourth century); F.436 (third century); F.363, upper fill, at least five vessels (Antonine); F.363 lower fills, at least three examples (c. A.D. 80–90).

(C)   *Other containers.*

30.   BFW73, F.47 (c. A.D. 75). Fragments of a two-handled flask in deep blue glass, rim infolded, edge of concave base, small and poor quality vessel. Mid first century.

Several vessels of this colour and shape were found in the 1960s at Colchester. Apart from the handles, the glass is thin and consequently very fragile, so the type is not easily recognised. Isings form 15.

TS72, L.521 (second century). Convex fragment of blue glass, with three slight blobs of marvered white decoration, may be from a similar vessel, as this is quite a common form of decoration on these flasks and single-handled flagons of the same period.

31.   RS75, F.289 (third century). Neck of a flask with remains of the upper part of the handle, rim infolded and flattened, mid first to third century.

RS75, F.363–6 (Antonine). Neck and part of a handle, fragment.

32.   TS72, L.536 (second century). Complete neck, infolded rim broken probably where the handle joined it, blue-green.

33.   This handle is from the same group as no. 32, but seems too heavy to belong to the same vessel. c, 60–200.

34.   Cathedral Close. Part of the horizontally ridged tail of the lower sticking part of the handle of a conical-bodied flagon, green glass.

VS74, F.606–4 (Antonine). Similar fragment.

There is a fairly distinctive feature among handles of flagons found in the north-west provinces c. 70–130. Their characteristics are a long narrow neck, constricted at the base, and a plain or ribbed body with a plain base or open pushed-in ring. Several other handle-fragments probably come from such flagons but cannot be identified with any certainty: Cathedral Close, 14: 1137 (Period 2A (construction)); 12: 1113 (Period 2B (construction)); foundations of wall blocking north end of passage from road (Period 2B (construction)). GS71, F.376 (late first century); L.44 (second or third century). SG74 F.1 (pre-Flavian). RS75, F.363–6 (Antonine).

35.   GS71, F.402 (third or fourth century). Fragments of a bath flask, with a spirally wound trail, blue-green. First to third century, Isings form 61.

TS72, F.139 (second century). Part of the eyelet handle of a similar flask.

36.   TS72, F.71 (second century). Complete eyelet handle from a similar flask.

VS74, unstratified. Colourless fragment with horizontal trail probably from a similar flask.

These glass flasks are copies of the metal containers used for carrying oils to the bath-house. The eyelet handle took a bronze chain or metal handle. A complete example with a handle was found in an Antonine pit at Corbridge (Charlesworth, 1959, 56).

37. TS72, F.193 (third century). Drop-shaped body of an unguent flask. First to second century.

38. GS71, F.395 (third or fourth century). Part of the drop-shaped body of an unguent flask.

39. VS74, F.484 (fourth century). Fragments of a 'pipette'—shaped unguent flask. Fourth century Isings form 105.

This is a very distinctive shape found usually in late graves. Half a dozen or more came from the York cemeteries (R.C.H.M., 1962, 137–8. Fig. 89).

(D) Funnels.

40. VS74, F.356–1 (*c.* 65). Fragmentary green glass, rim outsplayed, knocked-off and ground at the edge, bulbous top leading into an incomplete cylindrical tube. Isings form 74.

The type is not a common one, and is seldom recognisable from fragments. The only datable examples quoted by Dr. Isings are from Pompeii and Avennes (*c.* 100). Examples from Croatia (Zadar, Mala Mitrovica) are said to be first-century (Dameski, 1974, 69, Pl. viii, 3). Fragments from Watercrook (publication forthcoming) are also thought to be of this type.

41. Cathedral Close, unstratified. Fragmentary green glass tapering tube, possibly from a funnel as above, although that has a cylindrical tube below the bowl. It could be part of a rhyton or drinking-horn, but the identification is uncertain.

(E) The window glass.

There is a large sample of window glass but it is disappointingly fragmentary. No pane can be reconstructed and a probable size of only one pane, at least 16 by 12 cms, can be indicated. Both moulded and cylinder-blown (muff) glass was used; the moulded normally dates to the first and second centuries, the blown to the third and fourth centuries, but the period of change-over from one technique to the other is not clearly defined. These techniques are discussed in Harden, 1959, 8–16 and Boon, 1966, 41f.

One piece appears to be crown glass, Cathedral Close (Fig. 71, 42; 17: 22 (course of Period 2B)). It has a folded edge and is part of a disc, not a vessel. This is only the second piece to be recognised in a Roman context in this country. The other is from a fourth-century level at Chichester (Charlesworth in Down, forthcoming and Charlesworth, forthcoming).

Only one piece (GS71, F.402) shows any fixing material, a trace of mortar. This is quite frequently found on one side of an edge fragment, but many more are quite clean and must have been set in a wood or lead frame. Two fragments of blown glass may be parts of triangular quarries, one (Cathedral Close, 18: 64, Period 2A (construction)) with an apparently cut, not broken, obtuse angle and another acute-angled (Cathedral Close, 7: 32D, Period 2A (construction)). These small pieces would have to be fitted into lead cames to form a window, in the manner of the later church windows, for example at Jarrow in the eighth or ninth century (Cramp, 1975, 88–96). It is not certain that Roman glazed windows took this form, but there are various sites producing triangular fragments which appear to be deliberate and not the results of breaking a larger pane, e.g. Gadebridge villa (Neal, 1974, 203–4; see also Webster, 1959, 10–14).

Fragments of moulded panes occur in the following contexts (all panes in natural green glass except where the metal is stated to be colourless):

Cathedral Close:

Period 1A (construction), 6: 52H; almost colourless thin metal, 7: 32H.

Period 1B (construction), 17: 537; 4: gly. 8.

Period 2A (construction), 1: 9EA, corner fragment with a mark on the smooth upper surface where a tool has been used to press the glass into the corner of the mould; 18: 61; 18:64; 16: 1512; 16: 1520; nearly colourless, 22: 2126; 1: 9EB1; 1: 9EB1, 22: 2130; 4: 36B; 7: 32B; 1: 10EC.

Period 2B (construction), 17: 36; 13: 1405.

Course of Period 2B, 17: 22.

Period 2C (construction), 1: 1.

Course of Period 2C, 28: 195.

Period 3A (construction), 19: 516.

Fourth century deposit, 24: 18.

Some examples from graveyard levels.

Other sites:

GS71: residual in post-Roman features.

TS72, L.940 (fourth century); F.82 (third or fourth century); F.780 (fourth century).

Where there is an edge-fragment it is possible to be sure that the glass is moulded. In other cases it is only the roughness of the underside which is the determining factor. If this is only very slightly rough and pitted, it could be the result of contact with the floor of the annealing-oven when a cylinder-brown pane unfolded and lay flat on it to cool.

Fragments of cylinder-blown (muff) panes occur in the following contests, all in natural green glass, except where noted:

Cathedral Close:

Period 1A (construction), 16: 1531.

Period 2A (construction), 4: 46B1 and C; 1: 9EB1, almost colourless; 14: 1137.

(These fragments of cylinder-blown panes are noteworthy because they are securely stratified in first-century contexts; clearly this type of glass was employed in glazing the windows of the legionary bath-house. P.B.).

Course of Period 2A, 8: 29H2, almost colourless.

Period 2B (construction), 17: 37; 15: 1088.

Period 2C (construction), 17: 525.

(F) Objects:

Fig. 71.

   (a) Personal ornaments.

43. TS72, L.397 (post-Roman dark soil). An oval inlay white centre with dark brown or black surround. Probably too large for the bezel of a finger-ring but could be from a brooch.

44. BFW73, Pit 21 (fourth century). Ring in dark brown glass made by coiling a trail, overlap of ends clearly visible, inner surface smooth, outer rounded with tooled cross-cuts decorating it.

45. RS75, F.363–3 (Antonine). Small ring of colourless glass.

     These could be finger-rings or pendants on a necklace.

46. BFW73, F.84–1 (after c. A.D. 330). Two cylindrical beads, cut off from drawn rods, small perforations. One blue glass, the other green.

47. BS74, F.126 (third century). Opaque blue globular bead.

48. RS75, mediaeval pit. Small white bead.

49. Cathedral Close, 4: 46B1 and C (Period 2A (construction)). Half a large annular bead, off-centre core of yellowish-green glass with green covering it, marvered into the surface a serpentine trail of spirally wound deep blue and white. The bead seems to be made from

re-used metal, gathered from two different pots of fused glass. The first gathering of yellowish-green has apparently not been large enough for the maker's liking and so this has been dipped into more molten glass to add to its size before finishing the shape and decorating it.

50. GS71, residual in post-Roman context. Small blue bead, coiled trail and partly flattened to give a more-or-less square section.

Melon-shaped beads in turquoise glass paste:

Cathedral Close:

51. Unstratified, complete bead.

52. 18: 65 (Period 2A (construction)). Small bead.

53. 4: 46B1 and C (Period 2A (construction)). About a quarter remaining.

54. 4: 56A (Period 1A (construction)). About a half remaining.

55 and 56. 8: 49B (Course of Period 2A). About a half remaining.

Other sites:

57. Unstratified, about a half remaining.

58. RS75, residual in mediaeval pit.

(b) *Gaming counters.*

Complete sets of counters are found from time to time in graves. The earliest is from Welwyn, game requiring four sets of six pieces (Harden in Stead, 1967, 14f.). In the Lullingstone Mausoleum was the remains of a board and two sets, one dark glass, the other white, all decorated with marvered dots of contrasting colour (Taylor, 1959, 132f.) and a similar find, of 26 pieces, 15 white (so these are not two equal sets) in grave 1215 at Krefeld-Gellep (Pirling, 1966).

59. BFW73, F.69 (c. 75). Dark brown or black, plano-convex section, circular.

60. WS71, pit 22 (pre-Flavian). Similar.

61–3. GS71, L.422 (fortress levels). 3 gaming counters, 2 white, one dark green.

64. TS72, L.705 (fortress levels). Small blue-green roughly made counter.

(c) *Tessera.*

Cathedral Close, 6: 52E (Period 2A (construction)). Blue glass tessera.

Glass was used in wall- and floor-mosaics to provide detail in colours which could not be supplied in stone. An obvious possibility is for the eyes of any figure. At Aldborough blue glass is used for the inscription on one pavement (Smith, 1852, 42).

XII. SMALL FINDS

with contributions by D. F. Mackreth and H. Miles

BROOCHES (Fig. 72)

by D. F. Mackreth

Colchester Derivatives.

(1) The pin is hinged and the wings are thin with a circular section, each having two grooves at the end. The bow has a broad top and tapers slightly to a squared-off foot formed by a cross-moulding. There is a step down each side of the bow, while down the centre are two ridges each with diagonal cross-cuts which give a herring-bone effect. For discussion, see after no. 2.

Period 3A (construction); F.87.

(2) The pin is hinged and the wings have a circular section with four grooves at the end of each. The bow tapers to a squared-off foot. Down each side is a groove, while in the centre are two sunken mouldings which splay out at the top to leave a triangular space.
Southern *insula*; 9: 38F3.

There are no useful parallels: they belong to a widespread distribution of simple decorated brooches. There is no significance in the fact that they are hinged. This development had occurred by *c*. 50 (Brailsford, 1962, 10, Fig. 10, C95 and C96; Richmond, 1968,119). In the present cases, a date in the second half of the first century may be suggested, possibly restricted to the third quarter.

(3) The spring is held to the brooch by means of an axis bar through the coils and through the lower hole of a projecting plate behind the head of the bow, the chord passing through the upper hole. The wings are curved to seat the spring and each has a central flute lying between a sunken bead-row. The bow is plain except for a crest which is a continuation onto the head of the pierced plate behind. The crest has its top edge cut into a decorative profile.

Period 1A (construction); 4: 37C.

As for nos. 1 and 2, there are no useful parellels. There is a great variety of ornament to be found on Colchester Derivatives, and the most distinctive features here are the heavily moulded wings and elaborate crest. The former can be seen to be present, though not in a precise parallel, at Hod Hill (Richmond, 1968, 39, Fig. 31, hut. 56) where it must date before *c*. 50 (Richmond, 1968, 119). The crest itself is a skeuomorph of the hook of the Colchester type and attention may be drawn to another example from the Guildhall site at Exeter (unpublished), but neither of these wing and crest features is a definite dating characteristic. The approximate date of the deposit in which the brooch was found, *c*. 60–65, is entirely in accord with the general indications.

Strip.

(4) The bow has a flat rectangular section and widens where it is rolled under to house the axis bar of the hinged pin to form short wings. The bow tapers to a pointed foot and has a cross-groove about half-way down and shallow flutes down each side above this.

Period 2A (construction); 4: 46B1 and C.

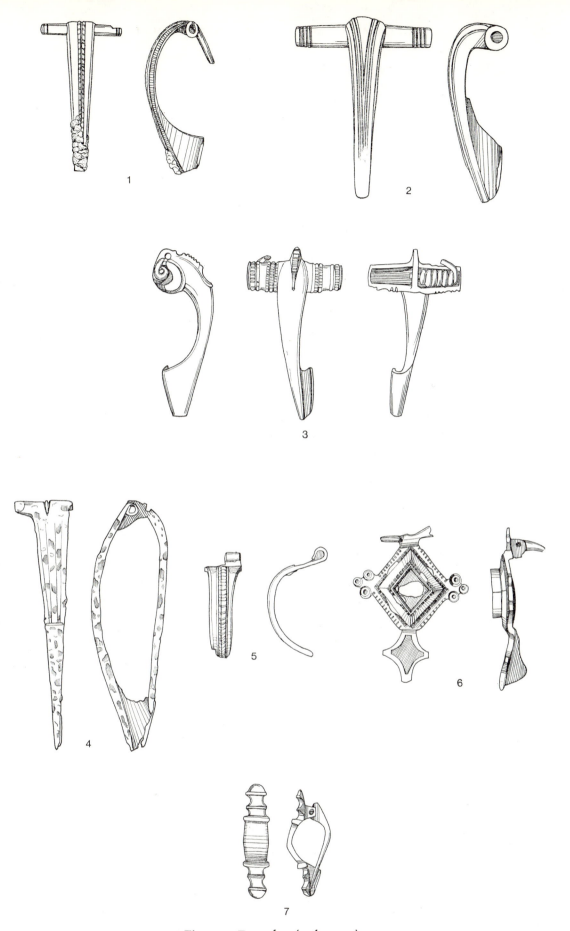

Fig. 72. Brooches (scale 1 : 1).

The Strip brooch has a wide distribution in Central-Southern England with a tendency towards the South-West. This example has parallels at Poundbury, Dorset, and Maiden Castle (Richardson, 1940, 441, Fig. 4. 1; Wheeler, 1943, 261, Fig. 84, 17) where it was dated to the first twenty-five years or so after the Conquest. In general, Strip brooches do not seem to have lasted much beyond the third quarter of the first century and were probably going out of manufacture well before then.

Aucissa.

(5) The main part of the bow and the head only of an uninscribed Aucissa. On the head is a groove lying between bead-rows, and at each end of the groove is a small cut-out. The bow has the normal design of a moulding down each side and a bead-row sunk into the top of the raised central section. The Aucissa is evidenced in Britain before the Conquest (Skeleton Green, Puckeridge, Herts., to be published) and was at the end of its *floruit* when the Conquest took place.

Period 2A (construction); 1804, levelling under floor of room north of the probable *curia* (see p. 70).

Unclassified.

(6) An elaborate brooch with a lozenge shaped boss raised on two steps. The boss once had an enamel setting; there are traces of white enamel in the bottom corners and there is a blob, possibly enamel, in the centre which may have been to 'glue' the main setting into position (c.f. Lethbridge, 1952, 182, Fig. 4.1). The main setting may have been prefabricated and most probably had small circular dots of black material set in it (e.g. Dudley, 1967, 50, Fig. 19, 152). The first step down had one row of square punch-marks along it and the bottom one two. Attached to the points of the base lozenge on either side of the brooch is a projecting wing shaped to a trefoil with concentric circles on each lobe. At the head of the brooch, and rising above the hinged pin, is a fragment or ornament which should probably be restored as an open circle with small projections radiating from it (e.g. Exner, 1939, 88, Taf. 9.7.1.52). From the lower point of the lozenge, and carrying the catch-plate behind, is another lozenge but with concave sides. The central area of this has been hollowed out and is filled with red enamel.

Precise parallels for any brooch which belongs to this family are hard to find. The range of motifs is limited, but their combination is such that a great many designs resulted. The central element can be seen on a brooch from Nor'nour (Dudley, 1967, 62, Fig. 25, 253); the probable form of the ring on the top is shown by a brooch from Andernach (Exner, 1939, 87, Taf. 6.1.48); the trefoils on either side are on another from Nor'nour (Dudley, 1967, 48, Fig. 19, 143). The bottom element has no parallel known to the writer, but the use of simple shapes filled with a single colour enamel is not unknown, as a brooch from Saalburg shows (Böhme, 1972, 104, Taf. 25. 962).

Once the association of these various features in a single family of some diversity is realised, these brooches are more common in Britain than at first appears. Very few have been dated but one from Verulamium belongs to the mid-second century (Frere, 1972, 118, Fig. 31, 23) another from Camerton dates to before c. 180 (Wedlake, 1958, 230, Fig. 53, 48). They appear to be largely second century and, as is clear from the numbers found on the Continent, they are imports.

Course of Period 2B; 17: 22.

(7) A hinged brooch which has a central panel with an arris across the middle. To top and

bottom is a cross-moulding which projects slightly on each side. The top and bottom are finished off with two cross-flutes terminating in a boss based on a ridge.

Period 2B (construction); 17: 528.

Symmetrical unenamelled brooches are much less common than examples of the family to which no. 6 belongs, but it is likely that the date range is much the same.

OTHER BRONZE OBJECTS (Figs. 73–74)

The measurement at the end of each description is of the maximum length of the object.

Military fittings.

(8) Part of a buckle (Hawkes and Hull, 1947, pl. 102, 18–23). Course of Period 2A; 9: 39A. 3.1 cm.

(9) Fleur-de-lys tongue from a buckle (Frere and St. Joseph, 1974, Fig. 27, 37). Period 2A (construction); 1: 10ED. 2.9 cm.

(10) Tongue from a buckle. Period 1A (construction); 1: F.34. 2.4 cm.

(11) ? Belt-plate. Period 2A (construction); gly. 10, packing around pipe. 3.4 cm.

(12) Lower part of pendant. Period 1A (construction); 1: F.34. 2.7 cm.

(13) Apron-mount. Similar to Richmond, 1968, Fig. 56, 15. Period 1B (construction); 5: F.30. 2.9 cm.

(14) Girdle-plate tie-hook from *lorica segmentata* (Robinson, 1975, Fig. 183). Period 1A (construction); 16: 1534. 5 cm.

(15) Buckle (tongue missing). This military buckle from a late third-century context is not a type current during the fortress period at Exeter. There are similar but not identical examples from Chester (Newstead, 1928, pl. 9, 13) and Newstead (Curle, 1911, pl. 76, 1). For the significance of second- and third-century military fittings from towns in Roman Britain, see Boon, 1974, 68. For another post-fortress military fitting from Exeter, see Fig. 74, 56, a bone scabbard-chape.

Period 2C (construction); 28: 209. 3.2 cm.

Miscellaneous

(16) Shank of a pin. Course of Period 2B; 17: 25. 10.2 cm.

(17) Part of a bracelet. Period 2B (construction); 13: 1402. 4.7 cm.

(18) Pin with flattened head which preserves traces of circular piercing. Period 2B (construction); 17: 36. 4.3 cm.

(19–20) Tweezers. Period 2A (construction); 13: 1409B–D. 5.5 cm. Graveyard levels. 3.4 cm.

(21) Nail-cleaner, rear flat and undecorated. From graveyard levels. 5.7 cm.

(22) Nail-cleaner. From graveyard levels. 2 cm.

(23) Pin. Third-century context; 8: 29 F. 7.3 cm.

(24) Key. Period 2C (construction); 17: 1. 2.7 cm.

(25) Lock-tumbler. From graveyard levels. 8.6 cm.

(26) Lock-tumbler. From graveyard levels. 2.6 cm.

(27) Bell with part of a bronze wire for suspension still surviving in loop at top. Four 'feet' extend from the rim of the bell; the interior is filled with iron corrosion. Period 2B (construction); 15: 1088. 3 cm.

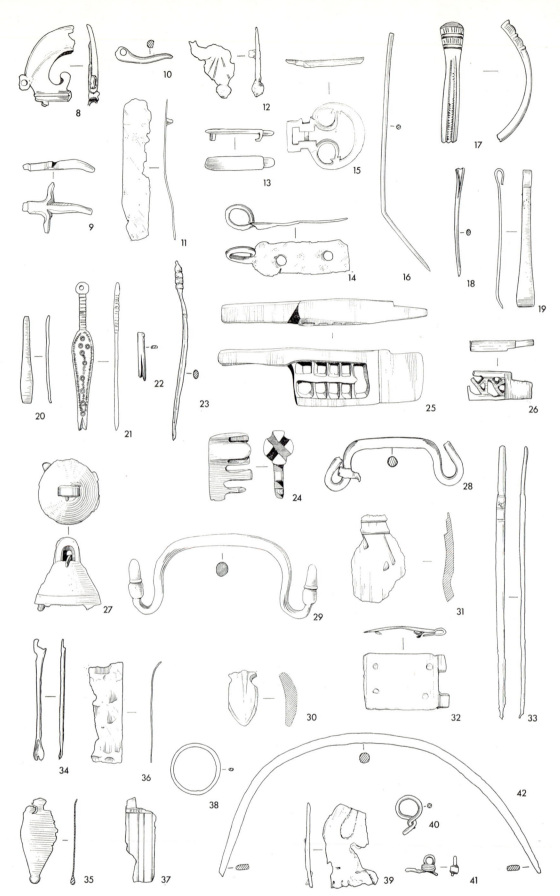

Fig. 73. Small finds, bronze objects (scale 2 : 3).

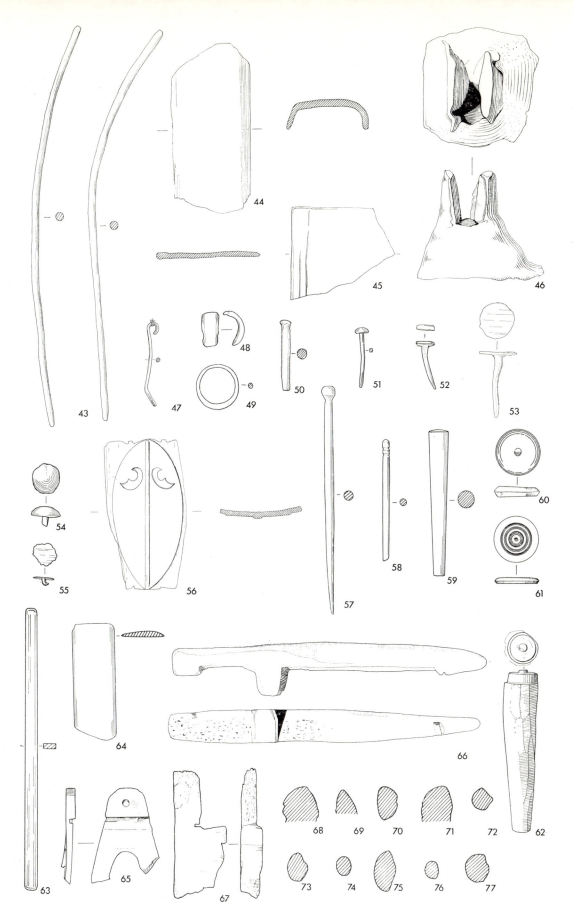

Fig. 74. Small finds, bronze objects (43–55), bone objects (56–67), shale objects (68–77) (scale 2 : 3).

(28) Handle with bronze strip for attachment. Course of Period 1A (? or 1B); 2021 (see p. 58). 5.7 cm.

(29) Handle with moulded terminals. Period 2B (construction); 17: 36. 7.7 cm.

(30) A cast leaf or petal, its underside only roughly finished. It has been broken away from a larger element at the top. For discussion, see no. 31 below. Period 2C (construction); 17: 514. 2.3 cm.

(31) Fragment from a cast object, its underside only very roughly finished. The upper edge is 'stepped' and there are two diagonal and one triangular impressions below. Period 2B (construction); 17: 36. 3.5 cm.

It is difficult to identify the function of the two small objects described above with any certainty. Both come from larger objects and one possibility is that they come from one or more statues. Flowers with distinct petals often decorate the muscle-cuirass of full-length Imperial portraits (e.g. fragments from Avenches, Furtwängler, 1969, Taf. 8 and 9, nos. 4 and 5); the flat fragment could perhaps be part of a full-size representation of a clothing-seam with stitches at the side or equally the top of a shoe.

(32) Hinge-plate cut from a thin bronze sheet, originally fixed in place by four small copper nails or pins, three of which survive. Period 2A (construction); 14: 1138. 3.4 cm.

(33) Stylus. Period 2A (construction); 1: 9EB1. 10.8 cm.

(34) Ear-scoop with loop probably for attachment to châtelaine. Period 2A (construction); 1: 9EB1. 4.8 cm.

(35) Leaf-shaped object thickened at tip. Period 1B (construction); 17: 537. 3.4 cm.

(36) Strip. Period 2A (construction); 1: 10EC. 4 cm.

(37) Moulded strip with transverse beaded row. Period 2A (construction); gly. 10, packing around pipe. 3.2 cm.

(38) Ring. Period 1A (construction); 16: 1532. 4.2 cm.

(39) Plate with white metal (presumably silver) inlay. Period 2B (construction); 18: 33. 3.3 cm.

(40) Wire loop. Period 1A (construction); 1: 9EC1. 1.7 cm.

(41) Wire loop fixed by a bronze strip grooved on one face. Period 2B (construction); 1: 36. 1.3 cm.

(42) Curved rod with flattened ends. Period 1A (construction); 8: 49J. 12.9 cm.

(43) Two rods of identical size, both with rounded ends; found side-by-side. 24: F.21 (post-trench associated with last phase of military structures north-east of baths). 15.6 cm.

(44) Fragment of bronze object, perhaps originally of tubular form. Period 2C (construction); 26: 208, 6.75 cm.

(45) Corner of square or rectangular flat bronze plate; upper surface very smooth (? polished) but with a raised edge along one side. Context as no. 44. 4.25 cm.

Nos. 44 and 45 were found lying together amid the tile and mortar debris of the road make-up together with other bronze scraps; it is possible that they all represent fragments from the same object.

(46) Rough bronze casting of pyramidal form with two tabs, their ends broken off, protruding from the top. Int. 22, quarry pit on site of *curia*, probably post-dating demolition of *basilica* but preceding development of cemetery. 5.25 cm.

(47) Shank, hooked end with thin bronze wire wrapped around it. Context as 46. 3.5 cm.

(48) Broad ring. Period 2A (construction); 14: 1138. 3 cm.

(49) Ring. Period 1B (construction); 8: 49F2. 1.8 cm.

(50) Nail with burred top. Period 2A (construction); 1: 10EC. 2.8 cm.

(51) Nail with square-sectioned shank and domed top. Period 2A (construction); 18: 65. 2.3 cm.

(52) Nail with square-sectioned shank and rectangular head. Period 2A (construction); 17:43. 1.8 cm.

(53) Nail with square-sectioned shank and round head. Period 1A (construction); 3: 46E. 2.6 cm.

(54) Tack with square-sectioned shank and domed head. Period 2A (construction); 14: 1137. 1.25 cm.

(55) Tack with circular-sectioned shank and round flat head. Period 1A (construction); 1: 9EC1. 0.9 cm.

Objects of bone:

(56) Scabbard-chape with pierced volutes. This is a companion piece to the second- or third-century bronze buckle (Fig. 73, 15). Bone scabbard-chapes of this type are common finds on second- and third-century military sites, e.g. Chester (Newstead, 1928, pl. 9, 1), Caerleon, where six were recovered from the Prysg Field site (Nash-Williams, 1937, 97, Fig. 43, 1–6), and Richborough (Bushe-Fox, 1932, pl. 9, 32). Three examples have been recovered from Silchester (Boon, 1974, Fig. 8, 5 and p. 68 and 309, n. 10). An almost exact parallel to our piece is provided by an example from Bonn, also with pierced volutes (Münten and Heimberg, 1976, 400, Abb. 12). Previously unpublished, in a bag marked 'C/east S.E. (Bath) June 2–1932'. From the site of the Public Baths, presumably from the filling of the *natatio* in the Deanery Garden. 6 cm.

(57) Pin. 24: 14 (fourth-century deposit found east of *forum*). 9.1 cm.

(58) Pin. Graveyard levels. 4.8 cm.

(59) (?) Pin. Period 2B ditch fills on north side of road (see pp. 97–8). 5.8 cm.

(60) Counter. Period 2A (construction); 18: 65. 1.9 cm. Another identical example from Period 2B (construction); 18: 33. 1.9 cm.

(61) Counter. Period 2A (construction); 22: 2134. 1.9 cm.

(62) Object with lathe-turned top, remainder knife-trimmed. Period 1A (construction); 13: 1417. 6.3 cm.

(63) Carefully finished strip. Period 1A (construction); 7: 32H. 11.1 cm.

(64) Strip. Period 2C (construction); 17: 1. 4.1 cm.

(65) Object with splayed arms, pierced at apex. Period 2A (construction); 1: 9EB1. 4 cm.

(66) Roughly-worked object, probably an off-cut. Period 2A (construction); 4: 46 B and C. 12.3 cm.

(67) Off-cut with knife-marks. Period 2A (construction); 14: 1138. 5 cm.

Objects of Shale.

Sections through bracelets (interior surface on the right-hand side):

(68) Period 1B (construction); 4 gly. 8. Dia. 12 cm.

(69–70) Both Period 2A (construction); 14: 1137. Dia. 9 cm and 13 cm.

(71) Period 2A (construction); 16: 1512. Dia. 11 cm.

(72) Period 2A (construction); 14: 1143. Dia. 9 cm.

(73) Period 2B (construction); foundation trench of wall blocking north end of passage from road to *forum* portico. 8 cm.

(74) Period 2B (construction); 4: 10B. 6 cm.

(75) Third-century context; 9: 38F3 (see p. 115). 11 cm.

(76–77) Fourth-century context; 24: 14 (see p. 119). 11 cm and 9 cm.

(78) Rim of a large dish or platter. An example from Wareham, Dorset, apparently from a first-century context, also has a projecting tab of identical form, and similar incised decoration, although the profile of the vessel is somewhat different (Baker, 1970, 148–50). Period 1A (construction); 8: 49G2. Approximately 40 cm dia.

(79) Rim of a large dish or platter. Period 2B (construction); 13: 1403. Diameter approximately 30 cm.

(80) Disc with irregular central piercing. Period 1A (construction); 12: 1161A. 2.8 cm.

Miscellaneous objects.

(81) Jet knife-handle. Graveyard levels. 5.1 cm.

(82) Pottery palette with lines incised before firing. Fabric resembles that of coarse-grained TN; the smoothly-finished exterior is dark-grey. Period 2A (construction); 14: 1137. 4.5 cm.

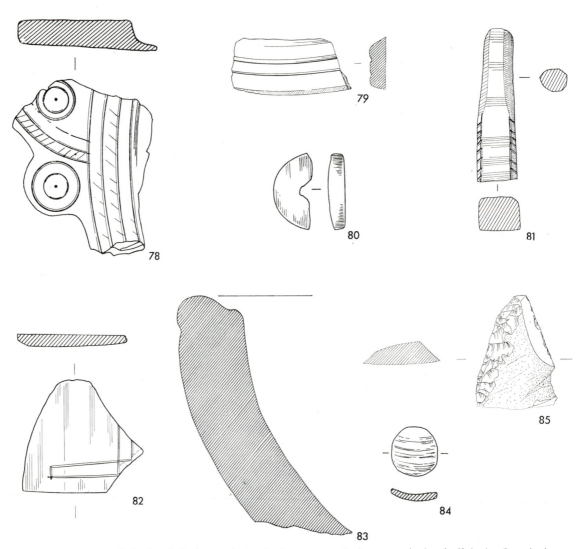

Fig. 75. Small finds, shale (78–80); jet (81); pottery (82); stone (83); shell (84); flint (85) (scale 2 : 3).

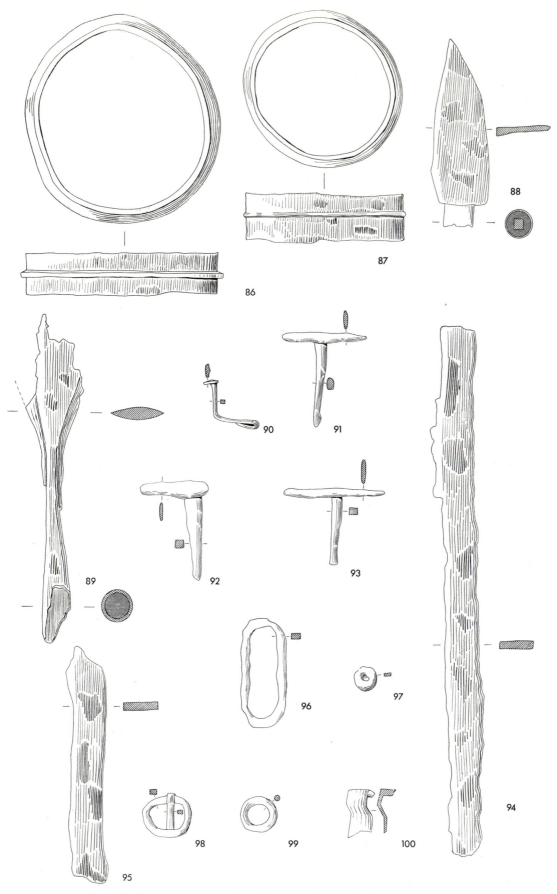

Fig. 76. Small finds, iron objects (scale 1 : 3).

(83) Rim of a stone bowl. The exterior has been worked to a fairly smooth surface, although no tool-marks can be made out; the very smooth interior surface shows that the vessel was used as a mortar. R. G. Scrivener has kindly identified the stone as an elvan of Cornish origin. This vessel belongs to a series of bowls thought to date from the third to the sixth centuries; they are fairly frequent finds on Cornish sites. The bowls are usually made from greisen, but examples in elvan have been recovered from a settlement site at Trethurgy, St. Austell (Miles and Miles, 1973, 28). Period 2C (construction); 17: 1. Diameter approximately 35 cm.

(84) Counter cut from an oyster-shell. Period 2C (construction); 19: 507. 1.8 cm.

Objects of Flint (H. Miles):

Only eight pieces of flint were recovered from the sites reported on in this volume. All of them appear to have been imported as components of levelling-up materials or gravel. The only diagnostic piece is a later Neolithic or Early Bronze Age knife but the general character of the other pieces (four flakes, two blades and a core) is consistent with the date of the knife.

(85) Part of a pressure-flaked plano-convex knife made on a cortical flake. Late Neolithic or Early Bronze Age. 3.9 cm.

Objects of Iron:

The condition of the iron objects retrieved from the site was in almost all cases extremely poor. Only the better-preserved items are illustrated below.

(86–87) Water-pipe junction-collars with central ridges. Both Period 2A (construction); 8: gly. 6. 12.5 cm, 11.5 cm.

(88) Knife. Remains of a wooden handle adhering to the tang are encased by a bronze ferrule at the junction with the blade. Fourth-century context; 24: 14. 16.7 cm.

(89) Spear. Hollow shank with wooden shaft preserved inside. Not closely datable, but the layer in which it was found contained no material obviously derived from fortress deposits and it seems likely that the spear is associated with the civil occupation. Course of Period 2B; 17:22. 28.5 cm.

(90) Nail. Manning Type 1. (Neal, 1974, 173). Period 2A (construction); 18:65. Overall length 9.3 cm.

Thousands of nails were recovered from the site but most were in such a corroded state that it was not possible to take accurate measurements of length, etc. The example above was completely uncorroded because it has been sealed beneath a clay capping which created an anaerobic environment.

(91–93) T-clamps for fixing box-tiles to wall-surfaces. Period 2A (construction); 6: 52A. 8.3 cm. Period 1B (construction); 6: 52G. 7.5 cm. Graveyard levels. 6.5 cm.

(94–95) Two iron bars from the hypocaust. These were used to support the floor above the transverse heat ducts (see p. 31); in order to serve this function their original length must have been in excess of 1 m.

Both Period 2A (construction); 16: 1524. 42 cm, 18.5 cm.

(96) Link, probably from a chain. Third-century context; 29: 228. 9 cm.

(97) Small ring. Period 2A (construction); 14: 1143. 2.1 cm.

(98) Buckle (?). Early graveyard levels. 3.7 cm.

(99) Ring. Period 2A (construction); 22: 2139. 3.4 cm.

(100) Binding (?). The curved part of the strip appears to have been wrapped around a wooden object, traces of which remain. Period 2A (construction); 16: 1524. 4.4 cm.

XIII. GRAFFITI

(Fig. 77)

by M. W. C. Hassall

(1) Brick 18 by 18 by 7.5 cm, corresponding in size to a *bessalis* which was two thirds of a foot, or eight Roman inches (19.7 cm) square, which will have come from one of the hypocaust *pilae*. Along one edge the first six letters of the alphabet have been traced with a stick before firing, with a superfluous upright at the beginning and the final letter repeated: IΛBCDIIFF

Period 2A (construction); 22: 2139.

(2) Part of the foot-ring and bottom of a platter Dr. 18. A graffito cut on the underside of the base, outside the foot-ring, reads either . . .]III or, depending on which way the graffito is,: . . .]IIΛ or ṖII[. . . .

Period 1A (construction); 6: 52H1.

(3) Part of the base of a platter, Dr. 18. A graffito cut after firing on the underside of the base within the footring reads . . .]LΛRI, *Hilari* or, less probably *Clari*, 'of Hilarus' or 'of Clarus'.

Period 2A (construction); 12: 1138.

(4) Sherd in dark brown fabric, the outside of which has been reduced to a dark colour and has been burnished (on the shoulder ?); below on the unburnished part of the vessel is a burnished lattice (?) pattern. A graffito cut after firing on the burnished zone reads:]ΛPRLI[, either *Apri* or *Aprilis*, 'of Aper' or 'of Aprilis'.

Mid or late second- to mid third-century ditch deposits on north side of road (see p. 97–8).

(5) Fragments of white painted wall-plaster. The surface of the plaster has been scored with a number of straight lines and casual markings (including a doodled 'pin-man' (P.B.)). Among these can be recognised:

(a)   The letters **KD**.

(b)   . . .]Ẹ CANEṂ[probably for *cave canem* 'Beware of the dog'. This slogan is found on a
        well-known mosaic pavement at Pompeii (illustrated in Toynbee, 1973, Pl. 43).

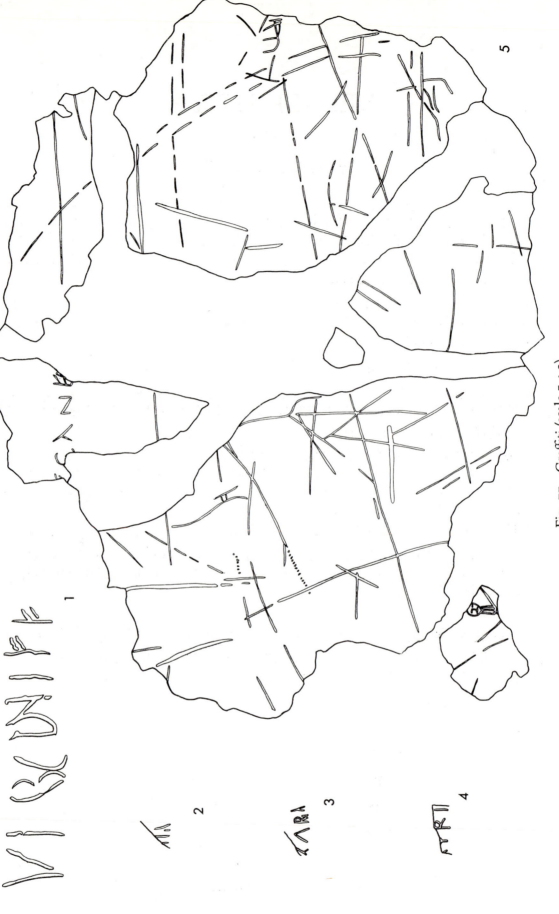

Fig. 77. Graffiti (scale 1 : 2).

XIV. REPORT ON FIVE POST-ROMAN SKELETONS

by the late Calvin Wells

(1) *Inhumation OB 278.*

Male, age: 40–50.

This consists of a badly smashed skull; vertebrae C2–7, T11–L5; pelvic fragments; pieces of rib; the scapulae; all long bones; some small bones of hands and feet. Almost all these remains are damaged, some of them extensively so, and are eroded by post-inhumation changes.

Reconstruction of the skull for the purposes of taking accurate cranial measurements is impracticable. From the various fragments it appears that the frontal bone rose moderately steeply from low brow ridges, passing in a low mid-sagittal curve to descend to a smoothly rounded occiput with no tuber occipitale. Markings for nuchal and other muscles are fairly strong; the mastoid processes are large and rugged; the superior orbital margins are thick and rounded. The sagittal sinus turns to the right, as is normal; a few wormian bones are present but their number cannot be accurately counted.

Teeth.

$$\begin{array}{c|c} 2\ 1 & \\ \hline -\ 0\ 6\ 5\ 4\ 3\ 2\ 1 & 0\ 2\ 3\ 4\ 5\ 6\ .\ ? \\ \text{P P} & \end{array}$$

Attrition is very heavy with much exposure and erosion of dentine. No caries. The cavity around the missing 7 tooth is perhaps due to simple recession and absorption of the alveolus rather than to a periodontal abscess. Large multiple bilateral mandibular tori are present.

The following long bone measurements were obtained:

	L	R
C1 L1	153.7	162.2
Hu L1	—	346.2
Hu Head	51.4	52.3
Hu Distal	66.1	61.4
U1 L1	286.1	—
Ra L1	259.0	—
Fe L1	c. 458.0	—
Fe D1	27.7	26.3
Fe D2	36.2	39.2
Fe Condyles	—	89.2
Metric Index	76.5	67.1
Ti L1	386.1	385.2
Ti D1	40.5	39.8
Ti D2	27.0	26.1
Cnemic Index	66.7	65.6

This corresponds to a stature of about 1753 mm (5 ft 9 ins).

No septal aperture is present in the humeri. Both tibiae have very large squatting distally.

Pathology.

There is widespread disease in this skeleton. The L. clavicle has been fractured and although the bone has healed solidly it remains 8.5 mm shorter than the R. clavicle. There is extensive oesteo-arthritis (O.A.) on the C4, C5 and L5 vertebrae and it is slight on L2–4. Oestephytosis (O.P.) is present to a well marked degree on all lumbar vertebrae and on the bodies of at least 7 scraps of thoracic vertebrae.

Osteoarthritis is present in both shoulder joints: early changes are found on the glenoid fossa of the L. scapula and a slight flange of arthritic 'lipping' or thickening extends around the head of both humeri. Arthritic changes are also present in both elbow joints: they are slight on the distal surfaces of the R. humerus and proximally on the L. ulna, somewhat more severe on the proximal surface of the R. ulna. At the wrists very early oesteoarthritic changes are present on the L. and R. radii.

In the lower limbs both hip joints were slightly affected—at the L. acetabulum and the two femoral heads. The knee joints were much more severely involved: both femoral condyles, both tibial heads and the R. patella have extensive arthritic lesions. In the femora this seems to have been secondary to a healed osteochondritis of the medial condyle. No pitting remains but a low ridge of new bone presumably indicates a filled osteochondritic cavity.

A small congenital perforation, about 4 mm in diameter, is present in the middle of the body of the L. scapula.

(2) *Inhumation OB 480.*

Female, age: 30–50.

This consists of a calvarium in fair condition; a fragment of mandible; the T10–11 and L4–5 vertebrae in moderately good condition; fragments of at least 6 other vertebrae (4T and 2L); the sacrum; 28 small fragments of rib; a fragment of sternum; a small piece of the L. and R.

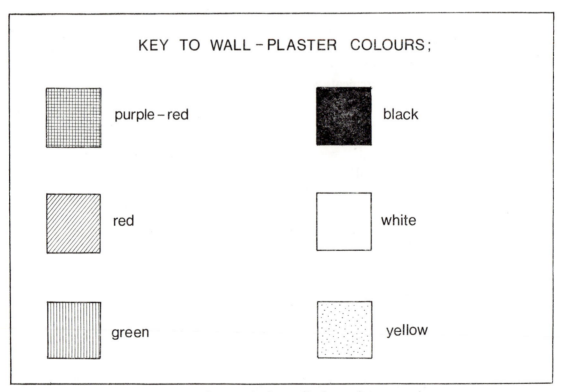

Fig. 78. Colour code for wall-plaster (Figs. 56–7).

innominates, in each case part of the acetabulum; fragments of clavicle; R. radius; a broken R. ulna; 4 carpals; 1 metacarpal; 4 phalanges of hand.

The skull is a long ovoid in norma verticalis. The frontal bone rises not very steeply from negligible brow ridges and passes in a low, flat curve through the vertex to descend into a slight 'bun-shaped' occiput which turns in a sharp angle to a very flat squama as it approaches the foramen magnum. There is no true tuber occipitale. Markings for the nuchal and other muscles are not strongly developed; the mastoid processes are small; there is a shallow inter-parietal groove; the orbits are somewhat trapezoid in shape and set rather obliquely. The palate is a diverging U-shape.

Teeth.

```
? ? ? 0 4 3 2 0 | 0 2 0 0 0 6 0 ?
_____|_____
? 0 0 ? ? ? ? ? |
```

Attrition is very light, hardly flattening the cusps. No caries. The teeth are small.

The following cranial measurements and indices were obtained (coding and method of measurement according to Martin (1957) and Morant (1922):

L	184.9	S'1	113.0	J	118.2
B	135.2	S'2	97.6	BOW	96.2
B'	88.4	S'3	98.4	IOW	89.6
B"	106.1	G'H	68.7	U	509.1
H'	112.8	GL	92.4	100B/L	73.1
OH	97.2	LB	93.2	100H'/L	61.0
Q'	264.3	NH	49.3	100H'/B	83.4
S	362.3	NB	22.7	100NB/NH	45.0
S 1	126.8	01	39.4	10002/01	82.5
S 2	106.4	02	32.5	100G'H/GB	81.8
S 3	129.1	GB	84.0		

The R. ulna was 262.8 mm long which would correspond to a stature of about 1700 mm (5 ft 7 ins).

Anomalies and pathology.

The L5 vertebrae has a detached neural arch.

There is a trace of oesteophytosis on the inferior border of the same vertebra.

(3) *Inhumation OB 485.*

(a) Male, age: 30–40.
(b) Unsexable, *c.*: 4 years.

(a) This consists of a severely smashed skull; a fragment of atlas; 3 pieces of ribs; L. and R. scapulae and clavicles; L. humerus; the condyles of the L. femur; L. and R. tibiae and fibulae; the tali; L. calcaneus, 3 metatarsals, 3 phalanges and a few other small elements. All these bones are damaged to some extent.

Reconstruction of the skull is impracticable. It is not metopic, has no supra-orbital notch, no foramen of Huschke. There is a slight malar tuberosity bilaterally but no malar tubercle.

Markings for nuchal muscles are strongly developed.

Teeth.

```
? 7 6 5 4 3 2 0 | 1 2 3 4 5 6 7 8
_____|_____
                | 1 2 3 4 5 6 7 8
```

Attrition is heavy on all teeth with extensive exposure of dentine and cupping of the molar crowns. No caries. There is slight overcrowding of the anterior teeth. A very mild degree of enamel hypoplasia is present on the incisors, canines and first molars. Tartar is negligible.

The following post-cranial measurements were obtained:

	L	R
Ci Li	? 147.5	—
Hu head	50.6	—
Ti Li	359.0	358.8
Ti Di	32.8	31.7
Ti D2	25.0	24.3
Cnemic Index	76.2	76.6
Fi Li	349.6	349.5

This corresponds to a stature of about 1687 mm (5 ft 6½ ins).

Pathology

There are some small pits due to post-inhumation erosion in the proximal surface of the L. navicular. One of these, c, 3.5 × 2.0 mm, may be at the site of a tiny osteochondritic pit.

No other pathology was detected.

(b) This consists of only two fragments of bone: a R. ilium and the proximal two-thirds of a R. femur which was probably about 200 mm long. There is nothing of note about these remains.

(4) *Inhumation OB 486.*

Male, age: 30–40.

This consists of a few small and eroded fragments of cranial vault; the R. supra-orbital margin and the R. mastoid process, both of which are strongly masculine in form; fragments of maxillae; a mandible in fairly good conditions. Post-cranial remains include: parts of the T3–12 and L3–4 vertebrae; c. 25 scraps of ribs; badly damaged L. and R. clavicles, humeri, tibia and a few other small fragments.

Teeth.

```
8 7 6 5 4 3 0 1 | ? ? ? 4 5 0 7 8
_____ | _____
8 7 6 5 4 3 2 1 | 1 2 3 4 5 6 7 8
```

Dental attrition is heavy with much exposure of dentine and cupping of the molars. No caries.

The following long bone measurements were obtained:

	L	R
Ti Di	35.2	35.3
Ti D2	21.0	21.1
Cnemic Index	59.7	59.8

The L. tibia and R. humerus were very tentatively reconstructed to give lengths of 360.0 and 330.0 mm respectively. This would correspond to a stature of about 1700 mm (5 ft 7 ins).

Pathology

There is a well-healed fracture of the body of a middle L. rib. Also a trace of oesteophytotic lipping on the T9 and T11 vertebrae.

(5) *Inhumation OB 20.*

Male.

This burial consists of the incomplete and damaged remains of a fully adult man. The surviving fragments comprise: the L. and R. metacarpals; six other damaged metacarpals; the L. acetabulum with a small fragment of ilium attached to it; the L. and R. femora (both damaged and incomplete); the L. and R. tibiae (slightly damaged); both fibulae in poor condition; the R. talus; a fragment from the posterior surface of the R. calcaneus; two metatarsals; a few other splinters of limb bone shafts and some small crumbs of vertebrae.

It was possible to obtain a few measurements from some of these bones:

	L	R
Femoral head: maximum diameter	44.8	
Femur: minimum antero-posterior diameter in the sub-trochanteric region	25.8	
Femur: maximum diameter at the same level	36.0	
Tibia: maximum length, excluding spine	374.1	
Tibia: antero-posterior diameter at the level of the nutrient foramen	36.4	38.3
Tibia: transverse diameter at the same level	21.6	23.9

The Meric Index of the L. femur is 71.6 (hyperplatymeric) and the Cnemic Indices of the tibiae are: L. 59.3; R. 62.4 (both platysnemic).

The tibial length corresponds to a stature of about 1725 m (5 ft. 8 ins),

Muscle markings on all the limb bones were strongly developed and it is clear that this was a powerful man.

No anomalies or pathology were detected.

Summary.

The numbers are too small to give significance to the sex and age distribution of these skeletons: one is female, four are male and one, a child of about 4 years, is unsexable. The age of the adults is difficult to estimate owing to the poor condition of many potentially diagnostic fragments. In the case of the woman, Inh. OB 480, there is marked contradiction between the almost completely fused cranial sutures and her negligible dental attrition.

Only with the woman is it possible to assess reliably her cranial architecture. She has a very interesting skull, notable for its extremely low vault. The height-length index is only 61.0 which is quite exceptional in the post-Roman period. In conjunction with the other features and measurements of this cranium it seems to indicate clearly that she was a survivor of an earlier, presumably Iron Age, stock. In so far as it is possible to assess the form of the male skull, OB 486, this too seems to have had a somewhat low vault though much less so than that of the woman.

Only for the males OB 486 and OB 485 can stature be estimated with any assurance. They were of medium height—1753 and 1687 mm respectively. The stature estimation of OB 486 depends on a very uncertain reconstructed length for the L. tibia. The height of the woman is based on the length of an easily reconstructible R. ulna: if the result is reliable she was, at 1700 mm, moderately tall for her sex. (The statures were calculated from the formulae of Trotter and Glesen).

The men's skeletons are of only medium build and robustness but they have, for the most part, fairly strong muscle attachments. This suggests that they were wiry, lithe persons rather than heavily built. The woman has muscle markings which are far less strong than those commonly found on many early females, e.g. the average Anglo-Saxon woman. Advanced cranial suture fusion, such as is found in this person, is a somewhat uncertain sign of advancing years because it may occur prematurely. Here, however, we can perhaps rely on it because she also has a trace of osteophytotic lipping on the inferior border of her 5th lumbar vertebra. In a woman who seems to have used her muscles only lightly and has no other evidence of arthritic change, this oesteophytosis is likely to be due to nothing more than advancing years. In which case the extremely light attribution on her teeth must suggest that she always selected an unusually soft diet, avoiding the tougher and coarser foods which eroded the other teeth in this group. If this was so, it may indicate either that she was of exalted class and could command the most succulent and delicate morsels or that she had some quirk of faddiness which led her to prefer soups and paps to nuts and hard-bakes.

Congenital anomalies and non-metrical variants are inconspicuous among these people, with nothing to suggest close family relationships between them. The overall impression is that they were of moderate physical variety and that they drew on a fairly wide gene pool: but many more skeletons, more completely preserved, would be needed to assert this with confidence.

In only two of the burials, the males OB 486 and OB 485 are the tibia well enough preserved to look for distal squatting facets. These features are large and bilaterally present on the former, bilaterally absent on the latter. No doubt this reflects some occupational difference between the two men, perhaps related to a difference of social class.

The woman showed virtually no pathology apart from the developmental defect of a detached neural arch. Of the men, OB 278 had a trace of vertebral osteophytosis and one well healed rib fracture. Little significance need be attached to these lesions: the first could represent a simple effect of ageing; the second might have been due to an accidental fall or a punch in the chest. OB 485 was also virtually free from any detectable pathology. With OB 486 the situation is very different. This man had well marked osteoarthritis and osteophytosis at all levels of his vertebral column. In his limbs it was present in both shoulders, both elbows and the wrists; also in both hip joints and both knees. This surely reflects a life of hard physical labour. It probably involved heavy lifting to produce the spinal lesions and violent strains or torsions as from ploughing, metal-working, horse-breaking, timber-felling and other occupations of this kind. The widespread nature of his lesions may suggest that he was of serf or slave status. The presence of an old osteo-chondritic pit in each medial femoral condyle probably indicates that he was already doing heavy work in his early teens. The severe fracture of his L. clavicle might be due to a blow from a cudgel. These fractures are common injuries when a blow aimed at the head is incompletely dodged or side-stepped; the club misses the head but falls on the shoulder girdle instead and shatters the collar bone.

The dental evidence here is very scant. Only 83 tooth positions are identifiable and from these 14 teeth have been lost postmortem, 1 antemortem and 1 third molar had failed to erupt. This leaves 67 teeth present in the jaws. Attrition was extremely heavy in all the males, hardly percept-ible in the woman. No tooth was carious. Occlusion, as far as it could be judged, was good.

XIV. GLOSSARY OF LATIN TERMS

Aedes A shrine where legionary standards were kept, situated within the *principia*.

Antefix A terracotta plaque covering the end of an *imbrex* at eaves level, and usually decorated with an apotropaic subject.

Apodyterium A changing-room in a bath-house.

Basilica and *forum* The administrative and commercial centre of a Roman town. The *forum* was a courtyard surrounded by porticos on three sides, behind which lay ranges of shops and offices. The fourth side was closed off by the *basilica*, a hall with one or more tribunals for magistrates; behind the *basilica* there was usually a range of rooms containing the *curia*, a shrine for the *tutela* and offices.

Caldarium A room in a bathing-suite with a hot, damp atmosphere, equipped with baths containing hot water and with *labra*.

Canabae A civil settlement under military control situated near a fortress.

Civitas peregrina A self-governing community of non-Roman citizens within the Roman Empire, often, but by no means always, based on pre-Roman tribal boundaries.

Contubernium Originally a tent holding eight men; the term also refers to the pair of rooms, one for storing equipment, the other for sleeping, which accommodated a unit of eight men in a barrack-block.

Curia The council-chamber of the governing body of a *civitas peregrina*, or of a community of higher status.

Fabrica A workshop.

Frigidarium An unheated room in a bath-house containing a cold bath and sometimes a *labrum* or emplacement for a cold shower.

Imbrex A semi-cylindrical tile used to cover the flanges of two adjoining *tegulae*.

Immunis A legionary with special skills who was exempted from routine duties; the special status of *immunes* was not officially recognised until the time of Hadrian.

Intervallum The space between the rear of the rampart and the *via sagularis*.

Labrum A large, shallow basin on a pedestal, usually carved from marble, granite or a fine-grained stone, and found in the *caldarium* (and sometimes the *frigidarium* or *tepidarium*). It held hot water.

Laconicum A room in a bath-house (usually circular in plan during the first century A.D.) with a hot dry atmosphere.

Natatio A swimming-pool usually found in the *palaestra* of a large bath-house.

Palaestra An exercise-yard attached to a bath-house.

Pila A support for the suspensura in a bath-house, usually consisting of a stack of tiles, *c.* 20 cm sq. and 80 cm or more in height.

Principia The headquarters building of a fort or fortress, consisting of a courtyard surrounded by porticos on three sides, behind which lay ranges of rooms, and a cross-hall (*basilica principiorum*) on the fourth.

Suspensura The floor above a hypocaust, generally of concrete laid over a layer of tiles 60 cm sq., which were supported at each corner by *pilae*.

Tegula A flat rectangular roof-tile with flanges running down its longer sides.

Tegula mammatar A rectangular tile with conical projections or flanges at each corner on one side. They were fixed to the surface of walls with clamps in order to form cavities through which hot gases from the hypocaust circulated.

Tepidarium A room of moderate heat lying between the *frigidarium* and *caldarium*.

Testudo A device used to maintain the temperature of a bath. It consisted of a water-container of half-cylindrical section with one end opening into the bath; the flat base of the *testudo* was placed above a furnace-flue forming its roof.

Tutela The guardian deity of a town.

XV. NOTE ON THE PLANS OF LEGIONARY FORTRESSES

The defences of a legionary fortress usually formed a rectangular enclosure, although some fortresses, for example Vindonissa, had irregular plans. A fortress of orthodox plan was divided into two unequal parts by a street, the *via principalis*, which cut across its entire width. The larger part was the *retentura*, the smaller was the *praetentura*. The latter was bisected by a street, the *via praetoria*, which joined the *via principalis* at right angles. At the junction of these two streets there stood the *principia*. A fourth major street, the *via decumana*, partly bisected the *retentura*, usually terminating at the rear of the *praetorium* (legate's palace) which generally occupied a position behind the *principia*. At the head of the *viae praetoria* and *decumana* were gates (respectively the *portae praetoria* and *decumana*). There were also gates at either end of the *via principalis*, which were referred to as the *portae principalis sinistra* and *dextra;* these were respectively at the left-hand and right-hand extremities of the *via principalis*, from the point of view of an observer stationed outside the *principia* and looking towards the *porta praetoria*. In addition to the *via principalis* streets of lesser importance divided the interior of the fortress across its width into a number of building-plots (*scamna*).

The buildings within the fortress were divided from the defences by a street, the *via sagularis*, which ran along the rear of the rampart.

INDEX

PLATES

ACKNOWLEDGEMENTS TO PLATES
R. Turner, Plates I–VII, VIIIB–XA, XI; N. Cheffers-Heard, Plates XIIIA, XB, XIIA–XXI.

PLATE IA. Interior of *caldarium* looking south-east; south-west wall of *curia* to left (2m scale).

PLATE IB. Central recess; to rear, left and right, patching of wall-core (2 m scale).

PLATE IIA. *Caldarium* hypocaust looking north-east (2 m scale).

PLATE IIB. North-east apse showing (centre) impression of *labrum* base; to the right, south-west wall of *curia* with threshold block; left upper centre, threshold block inserted at the beginning of Period 2B (2 m scale).

PLATE IIIA. *Caldarium* hypocaust looking north-east; arches to left and centre stopped up with earth in Period 1B; arch to right filled with modern concrete and rubble; mortar floor of Period 1B *frigidarium* to rear (2 m scale).

PLATE IVA. Tile *labrum* base in south-west apse.

PLATE IVB. Stone pier-base on north-east side of north-east apse; centre, bath supports with collapsed rear wall of bath above (30 cm scale).

PLATE V. South-west furnace-flue flanked by masonry bases; bath supports beyond with slots for iron bars running up to central piers, which preserve springing of arch; top, south-west wall of *basilica* with end of stylobate gutter and *forum* portico on extreme right (30 cm scale).

PLATE VIIIA. Slots for bedding-plates in the *forum*, Period 2A (30 cm scale).

PLATE VIIIB. Plank-lined lime-pit in the *forum*, Period 2B (construction) (30 cm scale).

PLATE IXA. Steps at east end of south-east *forum* portico, column-base and gutter-block to left (30 cm scale).

PLATE IXB. View of road (8 : 49B) showing trench for removal of wooden water-pipe (2 m scale).

PLATE XIIA. Mosaic in building south-east of *forum* (50 cm scale).

PLATE XIIB. Model of baths: *caldarium* looking south-east, with statue of *Fortuna* in central recess.

PLATE XIII. Model of baths: service area south-east of south-west furnace-house.

PLATE XVIA. Fragment of mosaic from Period 1B (construction).

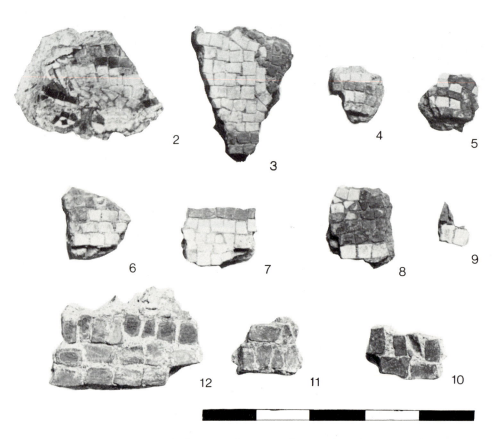

PLATE XVIB. Mosaic fragments from Periods 1B and 2A (construction).

PLATE XVIIA. Axe and *astragali* (?) carved on re-used (?) facing-block; from north-east face of south-west *basilica* wall (scale 25 cm).

PLATE XVIIB. 'M' inscribed on north-east side of south-west *curia* wall (scale 5 cm).

PLATE XVIIC. Inscribed marks on south wall of room in the south-east corner of the bath-house (scale 5 cm).

PLATE XVIID. Phallus carved on west wall of central recess at the level of the hypocaust basement (scale 5 cm).

PLATE XVIIE. 'X' inscribed on west terminal block of north flue-cheek of west *caldarium* furnace-house (30 cm scale).

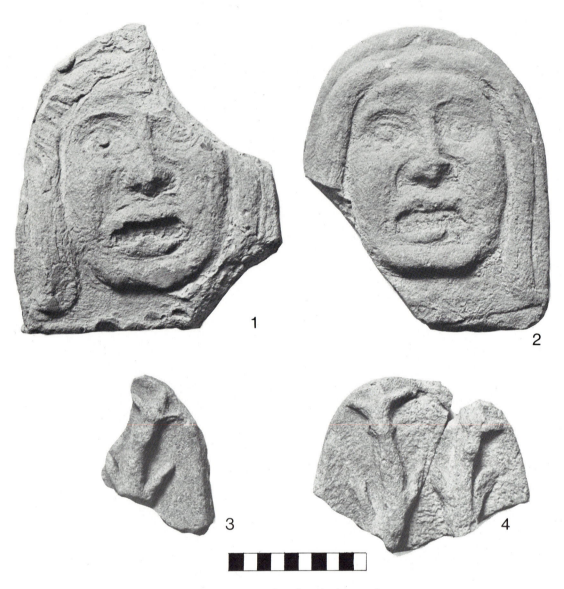

PLATE XVIII. Antefixes (scale 10 cm).

1

2

PLATE XIXA. Purbeck marble mouldings from the bath-house (scale 25 cm).

PLATE XIXB. Purbeck marble splash-board from the bath-house (scale 25 cm).

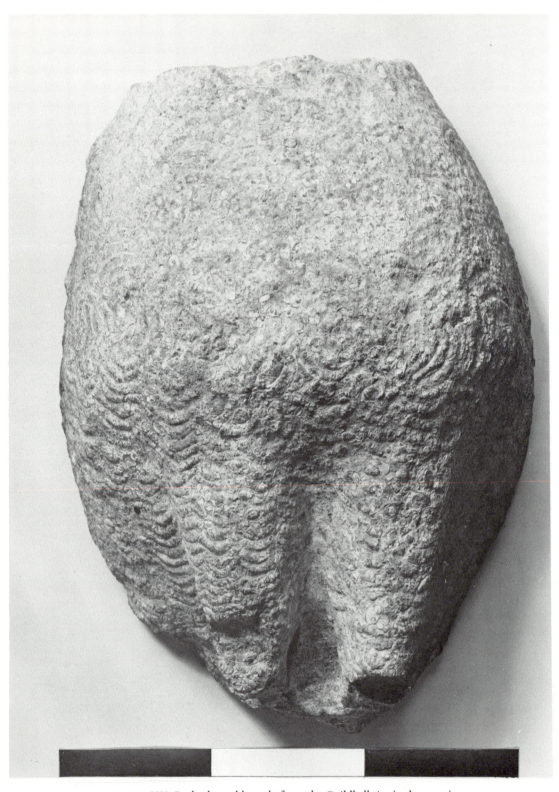

PLATE XX. Purbeck marble eagle from the Guildhall site (scale 15 cm).

PLATE XXI. Tile with soot-covered surfaces showing marks of iron bars (scale 25 cm).